Integrative Practice in and for Larger Systems

Integrative Practice in and for Larger Systems

TRANSFORMING ADMINISTRATION AND MANAGEMENT OF PEOPLE, ORGANIZATIONS, AND COMMUNITIES

Harold E. Briggs
Verlea G. Briggs
and
Adam C. Briggs

OXFORD
UNIVERSITY PRESS

OXFORD
UNIVERSITY PRESS

Oxford University Press is a department of the University of Oxford. It furthers
the University's objective of excellence in research, scholarship, and education
by publishing worldwide. Oxford is a registered trade mark of Oxford University
Press in the UK and certain other countries.

Published in the United States of America by Oxford University Press
198 Madison Avenue, New York, NY 10016, United States of America.

© Oxford University Press 2019

Library of Congress Cataloging-in-Publication Data
Briggs, Harold E. (Harold Eugene), 1955– author. |
Briggs, Verlea G., author. | Briggs, Adam C., author.
Title: Integrative practice in and for larger systems : transforming
administration and management of people, organizations, and communities /
Harold E. Briggs, Verlea G. Briggs, Adam C. Briggs.
Description: New York : Oxford University Press, 2019. |
Includes bibliographical references and index. |
Identifiers: LCCN 2018058359 (print) | LCCN 2019009335 (ebook) |
ISBN 9780190058982 (pdf) | ISBN 9780190058999 (epub) |
ISBN 9780190058975 (paperback)
Subjects: LCSH: Social service. | Management. | BISAC: SOCIAL SCIENCE /
Social Work. | SOCIAL SCIENCE / Human Services. |
BUSINESS & ECONOMICS / Management.
Classification: LCC HV40 (ebook) | LCC HV40 .B745 2019 (print) |
DDC 361.0068—dc23
LC record available at https://lccn.loc.gov/2018058359

9 8 7 6 5 4 3 2 1

Printed by Webcom, Inc., Canada

In honor and recognition of our parents, Hazel Loretta Goldsborough Briggs, Leatha Cave, Ida Elizabeth, and Frank Grace, and Aunts Carrie Louise Mines and Marion Christine Henson, and Aunt Mel and Uncle Clarence Goldsborough whose shoulders we proudly stand on.

CONTENTS

PREFACE

YOU'RE THE INTEGRATIVE AGENT
WHO MAKES IT HAPPEN!

Developing an integrative practice paradigm for use in and for larger systems involves the strategic use of model development research and an array of evidence-informed and best practices, which collectively form an evidence-informed performance management approach. This approach was used successfully in the administration, management, and delivery of a broad array of services and programs (Briggs, 1994, 1996, 2001a; Briggs, Feyerherm, & Gingerich, 2004; Briggs & McMillin, 2012). *Integrative practice in and for larger systems* involves the use of a model design and development process of information analysis, program development, staff development, and organizational development along with coaching and support of staff by leadership (Briggs, 2001a; Rothman & Thomas, 1994). Integrative practice begins at both the intrapersonal and interpersonal levels of macro practice. Intrapersonally, it involves the critical thinking and perspective building of the agency and program management practitioner. Doing so informs their strategic performance management practice lens by mapping the optimal multilevel interconnections between social policy, administration, management, and community practice that result in direct service effectiveness. Interpersonally, it involves "multilevel planning, implementation, evaluation, and quality assurance technology that is driven by the desirable outcomes and perspectives of families served by them" and is influenced by the perspectives of the staff, management, funders, legislators, and policymaking stakeholders (Briggs, 2001a, p. 371). Integrative practice in and for larger systems involves the strategic weaving of a panoply of multitasks within and across the multiple levels of a community-based agency's infrastructure (Briggs, 1994, 1996, 2001a). Multitasking is facilitated from the bottom up and from the top down (Rapp & Poertner, 1992; Resnick, 1978). Integrative practice also involves multitasking from the inside of a larger system to the outside of an agency or community, and multitasking from the outside of a larger system to the inside of an agency or community (Tolson, Reid, & Garvin, 2003).

Transforming the administration and management of people, organizations, and communities is accomplished through the strategic integration of a knowledge of the culture of oppression, social policy, theory, performance, and evidence-based management; infusing culture into roles for leaders and managers; and information literacy and synthesis resulting in a personal performance and problem-oriented practice model for use in larger systems. These represent the core generalist domains of this integrative approach for practice in and for larger systems. All in all, an integrative practice paradigm in and for larger systems involves (1) an understanding of the previously mentioned broader influences on larger systems serving smaller systems, as well as (2) the artful use of a larger system-wide behavior modification approach that positively impacts the service delivery processes and outcomes in larger systems (Briggs, 2001a).

In this book, our aim is to guide the reader in using these core generalist domains in establishing an integrative practice approach that prepares administration and management practitioners to competently achieve service accountability and service/program outcomes. The use of this approach allows the leadership of larger systems to emphasize the enhancement of the functional skill competencies and capacities of people, agencies, and community-level service beneficiaries. *Integrative Practice in and for Larger Systems: Transforming Administration and Management of People, Organizations, and Communities* is informed by the extensive practice knowledge and professional education of the first and second authors in social service and business administration. The book's comprehensive and cogent writing is due to the editorial assistance provided by the third author. Its roots and foundations are experiential, empirical, and inextricably linked to an atheoretical strand of empirical practice, behavioral theories, model development research, and a broad-based knowledge of the culture of oppression and culture's intersectionality with the implementation of performance management. The synthesis of these concepts allows leaders of larger systems to facilitate the use of evidence-informed and promising practices in direct services with families, youth consumers, and culturally specific communities (Briggs, 2009). The book's development spans a forty-year period; its origins, trajectory, and evolution constitute an organic and transformative experience tied to five essential drivers.

As the social worker in this project, the first driver was my initial exposure to the tensions existing between social policy and administration and direct social work practice. The elusive nature of this dynamic was unraveled in a discussion by George Hoshino (1973), where he carefully delineated the failure of the 1962 Social Service Amendments to the Social Security Act of 1935. The issue and study of threats to accountability in social services in this seminal work made an indelible impression on me. I was intrigued greatly by this discussion and was possessed of an avid curiosity about the legitimacy of both the public's jaundiced view of social workers as well as my own misgivings about the credibility of the profession. My initial exposure to a professionally trained and degreed social worker was a familial one that was not a positive or productive experience. He failed to ensure the health and well-being of his own family, yet he always remained highly vocal and was recognized for his beliefs about the injustices faced by others relegated to the bottom of the social welfare agenda. His apparent contradictory values and subsequent inaction significantly peaked my interests in the inconsistencies in social workers' competencies and overall effectiveness. As we see it, the competencies needed by social workers to achieve accountability to the systems they serve include an ethical obligation to use the best available evidence in problem-solving (Gambrill, 2004), along with the capability to strategically infuse the use of evidence with best and promising practice approaches. These include client-consumer voice, cultural knowledge, community engagement, information literacy, an agency culture of skepticism, and strategic learning by practice, trial, and error (Rzepnicki & Briggs, 2004). These core competencies and setting conditions enable the people, the organization, and the participating community to work as allies to strategically deliver and administer effective social services. To actualize these core competencies and proficiently achieve service effectiveness, social service administrators and program managers, as well as students seeking integrative practice competencies to lead and manage larger systems, need to adopt the strategies and lessons contained within this book.

The second driver involves a need to document the linkage of my formal education and first year graduate training in task-centered practice (TCP) (Tolson, Reid, & Garvin, 2003) with individuals, families, groups, organizations, and communities to my second year concentration in clinical problem-oriented practice (Pinkston, Levitt, Green, Linsk, & Rzepnicki, 1982). Through this venue, I learned to skillfully use the traditional problem-solving method along with single-case design research and applied behavioral analysis. Integrating TCP, a behaviorally based problem-oriented practice model, with the performance management organizational behavior modification (Komaki, 1982) and the social work administration and management practice literature bases (Briggs, 1994, 1996, 2001a; Pinkston et al., 1982) provides the core elements of integrative practice informed by evidence-based management approaches (Briggs & McBeath, 2009).

The third driver that motivated this book was an insatiable desire to memorialize this infusion of approaches into a unified, explicitly articulated curriculum. It constitutes the implicit curricula I used in my administration and management practice of nonprofit agencies. It was used to aid students and practitioners of direct care along with administration and management. The curricula also assisted parents who governed and led family support as well as advocacy organizations to actualize their intended service objectives and administer programs and agencies to achieve service effectiveness.

The fourth driver was to establish a macro practice approach that is agency- and community-based and that emphasizes cultural knowledge and customs as essential to the skill competencies of administrators and managers. The fifth and final driver was an overwhelming desire to sensitize readers, administration, and management novices to the significance of integrating business and social service administration perspectives through different ways of knowing. Given these events and conversations, we are eager to share this important work. It's our hope that you are enthusiastically anticipating the opportunity to learn more about *Integrative Practice in and for Larger Systems: Transforming Administration of People, Organizations, and Communities.* You may have questions, such as: What exactly is integrative practice anyway? What's it all about? Why is it so important? How does it work? How does it relate to me? And what's in it for me? If these are indeed your questions, this book will answer them all.

In the next few pages, you will learn all about the benefits of integrative practice in transforming the administration of people, organizations, and communities. In fact, your participation is so important that we have titled this Preface, "You're the Integrative Agent Who Makes It Happen!" This is because you—through your practical application of integrative practice—are what makes this curriculum effective. This book recognizes that each employee, relative to his or her line of responsibility for giving care to others, is absolutely critical to reaching successful outcomes in policies and programs. You are the most essential element in integrative practice in and for larger systems. So, let's get started.

Social Service Agencies and Programs

Social service agencies and programs work with people across

- *Five age groups*: Preschool/school children, young adults, adults, and older adults.
- *Five categories of disability*: Mentally disabled, physically disabled, developmentally disabled, health impaired, and others at risk.
- *Five service functions*: Clinical interventions, case coordination, case management, training/education, and employment.
- *Five functional capacities*: Superior, excellent, adequate, fair, and poor.

These twenty variables identify the "who" and "what" in service delivery. They interact dynamically because *no two people, and thus, no two cases* are exactly alike. Community organizations need a way to organize and manage the services rendered to their clients by the many thoughtful and caring individuals, like you. Integrative practice gives agency directors, program managers, and administrators the tools and abilities to monitor the quality of those services and improve outcomes through analyses of evidence and to direct resources toward those efforts that prove most effective. As a leader who incorporates the best analytical tools in the administration of program services, your direct involvement in decision-making is maximized.

This integrative practice book for managers and leaders of larger systems chronicles and memorializes the dual contributions of a scientific-based theory as well as an atheoretical empirical-based problem-solving practice curriculum. Each of these essential knowledge bases is a key aspect of this integrative and multi-level performance management practice model. It is a useful approach for training seasoned administrators and managers as well as aspiring executive directors, program managers, and program coordinators in the strategic implementation of best practices and evidence-informed treatments for individuals, families, and community systems of care through agency consortia arrangements. It is a field-tested approach that has been used in leading and managing the implementation of the science of behavior change through programs and services targeting client-consumers with culturally diverse backgrounds (see Chapters 1, 4, 5, 6, 7, 17, 18, 19, 21; Briggs, 1994, 1996, 2001a; Briggs & McBeath, 2009; Briggs & McMillan, 2012).

This book highlights the key integrative practice skill competencies of administrators and managers across four broad sections: (1) core generalist integrative performance management skill competency functions, as discussed in the chapters in Section I; (2) specialization stabilizing integrative performance management skill competency functions, as highlighted in the chapters of Section II; (3) enhancement of integrative performance management specialization skill competency functions, as presented in the chapters of Section III; and (4) program and organizational development integrative practice specialization skill competency functions, as provided in the chapters encompassing Section IV.

Section I: Core Generalist Integrative Practice Competencies for Administrators and Managers

Section I includes chapters on the core functions encompassing the administration and management of social agencies and programs. In Chapter 1, the authors identify the pivotal roles that social workers, social work administrators, and managers play in the delivery of quality services through attentiveness to social justice, cultural competency, collaborative organizational relationships, and client self-determination. Through program development and management, social service administration, and hands-on service delivery based on evidence-based practice (EBP), information analysis, culturally informed service implementation, and critical thinking, practitioners can best achieve agency effectiveness.

The authors identify an integrative, multilevel approach that involves eleven crucial skill competencies needed to lead and manage staff, programs, and the overall agency in an effective way. These skills include:

- Recognizing the role of the structural determinants of culture and the culture of silence and power as challenges to the leaders of larger systems who assess and address threats to civil and human rights and the social justice of service beneficiaries.
- Engaging in the integration of cross-cultural management practice and evidence-based perspectives across diverse larger systems.
- Using transparency and information literacy to define the integrative critical perspective of social work problem-solving, expand knowledge bases, and broaden the understanding of the complexities of social issues.
- Utilizing evidence to critically analyze ways to improve agency and program functioning and service effectiveness.
- Developing informed hypotheses about the root causes of agency, program, and client-related issues based on evidence.

- Using evidence to assess the contingencies of various solutions to resolve the problem.
- Investigating the costs and benefits of alternative options based on evidence.
- Making strategic decisions based on critical thinking and the "differential response system of care options" utilizing evidence.
- Tracking and monitoring client reactions to planned interventions as qualitative evidence to inform program efficacy.
- Critically assessing the agency's capacity to evaluate program successes and weaknesses, as well as its capacity to modify a course of action to assure quality service delivery.
- Using cultural knowledge and effective collaboration techniques to implement service coordination mechanisms within and across service delivery systems.

In Chapter 2, the authors discuss the relevance of deconstructing the culture of oppression by discussing the influence of the culture of silence, the culture of power, and the structural determinants of culture on white privilege on integrative practice in and for larger systems. In Chapter 3, the authors highlight the relevance of understanding social policy as a structural determinant that encompasses social/political and regulatory realities for clients and social workers while discussing why understanding policy is imperative to integrative practice in and for larger systems. This chapter outlines the systemic problems in policy development both within and outside of an organization. Paying close attention to the way social policy issues are identified, socially perceived, prioritized, and regulated is important in grasping racial disproportionality and its impacts on marginalized client-consumers, families, and communities. Forming a critical lens by which an organization and its team members evaluate existing agency and political policies, as well as how they work toward social justice through changes to and development of policy, encourages culturally aware problem-solving. The authors point out racial residential segregation, exposure to high-end restrictive services, lack of support system and services that improve client self-sustainability, social welfare, and lack of access to services that fully address the broad scope of needs for historically marginalized people. The authors describe 10 core integrative practice dimensions that must be a part of the evaluation of social policy effectiveness: (1) ethics, (2) efficaciousness/effectiveness, (3) efficiency, (4) equality, (5) equity, (6) ecologically based, (7) ecumenical, (8) empowerment-based, (9) economic participation, and (10) enforcement protections.

In Chapter 4, the use of theory is presented as an essential skill competency and driver for incentivizing performance as well as behavior change. As an aid to agency leaders and managers, theory is used to guide behavior change through direct management practice, and its overall relevance and importance are highlighted. The authors show how a leadership perspective is useful as a practical tool to use in guiding agency leadership's oversight of an integrative performance management practice framework that can be used along with the strategic use of applied behavioral analysis methods and organizational behavior modification techniques. This perspective entails five primary leadership competencies: vision, incentivizing others to act, team collaboration, facilitation of critical problem-solving, and promoting positive change. Administrators carry out functional analysis at different levels of the organization in order to make necessary changes, which are promoted by the integration of behavioral modification techniques that improve program functionality and client outcomes.

In Chapter 5, the authors break down into the key components, the unique framework they developed to assess the individual and collaborative roles of administrators, management, and staff within an agency with the goal of increasing efficiency and effective service delivery. By carefully examining seven core steps, the authors introduce the most purposeful means of dealing with multiple layers of organizational management for accountability, efficacy, performance, and culturally relevant service delivery. The seven steps include (1) defining the mission that clearly states the organization's purpose; (2) defining the structure, including the framework and staff relationships within the organization; (3) setting goals for expected performance that are observable, measurable, and specific; (4) establishing behavior strategies to assure efficiency, including continuity of care and time management; (5) incorporating "reinforcing events" that provide staff affirmation, proactive direction, and communicative space for staff to ask questions and discuss issues; (6) evaluating outcomes; and (7) a final enhancement and development step to refine service and service delivery to improve the organization's functioning and best meet the needs of clients.

Chapter 6 benefits from collaboration with Joy A. De Gruy and Risa Kiam. In this chapter, we address the importance of balancing management strategies with attentiveness to the nuanced complexities of social service programs that collaborate with culturally different staff, clients, and communities. Such balance can be acquired with the implementation of a comprehensive and yet flexible management practice methodology as proposed in this book. Ideally, organizations are culturally responsive service delivery organizations that are led by a management practice methodology that is based in relevant theories, adaptable intervention methods, and evaluator processes that result in an organizational culture that is responsive to its staff, stakeholders, and client-consumers. Incorporating core principles such as cultural competency, client voice and empowerment, and self-determination in an organization based on family-infused, strengths perspective, and evidence-based social work practice strengthens the functionality of the organization. The organization must value competence and capacity building in order to develop strong staff expectations to carrying out the organization's objectives. Each member of the organization must understand thoroughly each of the organizational objectives in order to establish reliable standards and best practices for effective service delivery that elicits positive responses from client-consumers.

Accountability happens at multiple levels within an organization. Understanding Maslow's hierarchy of needs in human behavior helps to establish a baseline of service delivery that is focused on addressing the physical and psychological needs of clients in a culturally responsive and accountable manner. Cultural competency is crucial in developing best practices that effectively meet the needs of diverse client-consumers, facilitate a sense of connectedness and collaboration, strengthen clients' problem-solving skills, and increase overall self-sufficiency. Organizations that strive to remain culturally responsive must do so at the micro, mezzo, and macro levels and incorporate these practices within the administrative, management, and service delivery interfacing roles of the organization, topics which are thoroughly discussed in Chapter 6.

In Chapter 7, and throughout this book, the authors draw on case examples to illustrate and discuss integrative practices in which EBP and evidence-based management employ the skillful application of cultural knowledge, science, client voice, and community participation to increase the agency's ability to provide exceptional programming that benefits the clients and communities in question. The authors highlight the importance of core integrative practice competencies, such as information literacy, critical thinking, synthesis, and decision-making skills, typically involved in agency and program management's use of evidence to manage and pursue multilevel behavior change.

Section II: Core Specialization Skill Competencies for Administration and Management

In Section II, the authors discuss the core stabilizing integrative administration and management practice skill competencies. In Chapter 8, leadership skill competencies are herald as fundamental and essential. Leadership is a social construct based on political/social interactions and is influenced by sociological, psychological, and institutional factors. The style of leadership is at the core of leadership sustainability. Sustainable and successful leaders must encompass three key skills: (1) they need to know how to nurture and build relationships, (2) they need to know how to engage and assist in developing individuals in the organization, and (3) they must motivate and promote the vision and expectations of the organizations. This chapter details both effective and ineffective modes of leadership for integrative practice in and for larger systems.

In Chapter 9, the authors point out the lack of an established prerequisite of proficiency standards, qualifying exams, and credentialing for social work practice and service effectiveness, as compared to the field of medicine. They examine how staff development encompasses three primary areas: (1) assessment and planning; (2) building capacity through training, continuing education, and professional development; and (3) performance accountability in order to reach ideal integrative practice results.

In Chapter 10, the authors examine the importance of interpersonal influence as a key integrative practice skill for incentivizing others to perform desirably. Political behavior and politics are an innate aspect of social work, and agency personnel need to be aware of the influence, both economic and political, that politics and social capital have on the design and implementation of effective social services. Change management strategies help to invest and motivate staff to changes by addressing sociopolitical factors that can help to create an environment of team collaboration. It is imperative to have a logic model plan of action in order to achieve assessment, new program implementation, and behavioral change and to assure smooth transition into a new protocol. This involves using existing social and economic capital, digital and media information sources, environmental scanning, research regarding EBP, careful monitoring of the implementation process, contingent thinking, succinct problem-solving, and strategic navigation. Being able to work with staff and draw from them the motivation to adopt new strategies and improve performance to move the organization in the right direction promotes positive attitudes about change and accountability.

In Chapter 11, the authors emphasize that workforce diversity is undergoing a multitude of changes and that organizational development and sustainability relies on keeping current with trends, competency, and inclusivity. The authors explore Mor Barak's theory of inclusion-exclusion and its four workforce propositions as related to organizational outcomes. At its core, an organization needs to have a well-honed human resource agenda that is attentive to the four dimensions discussed in this chapter: (1) the correlates, (2) causes, and (3) consequences of effective human resources, and (4) age diversity and its implications for workforce development.

This chapter discusses Zemke, Raines, and Filipczak's (2000) ACORN strategy for managing generations effectively, which includes, accommodating employee differences, creating workplace choices, operating from a sophisticated management style, respecting competence and initiative, and nourishing retention. Understanding generational motivations, workplace loyalty, desired incentives, and work ethics are important to gaining insight into employees' operational locus, which can help to develop management strategies, development plans, and effective workforce propositions. Incorporating the different perspectives of intergenerational employees can be an asset to the organization, one that is fostered by strong, nurturing leadership.

In Chapter 12, the authors show how inter- and intra-agency collaboration is an integral aspect of social services and how attention needs to be paid to collaborations that are beneficial to the integrative delivery of effective and quality services while enhancing the organization's functioning. Four different facets of service collaboration include (1) a definition and indication of the types of collaboration, (2) reasons for collaboration, (3) a general overview of organizational systems and power and politics theories as they relate to the collaboration process, and (4) a discussion regarding the conditions that enhance or hinder autonomy, authority, service accountability, and service continuity within the context of inter- and intraorganizational collaboration. This is an informed approach that taps into the various resources of multiple organizations or the departments of a single agency to support a full scope of care and service delivery. It also addresses the common problem of adequate funding, which an organization or department on its own could fail to attain, in order to fully meet the scope of client service needs. The chapter examines concepts of power and the politics of agencies or departments. Differentiation of power, once collaborators establish their relationship and implement change, can occur in respect to their different service provisions, provided it is carefully monitored for effectiveness.

Section III: Core Specialization Administration and Management Enhancement Skill Competencies

In Section III, the authors highlight the enhancement skill competencies for administration and management. In Chapter 13, the authors highlight the importance of using integrative practice performance measures in the administration and management of social agencies and programs. Performance measures that are built into programs and services are critical enhancements and time-savers when an agency undergoes accreditation assessment, program review, or evaluation, and for ongoing tracking of staff performance and client reactions to plans of care. This can be equally beneficial to management as well as staff in visualizing inputs, outputs, performance, and outcomes and is a valuable investment of time and energy. The authors outline the twenty-five skills that a problem-oriented practitioners needs to proficiently perform. Establishing performance measures of behavioral outcomes and desired performance at baseline helps to develop an anticipated trajectory of outcomes and outcome improvements, thus directing staff toward goals. Continuous use allows for more careful assessment and tracking of misplaced or wrong contingencies and the contraction of problem behaviors. Performance measures are an integral facet of problem-solving and are directly correlated to increasing program and service effectiveness. Furthermore, they provide clarity to the collection and analysis of data throughout all of the phases of programming and service delivery.

Chapter 14 is co-authored with Bowen McBeath. The authors highlight the importance and challenges of diffusing research to integrative practice implementation. The authors show how implementing EBP and empirically supported interventions (ESIs) can be difficult in social work due to resistance, uncertainty, and the demands of research. Furthermore, there are additional difficulties in implementing ESIs into child welfare settings due to feasibility, resources, and the disconnect between research and social work practice settings. ESIs are often viewed as not being fully developed for marginalized or culturally diverse populations or multi-issue clients, as being irrelevant in psychotherapy settings, or as not being flexible enough for systems of care that address extraordinary circumstances. The use of ESIs in lieu of

EBP can reinforce ecological fallacies and be too linear and universally presumed in some instances. There may be issues that agencies must face before being able to provide the necessary resources, adopt new practices, train staff, overcome staff resistance, provide clinical supervision, or implement a navigable database for assessment. To aid in the adoption of effective and innovative EBP and ESIs, an agency needs to follow several manageable steps to assure adoption and sustainability that are rooted in agency-based, social network, interprofessional, political, and education-related factors. These steps are outlined to highlight the benefits and challenges of transparent and thorough implementation of innovations in order to most effectively establish valid and reliable practice and interventions.

Chapter 15 chronicles the integrative practice professional development trajectory in program management and quality assurance skill competencies of the first author, Harold Briggs, in nonprofit agencies, a path that later culminated in a career in academia. His personal experiences shed light on the horrors of poor executive management skills that disrupted his and other staffs' abilities to perform their jobs effectively, repelled collaboration and client participation, and led to fiscal irresponsibility to the extent of breaking laws. This experience was followed by a positive position in mental health that involved intra-agency coordination, professional development, and proactive program management. Such experiences reinforced that key foundational elements need to be in place for effective program management, including (1) ethics and standards that clearly define performance standards inclusive of input from client-consumers, (2) communication of expected performance, (3) structuring and organizing agency performance-based work and implementation plans, (4) tracking and monitoring methods, (5) tools for performance appraisals, (6) a strategy for using performance appraisal data, and (7) the utilization of evidence in critical decision-making within program management.

In Chapter 16, the authors discuss integrative practice program review and program evaluation skill competencies. The authors illustrate the importance of program review and its focus on assessing the schedule of services and goods (inputs and outputs) and the consistency of these deliveries. Program review tracks for accuracy, feasibility, and the process by which outcomes are reached for quality assurance. Program evaluation is empirical in nature and looks closely at agency progress, service effectiveness, and program impact on clients. Both assess program fidelity and are learning processes by which organizations can use evidence and integrative practice to grow and thrive.

Section IV: Core Specialization Development Skill Competencies for Administration and Management

In Chapter 17, the authors present and discuss key development skill competencies. Preventative organizational development should be a key priority for an agency and a key component of integrative practice in and for larger systems. Implementing a culture of strategic evidence-based decision-making, participatory management processes, organizational transparency, checks and balances, shared accountability, and cultural competence is essential to meeting the goal of providing effective service delivery and program functioning.

In Chapter 18, the authors discuss the importance and relevance of program development skill competencies for integrative practice in and for larger systems. Program development includes three primary principles. First, critical perspectives include developing a statement of the social issue, culturally relevant value assumptions, and a plan of action proposal that acts to drive integrative practice program design. Critical perspectives entail stating the social issue, being clear about the practitioner's value assumptions about the problem, and stating the proposed plan of action and system support to address the social issue. Second, the critical perspective needs to be informed by knowledge development and dissemination to establish effective program design. Drawing from practitioner knowledge introduces experiences that reflect the evidentiary basis of the effectiveness of planned approaches. Also, knowledge development helps to eliminate program design elements that interfere with client self-determination. Finally, planning innovation and program change require that practitioners utilize a developmental research framework. The authors cite the model development approach as a practical framework in which current research is used to develop a set of procedures that are pilot tested and adapted as needed until ready for dissemination. The model development approach includes conducting a detailed problem analysis, gathering information from various sources, pilot testing design and development, undertaking evaluation and advanced stages of development, and, finally, initiating dissemination and implementation.

To illustrate the importance of grounding integrative practice in larger systems as an important macro problem-solving strategy, the authors use real community agency examples. In Chapter 19, they examine the existing disparities in that African Americans receive fewer and lower quality mental health services than do whites. In addition, the low percentage of African American practitioners is an alienating factor for clients who need to feel connected to and trust service providers. A major factor in these disparities is the lack of culturally informed evidence-based services that both address the cultural needs of African Americans and address the direct needs of the community through empowering community participatory approaches to better inform service delivery. Cultural stigma and a history of systemic health and mental health abuses resulting in distrust also impact utilization of services. Juxtaposed with the growing health and mental health issues that historically marginalized groups face, these disparities have become a public health crisis that is best addressed by taking a culturally informed approach to connecting African Americans to effective preventative and treatment services.

There are questions regarding current EBPs and ESIs and their limitations to being applied universally to diverse cultural populations or populations experiencing numerous service needs. EBP entails five steps: (1) designing answerable client-oriented practice evidence search questions, (2) searching for the best available evidence, (3) critically appraising the evidence, (4) using clinical judgment and expertise in considering client preferences and resources needed to implement each option, and (5) applying and systematically evaluating the services consistent with client preferences. Yet little development has been made in identifying EBP and ESIs that are grounded in the cultural experiences and myriad identity classifications of black individuals. As a result of enslavement and deeply rooted discrimination, black and African American identity is nuanced and dependent on factors related to acculturated identity, enculturation identity, and racial socialization or combination of any of these aspects that shape the cultural orientation of a black individual. Furthermore, with low participation in mental health services and few services to choose from, there has not been the effort put forth to develop an understanding of culturally relevant EBP and ESIs.

Experience has shown that community-based participatory action approaches tap into the knowledge base of diverse localized communities and enable the design of services based on the presence of disparities and the stated needs of community members. Community-based participatory research models are also better able to flesh out the authentic understanding and beliefs about mental health care and the particularities of mental health issues as the community understands them by using culturally relevant research team members made up of academics, mental health practitioners, and community residents. This helps guide the development of respectful interventions and services through local capacity building, social justice, and advocacy based on the voices of residents. This is highlighted through a detailed case study of an African American mental health initiative in Portland, Oregon.

Chapter 20 is co-authored with Bowen McBeath. The authors highlight the unique and nuanced perspective of community members as crucial to evolving human and social services and integrative practice in and for larger systems. Partnering community knowledge and scientific evidence will assist in developing services and capacity building. This entails, developing relationships with universities, maintaining transparency, using a trial-and-error method to assure the right fit, and putting into place the appropriate resources and financial supports for innovations. This is detailed in a case study involving EBP with African Americans in a child-care welfare setting in Chicago.

In Chapter 21, the authors provide a detailed chapter-by-chapter of summary of the highlights presented in each chapter of this book. Through the curriculum and multilevel approach highlighted in this book, the authors illustrate how it can be used in supporting individuals, families, communities, caregivers, staff, and managers to achieve better performance functioning and outcomes. The tools in this book can aid social work leaders and direct care professionals in demonstrating their effectiveness as well as in strategically planning and executing behavior change across the entire organization and within diverse communities.

This integrative practice book demonstrates how community-based agencies can deliver social services to people in the best possible ways. Each chapter covers one of twenty major subject areas crucial to a macro comprehensive social work curriculum.

Integrative Practice in and for Larger Systems

Core Generalist Integrative Practice Competencies for Administrators and Managers

The core perspectives and organizing tool kit that forms the foundation of *Integrative Practice in and for Larger Systems: Transforming Administration of People, Organizations, and Communities* is presented in this first section; which encompasses the strategic use of performance management, science, culture, information literacy, critical thinking, and decision-making guided by scientifically based theory. These keys are essential to integrative training. They are crucial to practitioners searching for multilevel organizing frameworks and compatible management approaches to guide the successful implementation of the science of behavior change to achieve service effectiveness. The chapters in this section provide a fundamental education for and preparation of administrators and managers of agencies and programs. They provide a sound, well-thought-out organizing framework for administrators and managers to follow to ultimately achieve intended behavioral change outcomes across a broad array of stakeholders, which includes client-consumers and their families, staff and management, as well as executives and boards of directors. Thus, the chapters in Section I explicate a structure, process, and outcome sequelae guided by the interplay of culture, policy, science, theory, and information literacy. Collectively, the chapters in Section I provide an integrative, multilevel blueprint for planning, implementing, monitoring, and evaluating performance progress and the outcomes for client consumers, staff, and management of an organization and social service program. The chapters in Section I, metaphorically serve as an architectural rendering that charts out a sequence of interrelationships between theory, social policy and social administration and management, the use of evidence, culture, critical thinking, decision-making, and problem- and performance-oriented practice for use across a broad array of organizational levels.

1 }

Integrative Practice in and for Larger Systems

TRANSFORMING ADMINISTRATION OF PEOPLE,
ORGANIZATIONS, AND COMMUNITIES

During the preparation of the initial draft of this manuscript, I was reminded of an end-of-year graduation party. As Chair of the University Graduation Board, for each of the 15 years I served in this distinguished and prestigious capacity, I co-hosted this event with my wife and second co-author, Mrs. Verlea Briggs. One of my former students, a recent graduate of the Masters of Social Work program whose studies were concentrated in social service administration, engaged me in a discussion regarding the relevance of culture as well as other knowledge paradigms. I was asked about the radical structuralism paradigm in relation to the use of scientifically based approaches and evidence-based management in social work. This recent graduate was interested in how I intended to introduce and unpack the central but often competing themes and knowledge paradigms used in the education of practitioners in social service administration and the management of human service organizations. These themes included the essential strategic decision-making and problem-solving elements: information literacy; use of evidence; research utilization; and nonscientific dimensions and factors such as culture, client empowerment, and community voice knowledge bases.

As an entry to answering her question, I shared with the graduate my disappointment surrounding an article that had been recently published in a public administration journal. The article grossly misrepresented social work's approach to the preparation and education of practitioners for the administration and management of social and human service organizations. I expressed my concern that the article misrepresented social work's capacity to educate and train students as macro-practitioners in administration and management. I also expressed my worries that social work programs have failed to adequately market themselves as a discipline preparatory for careers in administration and management. I reminded the graduate that the profession of social work is uniquely positioned to assist the government in establishing an effective interface between health and human

3

services, social policy and its implementation, and service provision to vulnerable or disadvantaged populations within their cultural context.

The graduate asked why public administration or business schools think so narrowly about our preparation for management. At that precise moment, a university student affairs department manager approached us and introduced himself. The gentleman intimated that he would soon be entering the university's public administration program. Although serendipitous, this chance assemblage of a recent social work administration graduate and an entering public administration student provided me the opportunity to address the question, "Why would a student pursue public administration as opposed to social work administration?" First, the previously mentioned article had a biased and traditional view of social work as a profession. It was obvious that the writer of the public administration article was not current with the advancements in social work education, particularly with respect to the use of evidence as a tool for achieving service effectiveness, one used by administration and management, as well as by direct service practitioners.

Aghast at my remarks, the public administration–bound student responded that his ultimate career objective was to manage a nonprofit organization. He further indicated that it was difficult for him to grasp the notion that a social worker had the competency to manage a nonprofit organization or a publicly financed health and human service delivery system. In his opinion, social workers are advocates for the poor, providing case management assistance and some therapy, but they do not possess the competencies of those with degrees in public or business administration. As Chair of the Social Service and Management concentration, his stated opinion gave me an opportunity to smile as I witnessed one of our recent graduates tear into this misguided soul. She passionately described her coursework in grant writing, leadership, human resources, program development, program management, and social service administration (with diploma in hand). I remarked, "Don't forget to tell him that it is our unique professional mission that embodies the commitment to the wellbeing of the vulnerable, the elimination of poverty, and the eradication of oppression that makes social work's social justice foci different than the social justice aims of public administration. Also, it is our Social Work Code of Ethics that distinguishes us from the public and business administrators of nonprofit and human service systems. Given social work's social justice mission, our well-prepared administrators and managers not only need to acquire competencies in the use of evidence to deliver services and programs aimed at achieving behavior change through the concerted efforts of staff. They also need to be able to use their influence and networks to broker linkages to other agency services and programs aimed at solving problems and issues that interfere with their clients' self-determination."

If I had the time, I would have shared with these students the impetus and origins of the writing of this book, which dates back as early as my first year in graduate school. As a first-year student of social work at the University of Chicago, I read and became enthralled with George Hoshino's work on accountability and the lessons learned from the shortfalls of the War on Poverty (in particular the failure of the 1962 Social Service amendments) during the Kennedy and Johnson presidential administrations (Hoshino, 1973). As a student of empirical social work practice, I learned how to transfer research knowledge into practice through three venues: (1) a behavioral practice orientation (Pinkston et al., 1982), (2) an atheoretical multi-level practice perspective and task-centered social work (Rzepnicki, McCracken, & Briggs, 2012), and (3) a theory-driven research lens using both group and single case methods as a context for planning and implementing effective practice (Marsh, 2004, 2012). For example, one of the first lessons taught by Jeanne Marsh as a new instructor of first-year social work research was the PLA-CHEK method. This ob-servational measure allowed practitioners to establish a proportion index to use to determine the level of engagement by members of a group by counting the number of people who were on task versus the total possible number of participants. Situations like the previously mentioned encounter between students and themes such as the use of evidence, tracking and monitoring staff decisions by examining staff and client behavioral reactions to management and staff decisions, the impact of effective programs on family life, and the achievement of youth fascinate me a great deal. This fascination and my early research investigation of a successful, inno-vative computer instruction program for inner-city youth with reading deficiencies demonstrated the importance of using reinforcing and nonthreatening approaches and their potential for achievement and learning through positive reinforcement and culturally enriching environments. From these early lessons, I sought to crystalize and synthesize the themes of use of evidence, decision-making, problem-solving, information analysis and processing, cultural empowerment, achievement, critical thinking, and service effectiveness into one overarching rubric. Borrowing from my quality assurance experience in medical social work, my formal education in task-centered practice (Rzepnicki et al., 2012), evidence-based practice (Gambrill, 2004), performance management (Briggs, 1994), and applied behavioral analysis (Pinkston et al., 1982), and my teaching experience in evidence-based management (Briggs & McBeath, 2009), I designed an integrative organizational practice method that incorporates each of these key themes.

In this book, management practitioners will learn the skillful use of cultural knowledge, scientific, and practice frameworks to achieve the goal of effectively managing staff, programs, and agencies. The comprehensive multilevel approach described in this book involves a number of important skill competencies, such as (1) the ability to engage in cross-cultural practice (culturally specific outreach, engagement, participation, collaboration), the skillful use of cultural knowledge, and evidence-based perspectives to develop interventions that achieve service effec-tiveness; (2) the ability to use transparency and information literacy to draw upon and utilize different ways of knowing, to gain a broad understanding about the contingencies of social problems impacting the disadvantaged; (3) the ability to use evidence to formulate a critical perspective about ways to improve agency and program functioning as well as service effectiveness to client and families; (4) the ability to use evidence to form an answerable hunch or hypothesis about the root causes of agency-, program-, and client-related issues; (5) the ability to use evidence to scan and comprehend the contingencies of the options and alternative solutions to the problem; (6) the ability to use evidence to investigate the costs and benefits of alternative options; (7) the ability to use evidence to make strategic decisions based on critical thinking about differential response system of care options; (8) the capacity to use evidence to track and monitor client reactions to planned interventions; (9) the capacity to evaluate and adopt program successes and capacity to modify or change a course of action that leads to no change or negative results; and, last, (10) the capacity to use cultural knowledge and effective collaboration techniques to skillfully implement service coordination mechanisms within and across service delivery systems. Although these do not complete the list of core competencies that will be addressed in this book, they are chief among the practice skills that will be emphasized for administration and management practitioners. It is unfortunate that many people, like the public administration student, maintain a myopic and limited purview of social work competencies.

At different points while completing this book, Verlea and I reflected on the aforementioned student encounter. I often wished for an opportunity to share an important parting lesson with our competent graduate of social work administration, one that I have always followed: No social worker should leave school and venture into professional life armed only with the certainty of knowledge gleaned from program studies. I strongly encourage students to leave school prepared to practice ethically and responsibly by using evidence. Given the state of social work research on evidence-based and culturally competent social work practice, I also advise with full assurance that students are expected to advance and expand social work's knowledge bases to areas that the profession does not fully understand and in which it has a need to be informed.

Furthermore, students must aspire to help others recognize the discoverer within by finding and never abandoning their thirst for discovery. The continuous learning obtained through reading should be a primary social obligation of practitioners. Also, the skillful and broad application of evidence in practice involves the enhanced cultural knowledge needed to advance volunteerism, promote a sense of community, and cultivate new methods of effective helping. The expanded reach and application of evidence-based practice may yet prove to be an important key condition, creating the tensions and skepticism necessary to sustain the adventurer in us all.

This book was written to aid instructors of social administration and management students and supervisors of direct practitioners, as well as students who administer agencies or manage a diversity of programs and services funded through public support. Its significance is principal to those social work administrators who seek service effectiveness through the administration and delivery of social services within highly politicized and economically conservative realities. To achieve their aims, managers of effective social service agencies must view the attainment of client goals as the product of the integrative practice sequelae; in the words of an artist, this is a completed landscape that results from finishing the unpainted portions of the canvas. To complete the painting, the artist pursues a series of expressions and angles which capture the exact image he or she seeks to convey. Some of the artist's initial efforts may produce great results, while others may prove costly and counterproductive. Even through such setbacks, all is not lost because the artist uses what he or she learns from practice errors and employs a culture of learning as a foundation for betterment. Errors are opportunities to pose thoughtful questions and critically appraise evidence while strategically choosing a course of action that leads to the competent completion of their masterpiece. This scenario is a salient metaphor that symbolizes the art and science of integrative practice in and for larger systems.

Practitioners who administer programs and services are given incomplete canvases. They are expected to ensure the quality and health of the program or agency in all its transactions. This kind of environment allows managers to define challenges as opportunities to transform contracts for social services into actionable, measurable, and sustainable service delivery systems. The character of the programs may vary depending on the clients served, as well as the administrative rules and mandates which govern programs. Policies mandating social services differ based on jurisdiction and law. Funding authorities may require the use of one approach or a combination of approaches in the delivery of eligibly funded community-based services. Requirements may include one or more of the following delivery approaches: culturally appropriate, evidence-based, proven, or promising practices.

Experience informs us that a need exists for a social work curricular model that prepares practitioners to balance, in their approach, the tensions between dimensions of managing for humanity and self-expression versus directing for service effectiveness within the context of cultural diversity. Each of these dimensions brings with it important external ecological considerations. Historical, social, economic, and political domains remain central to sustaining and managing the health of social service agencies and programs. Thus, effective organizational practice curricular models must focus comprehensively on these external ecological domains and their related contingencies. Curricula must support the competencies of administrative practitioners (1) across multiple levels of management, (2) through the use of practice theory within client-centered ethical frameworks, (3) by emphasizing the importance of data for critical thinking and decision-making, (4) by developing leadership with an emphasis on emotional intelligence, (5) within diverse cultural contexts, (6) in both internal and social network politics, and (7) through the identification of strategic means to establish interfaces between social policy, social administration, and service coordination.

Organizational practice curricular models must teach students useful tactics and strategies to establish cultures of learning aimed toward enhancing the structure, process, and outcomes in service delivery. Achieving this has significant implications for the continued reliance on community-based systems of care (care networks) for maintaining client-consumers in the least restrictive programs and services. In spite of the need for effective care networks for all clients who seek them, the research on organizational practice has not kept pace with care network innovations, such as those in the area of children's mental health. Again, based on ongoing practice research in nonprofit organizational settings, the authors wrote this book to assist others who administer agencies or manage programs. This is especially pertinent to those who manage politically charged, action-oriented, and accountability-focused organizational environments. Specifically, this book is also a helpful roadmap to guide both agency administrators and management practitioners through the complexities that come with administering human service agencies and managing social service programs across the life span and fields of practice. Finally, administrators play various roles conducting day-to-day responsibilities and agency operations. Political scientist, statistician, mentor, administrator, supervisor, partner and collaborator, planner, quality control agent, and human resource manager are among the many hats worn by effective social agency administrators and program managers.

This book offers perspectives on how to manage the myriad of conditions that administrators are both responsible for and subject to as typical daily challenges and struggles. If you are at a bookstore and have a few minutes, we invite you to read any chapter of this book at random. Each chapter provides both practically and experimentally based guides that are thoroughly researched and ready to be applied in your actual practice. The companion workbook provides a skill-building practicum of situational lessons that directly correspond to this text. The workbook's lessons address common administrative themes and agency dilemmas. In combination, they will serve as vehicles for use in developing your own administrative practice model.

Benefits of This Book as Advanced Curriculum for Social Work

The profession of social work is in need of an integrative, multisystemic, and evidence-supported agency administration and program management curriculum. Comprehensively defined, this curriculum should be grounded in theory and applied research and based on cultural responsiveness. This text, *Integrative Practice in and for Larger Systems: Transforming Administration of People, Organizations, and Community*, is written for students and teachers of social administration and program management who seek such a comprehensive technology. The book thoroughly addresses important ecological factors that similar texts ignore or fail to emphasize, and it provides a culturally responsive integration of the combined relevancies of theory, policy, research, and both internal and external politics. We believe that these are among the foremost factors considered in sound administration and program management practice.

Upon reading this book, students will learn that theory development is an ongoing pursuit of responsible social administrators and managers engaged in social work practice. This book emphasizes the interface between social administration and the varying dimensions of social policy in service coordination. These crucial social policy dimensions include development, implementation, evaluation, and advocacy for systems change through evidence-based management practice.

Based in a longitudinal model development process, this book contains a system for performance measurement and the management of information. This method provides rich quantitative and qualitative data, coupled with a permanent performance database for use by managers and staff members when making critical decisions. In support of developing strong managerial skills, students learn practical ways to think through a problem or to map goals attainment with performance data as their guide. Such an empirical foundation appeals to science-driven practitioners, journal editors, and funders.

Unlike other graduate books on social administration, this one targets the salient issue of agency environment and its impacts on sound integrative practice in and for larger systems. It also highlights the value of the organization and structure of the service delivery process. The latter impacts structural factors such as authority, autonomy, and accountability. This book acknowledges and examines structural conditions as vital knowledge components for managers when organizing service delivery within and between service-providing agencies.

Finally, this text appeals to teachers and students seeking sound management principles and effective administrative practice skills. Students who desire careers as administrators must develop important core competencies. Chief among these proficiencies needed in social administration practice are (1) the capacity to make decisions guided by evidence and critical thinking, (2) the facilitation of administrative practice, interagency service coordination, and social policy interfaces, (3) the management of inter- and intra-agency politics and negotiations, (4) a practical understanding of the role of theory development, and (5) the use of culturally responsive frameworks that support administrative practice at multiple levels.

Significance as a Textbook

So why do we need a new book like *Integrative Practice in and for Larger Systems: Transforming Administration of People, Organizations, and Communities?* Much of the macro social work body of literature evidences a major curricular gap. An article by Au (1994) reviews social work literature over a 12-year period from 1980 to 1992, examining (a) the state of social welfare administration in the discipline of social work, (b) the status of theory development, and (c) contemporary debates and challenges for people seeking careers as social welfare administrators and managers. This was a period of rapid growth of needs and reliance on social welfare administration at the federal, state, and municipal levels of government.

This growth resulted in the emergence of nonprofit and publicly managed human service agencies as vehicles to address many of the growing needs for the distribution and management of the goods, services, and products of social service systems of care. The development of knowledge in service delivery, like the social work profession in general, has been borrowed from multiple disciplines and has brought forth interpretive differences, controversies, and debates.

The initial theory base of social welfare administration is borrowed from business management, public administration, psychology, and sociology. A major challenge since the beginning of the social work profession has been how to borrow ways of thinking from other disciplines while remaining recognizably distinct in our own theory development. Achieving a definitive disciplinary identity remains a challenge. As a discipline, we have not been able to rely solely on management practice theory developed by social work practitioners as a basis to teach our students. Reasons for this include (a) the youth of the discipline itself, (b) the profession's heavy reliance on social welfare administration over the past 20 years, and (c) the lack of time afforded practitioners to integrate competing theoretical frameworks into a distinct and unified knowledge base.

These explanations are principal considerations, though these are not the only reasons. They help to explain the lack of coherent best-theory bases among practitioners for use in preparing students as administrators of agencies and managers of social services. To assess the nature of theory development in social welfare administration, Au's 1994 empirical study of 13 major texts on social service administration and human service management provides a thorough analysis. It represents an evaluation of the profession's theory development and measures the scope of knowledge provided by leading textbooks on social administration and program management. Au used a content analysis format to analyze the different theoretical frameworks used in the sample of 13 textbooks on human service management. These books were selected based on four criteria: (1) texts were all written by prominent scholars of social welfare administration; (2) the experience of the authors was based in research, teaching, publishing, and practice; (3) the texts were reviewed and cited in the academic press, such as *Administration in Social Work*; and (4) edited texts were excluded unless based in a common theme and framework. Au's findings considered eight variables: (1) interface between policy and service, (2) theoretical orientation, (3) management targets, (4) empirical support, (5) uniqueness of human service organizations, (6) normative assumptions about human service management, (7) major managerial tasks, and (8) levels of management.

Au's findings were informative. The data showed a marginal relationship between management practices and social policy. Few texts demonstrated how social policy influenced or shaped the management approach or the administrative methods used. Examples of books that considered the interrelationship between social policy and social welfare administration are Gates (1980), Gummer (1990), and Simyar and Lloyd-Jones (1988). The works that demonstrated little or no relationship between social policy and social services viewed social administration as a rational planning or implementation activity. The data indicated that textbooks on social administration focus primarily on the technical aspects of management. However, as the dates of the works become more recent, the focus on social administration as a function of social policy becomes more apparent.

Au's study revealed that the theoretical orientations used in most of the textbooks reviewed were based in a "rational approach or the resource dependence approach to human service management" (Au, 1994, p. 39). In this context, the rational approach to social administration is defined as a purpose-driven and coordinated activity generally connected to some organizational goal, social need, or problem. Textbooks that used the resource dependency model put emphasis on the broad ecological circumstances that shape the organization's internal and external relationships. Au points to the need for texts that blend these approaches, considering political and ecological circumstances along with the technical aspects of rational planning and implementation, so the student may get a broader framework to use in management practice. Au noted a few other concerns, such as the lack of articulation and consistency of ideas. In this sense, concern rests with the introduction of the ideas and terms that comprise theoretical orientations. He felt that, in many instances, the ideas were not carefully explained or consistently used throughout the textbooks reviewed. He concludes that:

> The above discussion suggests that the discipline of social welfare administration has to date attained a certain level of maturity in terms of theory and knowledge development, but not enough. As it stands, we have probably moved beyond the stage of simply relying on practice wisdom or knowledge imported from other fields in theorizing about human service management. However, it is also quite obvious that we have not progressed much further beyond that point. Apparently, there is still a lack of indigenous theories, which are coherent, conceptually sound, and can support social welfare administration as a professional practice. With respect to this, more efforts are needed to improve the situation. (Au, 1994, p. 43)

Few of the books reviewed identify the environment as a target for management intervention. Much of the foci lay in the organization, programs, or people. Another important finding was the lack of evidence or empirical support for the methods used in most books reviewed. Only 4 of the 13 texts had empirical foundations. Most of the texts reviewed defined human service organizations as entities that were distinct from other organizations. In that same spirit, most of the textbooks reviewed defined the assumptions or goals of human service organization in terms of outcomes, such as service effectiveness and efficacy.

Furthermore, Au identified five frequently cited managerial tasks emphasized in the textbooks. These included (1) planning and decision-making, (2) staffing and personnel management, (3) organizing, (4) evaluating, and (5) budgeting and financial management. The eight most infrequently cited managerial tasks identified included (1) managing organizational politics, (2) working with committees or boards, (3) resource acquisition and allocation, (4) managing interorganizational relations and transorganizational systems, (5) using and managing performance measurement and information systems, (6) managing organizational change within a generational perspective, (7) need assessment and protection of clients' rights, and (8) job completion and strategy implementation. Au's research clearly shows that most texts are written for an intended audience of only chief executive officers or executive directors.

Au concluded that two crucial curricular needs are unmet. First, theory must be developed that covers social welfare administration. The basis of this theory must be broad and encompassing of the criteria. Second, theory and practice methods, which account for the unique aspects of human service organizations, must be developed. The foci of rational perspectives, including planning and implementation frameworks, must be combined with theory and practice methods covering environmental, systemic, and ecological conditions and other relevant contextual dynamics such as culture.

This perspective is further elucidated by Edwards, Cooke, and Reid (1996). These authors describe the reduction in federal responsibility for social services and related phenomena, such as changes to the economy, social structure, and public policy as impetus that drives two different types of social welfare management approach: (1) total quality management and (2) reengineering. Neither of these technical approaches is sufficient to address the curricular needs of twenty-first-century students seeking careers in social administration and program management of services used across a host of different racial and ethnic context.

The literature just reviewed and referenced throughout this book provides conceptual support for students. This book exposes students to a social administration and program management integrative practice curriculum that (1) interfaces with culture and social policy; (2) considers multiple levels of management; (3) is empirically supported; (4) considers utilization of political skills, both inside and outside the organization, as a useful means to achieve goals; and (5) provides a technology to strategically lead, plan, and manage issues that are internal and external to the human service organization's environment. The methodology in this book was developed and tested over a seven-year period in a nonprofit organization (Briggs, 1994, 1996, 2001a). It was used in the successful training and development of family advocacy and systems change organizations (Briggs, 2009) incorporating many of the lessons included in this text.

Given what you have read so far, are you still interested? Does a curriculum that recognizes and addresses the real complexities of social administration and management appeal to you? Are you a teacher who desires the best methodologies to prepare future administrators for success? Are you a student who is considering a career as an administrator of a social service agency? If so, you'll want to ensure mastery of the core competencies that effective administrators use to secure funding and make social policy work for their stakeholders. Whether you have just been hired to supervise a foster care program, manage a system of care comprised of pooled funding from different organizations, or are currently working as a social work supervisor in an organization that provides family support and case management services, then you have selected the best book to help you achieve your goals.

We know that schools of social work must prepare their graduates in social administration and program management with curricula that will enable them to practice in a market that they now share with for-profit Fortune 500 companies, such as Lockheed International. In order to remain competitive and consistent with other graduate schools, social work schools must develop cutting-edge curricula that fill the gaps in our knowledge bases. This text does just that. *Integrative Practice in and for Larger Systems: Transforming Administration of People, Organizations, and Communities* provides a bridge to integrate knowledge bases and sound management approaches with organizational behavior management and program implementation.

Eight core themes permeate the chapters of this text. The first of eight themes is policy practice as an approach to and context for administering a diversity of social services. In this book, students learn what really drives the establishment of social policy and why the various regulations for program implementation have little to do with research and more to do with the politics of funding and competing power bases. The book provides students with an integrated view of social policy and social administration and includes an examination of critical factors involved in the administration of social policy and the management of its implementation through the task environments of nonprofit organizations. Yet, prior to our discussion on social policy, in Chapter 2, we turn our attention to what drives the establishment of social policy: the culture of power, the structural determinants of culture, and the conspiracy of silence shielding white privilege and power in larger systems. In Chapter 2, we chronicle the need for curricular innovations in cultural competence education that include an understanding of the conspiracy of silence and the ill effects of the structural determinants of culture. We believe that innovations in cultural competence education are needed now so that graduates may recognize the intractable nature of the ill effects of the structural determinants of culture. We highlight the education in civil and human rights that is needed by practitioners to affect access to the social determinants of well-being to realize the overall achievement of the mission of social work for racially diverse groups and communities. We examine the state of knowledge of cultural competence and discuss the strategies needed to educate social work students about the culture of power and the structural determinants of culture and their relationships to civil and human rights and social justice issues. Enhancing civil and human rights competencies and implications for social work are presented as a perfect entry to Chapter 3, which presents social policy as a structural determinant that influences integrative practice in and for larger systems.

Unraveling the Covert Aspects of the Culture of Oppression

THE INFLUENCE OF THE CULTURE OF THE
CONSPIRACY OF SILENCE, CULTURE OF POWER,
AND STRUCTURAL DETERMINANTS OF THE CULTURE
OF WHITE PRIVILEGE ON INTEGRATIVE PRACTICE
IN AND FOR LARGER SYSTEMS

Introduction

Rooted in the democratic value system and the Constitution of the United States
are the profession of social work's core mission and commitments to diversity
and social justice (Daniels, 2015). In the furtherance of these idyllic aims, here we
chronicle the need for innovations in cultural competence education in social work.
Social workers must be able to effectively practice with cultural humility and social
and emotional intelligence if they are to (1) enable access by racially diverse clients
to the social determinants of health; (2) enhance well-being across racially diverse
systems of all sizes; (3) utilize research discoveries that result in positive social
change across the life span and those systems of care involving health, behavioral
health, corrections, housing, education, and labor for racially diverse communities;
and (4) be active partners with these populations in achieving genuine social and
economic justice for vulnerable and oppressed people (Council on Social Work
Education [CSWE], 2015; Freire, 1970; Gil, 1994).

Revised and approved by the delegates of the National Association of Social
Workers (NASW) in 2008,

> The primary mission of the social work profession is to enhance human well-
> being and help meet the basic human needs of all people, with particular
> attention to the needs and empowerment of people who are vulnerable, op-
> pressed, and living in poverty. A historic and defining feature of social work
> is the profession's focus on individual well-being in a social context and the

well-being of society. Fundamental to social work is attention to the environmental forces that create, contribute to, and address problems in living.

Social workers promote social justice and social change with and on behalf of clients. "Clients" is used inclusively to refer to individuals, families, groups, organizations, and communities. Social workers are sensitive to cultural and ethnic diversity and strive to end discrimination, oppression, poverty, and other forms of social injustice. These activities may be in the form of direct practice, community organizing, supervision, consultation, administration, advocacy, social and political action, policy development and implementation, education, and research and evaluation. Social workers seek to enhance the capacity of people to address their own needs. Social workers also seek to promote the responsiveness of organizations, communities, and other social institutions to individuals' needs and social problems. (NASW Code of Ethics Preamble, p. 1)

As a context for moving forward, key concepts such as *oppression, injustice,* and *social justice* and their definitions need to be identified and understood. In this chapter, Gil's (1994) definition of oppression and injustice has been adopted. It "refers to relations of domination and exploitation—economic, social, and psychological—between individuals; between social groups and classes within and beyond societies; and, globally, between entire societies" (p. 233). Gil (1994) defines injustice as "discriminatory, dehumanizing, and development-inhibiting conditions of living (e.g., unemployment, poverty, homelessness, and lack of health care), imposed by oppressors" among marginalized and vulnerable people (p. 233). Alternatively, Barker's (1995) definition of social justice is adopted in this chapter. According to Barker (1995), social justice is "an ideal condition in which all members of a society have the same rights, protection, opportunities, obligations, and social benefits"(p. 354). According to Davis (2016), the issues of race, racism, and injustice have not been a focal point in this country. Citing recent setbacks in civil rights legislation and the marginalized plight of African Americans, Latino/as, and Native Americans, Davis (2016) believes that "for far too long, our society has elected to ignore the long standing elephant in the room—racial injustice" (p. 3).

To actualize the social justice mission of social work for racially diverse groups, such as African Americans, in larger systems, in Part 1 of this chapter we examine the state of knowledge in cultural competence education in social work. In Part 2, we highlight the culture of the conspiracy of silence. In Part 3, we examine structural social work and five structural determinants of culture, and, in Part 4, we articulate the culture of power and its influence on the structural determinants of the culture of white privilege. In Part 5, we draw implications for designing curricula in civil and human rights in Social Work. In Part 6, we present "next steps" that detail the social action and civil and human rights education needed by social workers to realize the competencies that will enable the systems they work with to realize and experience the social determinants of well being.

Part 1: State of Theory Developments on Cultural Competence

The recent changes to the Council on Social Work Education's (CSWE) Educational Policy and Accreditation Standards (EPAS) (CSWE, 2015) mandates accredited schools of social work to include a heavier saturation of content on diversity and difference in the educational preparation of undergraduate and graduate students seeking degrees in social work. The CSWE defines diversity as "the intersectionality of multiple factors including but not limited to age, class, color, culture, disability, and ability, ethnicity, gender, gender identity, and expression, immigration status, marital status, political ideology, race, religion/spirituality, sex, sexual orientation, and tribal sovereign status" (CSWE, 2015, p. 14). This broad definition of diversity supports an inclusive learning and social work practice paradigm that seeks "to affirm and support persons with diverse identities" (CSWE, 2015, p. 14).

One of the major threads that undergird this chapter is the extent to which this broad diversity filter ensures sufficient focus on the threats and challenges to cultural-specific well-being, such as the well-being of historically oppressed groups such as African Americans (Daniels & Patterson, 2012; Davis, 2016). The need to focus on race and racism and its deleterious effects on historically marginalized groups (e.g., African American and Native American communities) has been identified by Davis (2016) as America's grand challenge in his address at the 2016 Society for Social Work Research Annual Program Meeting. The dearth of emphasis on race and the issues impacting African American well-being is ironic given the contributions of early African American scholars in historically black universities and colleges (HBCUs) to social work education (Bowles, Hopps, & Clayton, 2016). Through contributions made by W. E. B. Dubois and E. Franklin Frasier, the profession of social work began to facilitate student learning in an inclusive environment and to focus on social justice, empowerment, and strengths perspectives, as well as the use of community-based research as a tool for the assessment and treatment of the social problems of African Americans in this country (Bowles et al., 2016).

Despite these landmark contributions by African American scholars, the focus of early social work was on the agenda of the Sufferage Women's Movement, which advocated equal rights for white women; a focus on the plight of European immigrants; and, later, a focus on child labor (Bowles et al., 2016). Social work pioneers avoided the struggles of African Americans during the profession's infancy, which occurred during the Jim Crow Era. It should come as no surprise that the passing of the first social policy was done with the deliberate intent and practice of disqualifying African Americans as eligible beneficiaries for social insurance (Poole, 2006). Social work's early insular emphasis on diversity and its current myopic diversity emphasis has only fueled the furtherance of the inattentiveness of social work toward issues of race and racism in general and has, in particular, encouraged an apparent de-emphasis on issues impacting the well-being of historically oppressed groups such as African Americans, Native Americans, and Latino/a communities (Bowles et al., 2016; Davis, 2016; Hopps, 1982).

The need for increased emphasis on the civil and human rights of racially and ethnically diverse groups seeking and receiving social services is our primary thesis in this chapter.

STATE OF THE SCIENCE AND RESEARCH DEVELOPMENTS IN CULTURAL COMPETENCE

Anderson, Scrimshaw, Fullilove, Fielding, Normand, and the Task Force on Community Preventive Services (2003) conducted a systematic review of the research on the effectiveness of five culturally competent approaches to healthcare. They were unable to reach any conclusions because of the low quantity of studies and the lack of methodological rigor used in the few studies available. Presently, healthcare is one of the key areas of interest regarding cultural competence as it pertains to institutions, providers, and the various disciplines that interface with healthcare. The absence of research about cultural competency in healthcare demands immediate attention.

A Dearth of Research on Culture-Specific Interventions

Sue et al. (2006) and Briggs (2009) highlight that few intervention and efficacy studies of evidence-based interventions for culture-specific groups exist. Even fewer studies of the efficacy and effectiveness of culture-specific interventions exist (Bernal & Saez-Santiago, 2006; Burns, Hoagwood, & Mrazek, 1999; Hoagwood, Burns, Kiser, Ringeisen, & Schoenwald, 2001).

Miniscule Attention to Structural Determinants of Culture

Aside from viewing culture from an anthropological and sociological perspective, culture has been recognized as a major social determinant of well-being and of other behaviors of systems of all sizes as far back as Galbraith (1960). Cultural competence is a central value and an ethical mandate in social work (NASW, 1999, 2001), and it is a critical feature of education in social work (CSWE, 2008, 2015), yet its relevance to the indoctrination of students into the profession is a subject of wide and spirited debate among academics and practicing professional social workers (Johnson & Munch, 2009; Park, 2005; Pon, 2009). Cultural diversity or cultural competence has been heralded as chief among the assets of professional social work training by some (Garran & Rozas, 2013; Saunders, Haskins, & Vasquez, 2015), while others view it as a perpetuation of symbolic and institutional racism (Abrams & Moio, 2009; Briggs, 2001; Johnson & Munch, 2009; Park, 2005; Pon, 2009; Razack & Jeffrey, 2002) or a platform from which to advance rhetoric with no action.

For example, there is growing evidence beyond McMahon and Allen-Meares (1992) treatise on the apparent absence of focus on racial diversity, which emphasizes the disjuncture between what faculties of schools of social work endorse as their commitment to diversity and social justice versus what they emphasize in their mission statements. A content analysis study of the 2012 top-ranked 50 schools of social work by Holosko, Winkel, Crandall, and Briggs (2015) showed that, on average, the schools had very long and vague mission statements ($N = 75$ words in length). Among their findings, they reported that the top 50 schools' mission statements failed to focus on diversity (41%), oppression (29%), policy (27%), advocacy (0%), ethics/ethical practice (0%), and evidence-based practice (25%). They concluded that the mission statements of schools of social work need to incorporate the profession's core values and emerging research. In a subsequent comparison content analysis of the mission statements of the top 23 HBCUs, the focus on diversity, service, and African Americans was emphasized more in HBCU mission statements, while research and scholarship were emphasized more in the mission statements of the top 50 schools of social work located in primarily white institutions (Briggs, et al., 2018). In a further analysis of undergraduate and graduate course titles in the top 23 HBCUs' BSW and MSW programs, the terms "race" and "African American" were not used (Briggs et al., 2018).

Training and education in the myriad structural roles and influences of the culture of white privilege broadens the social justice competencies of the professional social worker. It is one avenue the profession can use to reliably prepare social workers to attain civil and human rights competencies through learning the skills to mobilize and launch social action aimed at achieving and sustaining social justice. Providing students a fuller education on the structural determinants of culture, one that incorporates civil and human rights knowledge, policy, practice, and research competencies that comprise models of social action, is a strategic direction that social work leaders ought to pursue. In recently published research on the Diversity and Oppression Scale, the authors' focus on social work student knowledge of diversity and oppression included an assessment of students' confidence in their "knowledge of institutional oppression" and the ways "the misuse of power negatively impacts the human rights of individual and group" in client systems (Windsor, Shorkey & Battle, 2015, p. 64). Educating social work students about oppression is complicated by (a) the lack of a specific definition of either oppression or social justice in the profession's code of ethics (Gil, 1994) and (b) the adverse effects of lumping together the oppressive experiences of different at-risk groups (Hopps, 1982). Hopps (1982) recommends that social work develop specific and measurable definitions of "the unique types and levels of oppression and exclusion" (p. 3). According to Hopps (1982) "the blurring of the nature and degree of [groups at risk] oppression serves neither [each group at risk] respective causes nor social justice" (p. 3). Hopps (1982) believes that "social work needs to focus on the nuances, subtleties, and specifics of different forms of oppression"(p. 3). As a guide for social workers to determine which groups at risk should have preference through social policy for problem redress, Hopps (1982) recommends Daniel C. Maguire's social ethics perspective. Maguire, cited in Hopps (1982), believes groups at risks that meet the following conditions qualify for preferential attention: (1) alternatives to enforced preferences are not available, (2) bias is pervasive and detached from self-awareness by members of the dominant group, (3) bias has become institutionalized, and (4) the members of the groups at risk are without "an avenue of escape from their disempowered status" (p. 3).

The need for students to be educated in the assessment and redress of social injustices and civil and human rights violations has never been as evident as now. The changing demographics of the United States, access to the global knowledge economy, and an increasing emphasis on global education are all prerequisites for full citizenship in a globally centered society and will also be accompanied by a rise in threats to the social determinants of well-being and to the civil and human rights of socially, economically, and politically marginalized, vulnerable, and undocumented citizens (Baron, 1969; Briggs, Bank, & Briggs, 2014; Commission on Social Determinants of Health [CSDH], 2008; Katiuzhinsky & Okech, 2014). Such rising pressure will demand an organized social welfare response that will not be relegated to a lower priority status in the social welfare and national domestic policy agendas. A number of recent events have reignited the nationwide public debate on civil and human rights violations in this country. These include, for example, the gains made in legislation on marriage equality for same-sex partners; the passage of the Affordable Care Act (memorialized as Obamacare); the recent Supreme Court decisions that reversed the legislative gains in voters' rights made during the 1960s Civil Rights era; the rise in the number of dependent unaccompanied children and immigration issues; the nationally sensationalized homicides of Eric Garner by a team of New York City police officers aided by four emergency medical technicians in 2014, of Trayvon Martin by a neighborhood watch volunteer in 2012, of Michael Brown by a Saint Louis County (Missouri) police officer in 2014, of Tamir Rice in 2014 by two police officers, and of Freddie Gray by six indicted Baltimore police officers in 2015; the debate over freedom of religious expression and its ties to international terrorism rhetoric and platforms; the reframing of many social problems as determinants of the rise in incarceration (Briggs, Bank, & Briggs, 2014; Geronima, 2011; Golembeski & Fullilove, 2008); and the rise in racially disproportionate and disparate experiences in health, mental health, and employment, along with a reduction in financial resources for health and human services.

Part 2: Enhancing Cultural Competence Education in Social Work

In this section, we discuss the need for innovations in cultural competence education to equip social workers working in and leading larger systems that seek to achieve well-being and dismantle oppression. To unravel the elusive nature of the culture of oppression, graduates or soon to be professional social workers working in and leading large systems will need to recognize the challenges that come with addressing the conspiracy of silence and the intractable and sustained ill effects of the structural determinants of the culture of white privilege on vulnerable groups such as African Americans.

CULTURE OF CONSPIRACY OF SILENCE ABOUT CHRONIC OPPRESSION

A tension that complicates giving attention to racial diversity is the existence of a conspiracy of silence between historically oppressed groups such as African Americans and the larger society about the culture of oppression and white privilege and its harmful effects on marginalized groups (Danieli, 1998). Grounded in the history of slavery in the United States, this conspiracy of silence remains the "elephant in the room." It has been the double-down position of the Republican agenda since the apparent failure of the War on Poverty and the Great Society Programs of the Civil Rights era of the 1960s and 1970s. Despite right-wing conservative Ann Coulter's acknowledgment that the country owes something to African Americans, there is a rise in chronic, racially disproportionate burdens and injustices encountered by African Americans. It is also important to note that many of the federal protections achieved in the Great Society Programs have been eroded. In twenty-first-century America, the struggle for genuine equal justice by African Americans in the post-Civil Rights Era has been reprioritized as a lesser concern in the current political and racially indifferent climate.

Current political interest and sympathy is with protecting the economic elite and reversing the devastation of the poor and working classes who once made up the white middle class in this country (Carville & Greene, 2012; Loury, 2002). The recent focus on the white middle class's demise has been accompanied by a rise in many social problems that were once relegated to the inhabitants of inner-city communities populated primarily by poor African Americans and other historically marginalized groups. Given these realities and the broad-base emphasis on diversity in social work, there is a lesser emphasis placed on race and the injustices encountered by historically marginalized and oppressed groups such as African Americans (Davis, 2016) amid the growing protections and benefits accrued to white women (Hopps, 1982; Murray, 1984). Thus, the greater emphasis on diversity will fuel a de-emphasis and cause less attention to be paid to the protracted plight of historically oppressed racial groups such as African Americans (Hopps, 1982).

As far back as its humble beginnings during the Jim Crow Era and later recognized as contributing to the failure of the Great Society and War on Poverty programs of the 1960s and 1970s (Hoshino, 1973), the profession of social work has been inattentive in its design and use of curricula developments in the area of racial diversity. Social work has failed in pursuing a broad-base focus on the structural determinants of the culture of white privilege and culture of power (Themba-Nixon, 2001; Delpit, 1995). The structural determinants of white privilege involves accessing advantages and preferential treatmenat through the culture of power, intra-organizational and inter-institutional network relationship. These structural systems of influence continue to preserve racial inequalities which are manifested through policys and procedures that serve to establish interlocking systems of oppression. (Baron, 1969; Briggs et al., 2018; Gil, 1994; Themba-Nixon, 2001). These determinants and the conspiracy of silence that exists between the oppressed and the larger society requires strategic policy practice attention and broad base social change. The intractable conditions that sustain second-class citizenship and the denial of equal justice for African Americans need public exposure and redress through social policy and social work practice (Briggs, et al., 2018; Briggs & Paulson, 1996; Delprit, 1995).

Danieli (1998) describes the phenomena of silencing and the feeling of shame and further victimization that results when people who have not experienced similar forms of trauma and oppression cannot understand the plight of survivors or their aftermath (p. 4). With respect to Holocaust survivors, Danieli's (1998) interviews of survivors document what they encountered when recalling for others what they experienced, which included "indifference, avoidance, repression, and denial of their Holocaust experiences" (p. 4). Danieli (1998) posits that these reactions are an indication that the relived accounts by Holocaust survivors were thought to be too fantastic to believe. Danieli (1998) believes that the multidimensional silence that accompanies multigenerational legacies of trauma and oppression is applicable to the Jim Crow experiences of African Americans in Florida in 1923, when "the largely black town of Rosewood was burned to the ground, and many were killed and wounded, and others, especially children, were forced to flee and hide for days in the swamps. . . . We weren't suppose to talk about Rosewood" (p. 6). Others, such as Tammy Evans, reflect on the conspiracy of silence about illicit relationships among southern whites and blacks involving an underworld of illegal enterprises in Florida during the segregationist Jim Crow era. The torrid and unlawful relationships between blacks and whites in Florida were only exposed during the trial for a white man who had been murdered by his married African American female intimate partner. Heldke, and O'Connor (2004) referred to this phenomenon as a "culture of silence which is also known as a conspiracy of silence." By definition, a conspiracy of silence involves a numbing of reactions and indifference by members of both the victimized group and the larger society toward the horrific mistreatment and oppression of the victimized group (Danieli, 1998). Gil (1994) believes that "oppression tends to be more effective in achieving its apparent ends-enforcement of exploitation, social injustice, and constraints on liberty-when its victims, as well its perpetrators, are not conscious of the social dynamics involved, when the victims perceive their conditions as 'natural' and inevitable, and, especially, when they share illusions of being 'free'" (p. 231). Gil (1994) reminds us that there is precedent in history, where the consequences of the "denial and rationalization of oppression and social injustice, and their validation as sacred and secular 'law and order' may actually have been the most effective weapons in the defense and legitimization of unjust ways of life that tended to benefit primarily privileged social groups and classes"

(p. 231). Given the reality of unequal treatment through disproportionate burdens of threats to health and well-being (Hacker, 1992); the persistence of widespread social, political, and legislative marginalization of the poor (Loury, 2002); the apparent absence of legal enforcement protection and penalties for civil and human rights violations (Themba-Nixon, 2001); and a climate of apathy surrounding both victims of mistreatment and the ruling classes, accompanied by the criminalization of many social problems encountered by members of the victimized group (Davis, 2007), reinforces and sustains the conspiracy of silence between African Americans and the general society. Sadly, this protracted silence has existed since the ending of the Great Society Programs of the 1970s. Only recently have the heavily publicized homicides of unarmed African American young and adult men by police officers across a number of cities nationwide captured the general publics attention. These killings have engendered organized groups such as the Black Lives Matter and have led to expressions of concern and public outrage by other socially conscious citizens, even in the Northwestern city of Portland, Oregon, which is predominantly comprised of white residents. Residents marched by the hundreds throughout downtown Portland in protest and in solidarity with the Black Lives Matter movement occurring in other parts of the country.

While predictably, the silence is upheld by the people who intend on preserving white privilege, white supremacy, and racial injustices, it is also sustained by the good and civilized segments of society who know all too well about the struggle for genuine equality by black people in this country. Yet the lack of transparent social protest and activism by socially conscious people reinforces racial indifference while also contributing to and maintaining a broader climate of tolerance for the status quo and the perpetuation of second-class citizenship for African Americans by both whites and blacks.

Incorporating a structural determinants of culture theoretical framework in the training of social work students provides education and skill development training in (1) forming cultural humility, social and emotional intelligence, racial consciousness, and racial diversity while pursuing the well-being of African Americans; (2) understanding how to appraise structural determinants of the culture of white privilege and power (Briggs, 2016); (3) marshaling effective, socially responsible social action efforts and implementing best practices and culturally responsive models of practices to erode social justice protections to civil and human rights and social justice issues; and (4) learning evaluation skills to carefully document lessons learned through actual practice to inform research on effective culture-specific practice. Cultural competence curricula of this type is needed but often goes missing in social work education.

The absence of this important knowledge has serious ramifications. It calls into question the legitimacy of social work as a social justice profession. It also means that many graduates of professional schools of social work have been improperly prepared due to the absence of curricula content and instruction about the interrelationships among restrictive social policies, the reframing of social welfare problems as crimes, and the concomitant rise in disparate health and human services experiences, accompanied by a conspiracy of silence involving civil/ human rights violations. Consequently, social workers are ill equipped to advocate and organize broad social action that will result in positive change to uphold the civil and human rights of culturally different client systems. The broad effect of this inaction is that the entire social work industry, including the client-consumers we serve, are all captive actors of systems influenced by socially determined forces imposing a culture of inequality and white privilege. This results in a culture of despair and marginalization that is unequally distributed (Briggs, 2001a; Briggs & Leary, 2001; Themba-Nixon, 2001; Wheeler & Briggs, 2010). This culture of despair is exacerbated by a plethora of disproportionate burdens and cultural incompetence tolls imposed on its economically non-elite citizens (Briggs, Briggs, Miller, & Paulson, 2011; Coates, 2014; Feagin, 2010; Roberts, 2009). This is especially true for citizens from diverse backgrounds while the preservation of the structural determinants of the culture of white privilege continue to exist in this country (Briggs & McBeath, 2010; Briggs, Briggs, Miller, & Paulson, 2011; Randall, 2002; Themba-Nixon, 2001). Themba-Nixon's (2001) definition of white privilege, its structural manifestations and oppressive effects on African Americans and other historically oppressed groups, and the need to eliminate it was clearly articulated to the United Nations Convention on the Elimination of All Forms of Racial Discrimination (CERD). Themba-Nixon (2001) reports:

> Our focus is on the persistence of white privilege, a system that accrues to whites (or European Americans) greater wealth, resources, more access and higher quality access to justice, services, capital—virtually every form of benefits to be reaped from US society—than other racial groups. Conversely, white privilege has resulted in impoverishment and injustice for the vast majority of those belonging to racial minorities. White privilege is more than a set of attitudes or individual opinions. It is an overarching, comprehensive framework of policies, practices, institutions and cultural norms that undergird every aspect of US society. Too often, discussion of racial discrimination focuses solely on the effects on those who are oppressed as if there are no oppressors or beneficiaries. In this analysis, racial minorities are cast as "problems to be solved" instead of victims of an unjust system. Yet, as 19th century African American freedom fighter Frederick Douglass put it nearly a century ago, "There is no negro problem. The problem is whether the American people have loyalty enough, honor enough, patriotism enough, to live up to their own constitution. . . ." The US will come into compliance with CERD provisions—and other human rights conventions—only when it dismantles white privilege and makes the promise of "equality and justice for all" the letter and effect of the law. (Themba-Nixon, 2001, p. 5).

Part 3: Structural Social Work and the Structural Determinants of White Privilege

Any focus on the culture of white privilege and the conspiracy of silence surrounding it would not be complete without a discussion on its relationship to perspectives on structural social work (Mullaly, 1997). Structural social work offers a systemic perspective on the contributions of exploitation, power imbalance, and interest group politics in determining the plight, marginalization, and chronic oppression of the disadvantaged through institutional arrangements. Weinberg (2008) summarizes the contributions of the structural social work perspective as a theory for understanding the interplay between institutional arrangements and inequality based on race and gender. She states:

> The suggestion is that our institutions are structured in such a way as to discriminate against some people on the basis of class, race, gender, ability, sexual orientation, age, religion, etc. and that a function of the profession of social work should be on eliminating these disparities. Structural theory argues that these arrangements serve those in power, allowing them to maintain their power and privilege at the expense of others.

In furtherance of this view, Magee and Galinsky (2008) argue the inherently advantageous relationship between status and power as an important perpetuating mechanism for sustaining hierarchical belief systems in organizations. To illustrate the reinforcing dynamic of power and status manifested structurally as the covert ill effects of the culture of white privilege, five related structural effects come to mind: (1) intra-embedded relational institutional effects, (2) interactive "double-edged sword" effects, (3) inextricable effects, (4) interwoven effects, and (5) the interaction of iatrogenic effects.

INTRA-EMBEDDED RELATIONAL INSTITUTIONAL EFFECTS

The intra-embedded relational structural effect of culture involves an incestuous arrangement between two or more systems embedded within a single institution. This hand-and-glove interchange between distinct units of a larger system is administratively sanctioned. The embedded arrangements among systems within a cultural institution, such as law enforcement, can be used to sustain the status quo as well as lawfully sanction differential racial experiences. In many of the different homicide cases of unarmed African American male youth and men, law enforcement policies and procedures have been used to exonerate the police from any legal responsibility in or penalties for causing these deaths.

Law enforcement policies and procedures are the structural condition that both sanctions the use of excessive force while also shielding police officers from prosecution and incarceration for limiting the civil and human rights of people they arrest.

Another equally powerful structural condition which further shields law enforcement from criminal prosecution for causing or contributing to the death of citizens in their jurisdiction is the inherently biased partnership that exists between the local district attorneys' offices and the police departments.

Prosecutors use different legal theories and precedents to form the basis of the prosecution of individuals. A recent federal report by the US Attorney General's Office found evidence of patterns of excessive force used by law enforcement in Cleveland, Ohio, in community policing efforts to maintain law and order. They also observed insufficient check-and-balance accountability systems to address the apparent organized system of unrestricted privilege that sustained practices of excessive force and that resulted in the loss of lives without any legal redress for the victims.

An additional structural condition that is part of the chain of protection for law enforcement lies in the relationship between the grand jury and district attorney. In the Eric Garner homicide, the district attorney defined the case in terms of one officer and not the entire team of officers. By using the other officers involved as witnesses for the prosecution in the grand jury proceedings, which are sealed from public scrutiny, it is quite possible that the limited scope of the investigation of one officer and the limited instructions given to the grand jury for considering an indictment for reckless homicide could have been compromised by a number of conditions. One condition that prevented the arrest of the officer under suspicion was not allowing the jury to consider lesser charges, such as negligible homicide, against the single officer targeted for prosecution. The second condition was not considering the behaviors of all of the officers involved as equally implicated for prosecution. A third condition involved the repeated showing of the tape of the horrific and unjustified arrest of Eric Garner to the grand jury while using police academy policies and procedures as a cognitive filter that contextualized and justified all of the officers' actions. This aligned the testimony of the officers with immunity from prosecution, which gave them an opportunity to justify their actions as a function of their training and of the policies and procedures of the police academy.

All of these conditions served to desensitize the grand jury to the videotape arrest and to accept the actions of the officer under suspicion as justifiable. This insulated him from criminal prosecution and made it difficult for all of the officers to be found guilty under federal civil rights litigation. There is precedent in this area dating as far back as the Rodney King case of 1992, where, in the first trial, the all-white Simi-Valley jury found the officers not guilty and justified in their actions (Briggs, 2001). While the not-guilty verdict was later overturned, the structural conditions encompassing the unfettered discretion and privilege granted to the police through their academy training and standard operating policies and procedures, as well as the biased relationships between the district attorney, grand jury, and law enforcement, have not been understood as inter-institutional mechanisms that serve to sanction the use of differential treatment and excessive force in communities of color (Baron, 1969; Briggs & Paulson, 1996).

The last link in the chain of protection for law enforcement is the relationship of the prosecutor to the judiciary. There exist certain legal doctrines and precedents that judges and prosecutors subscribe to and that create the interpretative flexibility to determine whether or not to hold a given defendant accountable and/or culpable for acts that rise to the level of an offense or would be deemed criminal in any other circumstance. Judges are reluctant, whether directly or indirectly, to apply the legal doctrine of *res ipsa loquitur* ("the thing speaks for itself," a legal theory that holds that an injury is due to a defendant's negligence through the use of circumstantial evidence. It is analogous to evidence of a "smoking gun" without the hand). In many trials cases where a police officer's actions were found to be innocent of causing the homicide of an unarmed defendant, it is more likely that these cases involve the application of a legal doctrine and a legal test to determine culpability; these are, respectively, *respondeat superior* and *mens rea*. In *respondeat superior*, legal reasoning holds that an individual officer is not responsible, but his or her employer is responsible for the actions of employees performed within the course of their employment. In this context, by following police academy training, policies, and procedures, the officer's actions are administratively sanctioned. In *mens rea*, the prosecution has to prove without a doubt that the police officer's actions were motivated by criminal intent before the officer can be found criminally responsible for their actions.

INTERACTIVE DOUBLE-EDGE EFFECTS

A second structural effect of culture is its built-in interactive-based "double-edged sword" tendency to accrue benefits to whites for engaging cross-culturally while simultaneously "othering" people who are culturally different. Racial capitalism is an example that amplifies the benevolence and respect by whites that can be paid to racial difference while simultaneously accruing social and economic gains for associating cross culturally. Daniels and Patterson (2012), citing Bell (2003), echo this sentiment by describing the power of influence and incentives for whites to behave in accordance with the rules of democracy and civil rights. Sadly, there are no compelling social, political, and economic gains envisioned by the power and economic elite as incentives for investing in solutions that reverse the plight of racial and ethnic minorities, the homeless, abused and neglected children, the traumatized, or the clinically indigent who are at risk of behavioral health disorders. Public sentiment is with the decaying experience of the middle class (Barlett & Steele, 2012; Carville & Greenberg, 2012). Despite these downturns, ironically, federal policy continues to favor the economic elite and not the poor (Loury, 2002).

INEXTRICABLE EFFECTS

A third structural effect of culture is its inextricable countervailing determinants. People come from culture, while culture comes through people. Culture defines what constitutes mental health and what constitutes mental illness (Bowen, 2004; Briggs, 2014). Culture inhibits treatment access and influences its availability (Briggs, Bank, & Briggs, 2014). Culture influences the experiences of diverse communities while also influencing the general public's reactions to diversity. The relationship between capitalism and democracy is a perfect example of an inextricable relationship that favors the economic elite. The intractable relationship between political influence and privilege, economic status, and access to social capital as a result of membership in the economic elite is an example of an inextricable relationship to power. The ability of the economic elite to transgress and manipulate political processes is an example of an inextricable structural effect of culture. The assignment of minority status to communities of color and the stigma of second-class citizenship in America is yet another example of an inextricable structural effect of culture.

INTERWOVEN EFFECTS

A fourth structural effect of culture is its adhesive interwoven effects. The interwoven effects of culture involve the forced participation in reciprocal transactions. Through inter-institutional arrangements, the lack of participation or eligibility and the barriers encountered in one restrictive, highly regulated, public sector service system qualifies and ensures additional misery, taxation, and forced membership in other restrictive, highly regulated, service system sectors. For example, the lack of participation in and receipt of culturally appropriate health and mental health care has contributed to the disproportionate rate of child welfare involvement by African American families (Briggs & McBeath, 2010). The failure of at-risk youth to access modern health and human service innovations results in a number of consequences and poor adjustment in later life. Adolescents' contact with the criminal justice system is associated with a number of long-term negative adult outcomes: unemployment, substance abuse, and incarceration (Moffitt, Caspi, Harrington, & Milne, 2002). Factors that appear to protect youth from drug use include healthy relationships and open communication within the family, involvement in organized school activities, effective parental monitoring and limit setting, perceptions of future opportunity, educational aspirations, community support for drug avoidance behavior, and adult support for developing individual competencies (Briggs, Miller, Sayles, Tovar, & Dozier, 1997).

The "school-to-prison pipeline" based on school disciplinary policy and practice is an example of this kind of inter-institutional arrangement (Briggs & Paulson, 1996; Baron, 1969). The child welfare-to-juvenile justice system pipeline for African American youth is another example of an adhesive interwoven partnership between high-end, civil liberties–prohibitive service systems. Roberts (2009) refers to the effects of the inculcation of African American families and communities disproportionately involved in the child welfare and juvenile justice systems as representing a racial geography of participation of people of color trapped in dead end civil liberties–restricting service systems. Briggs, Briggs, Miller, and Paulson (2011) describe the assessment, diagnostic, treatment, and service delivery processes that result in culturally insensitive experiences for African Americans in public mental health systems.

The cultural and consumer challenges that accompany the adoption of research-informed treatments in social work and social agencies are highlighted by Briggs (2009).

Cultural Challenges

According to Briggs (2009), despite the introduction of research-informed treatments into child and family fields of practice, their cultural appropriateness remains unknown. A growing body of research raises cautions about research-informed interventions derived through pilot testing with Caucasian-only samples, in which no attention was given to analyzing their usefulness with racially diverse populations (Blasé & Fixsen, 2003). Additionally, too few racially diverse researchers, treatment outcomes, theories, and resources have been considered in the design, implementation, and research on the cultural appropriateness and responsiveness of research-informed treatments. Yet other researchers suggest that there has been insufficient attention paid to questions of how practitioners should allow for cultural adaptations, client collaboration, and client self-determination within empirically supported interventions (ESI) service frameworks (Briggs, 2009; Gambrill, 2007; Walker, Briggs, Koroloff, & Friesen, 2007).

Consumer Challenges

Consumer challenges that may limit the use of ESIs include a lack of knowledge of available effective services, limited advocacy skills of clients to request or access ESIs, and high consumer-borne costs for addressing the cognitive, family, social, and personal challenges that need to be managed during treatment (Gold, Glynn, & Mueser, 2006). Consumers may lack knowledge of the existence of ESIs, particularly if service providers or funding bodies do not inform would-be users of the existence and potential benefits of ESIs. Additionally, clients may not know how to access these services or may not be able to articulate what services and resources they need and that are available through ESIs. Furthermore, as Gambrill (2007) points out, a focus on ESIs derails attention to client values, experiences, and culture; informed consent; research utilization via electronic databases; and use of client choices.

ITERATION OF IATROGENIC EFFECTS

A fifth structural effect of culture is its iteration of iatrogenic effects, which are the cumulative adverse effects of culture. An example of this kind of compounding effect is found in Briggs and Paulson (1996). They illustrated the ill effects of a culture of inter-institutional arrangements in a public school setting example. In essence, it is quite simple—where you reside determines where you attend school, which influences what you learn and the quality of the instruction. This either prepares you for the knowledge economy or for college entrance, or it contributes to your limited education and the lack of skill sets required by any legitimate knowledge or service economy. This limited education relegates you to the "misery tax experiences" of the underclass, as depicted in *The New Jim Crow* by Michelle Alexander (2010). In her book, Alexander (2010) chronicles the iterative consequences of being an African American prisoner in the industrial prison pipeline/complex in this country. Another example of the unequal treatment experiences of children of color in the child welfare and juvenile justice experiences is reflected in their overrepresentation of these youth in powerlessness service delivery systems. Youth of color spend more time in juvenile justice custody, foster care, encounter more placement disruptions than white youth. What remains a matter of debate and contentiousness among researchers, policymakers, practitioners, and community advocates are the root causes for the racially disproportionate experiences of African Americans: research confirms the poor adjustment of African American foster care alumni while their white counterparts enjoy resilient and wealth-generating opportunities (Roberts, 2009).

As a structural determinant, culture encompasses intrapersonal, interpersonal, intra-institutional, and inter-institutional systemic characteristics and effects as highlighted earlier. The former two are typically the level and focus of training in cultural competence, while the latter two structural determinants of culture are not popular topics and are rarely discussed in the social work literature.

Part 4: Culture of Inter-institutional Racism and Culture of Power

The structural determinants of culture operate within institutional and inter-institutional spheres. They comprise the embedded characteristics and dynamic processes incorporated within the culture of power and the culture of the inter-institutional network of racism. The lack of emphasis placed on the influences of these structural determinants of culture derails social workers' abilities to comprehend the effects of these larger system forces on the social problems confronted by racially different systems of all sizes. Such ignorance adversely impacts the emphasis given to and the quality of advocacy for social justice and social action efforts aimed at achieving socially just and positive social change for racially diverse people and communities.

Thus, the underemphasized structural determinants of culture encompass core and valuable knowledge required by all professional social workers. Competence in the structural determinants of culture, such as knowledge of the culture of power and the culture of inter-institutional racism, is fundamental to marshaling resources to launch effective advocacy and social action against social injustice. Training in this area advances the acquisition of a fuller and broader base of comprehension of cultural competence learning outcomes by social work students. For social work students, education in the structural determinants of culture enhances their preparation for and attainment of advocacy and social action skill competencies. Culture, defined as shared ways of living, shapes the well-being of citizens in a civilized society in a number of ways. As a major social determinant of well-being in a society of ordered liberty and privilege, the broad structural influences of culture on well-being are not only a function of the culture of inter-institutional arrangements but are also influenced by the culture of power.

CULTURE OF INTER-INSTITUTIONAL RACISM

As far back as Baron (1969), Briggs and Paulson (1996), Themba-Nixon (2001), and Randall (2002), the culture of the inter-organizational network that sustains racial distinctions through the interlocking and reinforcing policies and procedures within and between organizations have been carefully and succinctly articulated. According to Baron (1969) and Briggs (1996), there are five major sectors embedded in any municipality: housing, labor markets, educational systems, welfare, and political sectors. While Baron (1969) and others (Briggs, 1996) believe that the political sector has influence over the welfare state, it is our contention that it has control over the other four sectors which are controlled by the economic elite that reside in or have influence over the municipality (Loury, 2002). Each sector is divided into dominant and minority subsectors, with the later being subordinate subsectors (Baron, 1969; Briggs & Paulson, 1996).

CULTURE OF POWER

Delpit (1995) defines the culture of power as a five-dimensional concept: (1) institutions, such as schools, possess power dynamics; (2) the culture of power is governed by rules of eligibility and codes of conduct; (3) the rules of the power elite mirror the rules that govern the culture of power; (4) knowledge of the rules of eligibility of the culture of power enables the acquisition of power; and (5) people with power deny it or do not acknowledge possessing it. Here is a good place to teach students about both privilege and power and the impact of its absence, as is the case in circumstances involving racial, class, and gender inequalities and unequal justice; as illustrated in Davis's (2016) perspective on race as America's grand challenge and Danieli (1998) narrative on the conspiracy of silence and structural determinants of culture concerning the struggles and plight of African Americans on all quality of life fronts in America.

Institutions and Power Dynamics

All institutional venues organized and structured through formal arrangements have incorporated within them power dynamics that reflect the influence of the people occupying dominant roles over people occupying subordinate roles (Baron,

1969; Briggs & Paulson, 1996). These power dynamics preserve the "racial controls and differentiation embedded in institutional arrangements" (Baron, 1969; Briggs & Paulson, 1996). For example, the bias and competence of instructors shapes the extent and character of learning acquired by the student. The role of the faculty in shaping the definitions, critical thinking, and content of the curricula used to educate students is another example of the power differential between teacher and student. In this example, white faculty who are uncomfortable with race or are racially indifferent can avoid addressing the issues and skills needed to aid social work students in advocating for the civil and human rights of African American and others historically oppressed groups. The role of the state in legislating and enforcing compulsory education in poorly resourced educational school districts over the self-determination of the family and child is another example of the power differentials that preserve racial differentiation and racial indifference that exist between individuals and institutions that operate on the basis of rule-governed behavior (Briggs & Paulson, 1996).

The impervious role of school discipline policies as a pipeline to the juvenile justice system is an example of the power dynamics contained within inter-institutional arrangements. Inter-institutional power dynamics serve to support the collaboration of youth-serving systems through restrictive mandates within each participating system. This results in the disproportionate burden borne by youth from racial minority backgrounds through the limits placed on their social capital, upward social mobility, and civil liberties (Alexander, 2010; Baron, 1969; Briggs & Paulson, 1996; Delpit, 1995; Roberts, 2009).

Rules of Eligibility and Codes of Conduct

Entry and admission to the culture of power is predicated on meeting eligibility standards and behaving in concert with the behavior codes that define acceptable styles of interaction, dress, and oral and written communication (Delpit, 1995). Restricted covenants and codes of behaving for residents in exclusive residential communities are examples of rules that define what is acceptable when living in high-end, wealthy communities. Adherence to written by-laws, restrictions, and the annual payment of membership fees are typically codified as rules for membership in and participation by members of exclusive private country clubs, golf clubs, and vacation resorts. In this context, they serve as additional examples of rules that accompany membership in the culture of wealth and influence.

Rules of the Culture of Power and Rules of the Economic and Power Elite Are the Same

Access to the culture of the economic elite and circles of power and influence improves the individual life chances of people attending schools located in areas of influence, wealth, and high tax bases (Baron, 1969; Briggs & Paulson, 1996; Delpit, 1995). Also, socialization by affirming and nurturing people controlling the contingencies of cultures of learning, employment, and quality of life improves one's overall success (Delpit, 1995). Additionally, repeated exposure to the social network of the culture of power enhances one's social capital and influence. Social capital is a major interpersonal determinant of well-being.

Knowledge of the Rules of the Governing Culture Improves Acquisition of Power

This is true only if the knowledgeable user of this information has direct access to the inner circle of the culture of power or social capital connections with the political clout that can influence the process of decision-making. The structural determinants comprising the culture of power have influence over well-being and status. The structural determinants of culture operate through the policies and procedures and governing institutional and inter-institutional collaborative arrangements that produce inter-relational, interactive, inextricable, interwoven, and iatrogenic effects (Baron, 1969; Briggs & Paulson, 1996). Clearly, the general public, particularly communities of color, are recognizing these structural effects of culture as forces that perpetuate civil and human rights violations while also observing that the system of privilege that protects unjust policies and procedures continues to operate unchecked. Without an organized response from social welfare entities and a demand for increased cultural competency, training, and collaboration between law enforcement and the communities they are designed to serve, these biased structural effects of culture will continue to disadvantage marginalized communities of color. The inter-institutional network of controls defined by members of the dominant group and sanctioned through institutional agreements, policies, and procedures are the structural determinants that preserves status and privilege for members of a dominant group while sustaining a culture of despair for those in the subordinate group (Baron, 1969; Briggs & Paulson, 1996). As questions are raised about the presumption of privilege at the expense and sacrifice of less-advantaged diverse groups, Ikard and Teasley (2012) educate us on the strategy referred to as "racial common sense" used by members of the dominant group to justify their white privilege.

Themba-Nixon (2001) offers another account of protracted, pervasive, and persistent white privilege in this country and chronicles its consequences on key quality of life indicators and social fronts for persons of color. She provides empirical evidence of the disparities and disproportionate experiences that African Americans encounter as citizens in this country. Themba-Nixon (2001) raises the injustices featured in the report to a level of critical concern given the sheer volume, breadth, and scope of the evidence reported and the nature and gravity of the disparate experiences of African Americans. Through this report, the federal government is urged to recognize the persistence of white privilege and its unequal effects on African Americans as a civil and human rights violation, one subject to oversight by the United Nations CERD program.

Another way to understand the culture of power is through its social network influence-making function. Institutions have both formal and informal structures that are governed by different chief executives. The reality is that if you want innovations to be adopted by members of the organization and take effect, you have to engage the social and political influences that enable the implementation of those innovations (Gold, Glynn, & Mueser, 2006). Political processes that are inherent to the organization's social network largely shape the decisions that lead to an organization's adoption and use of an innovation. The adoption of an innovation in organizations is rarely the result of an administrative directive handed down from the top to the bottom. This is especially the case if it involves a change in the status of the user; its complexity in use outweighs its benefits and ease in its adoption, and its social acceptance is either of no contest or viewed as a problem by influence-makers in the group (Gold, Glynn, & Mueser, 2006).

Denying the Knowledge and Possession of Power

People who deny having power do it to disavow any responsibility for participating in a dominant group whose actions limits the freedoms and autonomy of others subjected to the rules and practices of the dominant group (Delpit, 1995). The experience of white women in this country provides a perfect example to illustrate this key aspect of the culture of power. Hopps (1982) acknowledges the exclusion of white women from the ruling class that governs the "financial and power centers," but carefully describes the "derived power and material gains" by white women due to their personal relationships to the ruling class: namely, white men (p. 4). Hopps (1982) asserts that white women are in an inevitable position relative to people of color because of gains achieved through changes in legislation that ultimately favored them and advanced their opportunities "well ahead of all people of color"(p. 4). Murray (1984) documents the fact that white women were the primary beneficiaries of the War on Poverty and Great Society Programs. Hopps (1982) explains that "because of their individual and collective relationships to the power structure, [white women] are able to exercise leverage that people of color, regardless of their gender, do not have"(p. 4). In addition to derived power, white women, in Hopps's view, possess and exercise deferred power very much like that of a "sleeping giant" who postpones exercising his dominance (Hopps, 2016). Though not the ruling class in America, white women are privileged due to their connections to white men and their federally protected class status, which qualifies them as the diversity ruling class in America. As the diversity ruling class in this country, as well as holding ruling class status in the profession of social work, there is no evidence of them sharing their power with African Americans and using their favorable positions to champion issues impacting people of color. As far back as Du Bois, it has been noted that white women, like white men, have had no interest in, motivation for, or empathy toward changing the opportunity structure to enable advancements for African Americans. The dubious and tangential relationship between social work and its interest in and focus on the well-being of African Americans provides an opportunity for the practice of social work with African Americans to inform the research and education of practitioners who will be working in racially diverse communities as well as agencies working primarily with racially diverse people and communities (Briggs, Holosko, Banks, Huggins-Hoyt, & Parker, 2018).

Part 5: Implications for Designing Curricula in Civil and Human Rights in Social Work

Education in civil and human rights is relevant across all aspects of professional social work training. It should be incorporated in all classes and as a stand-alone course that focuses on cultures of power, politics, and economics, with emphasis added for other cultures of influence such as race, gender, and class. Banks (2003) believes that, at a minimum, instructors should teach students how to critically appraise injustices and aid them in formulating change processes. Training in civil and human rights and social justice should also extend throughout the curricula, being included in human behavior, practice, policy, and the elective courses in the foundation year.

Human behavior classes can be a useful place to educate students about these socially determined cultures of influence as they learn about diversity in the life span experiences of cultures of wealth, status, and privilege and non-privilege such as inequalities, disparities, disproportionalities, the cultures of white privilege, and institutional racism. Students of social work will be able to use the knowledge learned in human behavior class concerning the cultures of marginalization and white privilege in shaping their critical perspective and social justice plans of action. Knowledge and competencies in this area will assist them in preserving and gaining civil and human rights protection through social justice advocacy and practice methods for people and communities who experience social disadvantages and vulnerabilities. Students of human behavior require clear training in the coping and stress-invoking mechanisms contained in the triadic impact of intra- and interpersonal influences of behavior within the inter-institutional web of racism. These influences shape the quality of life system of care sectors such as health, mental health, substance abuse, housing, education, welfare, child welfare, juvenile justice, and adult corrections—in which social workers engage clients and communities. For example, the culture of institutional racism in the school-to-prison pipeline provides a useful example for students to comprehend the incentive structures and institutional arrangements within and between a network of institutions that result in suppressing and limiting the life chances of socially disadvantage youth and communities (Baron, 1969; Geronima, 2011). The important relationship between housing and quality of education and styles of school discipline and their relationship to the juvenile justice system is an important interrelationship to underscore. In each of these institutions, punitive policies and procedures incentivize the marginalization of minority youth in schools while serving as a conduit to the juvenile justice system and an array of disparities and disproportionate burdens that span generations and create a geography of racial disproportionality (Geronima,

2011; Roberts, 2009). Along this same line, students need to understand the intractable relationship between poverty and failing health (Braveman & Gruskin, 2003). Braveman and Gruskin (2003) highlight the effect of socially determined inequalities involving race, gender, health status, ethnic background, and disability status on the relationship between poverty and poor health and the implications raised involving issues of equity, human rights, and health disparities.

Students seeking a civil rights education need to understand the research on the culture of drug use that accompanies welfare recipients' experiences. Lee and Hines (2014) show that white recipients of welfare tend to be dependent on alcohol and nicotine, while African Americans and Latino Americans tend to have cocaine dependencies. Dependency on nicotine is associated with high levels of psychological distress among whites. The authors show how alcohol dependency is associated with high levels of psychological distress in African Americans, Latinos, and white welfare recipients. Social work students also need to know the relationship between internalizing mental health disorders and neighborhood safety (Zule, 2008a, 2008b). Zule's (2008b) research reports a strong link between crack cocaine use and risky urban neighborhoods.

CONTINUING EDUCATION IN STRUCTURAL ASPECTS OF CULTURE, CIVIL/HUMAN RIGHTS, AND SOCIAL JUSTICE

The existence of a global economy, global communities, and a global society requires continuing education that prepares social workers to effectively practice social work that will support well-being in systems of all sizes within and across diverse populations, communities, and nations. In our estimation, all graduates of professional schools of social work require a postgraduate course that provides professional socialization in social justice, civil and human rights, and the structural and interpersonal determinants of culture that impact the fields of practice and vulnerable populations in social work, broadly defined. This professional socialization should include a survey of the cultural group's strengths and customs; grief and loss issues; experiences with accessing the cultures of economics, power, and privilege; the extent of social and economic injustice experiences; and opportunities to both reflect as well as develop a personal value base that aids them in constructing a critical perspective that informs their social work practice with diverse populations, communities, and nations across systems of all sizes.

Banks (2004) argues that people require literacy skills that enable them to be "reflective, moral, and active citizens" (p. 298). Banks (2004) posits that multicultural literacy is lacking in basic education, but that such literacy constitutes a set of skills, knowledge, and affirmations that enables each individual to endorse global citizenship and social justice as well as preserve justice and humanity worldwide. He argues that students need to know how to pinpoint the origins and authors of knowledge perspectives and their interests and motivations. He also believes that students need to know the underlying assumptions of a perspective and to see and understand knowledge from a diversity of cultural lens if they are to use perspectives to engage in behavior change that will result in worldwide democracy. He argues that residents of a civilized, diverse democratic society require skills and competencies that will aid them to balance the aims of unity between diverse groups while preserving respect and allegiance to culturally specific communities and to endorse a brand of citizenship that encompasses cultural, national, and global identities (Banks, 2003, 2004).

Banks (2009) believes that education in human rights, diversity, and citizenship is challenged by the pursuit of assimilationist goals, which can be remedied by providing education that respects and reflects the cultural identities of the students. Clarke and Drudy's (2006) research on student educators shows that most student teachers tend to approach the teaching of diversity, social justice, and global awareness very conservatively and would probably not be effective with a classroom of diverse students. The authors argue that the belief systems and values concerning diversity that students bring to the teaching enterprise should be considered in preparing future educators.

Continuing education in human behavior in the social environment provides professional social workers opportunities to acquire training in further developing a theoretical formulation and critical perspective on social welfare issues that threaten social justice for vulnerable and socially and economically marginalized populations, communities, and nations. The anthropological approach to cultural competence in social work practice courses, which equips the practitioner to shape interpersonal skills competencies in working cross-culturally, requires additional training. The additional training needed provides the practitioner with productive approaches to engage in a process of professional self-reflection. It also provides opportunities for graduates of professional social work schools, as well as second-year students, to gain an understanding of the knowledge of self and the extent to which they have been socialized to carry preexisting biases and experiences that contradict social work values encompassing diversity. This checking-in process to cultural competence adopts an emphasis on cultural humility as a process for building an awareness necessary to rid the practitioner of bias, "-isms," and discriminatory practices that are embedded in the experience of "othering" members of diverse groups and communities. This process of cultural humility, however, does not go far enough to educate students on the structural determinants of culture and their linkages to civil and human rights violations (Tervalon & Murray-Garcia, 1998).

To reiterate, social justice is "an ideal condition in which all members of a society have the same rights, protection, opportunities, obligations, and social benefits" (Barker, 1995, p. 354). The narrative on social justice is derailed when it is not understood as a three-prong perspective that includes a value system and a set of skill competencies, inculcated throughout policy and service domains (Bent-Goodley & Hopps, 2017). When considered primarily as a value system with no social action, social justice loses its social responsibility. Mobilizing social action and intervening on behalf of historically oppressed vulnerable groups experiencing threats to their civil and human rights are aligned with our core social work mission.

As we see it, social justice professionals must avoid losing their focus on preserving the civil and human rights of vulnerable groups. To sustain credibility and ethical focus, social worker training ought to emphasize the intersection of social justice and civil and human rights throughout the foundation and concentration curriculums and programs of study in professional schools of social work. They can be inextricably linked to the profession's ethics and value base and to policy, both in practice and throughout all aspects of service delivery.

Education and professional socialization as a social worker will require ongoing difficult conversations about race. To do this will require addressing the animus and reactivity associated with focusing on race. It should also be emphasized that after conversations focusing on race in a concentrated way, those staff members who come from a non-white racial group are still left in the moment; they do not have the privilege of temporarily visiting with issues of race. Thus, ongoing education in and continuous professional socialization to issues of race will also require recognition that the structural inequality that accompanies being non-white continues to threaten the legitimacy of our democracy and the practice of equal justice.

The malignancy and debilitating effects of racism on African Americans is tantamount to assigning a "scarlet letter" from birth to an eternity spanning future generations. As an enduring and elusive social welfare theme, the nature of racism is unstoppable and has a lifespan commensurate with the survival rate of a cockroach, which is consonant with eternity. It is America's most horrific exemplar of protracted oppression and an exception to its democratic and equal justice ideals. It is because of our professional ethics and core social justice mission that each social worker must form, own, and practice a critical and comprehensive perspective on social justice informed by the three-prong perspective mentioned earlier. This is especially important as they work in and lead larger systems that seek to effectively serve racially diverse smaller systems through direct and clinical social services.

The challenge to actualizing this comprehensive view of social justice is multifold. There are proponents of a multicultural diversity perspective who view race as no more important than other diversity factors, such as gender, class, sexual orientation, disability, etc. The criteria to aid social workers in making difficult decisions about which diversity group qualifies for and is entitled to enforced preferences through publicly financed social services have been established by Maguire (1980), who recommends the following: (1) the diverse group requires enforced preferences since no alternatives exists, (2) the broader social structure and general society are predisposed to and have adopted racial indifference and negative stereotypes about the diverse group, (3) the general public lack cultural humility and social intelligence and have avoided social responsibility about the plight of the diverse group, and (4) the diverse group members are without options and resources to avoid the reality that accompanies their lack of power and privilege. By applying this framework, Maguire (1980) believes that historically oppressed groups and women in this country meet the preference criteria, with exceptions noted by Hopps (1982) regarding the derived power and advantages accrued by white women resulting from their close relationships to the center of power and privilege and the federal protections accorded them due to Affirmative Action legislation.

While Bent-Goodley and Hopps (2017) and others such as Du Bois believe that, in the twentieth-century, race was the major determinant of preference, in the twenty-first century, the direct and indirect intersectional influences of race, class, gender, and degree of vulnerability must be considered in determining which group qualifies for enforced preferences. Bent-Goodley and Hopps (2017) believe that the polarized and dynamic effects of these intersecting influences reflect a "multiple jeopardy" that encompasses the degree of economic deprivation, political disenfranchisement, lack of access to power and privilege, and the proclivity of "racism, sexism, and classism" experiences for certain diverse groups such as women of color (Hopps, 1982, p. 4). This is where Hopps, Pinderhughes, and Shankar's (1995) power to care perspective is instructive. From this vantage point, Hopps believes that the larger system policy limitation antecedents; political, economic, and social determinants; and consequences of environmental detractors (which are explained next) shape a powerlessness in clinical social workers working with racially diverse groups. In furtherance of this view, Hopps, Pinderhughes, and Shankar (1995) state that "clinical work is compromised by environmental detractors—drugs, violence, communities that do not provide adequate nurturing, and national policies that do not permit a sufficient range of programs and resources to address clients' multiple problems" (p. 3).

The lack of alignment between larger system policy and service delivery programs and services are structural impediments that interfere with the achievement of well-being. But they also present an opportunity to collect the evidence needed to meet with funders and lawmakers to discuss why the agency and client systems being served are experiencing the degree of entrapment and dependence on assistance (Hopps, Pinderhughes, & Shankar, 1995). These data and the collective influence and fund-raising actions of nonprofit associations, university faculty, business alliances and civic groups, client and family organizations, and supportive funding agencies are prudent allies to have as advocates. When needed, these various interests groups are important to larger system leaders executing a series of strategic offensive actions. These actions may manifest as a well-organized town hall, a massive interfaith and parent-to-parent telephone tree, a multijurisdiction legislative breakfast, and organized group protest along with well-placed political social capital who will use the publicized campaign as a staging opportunity to seek redress and change.

Thus, to actualize this important intersectional aim, clarity about what constitutes social justice is needed now. As alluded to earlier, Bent-Goodly and Hopps (2017), in their editorial on the interface of social work and civil rights, define social justice as a three-pronged stool comprising a value, a set of skill competencies that are infused throughout the policy, and a service delivery process.

To actualize Bent-Goodley and Hopps (2017) perspective on social justice requires modifications to the education of professional social work students. To ensure mastery of social justice and civil and human rights skill competencies, leaders of larger systems need to partner with professional schools of social work to establish a field-centric curriculum that emphasize social learning and capstone experiences for its students and continuing education for its field instructors and other staff. For example, a school could include cultural competencies in each BSW and MSW course's agency- and community-based assignments that focus on local civil and human rights and social justice issues. This can be done in any school of social work, regardless of nation of origin. For example, in the required community assessment first-semester community practice course at a school of social work located in Southeastern United States, the instructor involves students in the process of obtaining institutional review board (IRB) approval so that they can conduct actual community assessments through interviews, participant observation, and field-based assignments and use the data to assist the community in its development, enhancement, and problem-solving efforts. Imagine if the issues were primarily focused on civil and human rights or social injustice-related issues; then, through lectures and exercises, the classroom becomes a laboratory for enhancing the life of the community. The instructor could structure the assignment to allow the students to listen to the community leadership and membership about their experiences of social injustices and the insurmountable problems that require solving. The students could be taught a battery of tools for assessing the community's strengths; extent of powerlessness; degree of vulnerability; racial, gender, and class composition; and the resources needed to preserve the civil and human rights of communities that include economic and racial demographics of people with disproportionate experiences of barriers to health and well-being along with a bevy of financial and food insecurity stressors. The data collected by students are useful to agency leadership in furthering the development and enhancement of the community, as well as of the agency, staff professional development, and the education of emerging social work students.

Additionally, second-year field placement students, field instructors, and agency staff could establish and undergo a social policy project that assesses the nutritional and health promotion adequacy and usefulness of current food stamp policies (the Supplemental Nutritional Assistance Program [SNAP]). Through this social policy project, the student, field instructor, and other agency staff use the equivalent amount of approved food stamps to shop only in the periphery of a grocery store, where the health promoting and nutritional products and fresh produce typically can be found. By using reliable and valid assessment inventories to track their self-esteem; stress levels; and social, emotional, psychological, and health status for a thirty-day period that forces them to get in touch with the realities of food insecurity and poverty first-hand, students and agency staff will be able to authentically and credibly chronicle their experiences through single case studies. Through these data, they will be able to advocate for transforming food policies.

Advocacy can take on many forms, which can include writing letters to local, state, federal legislators, and lobbyists to describe food insecurity and the perilous efforts involved in making quality of life decisions while struggling to survive and thrive. Not only can students and agency staff get a first-hand experience through field-centric classroom assignments, but there are also opportunities for the faculty of schools of social work to partner with larger systems to conduct community-based practice and community participatory action research. Additionally, to help doctoral students get real post-MSW experience, an agency-based practice implementation practicum can be arranged for them to teach undergraduate and graduate field placement students clinical and community practice strategies to use in mobilizing the individual and community for problem-solving, social action, and social change. Including faculty and doctoral students as organizational development partners, instructors, and field liaisons can be mutually supportive. This can be done by structuring an academic–community or university–neighborhood partnership that emphasizes continuing education for agency staff, projects that involve listening to the community, structuring services and their provision through supervised field learning practicums, and field-centric classroom assignments in which doctoral students direct and supervise BSW/MSW students in aiding the community in planning and mobilizing social change interventions aimed at the elimination of social injustices. Linking doctoral students and their faculty mentors to agency and community programs enables the diffusion of research and best-practice models to practice. This supports agency capacity to achieve service effectiveness while giving doctoral students real-world practice experience and the faculty member a scholar-in-residence opportunity to do field-based practice model implementation, fidelity supervision, training, and evaluation with agency staff. Another way to teach students and agency staff civil and human rights competencies is to establish a community problem-solving/consultation lab within the school of social work aimed at supporting agency and community problem-solving and capacity-building efforts. The school of social work at the University of Maryland has such a model laboratory available to the urban community organizations in metropolitan Baltimore neighborhoods. Schools of social work with existing university–neighborhood and community engagement arrangements are in a powerful position to structure and launch community building and enhancement projects aimed at the education and training of community leaders and residents in knowing and exercising their civil and human rights.

The continuing education of social workers and graduating second-year students in civil and human rights competencies is still in its infancy, which means that it represents fertile ground for classroom, service learning, and other field-centric curriculum development efforts. One way to build a solid foundation in civil and human rights education is to link the articles of protection delineated in the United Nations Human Rights Declaration to sources of violations within fields of practice across social work. For example, in the State of Oregon, the overuse of foster care by African American and Native American children has been conceptualized as social injustice. The Governor's Task Force on Disproportionality in Child Welfare written by Briggs (2011) advances that "the overrepresentation of children, families, and communities of color in Oregon's foster care system represents a serious social injustice and an economic emergency" (p. 1). Briggs (2011) points to the differential reports of abuse and neglect among Alaska Natives, Native Americans, and African Americans. Removal of children from these racial and ethnic backgrounds was more likely than for children from other racial groups, rates of foster care are disproportionately higher for children of color, and the length of stay in foster care for children of color was more likely to be 2 years or more compared to the shorter stays, on average, observed for white children in Oregon. Briggs (2011) links the differential experiences of Oregon's children of color to structural inequalities; stressors external to the child welfare system such as poverty, health, education, housing, and employment disparities among families and communities of color; and the lack of sufficient workforce, training, and enforcement protections to ensure the accountability of existing child welfare policies and practices to guarantee culturally responsive systems of care. In this vein, Briggs (2011) is referring to the structural determinants of culture, the unfair and culturally incompetent public child welfare and juvenile justice systems of care, and the accompanying civil and human rights violations that shape the racial geography that Roberts (2009) and Randall (2010) articulate as differential experiences of communities of color in high-end child-serving systems. To prepare the next generation in aiding communities of color and vulnerable groups, such as children of color in the child welfare system, it will become essential to train agency staff and graduating students in content that helps them to understand social problems as civil and human rights violations as well as strategies for mobilizing for positive social change and social justice.

Continuing, advanced, and graduate social work education in social justice and civil and human rights can be provided by incorporating the knowledge bases of other professional disciplines. Curricula models in civil and human rights exist in the literature bases in other disciplines such as law, psychology, education, public health, and international studies. From a field-centric perspective, the Mandel Legal Aid Clinic, a partnership between the University of Chicago Law and School of Social Service Administration, provides a useful collaboration for educating students in civil and human rights competencies. Students learn assessment and practice competencies in civil and human rights while providing social and legal services to poor residents of Chicago. Along these lines, continuing education on the intersectionality of threats to civil and human rights and social injustices and their interrelationships with the structural determinants of culture and its impact on well-being is feasible. If at all possible, such education ought to be interdisciplinary, which requires the braiding of curricula from social work, law, education, psychology, and public health. Curricula models in these areas explicate the origins, causes, correlates, and consequences of poverty, health, education, employment and housing disparities, and the tax code in this country as examples of areas in which civil and human rights violations occur; these are useful knowledge bases to use in educating social work students and agency leaders and staff in larger systems. These literature bases are useful for teaching agency staff and students to use culturally themed assessments and practice approaches in addressing threats to civil and human rights and social justice. These same knowledge bases can be converted to continuing education curricula for agency leaders and staff to use to conduct assessments that pinpoint and track the interpersonal and structural barriers to accessing and utilizing mental health services by families of African American youth and their relationship to human rights violations as codified in the Universal Declaration of Human Rights of 1948 (McPherson & Cheatham, 2015). Additionally, these curricula models are useful in training the staff and leaders of larger systems in periodically assessing the racially disparate uses of the classifications of the *Diagnostic and Statistical Manual of Mental Disorders* (DSM) and the misdiagnoses of trauma cross-culturally. This training will provide both agency staff and students with a broader understanding of the lack of enforcement protections in federal policy that sustain disproportionate and disparate burdens of trauma and mental illness for communities of color. Moreover, the changing landscape of rates of educational failure, foster care, and incarceration and their deleterious health and economic disparity consequences on inmates and their communities of origin represents a racial geography of participation in powerlessness systems by marginalized communities such as African Americans, Native Americans, Alaska Natives, and Pacific Islanders (Briggs, 2011; Golembeski & Fullilove, 2008; Nicosia, MacDonald, & Arkes, 2013; Roberts, 2009; Sawrikar & Katz, 2014; Williams, 2010; Williams & Sternthal, 2010).

Thus, students as well as agency staff and leaders need to both understand civil and human rights violations and how to assess for their existence. They need a proper foundation in the historical and contemporary developments of civil and human rights legislation and protections for communities of color. Such an education is essential in establishing an understanding about why the United States is perceived as shielded from sanctions and consequences for lack of enforcement of human rights protections (Grant & Gibson, 2013; Themba-Nixon, 2001). Similarly, to gain a more comprehensive foundation in the history and shaping of social justice as a concept, students should be familiarized with the works of writers such as Audrey Lorde, bell hooks, Patricia Hill Collins, Plato, Aristotle, Thomas Aquinas, Immanuel Kant, John Stuart Mill, Jean-Jacques Rousseau, Jeremy Bentham, John Locke, Thomas Hobbs, John Rawls, and Maxine Greene (Zajda, Majhanovich, & Rust, 2006). To build field-centric cultures of learning through field practicums, service learning, and capstone experiences to attain advocacy, civil and human rights, and social justice competencies, leaders of larger systems will need to partner with social work educators and law to examine the role and effectiveness of using human rights clinics in legal training and education (Kestenbaum, Hoyos-Ceballos, & del Aguila Talvadkar, 2012). From a social work perspective, Hodge (2010) suggests that social work students examines the profession's role in the perpetuation of social injustice through the field's misuse of universal frameworks to solve complex social problems, misinterpreting customs and norms that comprise diverse cultural groups, and being driven by interests that preserve the professional status of social work (Hodge, 2010). On the other hand, in the field of education, Johnston (2009) posits that the social justice curriculum used cannot condone or support "social practices that interfere with human rights, nor can they teach otherwise than this" (p. 119). Pewewardy and Almeida (2014) describe the way white supremacy influences and impacts structural, organizational, and professional interactions in social work. They highlight the need to liberate the profession from these counterproductive practices.

Part 6: Next Steps

In furtherance of the previously stated aims, leaders of larger systems need to partner with the research faculty of schools of social work to explicate and study the direct and indirect relationships between the manifestations of the culture of white privilege in larger systems as moderators and mediators of the relationship between the social determinants of well-being and key factors such as race, cultural diversity, social justice, civil and human rights, discrimination, and oppression (Davis, 2016). Barker's (1995) definition of social justice is a good one to use: social justice is defined as "an ideal condition in which all members of a society have the same rights, protections, opportunities, obligations, and social benefits" (Barker, 1995, p. 354).

Second, the leaders of larger systems, as field instructors for schools of social work, ought to avoid providing field education in silos that demarcate and distinguish clinical social work practice, social administration, and community practice. Instead, larger system providers should work with the field faculty in schools of social work to retool field education to make it meaningful for students and their particular system needs. Such retooling should be done to educate students to achieve competencies in (1) critical thinking and human behavior theory, to build capacity for assessing privilege and power, racism, human and civil rights, and social injustice; (2) critical thinking, policy analysis, and translating research; (3) cultural humility, social and emotional intelligence, social advocacy, and intervening in systems of all sizes to achieve positive policy and practice outcomes; (4) evaluating practice in small and larger systems; and (5) service learning and field practicums that afford opportunities to use classroom instruction in actual practice, which leads to service effectiveness. By doing this, social workers will be taught the necessary skill competencies to (1) understand and respect cultural diversity with a capacity to practice with cultural humility and social and emotional intelligence, (2) critically think and effectively intervene across racially diverse client systems of all sizes, and (3) navigate publicly financed social welfare and healthcare systems to obtain access to the social determinants of health while (4) engaging in meaningful social action partnerships globally with organizations such as the World Health Organization (WHO), nationally with organizations such as the Centers for Disease Control and Prevention (CDC), and with local municipalities and community-based organizations to eradicate social injustices and reform institutional practices that do not enable client systems to experience well-being.

Third and last, faculties and larger systems leaders need to conduct research to assess whether field-centric and continuing education curricula result in the attainment of the aforementioned skill competencies upon follow-up evaluation with alumni and staff in larger systems.

Implementing these steps will involve teaching students and professional social work practitioners how to appraise, assess, and intervene in resolving human and civil rights violations. Larger system leaders should ensure that social workers should continue their civil and human rights and social justice training as professionals receiving continuing education in human behavior, social policy, and practice courses that emphasize assessing, intervening, and evaluating social work practice that seeks to eliminate civil and human rights, and social injustices. Both staff in larger systems and students need to know how to communicate the evidence of civil and human rights violations and their problem-solving plans to address them. In confronting ethical dilemmas, social workers should always seek professional opinions (Reamer, 2001). It is entirely prudent to seek counsel, support, and any problem-solving assistance that is required to achieve alignment between social work ethics and socially responsible behaviors. Along these lines, it is useful to stay active by aiding in a grassroots positive change effort. To quote Martin Luther King, who put it best, "a threat to justice anywhere is a threat to justice everywhere!" It is important for social workers to not allow inaction to triumph over the change that is needed when social injustices exists. As champions of a just society, social workers responding to Davis's (2016) call to action to address issues of race and racism against African Americans ought to be guided by the words of President John F. Kennedy, who aptly stated "for its is not what the country can do for you, it is want you can do for the country!"

Ensuring a focus on civil and human rights competencies through field education will require agency leaders to aid the faculty of schools of social work in adopting field-centric education models. Field-centric education reinforces and supports the agency leader's use of industry examples of the structural determinants of culture that contribute to the furtherance of civil and human rights violations. The field education on the conspiracy of silence surrounding white privilege and power can begin in the foundation social policy classrooms, with assignments tied to their field placement setting. The 1911 Mothers Pension Movement and the making of the first social policy in this country—the 1935 Social Security Act—provides a solid example to apply the aforementioned structural determinants of the culture of white privilege against a backdrop of social ethics, social responsibility, and social work ethics and values frameworks. For advanced social policy courses, a field-centric assignment for second-year students involving the examination of the relationship between the Affordable Care Act and the Social Security Act could be useful. This assignment would help concentration with second year specialization articulate the provisions and regulations and conduct analysis of each of the policies' contributions to social work's mission of well-being for disadvantaged or oppressed groups. In both foundation and concentration social policy classes, students can be given field-centric assignments that allow them to identify and assess for civil and human rights issues that threaten the achievement of civil and human rights for client systems of all sizes. The Flint, Michigan, water crisis is a perfect example fraught with white privilege for the economic elite. One of the major motivations for switching the water supply in Flint, despite the known public health threats, was as a cost-saving measure for the State of Michigan and its tax benefit for the wealthy. While there is a debate as to whether the temporary fix of filtered water is actually a safe alternative or not, the same pipes used to deliver the tainted water are still being used to deliver the filtered water. Herein lies a protracted human rights issue that has exacted major health and economic crises. The toxic water crisis in Flint, Michigan, will certainly threaten revitalization and recovery from the cumulative brink of disaster for the state and its residents for the short term and for a number of years to come.

In creating field-centric assignments for use in larger systems, it would be very useful for leaders of larger systems to work with social work doctoral students and faculty instructors to draw on the growing practice of research literature. Such a review will provide practice assessment and intervention tools to use to address civil and human rights violations and obstacles to achieving well-being. Sadly, the profession of social work is not without a host of civil and human rights violations that are manifested as health disparities and racial disparities in education, child welfare, juvenile justice, housing, employment, social security, and criminal justice systems (Themba-Nixon, 2001). Each of these field of practices is ripe with case examples to draw upon to teach assessment and intervention approaches to addressing civil and human rights issues throughout their two-year graduate education and their continuing education postgraduation. Gil (1994) recommends that social work educators prepare students to "explore not only the meanings and dynamics of these [social injustice and oppression] phenomena but also their own consciousness and values, the perceptions of their needs and interests, and their possible denials of oppression and injustice, as well as their unexamined, taken-for-granted justifications of established, oppressive, and unjust ways of life" (pp. 231–232).

The grounding of social work students in the industry narratives and meanings of what constitutes oppression, social injustice, and their opposites (Gil, 1994) serves as an instigating mechanism for nurturing cultural humility and social and emotional intelligence about historically marginalized groups. Gil (1994) suggests social work students learn about ways to organize nonoppressive cultures and practice through reciprocity of the client system with the distribution of resources and opportunities. This represents one way to merge the evidence of oppression and injustice with social work's ethical base and professional obligation for engaging in critical thinking and best practices, as articulated by McGuire in Hopps (1982), Gil (1994), and Gambrill (2004). Schools of social work will need to continue to inculcate their curricula in social justice and civil and human rights with field-centric projects and training tools for students while engaging in similar curricula development for the continuing education of professional social workers in larger systems. The goal of this enhanced training is to ensure that graduating and professional social workers better understand ways of not contributing to the conspiracy of silence and the structural determinants of the culture of white privilege. Schools can accomplish this by teaching students and professional social workers about the harmful effects of covert aspects of oppression; by teaching skills to analyze social injustices, oppression, and their opposites; and by teaching assessment, intervention, and evaluation skills and tools to use in their problem-solving efforts in addressing these and other civil and human rights barriers to well-being.

Conclusion

Educating social work students and professionals working in larger systems about the interrelationships of the structural determinants of culture and the threats to civil and human rights and social justice is a time-sensitive aim. Such education needs to underscore the role of social justice as both an organizing value (Marsh, 2005) and a set of practice competencies (McPherson & Cheatham, 2015). This will require a broad-based and concentrated dosage so that graduates of schools of social work can actualize the aims of the Universal Declaration of Human Rights and put social action back into the social work profession. Social inequalities never ceased to exist, yet the federal standard to prove racial discrimination became more stringent and set at a bar that would be difficult to prove in federal court. What also disappeared were the federal protections and administrative sanctions against individual, organized, and systemic experiences of differential treatments in public and private settings and rampant social injustices. Thus, the extent to which the professional socialization and training in social justice and civil and human rights competencies happens will largely depend on whether it is actualized as field-centric, classroom, and capstone activities annexed to each of the practice competencies sanctioned in the CSWE's educational policy and accreditation standards (EPAS) (McPherson & Cheatham, 2015).

IMPLICATIONS FOR POLICY, PRACTICE, AND RESEARCH ON CIVIL AND HUMAN RIGHTS CURRICULA

Infusing curricular content that links civil and human rights and social justice to the practice competencies will have a measurable impact given the rise in local and federal social policies that impact socially marginalized and vulnerable populations (for example, the rights of unaccompanied children and immigrants with permission to stay in this country will certainly be challenged and a subject of political debate in local, state, and federal arenas). We can expect a rise in social workers mobilizing and partnering with affected groups and communities through organized social action, seeking social justice remedies through legislation and in the courts. The character of social work practice should move away from a dominant psychotherapeutic framework to one that considers the broader environmental contingencies and ecological determinants that negatively impact cultural practices and well-being as targets for positive social change (Mattaini & Moore, 2004). By doing this, there will be an increase in social workers aiding their individual and family clients in joining community efforts to assist in social action programs that seek to achieve an enhanced social welfare experience that informs and enables improved individual, family, and community well-being for racially diverse community residents.

Also, if the call to action by Davis (2016) is effective, research studies that examine the efforts by larger systems to address and eliminate civil and human rights violations and the resulting effects and impact of legislation on individual, family, and community well-being among African Americans are expected to increase. Accreditation and empirical studies aimed at assessing the extent, quality, and impact of field-centric curriculums in preparing graduates in social justice competencies will also increase as a result of pressure within the CSWE to mandate a more saturated classroom-fieldwork hybrid educational emphasis in civil and human rights competencies among graduates of the profession.

Data from such future studies will be informative. Research in larger systems will not only advance the science on civil and human rights policy and practice, but will also inform curricula developments. Development of curricula in professional schools of social work, as well in their continuing education programs, will aid students as well as professional social workers practicing in and managing larger systems in the acquisition of skill competencies to further social justice. Data from future studies will promote new knowledge of the relationships between field of practice–specific social welfare problems, civil and human rights violations, and social injustices. As a result of this new knowledge and its careful application and appraisal, there will emerge an insatiable drive enabling the social workers and the systems we serve to pursue positive social change broadly defined (Freire, 1970; Heldke & O'Connor, 2004).

The consequence of this surge of individual and collective consciousness of the issues of social injustice and their threat to genuine equality will be followed by the ascendency of these issues as a priority in the social welfare agenda. This deluge of broad public scrutiny will instigate demands for deliberate changes in conditions that sustain oppression (Freire, 1970; Gil, 1994). Indubitably, such action advances research on issues of race and racism (Davis, 2016) while affirming Frederick Douglas belief that "Out of ignorance will come a desire for knowledge."

Intersection of Social Policy and Integrative Practice in and for Larger Systems

Social policy encompasses the social welfare values and socially responsible preferences of a society. It is chief among the myriad of structural determinants of the social welfare industry task environment explicated through legislation and administrative rules for policy implementation, and, subsequently, it sanctions the boundaries of management practice and the scope of service delivery authorization. Through social policy, society privileges policy beneficiaries with access to financial and quality of life resources, goods, and services to sustain and support well-being. These policy benefits come with a lot of regulation and bureaucracy and often result in organizations that are not always easily accessible, approachable, productive, efficient, or effective in their respective delivery systems. For process- and results-oriented leaders, how to be creative within policy boundaries becomes an arena for the integrative practitioner in and for larger systems to reimagine optimal ways to use policy to innovate and serve people seeking behavior change.

Social policy is the instrument by which leaders of social welfare regulate and administer the goods and services within their purview through administrative, legislative, and legal channels and subsequent mandates. Its content is shaped and influenced by the knowledge of the day. It is also subject to the larger political arena, the politics of its immediate task environment, and the competencies of the service provider responsible for addressing the particular needs of a population at risk. An example of how social policy is developed and shaped may illustrate the point. For example, the Social Security Act of 1935 was the first formal social policy guaranteeing social insurance to the people who paid into it. It was chief among the signature achievements of Roosevelt's New Deal for many—but not all—Americans. Now, some 81 years later, the issue of social security is chief among the complaints of the Republican Party. It is a political football of the conservative right (now including the Tea Party), seen as one of the financial disasters that obfuscates the ability of the country to balance the federal budget and reduce our national indebtedness. Under this type of political scrutiny, Social

Security, Medicare and Medicaid, federal unemployment insurance, and current healthcare policy all have exorbitant costs and are political issues.

It is a major topic of political upheaval, a national crisis that is as sensationalized as the current effort to socialize healthcare policy—not to mention the need for jobs for Americans. Each is chief among the areas of critical concern nationally. Issues of the poor, the elderly, and populations at risk of no health insurance are now being transferred from social to personal responsibility. This lack of sensitivity toward issues of the poor was a focal point in the 2016 presidential election for both major political parties. (In 2012, top Republican Party front-runner, Mitt Romney, openly admitted that he was not concerned with the issues of the poor; his focus was on Middle America.) In the 2016 presidential election, the important themes of arguments and debates for both parties were income inequality, the destruction of the middle class, corrupt campaign financing, changing the IRS Tax Code, the provisions of the Affordable Care Act, and increasing employment opportunities.

The belief by many people that the poor have had their contract with America and have not kept their word lacks understanding. Most people do not have the facts and/or training to comprehend the experience of the poor and vulnerable through social policy in this country. Mary Poole's (2006) account of social insecurity for African Americans highlights the vulnerability of social policy for the poor and populations at risk. It is an example of a political football that was used by Southern politicians who threatened to withhold support as long as social security benefits for occupations primarily obtained and available to African Americans remained eligible for benefits through social security. Also, Charles Murray's (1984) account of the failure of the War on Poverty and its impact documents the primary beneficiaries of War on Poverty programs involved the establishment and growth of the black middle class and civil rights opportunities accrued to white women. The poor were not the chief beneficiaries of the War on Poverty's 1962 Social Service Amendments to the Social Security Act of 1935.

It's these kinds of facts and realities that reveal the political "leaky bucket effects" that are the unintended consequences that accompany the process of designing social policy intended to reach populations at risk and most in need. The development of social policy has less to do with the science of assessment and best practices to address the needs of people at risk. Its development has more to do with the values and social, political, and economic clout of the people who control the creation of policy as well as their belief systems about the solutions needed to address issues impacting populations at risk.

The impact and influence of white privilege in US policy in education, child welfare, housing, employment, labor, and environmental realms, and their contribution to the experiences of racial disparities, is well documented in the exposé by Themba-Nixon (2001) as discussed in Chapter 2.

Sadly, Themba-Nixon's report "found gross inequities and discrimination along racial lines in every area of investigation" (p. 5). The problem of designing effective social policy is tantamount to finding a solution to the perfect storm, one that is the consequence of the collision course of racial disparities, racial discrimination, and the lack of enforcement protection. This conundrum continues to be justified as a sequence of elusive events and unfortunate actions. As a denied reality, it reinforces the ongoing practice of inequality and the conspiracy of silence about its existence, chronic devastations, and continuation.

In Rountree and Pomeroy's (2010) editorial "Bridging the Gaps Among Social Justice, Research, and Practice," the ambition of social justice was highlighted: "Many scholars have noted that social justice is a much needed goal; however, its conceptual formulation and application are often vague and abstruse. Operationally, there is often no singular definition of the term 'social justice.' Rather, the conceptualization is vague and open to various interpretations" (p. 293).

To achieve social justice, as well as to eliminate racial disparities and racial disproportionality, through social policy will require paying attention to the way these issues are identified, viewed, prioritized, and subsequently regulated. The value of cooperative action in the transformation of social policy cannot be briefly put into words; its relevance requires careful illustration through contemporary case example. For example, the issue of foster care overuse in this country is an exemplar for understanding the transformative dynamics involved in social policy development. Foster care overuse and the racial disparities and racial disproportionality that accompany it are fueled by structural racism within and outside of the child welfare system (Briggs, 2011). The lens by which to fully comprehend and understand it and its creation of a racial geography of devastation is best depicted by Roberts (2009).

As we view the issue of racial disproportionality through the joint lens of challenge and possibility, it in itself becomes an extraordinary opportunity to correct a long-standing wrong. The overuse of foster care and other residential services for youth and families of color is fueled by systemic inequalities endured by historically marginalized groups as a sort of "tax" that accompanies white privilege in US policy. The careful study of the overuse of foster care placement for children and families of color involves investigating the origins, causes, correlates, consequences, and implications of this overused practice for historically oppressed groups. The organized study of and reduction in the overuse of foster care for families of color is a national dilemma and an elusive social welfare theme that tops the list as the foremost nationwide child welfare industry problem. In Oregon, the persistence of racial disproportionality and its chronic negative consequences is of paramount concern to the judiciary, the executive, and the legislative branches of government.

The overrepresentation of foster care placements among children and families of color is a quandary of great proportion. It is a terribly burdensome experience for its child and family service beneficiaries, the communities of color and Sovereign Nations it directly impacts, corresponding child and family service professionals and service providers, and the taxpayers in each state of the union. As a far-reaching problem with exorbitant costs, and extraordinary and devastating effects, racial disproportionality is justifiably a time sensitive, noteworthy, and formidable multidimensional issue (Briggs, 2011). Given its intricate nature, it is gaining currency as a research priority across the social sciences, the legal profession, and the biomedical industrial complex.

Yet, as both an opportunity and a challenge, the elimination of racial disproportionality and the achievement of its alternative—the proportionate and equitable use of foster care placements—the improvement of the child and family service delivery system is undeniably a chief priority for state policy directors and lawmakers. As a broadly based and compelling challenge, it requires immediate attention by the legislature, priority status by local and state governments, and careful consideration by the federal administration, as well as swift, deliberate, and decisive executive sanction and administrative action.

As a challenge, the enormity of the problem of foster care overuse and racial disproportionality of child welfare service systems for Native Americans, African Americans, and other economically and socially marginalized groups will need different policy initiatives to direct its strategic elimination and its associated complexities. To do so effectively will require executive, administrative, judicial, and legislative leadership in states across the United States. Especially in Oregon, where foster care use is among the highest in the country, it is imperative to adopt former Oregon Senator Margaret Carter's perspective on leadership as guiding behaviors "transparency, trust, clarity of vision and purpose" as they form a critical lens. Establishing such a critical lens involves the use of data as key evidence for making decisions, including problem-solving and learning simultaneously. In this context, the data used in forming the critical lens are comprised of knowledge of the science of behavior change, knowledge of the unique people and particular situations involved, and a thorough understanding of the service systems experiences of Native Americans, African Americans, and other historically oppressed groups. To date, research on single child welfare agency (internally centered) approaches to eliminating racial disproportionality has not achieved its expected aims. Also, there is no science that endorses the notion that a transformed—internally centered— child welfare system approach alone can adequately eliminate racial disproportionality. Consequently, the research on disproportionality reduction in child welfare does not address the lack of attention paid to external system racial disparities and the essential participation of cross-system stakeholders. Unfortunately, this means that the accompanying adverse structural, cumulative, and clinical effects of the racial disparities that accompany the experience of disproportionality among children and families of color go undetected and lack proper attention and intervention.

For example, in Portland, Oregon the Black Women for Peace movement formed out of concern for the public safety given the rise in the frequency of shootings and gang violence issues. They commissioned a number of logic models. Based on these schemas, which reflect the research on the origins, causes, correlates, and consequences of juvenile justice involvement, this group endorsed the use of a community public health approach along with public safety methods as a change strategy for addressing all of the factors contributing to gang involvement and violence.

They uncovered that racial residential segregation impacts community economic viability and youth and family welfare and social sustainability. Since the early twentieth century, race and class have been used collectively to stratify people by residence. Bank practices such as redlining and culturally biased real estate practices, along with the systematic economic disinvestment of inner-city communities, is typically accompanied by residents who represent intergenerational groups of impoverished families and individuals with lower economic status. Typically, there are too few revitalization and community resources to stimulate economic viability. Residents of these communities are subjected to negative neighborhood coping resources that include fast food restaurants, liquor stores, and drug dealing, which are the results of economic disinvestment in these particular settings (Hare, 2008). The consequences of such economic devastation are generally the prevalence of self-medication, drug and alcohol abuse, poor housing stock, bad credit, tenants with suspicious activity or criminal backgrounds, and the lack of sufficient role models for youth. These community areas include many unemployed residents, experiences of racial profiling, gentrification, poor school districts, and insufficient health and fitness venues.

Racial segregation impacts educational system inequalities, and culturally insensitive practices impact parent and family well-being. Racial residential segregation limits educational school district resources and contributes to the use of differential discipline policies and teacher and administrator bias against poor and racially diverse school-age youth. These circumstances lead to the use of tracking, resulting in poor academic performance, school dropout, risky behavioral practices that complicate family stress, and, eventually, the onset of youth gang participation and violence. Poor and racially diverse youth come from families with multiple stressors and lack access to community activities that enable them to rebuild, fortify, and strengthen their capacity for problem-solving. These school-age youth and their families lack access to evidence-based mental health services or juvenile service providers that incentivize educational and employment opportunities for youth from lower income and racially diverse family backgrounds. Also, many of these particular families lack support on ways to navigate service delivery systems and connect to the key resources for which they are eligible to strengthen their capacities as parents and families. Also, these same youth and families are without resources and natural support systems that serve to build the self-efficacy and self-esteem capacities of youth and their parent caregivers as a foundation for minimizing experiences of marginalization and victimization (Bell, Wells, & Merritt, 2009).

Racial residential segregation leads to child maltreatment and child welfare and juvenile justice involvement. Racial residential segregation leads to poor community outcomes such as inadequate community and social justice promotion. The emphasis on public safety and the lack of emphasis on prevention, combined with insufficient positive youth development services and weekend and evening activities, results in youth accessing negative neighborhood norms and customs as a context for social and emotional development. The lack of sufficient individual and family health and mental health supports leaves the distressed family with no alternatives to ward off the negative threats to child safety and family stability. This results in child welfare involvement, the onset of risky behavioral practices sustained through repeated exposure to negative neighborhood coping resources, and the eventual participation in activities that lead to juvenile justice involvement.

One primary reason for a lack of any organized protests by social workers in changing the misery produced from these disproportionate experiences is that the field acts as if these issues are elusive social welfare problems that escape sound social policy and practice. The issue is treated as if it is too complex or enigmatic; current policy on disproportionality reduction is too narrowly focused on achieving proportionality and has not been held to higher standards.

For example, the use of racial proportionality as a benchmark would not make sense because you would have to put more white children and families into a system where they are currently underrepresented, given their proportion of the general population. It would be incorrect to legalize such a ridiculous standard. It would also be imprudent and unwise to subject white youth and families to unnecessary disruption and state scrutiny, and to produce an escalating and uncontrollable expense not supported by any real evidence of need. No one needs to bear that kind of trauma!

Yet, when it comes to the care needs of historically marginalized communities comprised of racially different groups and other populations at risk, the dimensions to consider in designing suitable and appropriate social policy and practice are not coherently linked with science and cultural knowledge. To date, the implementation of such social policy and practice has not been well-thought-out and orchestrated through a progression of logical thought that would lead to the use of reasonably sound remedies that include key dimensions which ensure access to the social determinants of health. Currently, historically marginalized communities and Sovereign Nations lack such access. Such access needs to be prioritized and included as an essential component in social policy and practices for residents and inhabitants of these disadvantaged communities and legally recognized Sovereign Nations.

As we see it, the core dimensions to consider for determining if a social policy or program is making a difference, especially for people with limited freedoms and privileges, need to include the 10 essential "E's" defined here.

1. Ethics
2. Efficaciousness/Effectiveness
3. Efficiency
4. Equality
5. Equity
6. Ecologically based

7. Ecumenical
8. Empowerment-based
9. Economic participation
10. Enforcement protections

ETHICS

Self-determination, transparency, social and economic justice, acceptance of difference, and self-awareness of bias are among the key drivers that shape the character and content of social services and its delivery by social workers. Yet the reality is that people run many nonprofits with training in areas other than social work. Also, in many instances in historically marginalized communities, the nonprofit executive director of an agency may not even have a college education. In these nonprofit settings, these circumstances present challenges to upholding the guiding practice principles that are governed by the Code of Ethics in Social Work.

There are a myriad of challenges, dilemmas, and conflicts for social work managers and administrators, direct care professionals, and student practitioners of social work employed in nonprofits that use alternative values and ethical standards to govern service delivery. Chief among the major threats to the unsuspecting public at large and the intended service beneficiaries is the delivery of services to address a problem (such as gang violence and weapon use) by a provider without the sufficient experience and background needed to qualify as a provider of dependable solutions. The provider chooses to provide a service not based in the best science available to address the problem, but instead they devise their own plan of action, with little known about its robustness compared to well-established science.

In the nonprofit arena, there are no ethical or legal mandates that legislate or enforce the protection of human subjects against the use of ineffectual approaches or experimental practices with unknown risks, harms, or unintended consequences. Nonprofit organizations are not required to use well-established practices to address a problem such as serious delinquent behavior. The provider may opt to develop its own approach without justifying its program selection to a human subjects review board or its reasons for departing from the best available knowledge and recommended science. Providers who are engaging in high-risk interventions without informed consent from the client consumers are engaging in an ethical violation.

Another related organizational ethical dilemma involves nonprofits that lack the skill competencies and capacities to provide a service. Yet, because of the ability to write grants and use political allies and alliances within a funding source, they are able to secure funding. Despite the reality that they are not able to do the job they are contracted to do, these nonprofits, through their high political and community leadership clout, find ways to neutralize and camouflage their inability to achieve service effectiveness or even deliver the goods and services competently.

Transparency and accountability by government and nonprofit organizations are key drivers behind Oregon Attorney General John Kroger's platform in managing Oregon's Department of Justice. There are structural issues that challenge his overall effectiveness. Oregon has evidence-based policies in place for the delivery of human, health, and social services. There is insufficient external oversight of the standard practices of organizational health, and there is less frequency of tracking strategic and well-reasoned decisions for overseeing the implementation and outcomes of evidenced-based and best practices through the efforts of trained and competent staff and program supervisors.

Despite this gross oversight in the regulations governing nonprofit organizations, transparency is the organizing ethical principle guiding the process of evidence-based practice (EBP) in social work. Misunderstandings, misrepresentation, and false claims that an agency is using EBP often occur in municipalities with evidence-based policies. The lack of incentives and penalties or enforcement protections against misleading or falsifying assurances of the claims of effectiveness of an approach reinforces the frequent occurrence of this unethical practice.

A bevy of unethical decisions occur in the administrative and management practices of nonprofit organizations. For example, agency directors and their fiscal managers may use funds reserved for agency payroll taxes to cover other agency bills. They make this critical decision in the hopes of replacing these restricted funds with pledges made by individual and corporate donors; as soon as these pledges are collected and credited as accounts receivables, they are used to pay payroll taxes to federal and state authorities. Other unethical decisions also appear, such as executive directors hiring people knowing that they do not have the skills to do the job. Buoyed up with their increase in salary and formal authority, these directors knowingly go along with the deception despite its ill-fated consequences. Unethical practices among unskilled and non-professionally trained personnel occur when they exploit their client-consumers and use them as minions in conflicts with co-workers. Their relative low power among co-workers, but their differential power over young clientele, affords the nonprofessional human service worker with control over the life chances of young client-consumers. As a gatekeeper, the non-degreed staff person extends to his or her young accomplices access to noncontingent reinforcers and unearned privileges as compensation for carrying out the misdeeds assigned them through staff manipulation. In this role, the non-degreed staff that is misbehaving now has an opportunity to manipulate and abuse the power relationship. In this instance, the staff actions are an inappropriate use of the young clientele to disrespect and harass co-workers.

There are countless examples of executive directors screaming and yelling at employees or using harassment, threats, and intimidation as employee management tactics for achieving compliance and loyalty. Staff feedback concerning the strengths and challenges of an organization ought to be a requirement of its funding source or of regulatory agencies such as the Departments of Labor or Justice. The lack of independent evaluation by staff gives permission to agency directors to behave without the threat of sanctions or the assurance of penalties. The realities of poor accountability as well as ethical violations transcend professions and organizational types and occur at the highest forms of state and federal government (Kroger, 2012; Themba-Nixon, 2001).

The Convention on the Elimination of All Forms of Racism in US Policy is a committee of the United Nations who published a report by Themba-Nixon (2001) articulating what it considers human rights violations. These violations and the lack of enforcement protection against them reinforce and perpetuate the culture of racism in the planning and delivery of publically financed health and human services. They are a direct result of the perfect storm comprised of the rise in racial disproportionality experiences in education, health, welfare, housing, labor, child welfare, and environment, occurring amid associated racial inequalities and a chronic exposure to their cumulative and interactive effects; all of which interact with the structural racism in social and public policies that regulate the poor and disadvantaged. The report observed that US policy does prohibit racial discrimination and has identified penalties associated with the violation of equal opportunities and protection legislations. Regrettably, there are no personnel to track and monitor compliance or enforce it. Furthermore, there are no positive consequences or antecedents specified that serve to incentivize compliance, nor is there a vehicle that administers penalties defined by law as punishment for companies that violate the laws prohibiting racial discrimination and injustices. Given this scenario, whether agencies follow the law or violate it, there are no real consequences for either set of actions.

As social work administrators and managers assume leadership roles and responsibilities in nonprofit programs and agencies, they will need to confront a broad range of intentional and unintentional unethical conduct by staff, management, and organization; the preceding examples are only a small sampling of possible unethical behaviors that may occur.

The ethically bound administrator of a nonprofit using social work values, ethics, and practices must always prioritize the establishment of tighter reins and check-and-balance vehicles to standardize the enforcement of ethical practices. Such a steadfast commitment and assurance needs to be an expected behavior in the management and administration of social services in nonprofit organizations. The lessons described in Chapter 16 on organizational development are important for these particular administrators and managers to follow if they are to uphold both the ethical and sound management of nonprofit organizations. Chapter 16 contains strategies and lessons learned from formal training in social services and business administration by the authors. It is based in the first author's research and publications on nonprofits governed by professionals, community residents and indigenous non-degreed parents of youth with disabilities alongside 30-plus years of managing professionally led nonprofits and consulting with their policymakers and executive leadership on transformation through the use of information literacy.

Along with the rest of the book, the lessons of Chapter 16 provide rich experience to guide and educate new social work managers and administrators to the power of the "*N*" of one. The informed thinking and practices that come with the first author's practical experiences and scientific study of nonprofit organizations, their development, processes, and outcomes is invaluable. These lessons provide rich case studies, aggregate data, as well as practice illustrations that should enable others to use as examples to critically think out solutions to organizational dilemmas. If standardized, the lessons and guides referred to in Chapter 16 would help managers and administrators improve ethical and innovative practices in the administration and management of social services in nonprofit organizations.

The use of evidence and science as a standard practice is expected to increase as more states and municipalities legislate the use of evidence-based programs in the administration of social services.

EFFECTIVENESS

There is growth in legislation requiring the use of evidence-based programs and interventions as more funders and government agencies set standards for the delivery of high-quality human, health, and social welfare services. A misguided belief that often is used to encourage municipalities to legislate the use of scientifically based programs is the falsehood that the delivery of evidence-based programs will guarantee effective outcomes that are also cost effective. If only this were the single most daunting challenge that accompanies an emphasis on the use of well-established science for people administering and managing programs and services through nonprofit organizations! The administration and management of evidence-based programs and best practice carries advantages, challenges, and limitations.

The advantages of using evidenced-based programs include the fact that they are well tested in both laboratory and natural and real-world settings with favorable and desirable results. Although not researched through random clinical trial research, programs that have been tested and that become standard, promising practice yielding positive benefits are also becoming preferable over approaches based on intuition or those with lesser scientific support.

The rise in the use of best practices and evidence-based programs and practice is accompanied by misrepresentation. To stay in vogue, many providers make claims that what they do in fact meets the criteria of a well-established scientifically based program. In many cases, what they report as an evidence-based program fails to meet the criteria. Commonly, we have come across people who believed that any program that has some reported empirical experience is an evidence-based approach. In some cases, people believe that they are using best practices or an evidence-based program because of the celebrity associated with the person who initially designed and used it. I recall one such instance where a grant monitor disagreed with her supervisor about an approach that had widespread local acclaim.

However, it didn't have any published research, but it did have an alleged evaluation by a local, highly respected person who orally and through some unpublished narration reported positive results that they attributed to the approach. Although no control group design was reported as the methodology for the study, she recalls hearing, "it must be evidenced-based if X used it and says it is."

Another problem with the administration and management of best and evidence-based programs is the fact that many of them are not within the immediate reach of the public and are commercial property intended for sale. Too few people are trained in the these evidence-based programs because many schools of social work do not include standard curricula courses devoted to the teaching of these proprietary approaches. Thus, the costs associated with hiring staff and management already trained increase personnel costs beyond what is typical because the market drives the costs up, thus reinforcing the value of employing people with training in evidence-based programs. If the agency directors are unable to secure already trained personnel, they must bear the costs for hiring consultants to train staff and management.

Another challenge for the administration and management of evidence-based programs is the need to ensure program fidelity. This is accomplished by having trained staff or consultants experienced with their use and supervision, and who have ability to troubleshoot areas where there is a problem of fit between the steps of the program and its use with a particular client-consumer. To implement a strategic arrangement of tasks and activities procedurally requires a well-laid out, measurable, and stepwise change process with built-in alternative strategies that may need to be included in working with a client to address a particular problem.

This process involves the use of scientific methods for the collection of data needed for a host of functions, one of which is to assess the client's reactions to change. Staff and management should be able to examine client data to analyze frequency, trends, duration, and qualitative changes in quality of life indicators for the client-consumer. These analyses allow them to determine if it is prudent to continue a course of action or if going in an entirely different direction is indicated.

The accumulation and use of data will require ongoing assistance from social workers or other staff comfortable with research and program evaluation methods. Typically, the function of program evaluation is added to other duties since funding sources rarely pay for full-time data management or program evaluation support staff. The additional responsibility of program evaluation by a person already overburdened or topped out will inadvertently be overlooked or not performed as feasibly and optimally as it should.

Another challenge for the administrator or manager of evidence-based programs is the difficulty of adhering to continuous quality improvement efforts when there is a high degree of staff turnover and change, which can threaten and interrupt the regular practice of institutional norms and memory. The ability of the director to administer a culture of learning in an organization that depends on all stakeholders being able to hold each other responsible for the competent use of data, transparency, and skepticism is critical. The inability to achieve buy-in by stakeholders and overburdening them with multiple duties without adequate resources may overtax the organization's human resources and negatively impact its program intent. These kinds of directors need training and consultation, or both.

Consultations working with social administrators and program managers will need to be strategic in how they assist the agency in becoming competent about the systematic collection of data, its important uses, and its challenges and limitations. The sustainability of the implementation of evidence-based programs and best practices hinges on the extent to which systematic data gathering and use by staff are sustained. This requires that staff data collection and data use in decision-making be incentivized by management as normative and standard agency practice. The use of data allows the staff to keep refining their operating hunches and practice hypothesis about what will work and what to avoid in practice.

An alternative to ongoing outside consultation is to make an arrangement with faculty at a local university. There are all sorts of bartering and fee arrangements for student assistance and contractual agreements with faculty that executives of nonprofits are able to negotiate and arrange.

EFFICIENCY

The extent to which the distribution of goods and services is done in an orderly, feasible, and time-sensitive manner is the aim of social welfare policy implementation. The extent to which social policy is administered efficiently means that care has been taken to address the needs of an eligible group in an expedient fashion. The efficiency of a social policy permits the distribution of goods and services to as many people as possible who need its provisions and are deemed eligible to receive them. The efficiency of a social policy includes a focus on the extent to which it is productive in its aims of reaching as many eligible beneficiaries as practically possible.

The efficiency of a social policy also involves the extent to which it is proficient in its administration. The litmus test for such competency involves its overall sound management, implementation, and regulation of those policy provisions that ultimately achieve intended effects. An example of inefficient social policy can be found in the child welfare policy to reduce foster care. Identifying the problem and its solution as an internally focused set of issues reinforces the silo approach to serving children and families. This approach is not the most efficient lens or method, as articulated by Briggs (2011). The lack of cross-system joint efforts is one of the reasons for its apparent failure. Also, the myopic view from within the child welfare system on the factors that sustain racial disproportionality and racial disparities reduces opportunities for a community psychiatry public health approach. A public health lens would define the multivariate character of the problem of racial disproportionality and racial disparities. To eliminate the problems of racial disproportionality and racial disparities is through this lens involves directing resources to buttress and reverse the ill effects of cumulative risks. Such a broad-based approach is needed given the chronic lack of educational, primary health, behavioral health, and financial illiteracy capacities of historically marginalized groups and communities.

Bartholet et al. (2011), a highly published critic of the reduction in the use of foster care, believes this approach has historical roots and philanthropy support. She recognizes the main culprits for this misguided policy initiative and its chief funders and proponents as the Casey Family Program Foundation. It is through their financial incentives that this perspective on reducing foster care has been able to flourish. She believes that the premature removal of children from foster care is short-sighted. Also, she understands the devastating negative consequences on families as well as racial groups such as African Americans, Native American, and Native Hawaiians and Other Asian Pacific Islanders (N-HOPI). The basis of the argument advanced by proponents of the Casey Family Foundation program is the use of decision point analysis data that highlights the differential experiences by racial groups at different child welfare service system.

Alternatively, Roberts's (2009) depiction of the racial geography created as a result of biased decisions in child welfare systems shows that it contributes to unnecessary family disruption for children and families of color. In some cases, Littell (2009) and others, discussed in Briggs and McBeath (2012), have pointed to decision-making in child welfare protective custody that has been discriminatory to African Americans, both in terms of its effect as well as its intent.

As we see it, the problem is with the inefficient use of decision point data to track biased decision-making in child welfare. It is the inability of this internal data to represent the impact and influence of societal inequalities on family disruption that is of major concern to Briggs as well as Bartholet (2011). These stressors contribute to parental stress and the eventuality of child abuse and neglect. They go undetected or accounted for because they are external factors not directly under the purview and control of the child welfare authority. Subsequently, these key triggers of abuse and neglect among fragile families from historically marginalized groups and communities are ignored. Their influences on the dismal realities for many children and families become the cumulative stressors that ultimately link them to both the child welfare and juvenile justice authorities. In many cases, children and parents may need to be separated. This temporary inconvenience will ensure child safety until the protective resources necessary to reunite and sustain families of origin can be established. To achieve the intended effects of reducing threats and harmful conditions to the children and parents, foster care is often used to avoid the eventuality of child and family endangerment. In a number of instances, its value and overall contribution to the socialization and preparation of youth as law abiding and academically achieving students is not always realized, especially for African Americans (Harris, Jackson, O'Brien, & Pecora, 2009).

Current policy on racial disproportionality reduction in child welfare is unproductive in other instances. For example, its emphasis on child safety and protection is done at the expense of also addressing issues of paramount importance, such as the lack of access to the social determinants of health. This reality comprises the sum total of the chronic consequences of the societal inequalities faced by historically marginalized groups and communities (Briggs & McBeath, 2012). The child welfare system has been outstripped in its ability to address the societal inequalities that accompany the prevalence of child abuse and neglect among African American children and families (Schueman, Rzepnicki, & Littell, 1994). The consequences of myopically defining and solving the problem of overrepresentation of African Americans in foster care as opposed to the conditions that give rise to the need for foster care use is not only inefficient, but also inept.

For example, Oregon's Child Welfare Equity Task Force comprehends the extraordinary costs involved in the use of foster care, seeing it as an expensive proposition with skyrocketing human and financial costs. Foster care in Oregon is used much more often and for much longer periods for African American and American Indian/Alaskan Native children than for white children. The overrepresentation of children, families, and communities of color in Oregon's foster care system represents both a serious social injustice and an economic emergency. In a task force report by Briggs (2011), it states that

> [t]he Task Force takes the position that there are at least two primary reasons why ending disparities in foster care must be a priority for the State and for the Legislature. The financial consequences to the state and its citizens when disadvantaged children become part of a system that will virtually guarantee a further decline in opportunities available to them when they exit the system; and, the unacceptable human impact to African American and Native American children who languish in the foster care system and their families. (Briggs, 2011, p. 5)

Briggs concluded that the root causes of disproportionality are complex and have been investigated from a broad range of perspectives. Based on its review of the data and the research provided by Briggs, the Task Force found that the disparities and overrepresentation of children of color in the child welfare system result from three primary causes:

1. Structural inequalities (in policy/practice), budget deficits, staffing challenges, and culturally biased decision-making *inside* the juvenile dependency system;
2. External disparities (poverty, healthcare, education), related consequences, risks and stressors *outside* the child welfare system, impacting child safety and family stability and leading to an increased need for state intervention in various communities; and,
3. Lack of a diverse workforce, training and *accountability* for existing policies and mandates designed to improve the cultural responsiveness of the system and eliminate disparities.

EQUALITY

Social policies that make equal provisions for everyone with a particular need and that are not concerned primarily with people with the greatest need are attempting to ensure that everyone defined as eligible gets the same response. The use of equivalency as a standard to guide the design and implementation of social policy raises concerns. The challenge with the distribution of goods and services under this arrangement is the issue of waste. Not everyone who is eligible requires the same distribution. This means that some people over-benefit while others fail to receive what they really need to resolve the problem they are experiencing.

Equity

Issues of lack of equity occur when social policy does not address issues of fairness and parity. Issues of equity in policy implementation as well as its administration also arise when policies do not ensure the greatest distribution of goods and services to the people with the greatest need. For example, the extent to which populations at risk are underrepresented in prevention services and overrepresented in most restrictive modes of service delivery presents an uneven picture that begs the question of equity.

For example, in a presentation on racial disparities and racial disproportionality, Julia Littell (2009) pointed to the reality that prevention services typically are provided to white families. Concomitantly, she recognized that substitute out-of-home care statistics reflect an overrepresentation of children of color in the foster care systems.

Hill and others who noticed the availability of least restrictive services and funding for family preservation of many programs serving white families raised the concern about lack of fairness in child welfare policy when they did not observe the same practices applied to African American families with child welfare involvement. The local Child Protective Services authority identified more African American families as eligible for services that typically involved out-of-home or residential placement.

The concern about justice in social policy is raised when the effects and unintended consequences of a policy on a particular group of people is experienced as if it carried the intention of injustice. For example, the creation of the subprime loan market made it easy for people to get loan approval for home mortgages even though they predatorily targeted people without capital who were more likely to be attracted to high-risk loans as an avenue to get a home. Yet, these same people were also more likely to get hurt from the crash of subprime lending, given the reality that they were already financially vulnerable and at high risk. Now, the additional cost of their home due to foreclosure puts an already financially strapped family further in debt. Their financial blunder carries additional penalties and taxes involved with the processing of real estate foreclosures.

Another example of inequity in policy can be found in the example of the harsher sentencing practices of people who violate drug policy legislation on crack cocaine, which carries longer prison sentences for its violation, than for people who violated drug laws by using or selling the more expensive powdered cocaine. The effort to disincentivize the use and distribution of crack cocaine only impacted the wealthy or other people who could avoid it by using a more expensive, less penalized and legally inexpensive drug of choice alternative.

The real estate and banking practices during the Jim Crow Era are examples of private industry policies that were not evenhanded. Real estate property in areas with no corporate investment or social, economic capital and with high crime rates were shown by realtors exclusively to African American families. Residential areas with above-average school districts with upper middle class and high-income families were reserved for exclusive showing to white families.

The lack of evenhandedness is an issue with a history as recent as 2009, when Dr. Andrew Grant Thomas of the Kerwin Institute showed the difference in racial residential patterns in Portland, Oregon. The Institute showed that African Americans with the highest income live in communities with a concentration of poor African Americans. In contrast, the wealthiest whites in Portland only live among the wealthiest whites and the white poor live among other white poor. His presentation provided evidence of the importance of the racialization of place.

A lack of justness is also experienced by persons with felony convictions who serve their formal sentences only to return to community life with no access to legitimate wage-earning labor markets and industry due to having a criminal record. These same ex-felons are not eligible for educational loans to attend school to learn a trade or acquire a skill competency so they will be able to secure meaningful employment. Their lack of employment means that they are unable to secure health insurance. They are unable to locate safe and affordable housing because the only landlords who will rent to them manage properties in high-crime and drug trafficking areas. The effect of a felony conviction carries the same discriminatory experience that comes with race. Sadly, the experience of a felony conviction is uneven and more disproportionately encountered by African Americans than Hispanic and white adults and juveniles. This statistic holds true in all states except for Idaho, where there is not enough diversity for the experience of overrepresentation in jails and prisons by people of color to occur (Iguchi, Bell, & Fanchan, 2005).

The lack of impartiality in the judicial court decisions can be seen in the racial makeup of participants of drug court versus the census of the jails and prisons in Indiana. Statistics show that white defendants are more likely to have plea deals that include drug court and community residential housing placement and probation, while African Americans receive lengthy jail and prison sentences.

An example of the lack of parity in the outcomes of a social policy is available in the statistics on foster care alumni by race in Washington state. Harris, Jackson, O'Brien, and Pecora (2009) show that white foster care alumni were statistically more likely to be home owners and long-term apartment renters with income significantly greater than their African American alumni counterparts, who were less likely to have their high school diplomas and were more likely to be in poverty, receive public assistance, and be unemployed.

ECOLOGICALLY SOUND

Social policy that includes provisions that are compatible with the task environment, the participating community needs and values, and the cultural and geographic customs of the client systems are more likely to produce intended program effects. The extent to which policy does not consider these crucial factors will result in negative and undesirable consequences for its targeted beneficiaries.

For example, juveniles who are suspended from school and have community detention and probation are enrolled in a school reconnection program housed in a residential locked facility where the youth are able to leave without restriction. The locked residential compound houses youth from the same neighborhoods and communities where the youth on probation reside. While a great deal of effort is done to keep both populations in separate cottages and from having any opportunity for verbal or physical contact, the setting provides a badge of honor for being rebellious and behaving outside the law. Consequently, it reinforces the attitude of being a tough person who cannot be controlled or threatened by fears of incarceration.

Another example is the location of juvenile court in some areas where public transportation does not operate with regular frequency, and the next available scheduled bus makes the youth too late to appear for a detention review meeting first thing in the morning. This violation of the court order adds another strike. For youth in Oregon, the Measure 11 Mandatory Minimum Sentencing policy and legislation carries harsher and longer sentences for people with three misdemeanor strikes. A third example of the importance of cultural and geographic customs in client systems is the lack of diverse cultural resources to wash and groom hair in group homes for youth, which results in penalties by home parents for untidy self-care skills.

A fourth example is a detention program where group probation counselors use talk counseling approaches comprised of storytelling about old-school values and cultural rights of passage as a programming approach for addressing violent behaviors among youth living in high-risk families and communities. The science is very clear on matching the triggers, precipitating factors, and contingencies that instigate the onset of and maintain the participation in criminal behaviors among youth with histories of serious delinquent youth behaviors. On the other hand, the community social service provider and the funder have agreed to a plan involving an experimental approach that includes cultural rights of passage and culturally specific activities. This experimental approach has more political accountability and support and lesser foundations in science. It ignores the prescriptions based in the science of addressing the serious delinquent youth population, their criminagenic factors and tendencies, and what actually works and does not work in achieving recidivism reductions (Latessa, Cullen, & Gendreau, 2002). Although the experimental approach is the popular choice politically and has endorsements from many groups in the community, this is an example of where those supporting a sanctioned grassroots approach to community problem-solving of serious violent crimes and activities may want to rethink their priorities and emphasis.

To insist on what the community thinks they want instead of what science, sound reasoning, and clinical trial research says will work, flies in the face of drivers for designing and implementing effective approaches. This is a risk management, informed consent, and institutional review board matter that needs external review and independent oversight. Such oversight will need to weigh the value of using well-established approaches based in the best available knowledge on solving the problem compared to an alternate approach. The important lesson is that organizations must use robust approaches as opposed to reinventing the wheel and using novel methods with less research support, unknown risks, potential harm, and unintended consequences.

ECUMENICAL

The faith-based community has become a major partner and ally in the delivery of human and social services, advocacy, and support to individuals, families, groups, organizations, and communities facing a myriad of social problems. In Oregon, the faith-based leader of the ecumenical congregation sits on the state commission for the Oregon Commission on Children and Families. He helps set policy for child-serving institutions receiving state funding. He also sits on the board of directors of the Northwest Health Foundation, a philanthropic charity that gives grants and contributions to organizations promoting access to the social determinants of health and primary healthcare for all citizens, especially those from high-risk, historically marginalized communities. For example, to combat the denial that is pervasive among many people in the African American community about the rise in HIV and AIDS infections among African Americans, the pastors and ministerial alliances sponsored a well-publicized HIV testing and AIDS awareness project. This was done to keep the conversation front and center in as many places as possible to break the silence and reverse the growth in HIV and AIDS infections among African Americans.

The importance and role of the faith-based community in its efforts to increase the use of mental health and psychiatric services among African Americans in Portland, Oregon, was a main mission of former State Senator Avel Gordly and Reverend William G. Hardy of Highland Baptist Church. As the chair of the African American Mental Health Commission in Oregon, Reverend Hardy was successful in joining with leaders of the Oregon Health & Science University's Division of Psychiatry and others to secure needs assessment research funding that aided the first author of this book in studying the needs for and design of a clinic.

In the needs assessment research by Briggs (2004), African Americans would rather seek the support of a friend and pastor instead of seeking services through the traditional mental health service system in Portland. Briggs received state and county funding of well over $1 million for the annual operations of the now established Avel Gordly Mental Health Clinic.

Beyond its many influences and contributions to the achievement of mental health, the role of the faith-based community in its positive contribution to therapeutic outcomes is also well established through scientific investigation. Nationally, faith-based organizations have joined the discussion in and efforts at increasing healthy marriages and reducing child poverty through sponsoring many of the fatherhood initiatives that are also receiving federal funding support. These initiatives cross racial lines and organize programming and services to combat the fragility of the family and the propensity of the family and children to remain in poverty and experience disruptions due to a breakdown in relationship-building. These initiatives also value clarification skills among unmarried parents and address the lack of effective parenting, financial illiteracy, and unstable employment that trigger the onset of poor parenting and family management.

EMPOWERMENT

The actualization and demonstration of the capacity of seeking and securing one's own life chances and choices is one of the moral imperatives that undergird the ethical practice of social work. Aiding clients to act within their own personal power to actualize their choice, dignity, and self-worth is a paramount aim of social workers working on behalf of and with populations at risk. Helping client-consumers achieve these essential life-preserving skills by learning from social workers how to successfully modify their personal, family, and social environments through the completion of therapeutic and time-sensitive tasks is the purview of the task-centered approach (Tolson, Reid, & Garvin, 2003) and applied behavior analysis in social work practice (Briggs, 1994, 1996, 2001; Pinkston, Levitt, Linsk, & Rzepnicki, 1982).

Briggs strategically and successfully included the perspectives, participation, and voices of client-consumers and families in the planning, implementation, and evaluation of the effectiveness of child welfare and gender-specific residential group home programs in inner-city African American communities. He taught these same management, organizational planning, and development skills to parent leaders nationwide (Briggs et al., 1993; Briggs et al., 1994), developing statewide family support and advocacy organizations in the field of children's mental health (Briggs & Koroloff, 1995; Koroloff & Briggs, 1996).

The use of youth client-consumers and families has contributed to the transformation of practice in the field of children's mental health. Families have contributed to the change in policies, legislation, funding, and the roles families play in non-traditional activities in the design, implementation, evaluation, and improvement functions of systems of care. Family participation in these nontraditional roles has contributed to a family knowledge base and expertise. Its emphasis has also grown in popularity in federal policy since Congress passed legislation in 1984 approving the Child and Adolescent Service System Project in the field of children's mental health (Friesen, Koroloff, Walker, & Briggs, 2011). Jane Knitzer's original exposé (1982) on the state of children services and the efforts of Barbara Friesen and Associates of the Portland Research and Training Center on Family Support in Children's Mental Health, along with concerned family members, professionals, and researchers under the direction of Robert Friedman, former director of the Florida Research and Training Children on Systems of Care in Children's Mental Health, aided the transformation in the roles of families use of cultural competence and principles of systems of care to organize and deliver services to children and families (Briggs, Briggs, & Leary, 2006).

Families, youth voice, and participation have been key to system reforms in children's mental health, such as in the Alcohol, Drug Abuse, Mental Health Administration Reorganization Act (ADAMHA). This act provided more than $120 million of federal funds for states that have adopted the principles of the Child and Adolescent Service System Program (CASSP), which involves the use of coordinated, culturally competent, family-centered systems of care for improving services to children with serious emotional disturbance and their families (Briggs et al., 2006). Both family and youth participation in family support and advocacy organizations has contributed to the sustainability of family knowledge and expertise, family-to-family peer support, and the achievement of transforming policies and children's mental health service systems (Friesen et al., 2011).

Briggs, Briggs, and Leary (2006) articulate how families and youth pursue systems change through statewide family advocacy organizations. They say that, "As agents of change, Statewide Family Networks [sic] are examples of radical structuralist organizations. . . . As radical structural organizations, SFN's involve family members who share a collective ideology about change. This collective ideology represents for them a 'universal truth'" (p. 46). Highlighting Netting and O'Connor's (2003) perspectives on the characteristics and approaches used by radical structuralist organizations as a framework for understanding the nature of statewide family support and advocacy organizations, Briggs et al. (2006) further explain that "the radical structuralist organization uses these external truths as guides in raising awareness and consciousness. . . . The basis of such awareness-raising in SFN's [sic] is done through education that focuses on the contributions and experiences of parents in the design of family-centered legislation, policies, and service systems. In short, radical structuralist organizations work from the inside out" (p. 46).

The empowerment and involvement of culturally diverse families in the aims and pursuits of statewide family support and advocacy organizations is a major aim that family leaders nationwide have aspired toward and one in which they have made considerable gains. The chief executive officer of the National Federation of Families for Children's Mental Health is African American. Also, research by

Briggs, Briggs, and Leary (2005) and others (Friesen et al., 2011) clearly articulates the involvement and penetration of diverse parents and youth in the systems change, family-to-family peer support, youth leadership, and youth-to-youth mentorship activities of statewide family support and advocacy organizations. Additionally, youth voice has been instrumental in the evaluation of culture-specific children's mental health services for Native American youth (Cross et al., 2011). It has also been instrumental in the broad agenda of the youth and family movement organized through the National Federation of Families for Children's Mental Health (Friesen et al., 2011).

Yet, there is still more to be done if the profession of social work is to use the best available science to improve behavior management and illness-related issues among children. Modifying family and youth voice in the use of evidence-based practice, initially, in step 1 of a five-step process, instead of including them at step 4, the next to the last stage of the process, was one of the editorial observations made by Walker, Briggs, Koroloff, and Friesen (2007). As a way of empowering parents involved in a statewide family support and advocacy organization to use evidence-based practice, Briggs (2009) taught an African American foster parent and family advocate how to use EBP successfully in addressing mental health issues and crises in her care of a teenage African American female foster child. He developed a technical assistance approach for assisting and coaching other parents in the use of evidence-based practice; this is fully delineated in our discussion of diffusion of innovations in Chapter 13.

ECONOMIC PARTICIPATION

The job of social workers involves aiding the poor and people in vulnerable populations to achieve social sustainability in their functioning and independent self-determination capabilities. Since the days of the Great Society and War on Poverty, the financial aid needs of the poor and their social service needs have been addressed separately through social policy (Hoshino, 1973).

The absence of aiding people in vulnerable situations to be financially literate and empowered is strange, given the role that poverty and financial stress play in the lives and conditions faced by people who come to the attention of social workers. Financial stress in this country is an equal opportunity problem. A study by the Personal Financial Employee Education Foundation reported that 1 out of every 4 employees are in serious financial distress. More than 80% of those with financial distress use work time ranging from 12 to 20 hours per month to deal with personal financial issues. The cost of lost productivity among these employees is estimated to be $7,000 per year for each affected employee, according to a study by the Financial Literacy Partners.

Also, the 2009 Society for Human Resource Management study reported that its survey respondents had witnessed an increase in wage garnishments, requests for loans from their 401(k) plans, and requests for payday advances. Additionally, as reflected in the 2009 Federal Deposit Insurance Corporation's (FDIC) national survey, more than 25% of all households in this country either did not have a bank account or had a bank account, but no banking products, such as a loan. Of this number, about one-third of these households were people who identified as black (31.6%), almost a third (28.9%) identified as American Indians, and 24% identified as Hispanic. Of the households with incomes less than $30,000, about 20% did not have bank accounts. More than two-thirds of the people without bank accounts use alternative financial services such as check cashing stores, pawnshops, payday loans, refund anticipation loans, convenience stores, and postal money orders.

Ignoring the problem of financial distress and financial illiteracy is not an option due to the shift in the larger economic context and the growing emphasis in this country on personal as opposed to social ethics and responsibility. There is also a growth in the complexity of financial products, and the gap between who is eligible to access these products is also widening. The financing of retirement and health-care is shifting away from employers and government to the individual employee, while health costs continue to soar. Additionally, there is a growing distrust among consumers of banks and banking, in general, and with the policies and practices of Wall Street and other financial institutions.

If early pioneers of social work education and architects of social policy would have known what we know now about financial illiteracy as a public health threat, it is conceivable that its interrelationship to other social problems could have been realized. Perhaps then the inversion of Maslow's hierarchy of needs (1970) and its inextricable linkage to the assessment of the social determinants of health would also have been included as threads and key drivers of the ecological systems perspective in social work. It is only through a public health analysis of the absence of social and economic capital by people and what is subsequently learned about the associated origins of the problem and its causes, correlates, consequences, and implications, that the relative importance of the intersectionality of public health and social work will be realized.

To reverse the experiences of financial distress, it would be prudent to include financial literacy and financial wellness and empowerment education in primary, secondary, and higher education. Social workers and others helping distressed and historically marginalized communities must be knowledgeable and experienced and also become empowered financially. There is institutional support and financial incentives for social workers and participating social service organizations through Public Law 109-173, Section 7 of the Federal Deposit Insurance Reform Conforming Amendments Act of 2005. This legislation mandates the FDIC to engage in and provide proof of transforming the financially illiterate and moving them into the conventional system of banking and finance. There are four avenues through which social work can link with financial institutions to increase financial literacy, financial wellness, and empowerment among its students, professional practitioners, educators, and the beneficiaries of social services. These include banks, insurance companies, mutual funds, and independent financial education programs.

ENFORCEMENT PROTECTIONS

The absence of enforcement protection accountability mechanisms in US policy has been blamed for the rise in racial disparities and white privilege on all quality of life fronts (Themba-Nixon, 2001). The need for enforcement protection is fast becoming a necessity and is increasingly dependent on the extent to which it is sanctioned and mandated by funding sources. Assuring the provision of high-quality services through continuous quality improvement efforts that eventually result in the achievement of the intended program effects involves a degree of accountability that has been difficult to sustain in social work.

The discussion of the issues and threats to accountability in social services originated with Claghorn (1927). She described the lack of measurement, follow-up, tracking, and monitoring of the errors and successes of a change process as contributing to the revolving door of new, but short-lived solutions for historical social problems such as juvenile delinquency. The lack of accountability was the major setback that contributed to the overall failure of the 1962 social services amendments to the Social Security Act (Hoshino, 1973). Hoshino explains:

> The problem of accountability points up the paradoxes of social policy and the dilemmas of social welfare. Until the goals of policy can be made more coherent and consistent and criteria of performance more explicit and realistic, there is little hope of attaining accountability in any real sense for either the services program as a whole or for the individual worker. Even more problematic is the question of accountability to the client population—of serving the interests of the consumers of social services, as they perceive their problems and needs. (p. 381)

Since our humble beginnings, the profession of social work has improved its ability to measure its effectiveness, as well as its capacity to track and monitor our errors and successes. In the empirical practice movement, the current foci on evidence-based practice and evidence-based interventions is evidence of advancements in social work. Now, in social work education, there is increasing emphasis placed on educating practitioners competent in methods that allow them to evaluate their own practice as well as learn to provide interventions with a robust research foundation. While goals and performance of management, staff, and client-consumers are more clearly and measurably defined, there is still no change in actualizing the assurances that they will perform as expected. Also, the failure of the 1962 Social Service amendments left a bad impression of social work with the American voting and political camps, especially Republicans and conservative Democrats (Hoshino, 1973).

The extent to which performance problems exist, Mager and Pipe (1970) argue, is accompanied by a lack of reinforcement, incentives, and disincentives for poor performance, lack of performance, or the punishment of good performance. Mager and Pipe (1970) and Baer (2004) would argue from a behavioral analytic perspective that the wrong contingencies are sustaining the wrong behavioral performances that comprise the environments of poor and underfunctioning nonprofit organizations. From a systems point of view, Kim (2005) argues that placing greater emphasis on legal and hierarchical accountability impairs political and professional accountability. Kim would argue that the different types of accountability compete and mutually interact. He believes that any manipulation of that interaction to establish a preference for one set of accountability relationships over other types complicates and nullifies the balance between competing accountability relationships (p. 145).

The issues and problems in achieving accountability in the practice arena of social work are also tied to its missteps in social work education. Arguably, the overall failure of social work education to establish interconnections between faculty inputs (instruction and research), student outputs (skill competencies), and field practicum agency-based outcomes (service effectiveness) is one of the barriers to sustaining accountability in professional social work practice and human service organizations. However, in the profession of medicine, proficiency in medical education is tied to the health outcomes that practitioners achieve as student interns, residents, and specialists. In the medical education scenario, it is clear that a functional relationship exists between the effective resolution of the health needs of patients in the teaching hospitals and clinics, the skills of the student interns and residents, and the instruction based in research and evidence-based medicine.

Alternatively, the rational ordering and logical reasoning that are the characteristics of the positivist paradigm are not the prevailing approach used in the education of students of social work. Allegiance to authority-based approaches dominates and inflames the passions; they are the most commonly used and preferred theoretical paradigms by members of the National Association of Social Workers (NASW). Referred to by Gambrill (2004) as authority-based approaches to social work practice, these methods are based in perspectives that explain human behavior in terms of internal motives and drives and other assumptions that have not been subjected to rigorous random clinical trial research. The poor research foundation of many of these authority-based approaches increases the propensity for a kind of pseudo-science and quackery in the practice of social services (Gambrill, 2004). For example, in some practice settings, people are camouflaging their actual use of authority-based approaches by claiming to use other approaches that have greater appeal and wider acceptance as emerging, promising practices or a newly recognized evidence-based interventions. In other words, just because people claim to be using evidence-based approaches does not always mean that there is truth in advertising!

Another shortcoming in the education of students in social work, and one that undermines their ability to be accountable, is their limited exposure to public health curricula. Such information allows them to acquire a thorough grasp of how to assess and analyze the public health threats to individuals, families, groups, organizations, and communities at risk and with high risks of social problems. To some extent, the skill of understanding how the environment threatens, exacerbates, and gives rise to problems encountered by client-consumers of social services is provided through courses on human behavior in the social environment. However, in much of the published materials in that area, there is a dearth of literature that articulates the multicontingency behavioral analytic perspective on this phenomena in social services, with the exception of Briggs and associates.

The lack of focus on curricula that articulates a behavior analytic multi-contingency analysis of the interlocking and inter-institutional web of urban racism permeating social and public policy presents students with a handicap (Briggs & McBeath, 2012; Briggs & Paulson, 1996). This handicapping condition, along with not understanding epidemiology and training in public health assessments, enables institutions to sustain the status quo of inadequate, race-based, inept, and ineffective social policies. The preservation of the current status quo contributes further harm in the way of sustaining both racial disparities and white privilege, as articulated in the report by Themba-Nixon (2001). The authors of that report believe enforcement protections would decrease the rise in these issues.

The former Attorney General of Oregon, John Kroger, and the authors of this book share the same passion for transparency and accountability in social and public policies within the governments and nonprofit organizations that receive public funds. In Kroger's estimation, people in government and nonprofits will not do anything unless it is mandated. In our opinion, we would extend that one step further: people will not do what you expect or want them to do unless you both mandate and enforce the mandates incentives, disincentives, and penalties.

Enforcement protection mechanisms should be built into every level and aspect of an organization and maintained through external monitoring, sanctioned by administrative rules governing nonprofit organizations. Wandersman, Imm, Chinman, and Kaftarian (2000) delineate an approach to achieving accountability at each stage, beginning with the needs assessment and planning phases, continuing through the implementation of best practices phase, to the quality assurance and evaluation phases. Their approach is driven by 10 accountability questions that cover these three phases. Funders should require these questions to be completed by nonprofits as a standard boilerplate plan for getting to outcomes through a results-based accountability approach. They should be completed prior to final grant awards and the commencement of the funding and at the end of each annual funding cycle of social service programs and services. The 10 questions are listed here (Wandersman et al., 2000, p. 393).

1. What are the underlying needs and conditions that must be addressed?
2. What are the goals, target populations, objectives, and desired outcomes?
3. Which science (evidence)-based models and best practice programs can be useful in reaching the goals?

4. What actions needed to be taken so that the program "fits" the community context?
5. What organizational capabilities are needed to implement the program?
6. What is the plan for this program?
7. How will the quality of program/initiative implementation be assessed?
8. How well did the program work?
9. How will continuous quality improvement strategies be incorporated?
10. If the program is successful, how will it be sustained?

As a standard practice, the nonprofit agency should engage in a continuous assessment of organizational health as well as implement an ongoing organizational behavior modification process. Also, to ensure their completion, both the organizational health assessment and organizational behavior modification plans should be mandated and completed annually by the nonprofit. The annual organizational health assessment is a performance review by the nonprofit covering its staff, management, and resource capability, capacity, effect and impact, areas in need of improvement, and progress on existing organizational behavior modification plans. Organizational behavior modification plans identify areas targeted for change and improvement, the change strategy, the parties responsible for change, and the target outcomes. At each level of the organization and among the stakeholders, the certainty that what gets monitored gets done should be the reality.

In Oregon, the lack of enforcement protection and accountability mechanisms that consider cultural knowledge and practices has contributed to the rise of the use of foster care for children and families from Sovereign Nations and historically marginalized communities.

4 }

Integrative Practice

THEORY AND INTEGRATIVE PRACTICE MODEL DEVELOPMENT IN LARGER SYSTEMS

To recap, so far you have been introduced to three core foundational areas of integrative practice; (1) the importance of integrative practice in and for larger systems to enable social work agency, program, and community leaders to strategically obtain service and client level accountability; (2) the significance of culture as a structural determinant of resiliency, power, and privilege and the lack of power and privilege in historically oppressed groups; and (3) the influence of social policy in shaping social welfare responses, boundaries, and regulations in larger systems providing an array of social services. We now turn our attention to the fourth core integrative practice competency: theory as a guide for problem-oriented practice model development in and for larger systems.

For many leaders of social service agencies, the paucity of a well-defined theoretical framework to use to both incentivize and effectively guide all aspects of the social service agency leaves administrators in community organizations to practice myopically and prophylactically instead of innovatively, multisystemically, and strategically focused. For instance, direct care staff who join agencies mandated to apply evidence-based interventions may continue to follow a familiar case management approach based on loyalty to and belief in a particular practice theory. Typically, agency direct care staff use methods they are most knowledgeable with, and we believe the same holds true for executive and program management personnel.

What is missing in the preparation of the social agency administrator and program management is education in the science of leadership along with training in the careful use of theory to guide the implementation of integrative management practice through the science of behavior change. To successfully incorporate best practices and evidence-based treatments into the service delivery process, social agency heads need to know performance management technologies that allows them to skillfully use evidence to incentivize and lead the staff's implementation of the science of behavior change through evidence-informed approaches (Briggs, 2001, 1994, 1996).

Social Work Theory

Holosko's (2009) leadership perspective, which includes leadership competencies, is applicable across layers of an agency: leaders in this context (a) are mission and vision driven, (b) incentivize and influence others to act, (c) facilitate teamwork and collaboration, (d) facilitate problem-solving, and (e) promote the achievement of positive behavior change. Competency in these issues, combined with the competent use of the science of behavior change, is sufficient preparation as a guide to launch leaders of social agencies. Without this competency, the lack of such a unifying approach by staff and management provides very little direction to the individual administrator seeking to strategically administer a larger system, while solving managerial dilemmas that impede progress.

Marsh (2004) explicates the value of theory as a vehicle to chart the specifications of the problem as well the change process needed to reduce or eliminate the problem. The unification of Holosko's leadership perspective with Marsh's perspective on the role of theory in directing the implementation of the science of behavior change is a useful organizing theoretical framework that supports management in conceptualizing common problems that interfere with program implementation. Such interference is in direct conflict with achieving service effectiveness.

In this book, such a unifying theory exists. Holosko's perspective is a useful framework that administrators can use along with the strategic use of task-centered practice, applied behavioral analysis methods, and organizational behavior modification techniques. All of them are inextricably linked and share a common point of reference: the achievement of client and staff performance outcomes are contingent upon a supportive, well-managed agency environment. Repeated applications of these methods with staff, management, and families modifies agency practice in a favorable direction. It is the repetitive use of a functional analysis at different levels and over time that is of greatest value. It allows management to make strategic decisions based on the evidence of the contingent relationship between staff inputs and outputs and client behavioral reactions. In this instance, the bottom line of administration and management is actualizing better functioning programs, which result in better functioning client systems, which includes individuals, families, small groups, organizations, and communities (Briggs, 2001a).

The theoretical approach used in this book is different from most texts on management. In this book, we emphasize the overall importance of combining direct practice and management practice driven by a unified multilevel performance management methodology. This methodology is driven by actionable theories about the situation and theories about changing the situation. It is a knowledge acquisition, knowledge synthesis, and knowledge use paradigm triggered by incentivizing behavioral expectations and interlocking contingencies that binds each of the stakeholders of the organization to one another, such as the funding sources, management, staff, and the client-consumers of social service agencies. The strategic and consistent implementation and performance feedback loop used to make decisions and guide staff behavior enhances the likelihood that when you introduce a knowledge-driven change process and monitor its progress, what gets monitored gets supported and done!

In this chapter, several organizational behavior modification techniques based in behavioral theories are combined with the use of evidence and other theories for developing and refining relevant theories of situations and for changing situational dilemmas in administration and management practices. This includes operant and social learning theories, which have been used in recent years as solutions to service delivery (Reid, 2001, 2004; Thyer, 2004) and its administration and management (Briggs & McMillan, 2012).

Operant Theory

Baer, Wolf, and Risley (1987) suggest an entrepreneurial stimulus approach exemplified by arranging the antecedent and consequences of desirable behavior. Enhancing the rate of desirable behavior and a process of events can be influenced by changing their antecedents and consequences (Baer et al., 1968, 1987; Skinner, 1953; Thorndike, 1998). Applied behavioral procedures are valuable as a methodology for resolving service delivery problems (Baer et al., 1987; Komaki, 1982). Derived from operant theory, these procedures are applied with the expectation that they will influence the rate of behavior. Defining the environment is an essential antecedent to selecting behaviors to increase, decrease, or maintain. The environment in which these procedures are expected to operate must include (a) a well-defined operating structure, including auxiliary community services and linkage agreements; (b) program policies and procedures congruent to the proposed treatment models; (c) an ongoing data collection system; (d) intervention system; (e) feedback technology; (f) planning methods; and (g) the evaluation of behavioral events across time and subjects.

In examining the client level of performance, the process that is used to select behavior change and target staff performance and other environmental variables yields important program development information. Patterson (1982) in his research on aggression found that examining events spatially explained, and explicated, the structure and process of family interaction. This supports the importance of model development research in testing behavioral procedures for teaching families behavior management and communication skills. His research provides evidence that the more information therapists have about the antecedents and consequences of specific behaviors, the more useful the information is to developing family management programs by increasing the options for intervention. In generalizing these findings to management, the same may be expected to be true.

Influencing the antecedents and consequences or process and outcome variables enhances the structure, process, and outcomes in institutional residential settings (Andrasik & McNamara, 1977). Christian (1984) studied the influence of a package of behavioral procedures on institutional behavior change and found that client, staff, and management outcomes were positively related to applied behavioral procedures. In a similar study, Glahn, Chock, and Mills (1984) reported the positive relationship between the teaching family model, staff performance, and specific client outcomes.

In research by Briggs (1996), the structure and process of a community residential program was examined over a 30-month period. Pinpointing the interaction between behavioral events of clients, staff, and organizations provided a qualitative and quantitative database with which to study the general usefulness of the preceding assumptions.

Social Learning Theory

Procedures derived from social learning theory have also been used to develop appropriate learning environments for the developmentally disabled. Observational learning is a natural and efficient method for teaching new skills (Bandura, 1969). Aggression studies represent an appropriate example of the influence of antecedent and consequences. In Patterson's study, the future probability that a child would engage in a behavior was influenced by the parents' previous actions. The combination of positive reinforcement and modeling procedures has been demonstrated as having practical utility for designing effective interventions aimed at enhancing process and behavior change in natural settings (O'Dell et al., 1982; Pinkston, Levitt, Green, Linsk, & Rzepnicki, 1982; Pinkston & Linsk, 1984). Using observational learning procedures and corrective feedback can be advantageous to practitioners interested in developing broad-scale programs for enhancing process and behavior change (Luthans & Martinko, 1982; Sims & Manz, 1982). Modeling procedures are also cost-effective because they can be used to reach a larger audience more quickly. This enhances the maintenance of behavior change over time when compared to didactic procedures (Adams, Tallon, & Rimsell, 1980).

In studies by Page, Iwata, and Reid (1982) and Burgio, Whitman, and Reid (1983), modeling procedures have been used in organizational settings to enhance process and behavior. Page and his colleagues found that improvement in staff performance influenced the rate of client level of functioning. Maintenance of improvement was also observed. Burgio and his colleagues found that observational learning procedures can be effectively used to enhance staff participation in goal-setting, activity planning, performance feedback, program evaluation, and appropriate interaction between staff and clients during unstructured time periods (Burgio et al., 1983). These procedures have been used effectively to address service delivery process variables and specific outcomes.

Task Analysis

Task analysis procedures have been used effectively in research aimed at increasing behavior change to improve staff performance (Bacon, Fulton, & Malott, 1983). Task analysis has also been useful in research with severely handicapped students. In these studies, task analysis is used to measure a chain of desired behaviors within a set of successive steps and time (Browder, 1987). Task analysis has also been used to examine the rate of recreation, social activities, use of community facilities, travel, and vocational rehabilitation (Browder, 1987). Results from these inventories provide a profile of the level of community support for individuals with severe handicaps. Tracking data is useful in the development and evaluation of group interventions that enhance normalization and independence.

The influence of detailed task analysis procedures on the quality of behavior change, accountability, and maintenance of a problem-solving capability has been clearly identified by Foxworthy, Ellis, and McLeod (1982). In other studies, simple task analysis procedures (i.e., assigning due dates) was a superior intervention with respect to staff training in increasing supervisory task completion (Conrin, 1983).

Performance Feedback

Performance feedback has been recognized as a very effective procedure to use for improving performance among staff and management (Frederiksen, Richter, Johnson, & Solomon, 1982). Performance feedback (a) increases on-task behavior, (b) is effectively used as a positive consequence, and (c) increases self efficacy (Karl, O'Leary-Kelly, & Martocchio, 1993). In the Repp and Deitz study (1979), performance feedback was responsible for increasing the rate of (a) on-time progress reports, (b) on-time attendance, and (c) completion of time sheets. Christian (1984) found that performance feedback was an essential intervention for changing client, staff, and management behavior over a 5-year period. Greene, Willis, Levy, and Bailey (1978) developed staff performance feedback procedures that were used effectively to (a) increase the rate of staff activity, (b) increase the rate of client level of functioning, and (c) decrease the rate of off-task behavior. Performance feedback procedures were found to be effective for increasing the rate of correct individual habilitation plans (Maher, 1982). In Maher's (1981) earlier study, managers who received performance feedback and were able to behaviorally rehearse and role play were superior in developing program plans and accurately evaluating activities to those exposed to didactic procedures.

Time Management

Systematic application of time management procedures increased on-task behavior among teachers (Maher, 1982, 1985). The effectiveness of time management procedures for improving service delivery processes and specific outcomes is not discussed as an essential variable, but logic dictates that it is important when trying to juggle heavy work loads. In the Briggs (1996) study, weekly residential time management schedules were used to (a) identify group activities, (b) plan habilitation services, (c) schedule community contracts, (d) plan family and home visits and (e) plan special events.

Work Performance Contracts

Work performance contracts have been used effectively with other behavioral procedures to change the structure, process, and outcomes in an institutional setting (Christian, 1984). The application of work performance contracts to community service delivery problems is rarely mentioned in the literature (Christian, 1984). In the Briggs (1996) study, written, behaviorally specific job descriptions are used to define expected and desirable performance. Furthermore, staff received verbal feedback, expense-paid lunch, special days off, promotions, and other consequences of desirable performance.

Supervision

The influence of supervision procedures on process and outcomes has been carefully studied in the applied behavioral literature. Burg, Reid, and Lattimore (1979) found that self-management techniques have been known to influence the rate of staff performance and disruptive client behavior. In the Burgio et al. (1983) study, self-management, goal-setting, self-monitoring, graphing, and self-praise procedures influenced the rate of staff and client performance. Quilitch (1975) used activity scheduling and feedback effectively to increase the rate of staff and client performance beyond rates reported during memo and training phases. In this study, an evolving supervisory process was used. Weekly, the supervisor reviewed habilitation plans, program operations, and licensure compliance. Resource development, program planning, appointments with key people, task analysis, and milestones were also arranged weekly.

Administrative Policies and Procedures

The influence of administrative policies and procedures as a component of the process of systematic behavioral change on staff and client behavior in institutional settings has been established (Andrasik & McNamara, 1977). In the Briggs (1996) study, policies and procedures were developed to assure proper structure, process, and expected performance for staff, clients, and management.

Program Planning

Social learning and reinforcement procedures have been effectively used to influence the variance in the number of accurately completed individual educational plans (Maher, 1981; Page et al., 1981). Individual habilitation plans have become an important and major vehicle in the design of behavior change technology for developmentally disabled adults in the United States. While there is a great deal of consensus about the importance of having a plan of care that is least restrictive and that normalizes behavior, there is little evidence that having a plan will result in service effectiveness (Schalock, Foley, Tolouse, & Stark, 1985). In the Briggs (1996) study, the individual habilitation plan is used in combination with other procedures to enhance structure and process and to evaluate outcomes.

Program Implementation

Program implementation procedures have been used to influence process and outcome in several studies (Brown, Willis, & Reid, 1981; Christian, 1984; Coles & Blunden, 1981; Maher, 1983). Many studies, in general, found improvement in staff performance, process, and organizational outcomes to be related to implementation procedures, although, they often failed to include outcome data for clients' achievements. None of these studies was focused on improving organizational process and outcomes within a community residential setting.

In the Briggs (1996) performance management study, program implementation technology included (a) a weekly meeting by supervisors to review tasks, (b) planning staff activities, (c) planning behavior management procedures, (d) developing time management plans, (e) arranging material resources, (f) talking with key people involved in decision-making to facilitate performance, (g) planning maintenance of client progress, and (h) giving verbal feedback.

Involving Families in Service Delivery

The rate of family contact decreases over the life cycle of mentally disabled persons (Suelzle & Keenan, 1981). Including families in planning activities with staff has been shown to improve the rate of family contact, client participation, and staff performance (Porterfield, Evans, & Blunden, 1985). In the Briggs (1996) study, family contact and home visits were two interventions used to establish and maintain behavior change.

Generality and Maintenance

The way in which behavioral change is extended beyond experimental conditions differs for clients, staff, and management. Procedures aimed at generalizing behaviors across time, subjects, and setting have been offered in the behavioral literature (Kanfer & Goldstein, 1975; Lakin & Bruininks, 1985; Pinkston et al., 1982). Changing the rate of desirable behaviors, decreasing negative behaviors, and establishing new behaviors requires a different set of procedures to be followed. Depending on the particular behaviors targeted for change, practitioners must plan a very specific and well-defined system that arranges stimuli and environmental contingencies that generalize and maintain behavior over long periods of time. In the Briggs (1996) study, procedures for enhancing generality and maintenance were adapted from Kanfer and Goldstein (1975) and Pinkston et al. (1982). These procedures are concerned with how program goals are defined, implemented, and evaluated.

Building an Integrative Practice Theory of Agency Service Effectiveness

Achieving a client perspective in human service management depends on the degree to which the actions and actors of social service agencies "reflect a preoccupation with clients and their wellbeing," as well as, "the design and implementation" of a care cycle that favors client positive outcomes (Patti, Rapp, & Poertner, 1988, p. 23). The lack of preoccupation with client outcomes is due, in Patti's estimation, to four important myths: (1) client outcomes in human service organizations are individual phenomena, (2) client outcomes are not measurable, (3) agency accountability cannot be assessed in terms of client outcomes, and (4) assessing client outcomes is not efficient and would require additional time and resources (pp. 26–37). These ideas are not supported by any conclusive evidence, and, to the contrary, they only serve to maintain the status quo of organizations.

One of the major challenges to human service organizations seeking to be client focused is reaching an agreement about what constitutes service effectiveness.

According to Reid (1988), "although the typical effectiveness study is conducted as part of an agency program, the focus of the investigator, the report, and subsequent critique is on the particular population and interventions studied" (p. 41). Agencies often fall short of meeting scientific conditions for assessing service effectiveness. Of those programs that have established criteria, if they show some growth based in criteria, this growth measures only a fraction of the larger agency goal (Reid, 1988). To measure service effectiveness, Reid recommends "monitoring and data utilization" as key strategies for mangers seeking ways to evaluate their practice (pp. 49–57). Hudson (1981) elaborates on the various types of tools and methods to measure client outcomes in social service agencies. He recommends the measurement of client problems and goals by "(1) binary status (present or absent); (2) frequency; (3) duration; or (4) magnitude (intensity)" (Reid, 1988, p. 64). Two ways to measure problems and goals, as defined by Hudson, include "(1) direct observation and (2) self-report" (Reid, 1988, p. 64).

Grasso and Epstein (1988) examine the dilemmas and opportunities of management in measuring client outcomes in social service agencies. They argue that, in some cases, quantitative measures are not adequate in describing change in client behavior and situation. This is particularly true at the direct service level where the goal is not based in a measure of how often staff did something, but whether if the crisis or suffering of the client was relieved.

Why do community-based service agencies need a scientific methodology for managing their programs and services? Science or rules of scientific proof require sufficiently precise definitions to transfer private information into objective information that can be judged on its merits. These definitions provide information regarding effectiveness that can test the efficacy of procedures and programs. The commitment to using scientific methods means that an agency may know about and use the most advanced technology. Failing that, agencies that have the capacity to develop and evaluate technology on their own, based on the emerging needs of their client populations, are committed to achieving service effectiveness through the use of scientific methods (Pinkston et al., 1982).

A successful community-based social service requires a method of management that can accomplish both client case management and organizational staff management. These are complex organizations, comprising many individuals who must work together to accomplish client service goals. This requires multilevel interventions to design and implement programs. It is our assumption that the primary goal of these programs is to help clients move toward greater degrees of functioning, independence, or possibly empowerment.

The purpose of this book is to present an incentivizing performance management model of sufficient specificity, breath, and generality. The performance management model is an incentivizing mechanism and behavior change framework that incorporates behavioral treatment, task-centered practice, and organizational methods. This framework allows us to examine the performance of all areas from a unified point of view. Within this model, we can examine the performance of clients, family, and community as they relate to the society. Each level has its specific task in taking the client from a dependent, nonfunctioning state to one of independence through improved functioning within the context of the community.

To accomplish this, practice-related evaluation becomes a component of every aspect of the organization. Systematic, ongoing evaluation informs problem definition and intervention methods. Although some practice is mildly affected by the glut of behavioral research with children, families, and adults, this model uses practice-based research as the foundation.

Who is the consumer? The consumer of social services resides within three categories: the client, the community, and the society. One level of consumer is often the complainant of the behavior or the condition of another consumer. A family may consult the agency because the community, represented by their child's teacher, has found the behavior of their child troublesome. Whether the focus of intervention will be the child, the parent, the family, or the context of the child's behavior, the teacher, and/or the classroom, it is clear that the client and the consumer may not be the same. The question is then: Who will need to be satisfied with the outcome to assure that the outcome is positive? Could it be, as posited by Baer (1999), that the success of the intervention is assured when the complainant stops complaining?

When the community is dissatisfied with the state of affairs in which adequate responses are not present for adaptive functioning to occur, or when a problem is not being solved to their satisfaction, it may be defined simultaneously as the complainant, the client, and the consumer. As the complainant, the community may define both the problem and, through policies established to spend its money, the solution.

There is an emerging gold standard of evidence for effective social work practice. Evidence is based in random, controlled, clinical trial investigations or practice-based experimental designs with control features that allow for cause-and-effect observations (Feder, Jolin, & Feyerherm, 2000). While it is often difficult to achieve this gold standard, we aspire to it, nonetheless. In doing so, many social workers use or collect physical data in their social work practice. There are many who feel that they are using a technology that is compatible with an oral tradition that incorporates the basic communication customs of people of color. These particular practitioners feel that they do not need to critically track data elements. Yet, while culture and approach need to be compatible, the field of social work is in need of information to support why practitioners who use these techniques feel that these approaches have particular merit or optimal use in these specific cultural situations.

The need to effectively learn what may work and how to make it happen has been addressed in several social work venues. The report of the October 1997 Symposium, held by the Brookings Institution (Schorr & Mann, 1998), spells out in detail the practical and methodological issues that come with learning about what works. In this report, Schorr and others indicate that the large-scale, complex interventions that do work cannot be explained using typical rigorous methodologies. She says that these "promising interventions . . . intervene in more than a single facet of people's lives and change more than one thing at a time. They are designed to impact not only individuals, but also neighborhoods, institutions, and systems" (p. 2).

Darman in Schorr and Mann (1998) agree that "social scientists who have taught policymakers to dismiss information that may be relevant, timely, and informative, but lacks certainty, have contributed to the widespread sense that nothing is known about what works—because the certainty we demand is not attainable. Thoughtful observers with access to a wide array of data about what happened and what might have happened under different circumstances can combine that information with an understanding of similar intervention and build a strong and useful knowledge base" (p. 2).

Advocating for looser definitions of evidence and, "while conceding that such a body of information would lack certainty about causation," Schorr predicted that it "would be more likely to lead to effective action on urgent social problems than conclusions based on a narrower definition of what is credible and scientific" (p. 2). Within that same vein, Darman in Schorr and Mann (1998) argues that, in practice, we need to ask about "what may work, learning what some people think may work. That's a stage you have to be at on the way to learning what works" (p. 2). Asking for a step backward, Darman believes that "jumping prematurely to say we know it works stirs up distractive controversy about methodology" (p. 6). He affirms that "if you're slightly more humble and you say that now we really have support for an interesting hypothesis, then it's informed judgment. And over a much more extended period of time, the society increases its intellectual capital and works its way towards knowledge about what works" (p. 6).

To address the conflict between rigor and usefulness, Hollister in Schorr and Mann (1998) describe a number of key responses that all have their benefits and limitations. He points out that the standards of evidence have been lowered. This has created a dilemma about "How far do you back off, and under what circumstances" (p. 14). He recommends an increased use of theories of change approaches. This strategy is not fail-proof, either; Hollister says it best: "if we're really concerned about the impact of this problem in the sense that it changed the outcomes from what they would have been in the absence of the program, these methods (theories of change approaches) do not solve the problem" (p. 14). Finally, it is important to use several but different types of evaluations, such as single-case and quasi-experimental design evaluations, although using multiple data sources through different evaluation types could produce contradictory results.

The urge to use science has not lessened in the profession of social work. If anything, the exact opposite has taken place. There is a greater emphasis placed on the use of science in social work practice and social work education. In fact, the Council on Social Work Education's (CSWE) new accreditation standards call for schools of social work to demonstrate use of evidence-based theories. The CSWE also requires a more intensive and precise definition of indicators of what the student should be able to do as a result of the integration of science in field, practical, and classroom experiences.

Evidence-based social work practices are often confounded with behavioral practices. This common misunderstanding arises out of accepting, or believing, that others accept behavior as the only valid evidence upon which practice approaches and research methodologies can be based. Perhaps one of the most valuable contributions to the profession by the behaviorialist is our acute attention to and assiduous collection of data. For it is this collection of data that provides the evidence necessary to an evidence-based approach to social work. Behavior, however, constitutes only one kind of evidence—one kind of data. What evidence-based social work practitioners advocate is a systematic collection, rigorous analysis, and careful evaluation of all relevant data to guide a process that ultimately results in the achievement of a set of outcomes. The POP concentration at the University of Chicago's Social Service Administration provided an early training ground and curriculum to prepare practitioners to use evidence to guide problem-solving with individuals, families, groups, organizations, and communities.

Problem-Oriented Practice (POP): Behavioral Successor to Task-Centered Practice

The School of Social Service Administration (SSA) at the University of Chicago's social work graduate program had a core curriculum in the late 1970s. Students' interests were used to match them with learning experiences consistent with their paradigmatic perspective. Students were placed in sections and learned the foundation of social work in the first year with a focus on theory-based or scientifically derived practice perspectives. In the second year, they specialized in a concentration of personal choice and selection. POP served as an early behavioral prototype used in social work practice as a second-year concentration successor to task-centered practice, a first-year problem-based learning approach and early prototype in the evolution of evidence-based interventions and evidence-based practice in social work.

POP involves the use of a theory of human behavior as well as a behavior change practice theory within the framework of a single-case design methodology as tools for use by social workers in the assessment, intervention, evaluation, and follow-up stages of social work practice with vulnerable families with young children and older adults with dementia (Briggs, 2005).

Using her early work on the design and development of single-parent behavioral training methods, Pinkston demonstrated the utility of the integration of single-subject research designs, operant and social learning theory, and behavior modification as containing a core concentration practice curriculum for social work students. Beginning in 1972, she joined the faculty of the School of Social Service Administration at the University of Chicago. There, she provided technical assistance to Laura Epstein and William Reid, which resulted in the shaping of one of earliest forms of evidence-based interventions: the task-centered practice model, which included a robust behavioral orientation and reliance on the single-subject design methodology.

The value added by her contributions to the task-centered practice approach is not the only barometer by which we measure her merits and significance to the discipline of social work. It was also found in the skillful way in which she articulated and demonstrated the role of applied behavioral analysis to the education of second-year clinical social work students. While it began and was known as *applied behavioral analysis*, it was subsequently adapted as SSA's behavioral as well as its empirically based social work concentration, which she entitled Problem-Oriented Practice (POP). It was her contributions to the development of task-centered practice and her deliberate and passionate use of applied behavioral analysis and the establishment of the POP concentration that qualifies her as an early pioneer in the creation of scientifically centered, problem-based learning in social work as a precursor to what is now coined the "process of evidence-based practice."

How the Problem-Oriented Practice Approach Works at the Agency Level

To promote service effectiveness throughout the organization, we use the combined content of the problem-oriented practice (POP) and multilevel performance management practice theory approaches within a problem-solving framework: (1) problem identification, (2) assessment, (3) planning, (4) application, (5) mastery, (6) evaluation and adoption. It is used in practice as a problem-solving technique, whereas, in a developmental research context, it is modified to solve and evaluate the problem.

The utility of implementing the combined POP and multilevel performance management practice theory approaches within a problem-solving framework is its generality of application. We may use it as a framework to handle management and staff difficulties, to handle community difficulties, and more. Identifying the problem is the first step. Though seemingly obvious, there are many recent examples where individuals have launched into a planning exercise without making an adequate identification of the problem.

Problem Identification

Identify the problem to be solved. In an administrative and management context, the problem or dilemma can be stated as a performance discrepancy (Mager & Pipe, 1970) that can be addressed through problem-solving and applied behavioral analysis techniques.

As an issue or dilemma, the problem represents a challenge that brings many contributing factors and conditions that cannot be ignored. For example, Agency X promotes the use of culturally responsive programs and services, although its current operating practice principles and implementation system do not include methods that focus on building productive cultural relationships between clients and staff and among staff and management. As shown in the earlier example, as a discrepancy, the problem statement includes an observation about what is actually occurring versus what ought to occur.

For example, Agency X lacks a check-and-balance system to use in collecting data to use in critical decision-making and program evaluation; it currently uses staff opinions to judge if what is contractually agreed upon is being done.

Assessment and Problem Analysis

Assess the problem's impact. What are the consequences of not solving the problem? Here, the manager or administrator is using some form of risk assessment or cost-benefit analysis to determine if change is necessary.

Corcoran, Grinnell, and Briggs (2001) recommend seven steps for structuring and implementing the foundations for change in social work practice: (1) setting goals, (2) setting objectives, (3) selecting interventions, (4) structuring the intervention, (5) developing a contract, (6) monitoring and evaluation, and (7) maintaining products of planned change (p. 3). Based on their analysis, a problem should not be ignored if the it interferes with the way you envisioned the implementation and conclusion of the change process. Before setting goals, Corcoran and colleagues recommend that the goals be specific and challenging, involve persons affected by goal in the planning, and that the goals you set be reasonable and capable of being reached.

Reasons for establishing goals by managers to address administrative problems are similar to reasons given by Corcoran et al. (2001) for establishing objectives for change. They include, (1) involving managers and key personnel in goal-setting, thus increasing the likelihood that each will share a mindset of similar expectations and aims, (2) setting clear goals to facilitate the selection of helpful ways and means, and (3) defining outcomes to provide a framework for tracking, monitoring, and evaluating the change strategy.

If deciding not to ignore the problem is the only option, then the motivation to address the problem is determined by deciding the degree of its priority. Corcoran et al. (2001) cite literature that identifies three criteria for establishing priorities among goals: (1) establish the relative importance of outcome to client. In the case of an organization, is this problem an issue for management? (2) Know the degree to which solving the problem will be of benefit, or if solving it further will complicate issues and produce other problems for management. (3) Know the advantages, assets, and strengths that will be realized as a result of addressing the problem.

Planning

Plan a course of action. That is, take a complex goal and identify a route for achieving it. This route should consist of a sequence of small, relatively achievable steps. Pinkston and associates highlight intervention planning and its nine associated components as a function of behavior modification. These include

(1) defining desired behaviors, (2) setting and using a schedule, (3) providing response opportunity, (4) prompting correct behavior, (5) allowing time for behavior to occur, (6) praising appropriate behavior, (7) assessing if the behavior does not occur, (8) ignoring inappropriate behavior, and (9) recording.

Defining desired behaviors includes the identification of expected performance through the use of target behaviors, actions, or processes. Administrative and line staff seeking to achieve expected or improved performance need to know what they will be able to do after the intervention has been judged to be effective.

Application

Setting and using schedules involves establishing realistic time points for engaging in the desired behavior. Identifying the expected frequency or repeated episodes of desired behaviors requires the use of a temporal sequence of events as follows:

1. *Provide response opportunity*. Opportunities to engage in the desired behaviors need to be scheduled in multiple environments. This is needed so that the frequent occurrence of desired behavior is achieved naturally across different settings.
2. *Prompts and cues for desired behavior are essential*, given the breadth and depth of staff and management responsibilities in community organizations. Program plans, service contracts, time management tools, feedback in supervision, appointment books, calendars, things-to-do lists, job descriptions, and policies and procedures are examples of permanent product cues and prompts that, when followed, provide reminders to staff and management as to what, when, why, where, and how desired behavior is expected.
3. *Application*: Apply the plan.
4. *Mastery*: Master the steps. Do the technique described in the plan well.
5. *Evaluation and adoption*: Evaluate how well you are doing. Is your mastery sufficient?
6. *Enhancement*: Enhance, with the feedback of your evaluation, your technique. Refine your approach.

Agency Case Example

The inventor and founding executive director of Agency X sought to use the science of behavior change as the foundation for providing services through a careful collaboration of families, community leaders, and professional service providers as allies aimed at achieving economic and community empowerment and functional behavior change among inner-city community residents. He wanted his staff and management trained in scientifically based interventions that will eventually result in the achievement of service effectiveness and positive behavior change. In his estimation, he wanted the direct care staff to be able to engage the community and agency service beneficiaries and other stakeholders in the life of the agency while the staff aided them in developing skill competencies to achieve self-reliance and self-sufficiency. To test many of these assumptions, the first author incorporated his training in applied behavioral analysis, task-centered practice, POP, and social administration into an incentivizing performance management practice theory model that was initially tested by the first author in child welfare and mental health and later applied agencywide.

PROBLEM IDENTIFICATION

The Child Welfare Division of Agency X, Inc., was experiencing a lack of sufficient resources and family supports for youth who did not have any other option but long-term foster care. While some thought that was a decent goal, others felt that permanent relationships were more beneficial to the overall future, development, and growth of these African American youth. The issue was one of program development opportunities. Some foster parents and youth had bonded and were ready for adoption, but the state had not advanced this opportunity to all agencies until 1986, when it contacted private agencies with a training program that the state wanted to share with private agency child welfare workers. At Agency X Inc., the idea of certain homes becoming foster parent adoption homes was timely, and the opportunity for state training on how to convert those homes came at a time when the agency was undergoing staff turnover and multiple placement blow-ups.

ASSESSMENT AND PROBLEM ANALYSIS

The upper management felt that the issue was a lack of appropriate administration and management methods used in the delivery of child welfare service systems. They based this finding on an internal and external audit that showed the clinical mismanagement of delivering child welfare programs that made it difficult to track cases with staff and personnel records. They recommended that the child welfare division be reorganized into a system that would meet licensure standards and use sound management practices.

PLANNING

In several brown bag lunch meetings, the executive operations manager met with secretaries, child welfare staff, foster parents, and community representatives to describe a course of action: a time-managed case management and staff development infrastructure with clinical and administrative supervision. The plan included training for all parties involved in the delivery and administration of services to children and families involved in child welfare services. The program administration, clinical care and consultation, staff training, supervision, and quality assurance of all the contributing parties and functions would need to meet agency-adopted permanency planning and state licensure objectives. This meant that the agency would find longer term solutions for children and families involved in child welfare programs and services. The aim of the division of child welfare would be to provide a continuum of care, including lesser and residential treatment services for youth and families involved in the child welfare system.

Staff were trained by experts from the University of Chicago School of Social Services Administration in permanency planning, behavior modification, task-centered treatment, and intensive case management methods. Additionally, the staff were taught ways to skillfully conduct risk assessment at intake, assessment, service planning, and home visiting and how to provide reinforcement and support. A clinical consultant was hired to provide staff with training on ways to assess for family functioning, the effects of role strain or issues with foster parents on child behavior management, and the influence of the foster family dynamics on foster parent and child interaction.

A permanency planning expert was hired to train foster parents, child welfare staff, youth, and administrators together on ways to promote better relationships and longer term care options for youth in substitute care. Changes in hiring policies were instituted, and a selection of staff who were recent graduates and had a field internship with youth and families were hired and deemed trainable and ready for supportive and regular supervision and agency management. Finally, policies and procedures for the delivery of all of these new methods and approaches had to be written and administratively sanctioned by the board of directors and executive director.

MASTERY

Routinization of program procedures occurred as new staff were hired and a new program structure emerged with a supervisor, staff, and training resources for staff and management. As management received consultation and training on using incentivizing staff management, organizational behavior modification procedures, and techniques for designing data based on supervisory checklists and quality control systems, staff were also receiving training. This training was specifically focused on key child welfare, behavior modification methods, case management, and task-centered strategies for making critical decisions in providing services to youth and families.

EVALUATION AND ADOPTION

This performance- and evidence-based management approach was continued for a period of 6 years and was well-documented by Briggs (1994, 1996, 2001a) and Briggs and McMillan (2012). It is presented next, in Chapter 5.

5 }

Using Performance and Evidence-Based Management to Transform Administration of Multiple Agency Layers

Community-Based Systems of Care

Community-based social service organizations are complex instruments comprised of many individuals who must work together in a coordinated and coherent fashion in order for the organization to accomplish its goals. Although there are many goals that are specific to the particular set of clients and communities being served, there is nevertheless one goal that is paramount. This aim is assisting clients to move toward greater independence and increased ability to function within their community. Is there any one overall approach that can help us meet this and other goals? We have found that the performance and evidence-based management process described by Briggs (1994, 1996, 2001), Briggs and McBeath (2009), and Briggs and McMillan (2012) has sufficient generality and applicability to be a useful framework on which we may hang other specific approaches (evidence-based practice, family and youth empowerment), practices (strengths perspective), and other organizational methods (such as task-centered practice, organizational behavior modification strategies). It represents the fifth integrative practice competency to include in your leadership and management toolkit.

The generality of this performance and evidence-based management framework allows us to examine the contingencies and evidence of performance in all areas from a single point of view. We may look at the contingencies and the performances of management, staff, family, and community. Each of these practice domains has a role to play in taking the client from a dependent, nonfunctioning state to one of independence and increased ability to function within the community (Briggs, 1996). For us, the next few pages have encapsulated the driving force behind our approach to the training and teaching of individuals in carrying out their respective roles within the overall organization. Finally, this chapter exposes students to strategies for managing multiple layers of an organization through a seven-step process. Given that this process is so important to the manner in which accountable community organizations operate, we will take a finer look at each step.

STEP 1. DEFINING THE MISSION

Arguably, the mission of any organization is its unique reason for being; therefore, a well-managed company or organization has a mission statement. This is simply a statement that describes the long-term, overall purpose of the organization. It answers the following questions:

- Who are we?
- Why are we in business?
- Where is the business going?
- What is the nature of our business?
- Who will receive our services?
- Why do we provide these services?

Having a mission statement is a sound management practice because it helps all members of the organization to understand the purpose of the agency and their part in it. Every activity of an organization should follow logically from its mission statement. If an activity does not agree with this statement, there will be confusion among the managers and employees. People will be working at cross purposes; time and money will be wasted; employees will be frustrated; and needy people will not get good service. In sum, to ensure that everyone is "singing from the same song-book," the mission statement needs to be communicated throughout the organization and understood by each of its members. For instance, the mission of Agency X is to enhance economic development, political empowerment, and, ultimately, community development by assisting less advantaged individuals become more capable and self-reliant through the use of scientifically based intervention methods along with solid management practices. By drafting this mission, the organization provides clear expectations that guide the organization's members to align policies and practice that best reflect the core principles of the organization.

STEP 2. DEFINING THE STRUCTURE

The structure of an organization is the form it takes in order to meet its mission. The framework of an agency or institution refers to the way the work is divided into departments or divisions; it also refers to the reporting relationships of all the managers, employees, and volunteers needed to get the job done. There are as many ways to organize as there are businesses and social service agencies. Each structure is unique to the work that must be done. However, in every single case, the organizational structure must be in total agreement with its mission. Otherwise, it will be difficult for managers and employees to work at peak efficiency. In other words, when people don't understand the ultimate goal or how they relate to it, they may unknowingly duplicate the work of another area or overlook an important task that they should be doing.

The form of an organization is usually expressed in terms of a representational chart. This is a visual depiction of the organization, using boxes to illustrate the various positions. The head of the organization is at the top. The boxes immediately below this are the positions that report to that person, and so on with each successive level. Furthermore, each of them represents a position different from all others in the organization, with a specific set of goals and responsibilities that relate directly back to the overall mission.

In terms of the social service administration and management process, the step of Defining the Structure involves answering three questions:

- How should the organization be set up to meet the mission?
- What is the organization model?
- What is the operating structure?

STEP 3. EXPECTED PERFORMANCE

This next step in the Transforming Administration and Management process has to do primarily with setting objectives for the actual work that needs to be done during the coming period. Objectives are another name for goals, which are the desired results we want to achieve. Similar to the organizational structure, these goals should relate directly back to the mission of the agency. Also, they should be observable, specific, measurable, and achievable, and they should cover a certain period of time and be developed jointly between employees and manager, written down, and reviewed frequently. A good set of objectives tells you where you want to be, what you want to accomplish, what to aim for, and how long it should take. When a set of goals is agreed upon between a supervisor and subordinate, this is what is known as "expected performance."

Every person in an organization from the chief executive downward should have a set of goals for expected performance. The aims should be stated in such a way that they lend themselves to being measured, so that it is clear when they have been accomplished. Then it's time for setting new objectives. In fact, you will know when you have succeeded at Agency X when you find it's time to set new and more challenging objectives.

In the Social Service Administration and Management process, the Expected Performance step involves answering the questions:

- What are the specific objectives?
- What is the criteria for achievement?

STEP 4. BEHAVIOR STRATEGIES

Very simply, objectives tell us where we are going, and behavior strategies tell us how to get there. They are the actions and plans that delineate how objectives will be met. After you have a set of objectives and understand the performance that is expected, it's time to get to work to achieve those goals. To do so, you will need behavior strategies. There are many behavior strategies that can be used effectively to get work done. Two important ones that you will be using as an Agency X line employee are called *continuity of care* and *time management*.

Continuity of Care

This behavior strategy is used in case coordination to ensure that clients receive a continuous stream of good service throughout their relationship with Agency X. Continuity of care begins with the proper intake of new clients, assessment of their individual needs, placement with those who can provide them service, setting of specific client objectives, service delivery, evaluation, and adjustment of the care provided. The continuity of care behavior strategy facilitates the client's movement through the Agency X system. The *case coordinator*, acting on the client's behalf, is responsible for seeing that the client receives proper care at each step in the process.

Time Management

This behavior strategy is the key to accountability. Time management is how Agency X keeps track of the many activities and services provided to clients. Each line employee of Agency X has a time management plan (TMP). This plan is used in conjunction with the supervisory conference form to determine the most effective utilization of time for completing assigned tasks, duties, and responsibilities. The actual dates for completion on the TMP are determined by specific program requirements on a daily, weekly, or monthly basis.

STEP 5. REINFORCING EVENT

We all like to know how we are doing at work. We want to know the extent of our progress and how we can improve upon our job performance. That's the idea behind the Reinforcing Event step of the Transforming Administration and Management process.

Reinforcing events are actions taken to inform participants of their progress toward the mission. Some people call it performance feedback. At Agency X, we use the term "reinforcing event" because it is a chance to reinforce and congratulate the individual for progress made toward achieving goals. A reinforcing event is scheduled on a regular basis to review the activities and results that have taken place to date. The amount and nature of input given to the participant depends on the particular needs of the individual. Since no two cases are alike, it follows that no two reinforcing events are alike.

In general, however, a reinforcing event says to the participant "You're doing a great job. Keep up the good work!" It is also an opportunity to give additional direction to the individual for improving the rate of progress on a particular case. Such guidance is meant to be a positive reinforcement and is generally considered welcome input by people who have been through the process.

Finally, a reinforcing event is an opportunity for the participant to ask questions, discuss problems, and even to air complaints. Specifically, it is a forum for open communications. Many concerns can easily be cleared up at this time so that progress toward goals can get back on track. A reinforcing event is a positive and worthwhile experience that will make your job at Agency X far more satisfying.

STEP 6. OUTCOMES

Outcomes are the moment of truth in social service administration and management. This step is an evaluative one. The intervention and activities, which have been provided to clients, must now be evaluated. Success is a relative term in casework. Whether or not a participant has been successful depends on the specific objectives that were agreed upon earlier in the process.

You will recall that during the third step, "Expected Performance," we identified objectives for performance. At that time, we also determined the criteria for achievement, or what had to be done in order to meet the objectives. We agreed that the objectives had to be observable, specific, measurable, and achievable. Now is the time when a well-defined set of objectives and good performance pays off.

To carry out this step, it is necessary to go back and look at all the preceding steps to see how close we have come in the Transforming Administration and Management process. It involves answering the questions:

- What was the mission? Was it appropriate and clearly understood?
- What was the organizational structure? Was this the most effective way to organize for getting the work done?
- What were the specific goals? How were they observed? How were they measured? Were they achievable? How well did we achieve them?
- Which behavior strategies were used? How well were they applied? How well did they work?
- Was a reinforcing event scheduled? Was the project off track in any way? Did we get it back on track?
- How close have we come to achieving our mission?

STEP 7. ENHANCEMENT AND DEVELOPMENT

This is the final step in the Social Service Administration and Management process. We have come this far in the process, and we may even have achieved our mission.

But this is not the time to stop. It is the time to ensure that all the good work that has gone on before is continued and enhanced.

The world never stops changing. Given that change is a constant in our lives and those of our clients, we must always be alert to the ways in which this affects the positive outcomes that have already been achieved.

The Enhancement and Development step gives us the opportunity to further evaluate and refine the services given to clients in line with their changing needs. At this stage, we need to ask:

- Is it time to set new objectives?
- Is there a better way to organize to get the job done?
- Are the criteria by which we measure success still appropriate?
- Should reinforcement be increased or decreased?

It may be that no action needs to be taken if all is going well. The point is, we must always watch out for the changing situations that could prevent us from meeting our objectives and achieving the overall mission of Agency X.

The Enhancement and Development step of social service administration and management is essentially a quality assurance function. To aid in this effort, a special quality assurance monthly reporting form was created. It provides an easy to follow and consistent format for program managers and division directors to document information on the volume and quality of services rendered in their areas.

All in all, we believe that solving the problems of community-based social service organizations must be directed toward the needs of their clients if they are to survive. These clients are consumers of the organization's product. What is that product? It is a better functioning, more independent individual within the framework of a supportive community. If we cannot deliver that product in an efficient manner, we will not survive as an organization. More positively, if we can show our funding agencies, communities, and clients that we can deliver, perhaps this will yield continued support.

Viewed from an external perspective, the organization's efforts are directed toward consumers—those who are your clients. Policies are implemented by management through the activities of staff. Family and communities participate and, in fact, create the kind of environment in which your consumer-client perceives the actions of your organization (Briggs, 2001a).

As a result, you need support from all levels of your organization if it is to succeed. In order for you to obtain support, families and community must understand your agency's goals and methods. As manager, you will need to recruit from within and outside the organization to aid in this endeavor. You must answer the question, "How do we coordinate different individuals and their activities in order to achieve overall goals?" This is done by applying those seven steps described earlier. Within profit-making business enterprises, this approach is well accepted as a means by which to achieve an increased bottom line. All mechanisms of leadership, behavior modification, and motivation are used to achieve excellence, minimize costs, and maximize profits. Why not use similar techniques, grounded in relevant evidenced-based theories of human behavior, in order to have people help people?

Positivists organizational theorist believe that successful delivery organizational theorists is that successful delivery of human services in community social service organizations will require a stronger database and a more scientific approach to development, implementation, and evaluation of social service products (Netting & O'Connor, 2003).

Experienced inner-city community social service organizations have as their strongest position their presence and understanding of the communities they serve. Therefore, because methods have often not been developed for serving their particular clients, a community-based, client-driven, self-evaluating technology for enhancing performance by all parties involved is appropriate.

Managing social service agencies within this context requires considering the use of implementation frameworks that unify the work of the staff and the management in nonprofit community organizations. The dearth of such an important organizing framework creates factions of small interest groups focusing on process objectives, such as enhancing the number of clients in a particular program or service, rather than concentrating on both the "nuts and bolts" of establishing a quality program and desirable client outcomes. Considering that staff, management, and client-consumers make up the major internal players of an organization, it would be good for management to implement agency practices that define the expectations and environmental supports for positive behavior change at each level of the infrastructure.

A basic flaw in social work education occurs when you provide direct practice students with a fund of knowledge about client self-determination, but with little or no direction on how to integrate direct practice technology favoring clients in agency practice, given the political realities of bureaucracies. Further, there is very little direction given to management students about ways to incorporate the tasks and responsibilities of direct practice staff seeking to enhance client outcomes into agency operating policies and procedures. Since each practitioner, in both direct care and management, operates within his or her own domain of influence with minimal integration of approaches, the fusion of methods at both levels is often left to serendipity. The failure to unify direct practice and management efforts in agency operations is a problem stemming from an unclear purpose, inadequate structural support, process dilemmas, and the uncertain knowledge about ways to measure and use social service data.

Ambiguous mission statements will not allow the practitioner to skillfully modify and track his or her respective tasks and activities against the organization's primary purpose. Mission statements that are clearly defined include (a) measurable outcomes and (b) clearly defined strategies for achieving defined goals. The agency's mission serves as the primary function, and its infrastructure is the structural form by which it pursues aims.

Inadequate structural support hinders the ability of direct care and management personnel to deliver social services in an organized manner. Clearly, to achieve an organizational infrastructure that is compatible with the mission is important.

Too often, social service agencies define the infrastructure to meet the needs of constituents other than the client-consumer. They use a top-down approach to management, only to find that this approach will do very little to promote innovation in favor of the client (Resnick, 1978). A client-defined approach to managing social services begins with a mission statement that reflects the agency's objectives and thus is followed by a chain of command that facilitates exchanges of ideas and input from all levels of the infrastructure. Typically in organizations, the exchange of ideas and input for agency change comes from the top down. The result of this kind of hierarchical thinking minimizes the chances for client self-determination if the client is not allowed to contribute through participation in policy development and service delivery. This then hinders how these clients are empowered to influence the actual care received from the agency service delivery sector and to provide input on how the organization formulates its policies. In most organizations, there is a board of directors and an executive director; the sharing and use of client input in policy formulation and decision-making is a practice requiring administrative sanctions. Without this support, it will be difficult to facilitate the transmission of ideas and input to and from the lower ranks of the organization. Using a participatory management approach allows you to expose staff to critical thinking and repeated uses of data as a basis for decision-making regarding which steps to take and which actions to avoid.

Process dilemmas occur when the behavioral expectations are not clearly specified and sanctioned through internal policies and procedures. Policies and procedures are an example of environmental cues that define desirable performance. Time management, supervision, and staff training are three behavioral strategies that address the confusion that accompanies process dilemmas.

Time management methods can be useful under many circumstances. These methods have been used successfully to complete treatment plans (Maher, 1985). Also, they are useful to staff responsible for multiple tasks and functions. By using time management, each responsibility can be redefined into smaller tasks that are easy to manage and complete. Furthermore, time management allows you to track behaviors in five primary areas: (1) what you intend to do, (2) what you expect to accomplish, (3) what you actually did, (4) how you rate task completion, and (5) what are the next steps that need to be done.

Time management is effective in organizations that value the importance of planning and evaluating tasks as well as in organizations that encourage the use of data in decision-making. It is not so useful in organizations that do not hold staff accountable for their performance, use of time, planning, or monitoring client reactions to service delivery.

To ensure that staff perform their assigned duties, supervision is a promising organizational behavior management method that has been shown to increase staff performance. As an antecedent of staff and management behaviors, effective supervision provides support, technical assistance, and feedback. By supporting decisions and actions taken by staff, management is providing clear and desirable consequences for job performance. On the other hand, by providing corrective feedback and support around difficult tasks and job activities, management is creating a safe and nurturing environment in which staff can ask questions and learn better ways to perform job responsibilities without reprisals. Ineffective supervision occurs when personnel are not accustomed to supervisory contingencies and when they do not have supportive supervisory relationships with management. This usually occurs when personnel fail to develop an accountable relationship with management and use supervision time to discuss issues other than those directly related to the client and the organization.

Staff training enhances client outcomes and staff performance variables when management is included to a degree, allowing the transfer of the emerging skill to the work place. Staff performance is improved when training is sanctioned by administration and when there are cues that facilitate the transfer of learning from the training situation directly to work with client-consumers. The probability of effective transfer of learning occurs when it is programmed from the training session to the practice situation. Transfer of learning is enhanced for and accomplished by personnel when it is administratively sanctioned and competent training resources are arranged.

Sometimes staff training is not needed. It may be provided as a respite or morale builder when all that is necessary is routine, systematic performance feedback (positive or corrective) and other related administrative supports and sanctions for desirable performance (Mager & Pipe, 1970).

Case Illustration

An organization located on Chicago's Westside, is an Afrocentric community social service organization that served as one of the early testing grounds for the methods described in this book. Its early founder helped to blaze a trail for the use of data gathering methods and theories to be applied in the social delivery strategies aimed at helping individuals, families, groups, and communities be self-sustaining. From its humble beginnings, the organization sought to be a comprehensive social service delivery system. The organizations' central focus involves preparing people to problem-solve their barriers and challenges to life and to become self-sufficient by overcoming their problems and constraints to optimal functioning.

The organization has met much success in its efforts in habilitating persons with developmentally disabilities. Through effective community residential programs, the organization has been able to assist people to adjust and learn community survival skills (Briggs, 1996). These new skills have enabled the organization to link with natural families and caring communities to help persons with disabilities move to lesser restrictive and cost-saving care settings. Since 1978, the organization has developed a series of sound programs and services.

The organization has enjoyed a solid growth record during its twenty-five-year history. One main reason why it has enhanced its operations is because of its use of a behaviorally based management system developed in-house by Briggs and associates (Briggs, 1994, 1996, 2001). This system includes a seven-step process that is a formal system for designing, implementing, managing, and evaluating the delivery of vital social services. The process is organized into seven interrelated steps. Each of the steps centers around the implementation of methods and procedures that have been field tested (Briggs, 1994, 1996). The methodology includes a package of scientifically based intervention strategies for addressing the behaviors of clients, staff, and managers as they pursue behavioral process and outcome indicators. Nothing in any of the steps is left to chance: every planned activity or action is repeatedly monitored. The seven-step process is based in theory. The theoretical assumptions that support the process are simple, sound, and transferable. They are (1) operant theory, (2) social learning theory, and (3) organizational behavior modification theory. Each is based on the science of behavior, as defined by B. F. Skinner. The theory is capable of transfer to real-world application and has been applied at Habilitative Systems, Inc. to more than fifty programs and services. In this organization, process and outcome behaviors are defined along a continuum that ends, ultimately, with self-sufficiency as the chief behavioral indicator.

The unifying threads that weave the organization into a tight and soundly managed entity are focused on quality control. Through continuous case management and case coordination, both the client and systems providing services to them are scrutinized and evaluated routinely. To ensure client voice, engagement and satisfaction we use the client as a reference point because we feel that quality has no meaning unless it is defined by the client-consumer. The seven-step process relies on the needs and expectations of the client-consumer and staff. Since both groups are involved from the beginning, there is a sense of ownership and personal integrity about the product being sought: that is, a better functioning person, family, and or community. Also, this ownership is accompanied by the motivation to succeed that is respected and sanctioned by management. In this context, customer input and quality control is defined throughout each step of the process.

We realize that any system that relies on groups of people to carry out its stated objectives is at risk of getting off course from its original plan. To address this reality, checks and balances are built into the seven-step process as a means to solve problems and other issues before they escalate or compound into serious dilemmas.

The mission of the agency has evolved over its rich, almost forty-year history, from one of general welfare, "To help all people who lived in the community," to one that is clearly achievable and measurable, "To help people become more self-reliant and self-sufficient." The theories driving the mission include the early founder's philosophy on the interconnection and synergy that flows through individuals, families, small groups, and communities that are interwoven and bound together until, like a phoenix, they can rise from the ashes, thus freeing the human spirit toward self-sustainment and continued development. The early founder and others to follow, such as Briggs and Pinkston and associates, used evidenced-based theories to teach families, staff, client consumers, managers, and boards of directors.

The organization's mission is supported by an infrastructure that promotes quality control, continuity of care, culture-specific policy focus, and system of care delivery systems that assist youth and adults with HIV, persons with developmental disabilities, the homeless, the economically indigent who need assistance with paying bills, and the elderly who need housing and regular assistance with their activities of daily living and social companionship. The board of directors set policy and get their membership from the local community, philanthropy, civil and municipal authorities, business, industry, and the family members of persons using agency services. Executive management staff are responsible for general day-to-day responsibilities such as quality control and assurance, operating offices, fiscal management, management information systems, community relations, and resource development. Each of the four major service systems of care are managed by care directors. The structure supplies sufficient support staff to assist the systems of care in providing accountable services.

The expected performance of every person involved in an agency that uses evidence-based management is defined through job descriptions, program plans, and policy statements which clearly set boundaries. They use data sources daily in their decision-making, which allows them to advertise their achievements in annual reports as evidence-based outcomes and through accrediting standards such as the Commission on Accreditation of Rehabilitation Facilities (CARF) and Council on Accreditation (COA) national regulatory bodies.

The organization continues to have a relationship with the academy and uses staff training, supervision, and quality assurance in its daily operations as standard interventions. These particular interventions grew out of research regarding the design and development of inner-city organizations serving persons with disabilities by Briggs (1994, 1996, 2001).

The organizations' administration and management staff follow strict rules governing collection of evidence in their daily routines. It uses checklist and measurable progress reports as a basis to make decisions that affect policy development and service delivery. Finally, what gets evaluated and monitored gets done, even if they have to scrap one unworkable idea to test out a more critically thought out approach.

Overall, the organization provides services to African Americans and continues to employ the best practices of leadership, behavior modification, and motivation in the management of staff activities focused through systems of care aimed at the self-sufficiency of people with disabilities.

6}

Infusing Culture into Integrative Practice in and for Larger Systems

Harold E. Briggs, Joy A. DeGruy, and Risa Kiam

As stated earlier, community organizations deal with a wide variety of service beneficiaries, ranging from the physically disabled to the developmentally disabled. All age ranges are possible. Each situation may require one or a combination of case management, coordination, training, education, and employment assistance methods. Considering such a broad landscape of clientele, what context can we adopt that is responsive to culturally diverse players? This chapter covers the sixth integrative practice competency of infusing culture into your role as an agency leader or a program manager. As agency leaders and managers of programs and community service systems, you are tasked with the responsibility of coordinating the delivery of needed services, measuring the effectiveness of such delivery, and providing feedback to the individuals engaged in such services (including staff, families, clients, and communities). Leaders and managers also need to measure the effectiveness of the agency or program implementation and provide feedback to the individuals engaged in care to help them improve their own approach, efficiency, and overall job performance function.

According to Briggs (2001), involving nontraditional players such as family members and staff in critical thinking, decision-making, planning, and quality assurance activities presents interesting challenges to the administrative practitioner or student of organizational management. These essential functions are traditionally reserved for degreed professionals with middle or senior management responsibilities. To address these challenges, administrative practitioners require a comprehensive, flexible, seamless management practice methodology. This model needs to be based in relevant theories, compatible intervention methods, and evaluation procedures that allow for a responsive organizational culture. The tools need to be consistent with or incorporate the relevant aspects of a culture of learning, skepticism, and the principles of empowerment; they need to use a strengths perspective and be culturally competent, family-centered, and evidence-based social work practice. Using key relationships to promote the objectives of family-centered, culturally responsive accountable agencies, administrative personnel need to understand the particular nature of each of these organizational objectives in order to establish standards and best practices designed to enhance staff competence and the capacities relative to achieving those specific agency objectives.

Family-centered organizations are those agencies defined and governed by family members that may also perform the functions of support, advocacy, and service delivery. In some cases, a family-centered organization may include external professional staff, however, the board of directors is always comprised of 51% family members. On occasion, it is possible for a professionally administered social service agency to be family-centered. In this instance, as long as the mission of the organization is family-centered and the board is family-controlled, with family members involved in key functions, it is allowable for professionals to administer family-centered agencies (as in the case of Briggs 1994, 1996a, 2001a).

Organizations that are culturally responsive focus on the strengths of vulnerable segments of society by promoting the participation of members in key areas, especially those areas that promote the achievement of equal opportunities and a more level playing field (Briggs, 1996b). Accountable organizations are those that utilize standards of best practices in management theory and technology in order to facilitate the achievement of the above-mentioned agency objectives. These organizations, which are culturally responsive and family-centered, include roles and functions of management based on a relational model that provides teaching, supervision, and mentorship. Briggs and Pinkston collaborated in providing agency consultation related to implementing scientifically based intervention methods in several programs in an African American managed community organization in the Midwest. Briggs and Pinkston worked with the agency's executive director, managers, staff, board members, family members, clients, and consumers for a period of seven years in a culturally responsive context in order to implement the evidence-based and relational model that empowered and enabled the agency, staff, and community to achieve their mutually agreed upon objectives. In earlier publications (Briggs, 1996a), the scientific processes and outcomes were highlighted. Although the sustained relationships between the organizational layers and the specific roles and functions used to alter management's role and establish organizational buy-in were only briefly described, this subject is illustrated in table form by Briggs (2001a).

Accountable organizations have multiple and intersecting levels of accountability at all levels of infrastructure related to staff members, client systems, funders, and community representatives. All of these organizational components are accountable to each other. Satisfying these multiple agendas requires practitioners to understand key factors regarding needs, values, and customs based in philosophical perspectives on basic human needs in general and on culture specifically.

The interested administration or management practitioner needs to understand Maslow's hierarchy of needs (1970) and how it relates to the development and maintenance of a culturally responsive, accountable organization. Maslow suggests that practitioners initiating a helping relationship with clients must ascertain whether these individuals have the basic necessities, such as food, clothing, and shelter. People must have these primary needs met before other needs can be considered. Assisting clients in obtaining these necessities aids in establishing a working rapport of mutual trust and respect. A helping relationship that emphasizes mutual trust and respect establishes a safe physical and psychological environment where there is an appreciation for the cultural context of peoples' lives. The practitioner also works within these parameters to strengthen clients' problem-solving abilities and opportunities. Being responsive to the client's culture and background enhances their feelings of belonging and acceptance. Importantly, it allows them to invest in satisfying, productive relationships, which results in increased self-esteem and feelings of competence that could lead to further self-actualization for the individual in their family, community, and overall social structure.

With the application of Maslow's concepts to organizations attempting to implement a relational model and structure, we need to begin at the micro level where *individual staff* is committed to the agency vision, mission, and client service in a mutually respectful and safe environment that supports staff development. *Individual clients (family members)* strive to meet their basic and social structural needs and feel safe enough to utilize agency services to grow, change, and develop a sense of belonging and esteem. *Individual volunteers* develop a sense of belonging to a community and work to support the agency's vision, mission, and client services in order to improve the social structural life of their community and their own lives in that community. At the mezzo level in the organization, *families/consumers* collaborate with staff and engage in developing relevant client-centered programs and services (social structural and interpersonal) that benefit them and the community. Consumer groups invest in the success of the agency and its programs, which enhances everyone's esteem. At the macro level of the organization, the *agency* becomes an organic part of the community that serves by respecting consumers and inviting them to be active participants in their own healing and empowerment. Culturally responsive, accountable organizations will be respectful of participants and consumers. The characteristics of their responsiveness will automatically include the preceding components and/or the opportunities to develop various levels of actualization.

In family-centered, culturally responsive organizations, the opportunities for meeting these relationship-based needs are incorporated into various functions that managers and administrators perform. These roles, which will be explained shortly, are based in an axiological perspective developed by Nichols and later taught to DeGruy-Leary (1998), whose relationship management practice model will be presented later in this chapter.

Sociocultural Theoretical Perspective: Nichols's Model

Dr. Edwin J. Nichols (1976) created a model that emphasizes and explores four philosophical aspects of cultural difference that drive the way individuals in a culture interact with the world: axiology, epistemology, logic, and process. The differences related to these aspects are so fundamental that they lie below our everyday awareness, and the assumptions that they generate are almost never questioned. Of the four aspects that Nichols presents, axiology is the most pertinent for this discussion. *Axiology* is the study of the nature and criteria of values (i.e., what value a culture holds in highest regard).

Nichols's axiological construct identifies and elaborates on the concepts and themes that relate to values within specific cultural groups. The axiology of a people is largely determined by their survival adaptations over time. These adaptations generate the primary value systems of the particular cultural group and become the template upon which future generations derive their understanding of how to meet their needs. Nichols asserts that once the primary "values" have been established, they endure throughout millennia. Nichols identifies four major axiological constructs:

> *Member-Object*: Characterizes the European axiology in which the highest value lies in the object or the acquisition of the object.
> *Member-Member*: Characterizes the African, Arab, and Latino axiologies where the highest value lies in the relationship between people.
> *Member-Group*: Characterizes the Asian axiology where the highest value lies in the cohesiveness of the group.
> *Member-Great Spirit*: Characterizes the Native American axiology in which the highest value lies in one's relationship with the Great Spirit. (p. 1)

For practitioners working with African Americans, knowledge of the African axiology is helpful according to Nichols: the primary value system that dominated the African continent was member-member. This axiology places the highest value on the "relationship" between individuals; the relationship is the most important factor in regulating the majority of human activities within the culture. Still, it suggests that the survival of the group is primarily dependent upon the integrity of relationships among the members of that group.

The implication of the African axiology is that a fundamental level of "respect" exists among members. This respect becomes the linchpin for the sustained health and survival of the group. Given this view of the world, each individual is viewed as an integral part of the whole rather than as replaceable units. Therefore, we should treat each individual as crucial because altering the individual consequently alters the whole. Due to this perception, each person, in and of him- or herself, is seen as a cherished and vital entity, which is the foundation of the member-member axiology construct.

When these beliefs are programmed into the roles of the administrator or manager of an organization, they make it clear that we must respect one another, view each person as an important integral part of the whole, and understand that when the individual changes, it impacts their family at work and at home as well as their community. This managerial concept will provide a supportive, culturally responsive environment that reinforces peoples' innate strengths and motivates them to move toward self-actualization in all their family, work, and community relationships.

Culturally responsive, family-centered, accountable organizations are institutions that are community organizations. Unlike professionally trained providers of social services in community-based settings or clusters of professionally led organizations, a community organization is one that is defined by and governed by the residents, family members, and invited civic and philanthropic-minded board members. These organizations need to utilize appropriate technology in maintaining their accountability and credibility because this will contribute to the organizations' ability to successfully achieve their community sanctioned objectives. Such institutions use technology that promotes social justice, fights against oppression, addresses the unique concerns of vulnerable segments of the community, and allows for the inclusion of everyone in the decision-making process and power base of the organization.

DeGruy-Leary (1998) recommends a technology that at least bases the inputs by staff and management on cultural values and customs of inclusion, partnership, collaboration, and goal attainment. Briggs recommends a compatible technology that is derived from scientifically based intervention and sound management approaches. Though not reported, the consultation and supervision process reported in Table 6.1 (published in Briggs & Corcoran, 2001, p. 376) and used in the intervention is compatible with the relationship-based roles and methods described by DeGruy-Leary, 1998. In this chapter, both methods are combined to forge a technology that is a strengths-based empowerment approach that can be applied to all systems: micro, mezzo, and macro.

Micro, Mezzo, Macro Systems

MICRO

At this level, the administration practitioner is interested in using strategies that will allow them to reinforce the values and ethics of maintenance, restoration, or change of some staff behavior to promote the client- or family-centered aims of the organization. The administrator will need to do this by developing a productive working relationship with staff because they are liaisons between the agency's goals and the client's organizational experiences. The staff's buy-in and optimal participation in agency matters will depend on how their investment is shaped and motivated. They will need to learn the theories of human behavior that explain why their participation matters in helping others learn ways to help themselves. These theories of the interdependence between the human condition, communities, and society, when reflected in the agency's policies and procedures, communicate to staff the values and

TABLE 6.1 } Intervention design and development plan

	Information analysis	Program development	Staff development	Organizational development	Personal support
Staff	Staff perceptions Resource needs Supervisory support Case-management issues **Skill-training needs**	Social leisure activity program Assessment tools Tracking tasks Clinical consultation Case collaboration **Family participant and service delivery**	Case management **Record keeping Community** linkages **Implementation** tasks **Brief treatment methods**	Policies and procedures Methods to evaluate Focus on strengths and outcomes **Administrative support**	Advocate Advisor Feedback **On-the-job training**
Group home residents and families	Behavior management issues Activity planning **Positive and corrective feedback**	Weekly meetings between residents and staff Administrative support Training Quarterly treatment **stuffings**	Behavioral management Parent-training methods Collaboration with biological family and staff	Administrative support with case coordination unit Staff support Meeting with management **Joint activity between staff, residents, faculty, and management**	Advocate Training consultant
Upper and executive management	Staff performance indicators (or lack of) Negative licensure evaluations Environmental contingencies	Annual training program Additional training supports Performance evaluations Administrative participation Recognition **Organizational support**	Professional development Supervision Planning, evaluation **Quality assurance**	Staff support Management consultation	Confidant Advisor Volunteer Trainee Feedback Advocate
Board of directors	Feedback Recommendations Supports	Review of progress at **annual board, staff, and management retreats**	Participation in training with staff and management at annual retreats	Advisors **Consultants**	Advocate

Source: Briggs (1996b).

aims of self-sufficiency, self-sustaining families, and vital and wealth-generating communities. These values cannot be achieved without their finding responsive strategies for helping client systems achieve their self-determination.

To that end, staff are motivated by management to buy in to the agency's vision, mission, and client service in a mutually respectful and safe environment. Taught through supervision and staff development, helpful strategies for motivating individual clients (family members) strive to meet their basic needs and allow them to feel safe enough to utilize agency services to grow, change, and develop a sense of belonging and esteem. Individual volunteers develop a sense of belonging to a community and work to support the agency's vision, mission, and client services in order to improve the life of their community and their own lives in that community. Staff are taught methods and expected to use them to critically think through the use of theory to formulate the understanding of problems and goals. They are then taught data collection, data-based decision-making, and evaluation procedures for routinely tracking and monitoring their performances and client reactions to services delivered. In addition, these staff are provided opportunities for respite, training, and participation with agency leadership at retreats so that they can be part of planning, evaluating, and establishing the solutions used both agency- and program-wide.

The staff who work for these particular organizations are taught to understand the lack and scarcity of needed resources and to learn and apply principles of ordinary household budgeting skills to help clients stay within the bounds of fiscal realities. To help bring in additional resources, the staff work closely with the agency resource development/fundraising department to help shore up shrinking in-kind donations as well as provide contacts and leads regarding prospective donors. Staff are educated about the legislative and political processes, and they learn what politicians are supporting and what legislation is being drafted that might impact their community as well as the agency's achievement of its goals and objectives. Political education is most effective when it is facilitated by acknowledged community leaders, partners, and organizers who are all invested in the organizations' and communities' shared aims.

MEZZO

Families/consumers collaborate with staff and engage in developing relevant client-centered programs and services that benefit them and the community. Consumer groups invest in the success of the agency and its programs, which enhances everyone's esteem. Families are invited early on to share their perceptions, assumptions, and goals for relatives in care. They are encouraged to participate in agency and program training and in social and leisure activities dedicated to promoting their linkage to the broader community as well as providing them additional supports and resources. Through agency-wide meetings or specific training sessions, the agency's values and ethics are discussed in relation to how agency objectives are based in a culturally responsive context that emphasizes innate client strengths and empowers clients to develop the capacity for self-sufficiency in meeting their basic needs and moving toward greater self-actualization. Families are invited to participate as allies in the development of planned interventions with clients and staff. Their involvement provides other contacts, settings, and environments to use the new skills they acquire through agency services. The staff has the opportunity to observe the dynamics of and interactions between family and clients. Conversely, the families get an opportunity to witness interaction between staff and their relatives as client-consumers of agency services. Family members participate in program planning meetings when new services are being planned or existing services are reviewed for modification or enhancements. Families also participate in quality assurance committees for agency programs. In this capacity, they provide an opportunity for consumer-oriented scrutiny of program progress, client responses to services and resources used and needed, methods of services, and staff approaches to service delivery. The suggestions that family members make provide a realistic and rich data source that comes from their own experiences as family members and recipients of services. This information provides valuable assistance to agencies interested in providing relevant and effective services to their client systems.

MACRO

The agency becomes an organic part of the community and serves by respecting consumers and inviting them to be active participants in their own healing and empowerment. This value of community, family, and individual interdependence is reflected in the agency's mission, vision, and code of ethics. Through its bylaws, policies and procedures, and articles of incorporation, the agency spells out its perspectives, very much like an architectural rendering or blueprint. This blueprint provides a construction of environmental realities that impact the agency's ability to provide programs and services.

The agency administrator utilizes critical thinking strategies and provides vision and a sense of mission in leading and guiding staff, family members, and volunteers of the agency in their efforts to implement and achieve agency objectives. Administrators may use a combination of participatory management or team management strategies to secure staff investment and create the environment for family members and volunteers to participate in as equal players in program planning, program implementation, quality assurance, and evaluation activities. The administrator helps staff and others to understand that their performance is interconnected to others; they also encourage staff to examine their own particular actions in accordance with their overall objectives (content), methodology (structure), outcome (sustainable relational process), and results of the outcome (what permanent product, competencies, or capacities were established).

Administrators of these particular organizations rely on program management strategies and methods that are responsive to staff and client-consumer values based in sound, logical, and previously tested experiences with supporting evidence that demonstrates their effectiveness. They supervise staff routinely to reinforce and facilitate staff performance based in the ethics and theory that are logically connected to the agency interventions used.

Culturally responsive, family-driven, accountable organizations are respectful of all agency participants, including management, staff, family, and consumers. The characteristics of their responsiveness are automatically included in the roles of management (mentor, regulator, and guardian), which incorporates opportunities for staff to develop various levels of actualization (DeGruy-Leary, 1998).

Roles and Functions of Culturally Responsive Management

THE MENTOR ROLE

The primary responsibilities of empowered individuals as administrators or managers acting in this role include a focus on providing *encouragement, support,* and *advice* to staff. With respect to inspiration to achieve, the mentor is responsible for providing staff with incentives, motivation, reassurance, and stimuli based on an understanding of the individual and the axiological/epistemological perspective.

The mentor is always thinking about issues of self-awareness and tries to help others develop their own style, effective work habits, and performance achievements. The mentor serves as model and, through their own behaviors and attitudes, demonstrates to their employees standards of practice and performance expectations. These techniques are used to engender confidence building and encouragement, instilling hope and self-reliance using the individual's axiological reference.

According to Goleman (1998), self-awareness is one of the five components of emotional intelligence, which he and other researchers calculated to be the most important significant variable—twice as important as technical skills and IQ in demonstrating outstanding performance and leadership. In addition to self-awareness, Goleman states that there are four other essential components to emotional intelligence. *Self-regulation* involves integrity, openness to change, and the ability to think before acting and the ability to control impulses. *Motivation* includes an unswerving commitment to work for reasons that go beyond money or status, optimism, energy, and organizational commitment. *Empathy* is important in understanding people's emotional responses and developing compassionate relationships with others, which can be demonstrated through cross-cultural sensitivity. *Social skill* allows mentors to build relationships, partnerships, and networks that enhance the mentor's effectiveness in leading people to make changes in themselves, their families, organizations, and communities. In summary, Goleman's research indicates that mentors with high emotional intelligence will inspire self-confidence in their employees and empower their employees to believe in their own abilities, strengths, and capacity to achieve the agency's mission to serve its constituency with integrity and commitment.

Reinforcing Goleman's concepts about organizational leadership, the effective mentor/administrator can facilitate enhanced staff performance and can assist his or her staff in focusing on their career paths through guidance, goal-setting, and career decision-making. The mentor can further support employees through specialized training to promote self-confidence and greater understanding of personal skills. The mentor teaches the employee how to develop the emotional intelligence needed to improve opportunities for networking within the department, organization, or community as well as how to utilize their relational skills appropriately in order to work effectively with a variety of client systems and key knowledge sources.

With respect to helping the employee process difficult or corrective feedback, the mentor is responsible for sharing positive and negative critique that is specific to observable behavior and not influenced by bias or stereotype. If some of the performance difficulties lie in building relationships, the mentor can utilize Goleman's concepts about emotional intelligence to assist the employee in developing more effective interpersonal relationships with co-workers, including effective team participation, team building, individual learning styles, and improved performance. Another key area in which the mentor helps is by modeling cultural competence and responsiveness. They demonstrate to the employee various ways of understanding the thought processes and potential contributions of people from other ethnic cultures in order to gain a better understanding of interactional relationship dynamics and facilitate the development of more effective strategies for the team, department, or organization.

THE REGULATOR ROLE

The primary responsibilities of empowered individuals as administrators or managers functioning in the regulator role include providing information to the employee about the essential attributes of success in the organization and information about required job skills and expected behaviors. With respect to promoting staff performance and overall achievement, a regulator is responsible for communicating helpful tips for using policies, best practices, and procedures. In this context, the manager is opening the door to the "club," providing both the written and unwritten rules of expected performance. Also, the regulator uses an entrepreneurial approach to encourage the employee to invest in the organization and demonstrate his or her abilities. The regulator explains that there are equitable opportunities in the organization for staff to acquire helpful information about appropriate grooming and communication skills to enhance their chances for advancement and compensation. The regulator also explains that their performances are mutually linked and that accountability between employee and employer is inextricably woven into a whole mosaic that shows the importance of their relative and collective participation.

Regarding efforts to improve staff performance, the assessment, counseling, and evaluation activities that are natural to the supervision process are the primary duties of the regulator. The regulator as manager is responsible for job skill development as required by the individual based upon objective, unbiased observation; reinforcement of behavior through positive consequences and corrective action; bias-free communication; and proactive discussions of expectations, observations, goals, behavior, obstacles, problem areas, performance, concerns, advice, and instructions.

With respect to employee advocacy, a regulator is responsible for providing positive empathy; the freedom and latitude to make decisions and mistakes without fear of reprisal; and opportunities for staff to contribute, as well as for recognizing how individuals within different cultures view themselves and others in relationship to the world (i.e., the "process"). The regulator provides leadership in tearing down "isms," recognizing and denouncing the potential influence of dichotomous logic in creating assumptions which may be blatantly untrue.

THE GUARDIAN ROLE

The primary responsibilities of empowered individuals who are acting in this role include aspects similar to those of a parent. A guardian is responsible for ensuring environmental and physical safety, providing challenging work, and teaching and assisting in conflict resolution related to psychological well-being and work stress. In this capacity, the guardian demonstrates respect for the individual and self-esteem, and tries to see each employee as an individual with different values, styles, and needs. The guardian demonstrates openness and honesty regarding the social well-being of employees, but limits their interest to the genuine welfare of the employee and not to personal areas that are prohibited through harassment, civil rights, and equal employee opportunity regulations. To this end, the guardian participates in establishing environments that reflect the celebration of differences regarding spiritual well-being.

In relation to legal rights, a guardian is responsible for ensuring the rules involving employee "contract" rights. This includes employment contracts, employee handbooks, unemployment compensation, and other personnel, and ensuring that program policies and procedures are implemented, evaluated, and changed with input from staff, family members, and other key agency stakeholders. The guardian is responsible for ensuring all rights under the constitution, including free speech, due process, the right to privacy, and more. They ensure the protection of civil rights, including in cases of racial, sex, age, lifestyle, and handicap discrimination. The guardian teaches employees their rights under wage, hour, and labor laws, including wages and hours, labor unions, immigration, worker's compensation, and other related elements.

With respect to moral and ethical interventions, a guardian is responsible for establishing an environment that promotes employee empowerment. In this empowerment-oriented environment, the employee's future success is based on his or her actions, the employee is both responsible and accountable for work and performance, the employee's purpose is strongly felt and compelling to others, and the employee makes a commitment to role, functions, job, project, or organization.

In the event that the employee does not demonstrate acceptable performance, the guardian as manager is there to provide employee assistance. As a sympathetic listener, the guardian helps the employee utilize the personnel policies and procedures to gain support and services to address their personal problems. Sometimes the nature of the problem could be work or a combination of work and personal issues that result in stress. Then the guardian's role is to assist the employee in securing ways to reduce stress wherever feasible and within reason.

The Relationship Model of Managerial Intervention

The Relationship Model of Managerial Intervention developed by DeGruy-Leary (1998) utilizes three primary relationship roles as a basis for intervention with the employee. These roles are the Regulator, the Mentor, and the Guardian. Additionally, briefly discussed here are the associated managerial responsibilities, reciprocal employee motivations, and interests given the role of management.

THE MANAGER AS REGULATOR

Managerial responsibilities ensure the organization's accountability to the employee. In effective organizations, managers as regulators are coaching the attributes of success, engaging in employee assessment, and providing counseling and evaluation, employee advocacy, employee and staff coaching, and professional development. *Employee reciprocity* addresses the reciprocal behavior of the employee, including trust in the organization and management, personal growth, acceptance of negative feedback, demonstrating a willingness to stretch and to extend beyond previous achievement, and engaging in guiding and leadership behaviors. The Regulator relationship is motivated by the value of the information, the attainment of new skills, personal feedback, and specific opportunities to achieve and advance. The Regulator is also motivated by demonstrated efforts and personal commitment to ensure organizational accountability to the employee and by a more in-depth understanding of the inner workings of the organization.

THE MANAGER AS MENTOR

In this role, the manager serves as an advisor responsible for employee growth, and he or she provides inspiration for the employee to achieve, along with stimulation to perform, in order to accomplish a personal sense of alignment between the employee's sense of self efficacy and career aspirations. Employee reciprocity, the reciprocal performance and growth resulting from this guidance, includes long-term career goals and objectives, enhanced performance, and cultural awareness. The Mentor relationship is motivated by joint employee–manager efforts to transcend current attainment and understanding of business activities by the setting of attainable goals, measurable performance, and expanded opportunities, and by the clear intent to nurture employee skills. Grooming for greater responsibility is perceived as personal and not business.

THE MANAGER AS GUARDIAN

In this role, the manager provides protection for the physical, mental, and emotional well-being of the employees. This includes personal well-being, legal rights, and moral and ethical intervention. Employee reciprocity for this protection includes high morale and a well-balanced outlook, trust in the ethical and moral code of the management system, providing best possible effort, loyalty, and dedication. The Guardian relationship is motivated by safety procedures, accommodations, useful advice and counsel, and managerial intervention in team dilemmas. It is also motivated by the observed use of hierarchical power and authority, as well as ethical and moral conduct to protect personal and family interests. It is finally motivated by a sense of belonging and well-being as part of an organization.

Infusing Culture into the Problem and Performance- Oriented Practice (POP) Approach

The roles and strategies recommended by Briggs (2001) illustrate the importance of "working as mentor, teacher, parent" (p. 375).

GUARDIAN AS INFORMATION ANALYST

In the role as guardian, accountable practitioners will employ data collection tools that allow them to understand the issues and challenges that interfere with achieving the organization's aims. They do this by gathering and assessing the information collected from each level of the organization's infrastructure. In collecting information from staff, the guardian administrator gains perspective about their resource needs, their ideas about what works and what does not work, and the respective reasons for their beliefs. These individuals identify what they need as supervisory support, their skill training needs, and the internal and external factors that help or confuse the case management of client consumers.

The guardian as manager meets with the client-consumers to gain understanding on similar issues from the client's perspectives. They seek clarity from the clients as to the triggers, behavior cues, and circumstances that lead to and maintain client-consumer behavior management issues. They ask client-consumers about the activities they would like to have developed. Also, the guardian as manager seeks positive and corrective feedback.

In this role, they provide opportunities for all levels of management to share their analysis of those organizational conditions, broadly defined, that need alteration, modification, or elimination. They seek clarity from managers about staff performance. In this discussion, the guardian as manager solicits data about the indicators or lack thereof of desirable and positive performance. They inquire about the nature, frequency, and manner in which supervision is instructive, supportive, corrective, and encouraging. The guardian reviews licensure and administrative standards governing programs as well as recent evaluation and licensure studies that pinpoint the extent to which the staff and managers are doing what they set out to do. Last, the guardian as program manager obtains suggestions and feedback from different levels of management on how to arrange the environmental contingences that correspond with the planned accomplishments of the organization, broadly defined.

The guardian as manager meets with the CEO, executive committee of the board, and, later, the full board of directors to secure their feedback and perceptions regarding the key functions of the organization. This person seeks their advice and recommendations on how to proceed, and, finally, the CEO and guardian as manager encourage the board to establish routine functions, such as data analysis, performance feedback (program, staff and management), critical thinking, and planned organizational change, as typical board activities.

PROGRAM DEVELOPMENT

The guardian as manager synthesizes all of this material in a committee comprised of people representing different levels of the organization's infrastructure. This committee works with the program staff and client-consumers to plan the implementation of their suggestions regarding the program and organization. The implementation plan includes the design and scheduling of social leisure activity programs, assessment tools, and tracking tasks. Other aspects of the implementation plan are clinical consultation, case collaboration, and family participation in service delivery.

The guardian as manager and the planning committee establish an implementation plan that involves weekly meetings between residents and staff, administrative support and training, and quarterly treatment case reviews. With all levels of management (including upper and executive management), the guardian as manager recommends annual training programs for all levels of the organization's infrastructure. The basis of this training is to establish synergy in vision and methods, as well as opportunities to iron out contradictions, duplications, or conflicts between different levels within the infrastructure. The reason for this is obvious: in order for the implementation plan to work, all participants must work as a team. By doing this, the guardian as manager establishes a work culture that depends on reciprocity, collaboration, partnership, and teamwork. At times, additional training supports are necessary, and the guardian as manager arranges for specialized training whenever needed and financially feasible. To ensure accurate implementation in addition to determining if what was planned needs to change, performance evaluations are included as regular feedback loops and vital data sources for critical thinking, decision-making, and subsequent action. So that this management process is respected and followed, administrative sanction from the board of directors as well as buy-in from other levels of the organization are necessary. Recognition for ideas, performance, and accomplishments are institutionalized both formally and informally. Formally, recognition happens through pay increases, bonuses, positive performance appraisals, and through promotions and job changes. Informally, recognition is provided through the use of indirect feedback. This works through the guardian as manager telling key people at each level of the organizations infrastructure about the good work performed by particular individuals. This inexpensive means of communicating staff progress and achievements is very powerful because it motivates others to do the same. Also, it provides the targeted employees additional social reinforcement and support for their work. The guardian as manager plans opportunities for organizational support in areas needing assistance. The guardian does this by attracting university professors, volunteers with expertise, and may even by establishing an ad hoc committee to assist the fundraiser in writing grants and proposals for in-kind and financial contributions.

The guardian as manager, along with the CEO and various committees comprised of people representing all levels of the organization, establishes annual and quarterly board, staff, management, family, and community retreats. This mosaic of nontraditional partnerships activates people to use their talents and personal resources as well as fortifies their willingness to work toward organizational aims. Also, by having all of these players in the same room at the same time repeatedly throughout the year, an arsenal of action-packed, knowledgeable, development-minded, community, civic, professional, and non-degreed professional participation is created. These people collectively demonstrate an interest in program development that results in sustainable solutions and vital and self-sustaining client-consumers, families, and communities.

STAFF DEVELOPMENT

As the regulator, the manager is responsible for enhancing the skill development of all people involved with the organization. The regulator establishes staff development programs for staff, management, board of directors, and family members as a means to effectively model behavior change of the client-consumers, programs, and organization. Staff development may include training in case management, record keeping, community linkages, implementation tasks, and brief treatment methods.

For client-consumers, the regulator as manager is also responsible for planning training programs in areas such as behavioral management, parent training methods, and collaborative sessions with staff and biological family. The net effect of this training is to establish the client-consumers' competencies and capacities as they relate to treatment goals and objectives.

For various levels of management, the regulator as manager is responsible for the development of training in areas such as professional development, supervision, planning, evaluation, and quality assurance. The basis for this administrative skill development effort is to promote better functioning administrative staff. When this particular set of personnel gets the training they need to monitor what gets done and help others improve their performance, then they are able to maximize everyone's contributions to the organization.

ORGANIZATIONAL DEVELOPMENT

With respect to organizational development, the regulator as manager meets with staff to establish useful policies and procedures. These are established and, if available, modified to communicate expected performance to staff. Also, the regulator as manager meets with staff to secure their input and suggestions for planning evaluation methods for the organizations, programs, and services. Through this vehicle, the staff is taught to focus on strengths and positive outcomes. They are discouraged from using crises and behavior management episodes as the typical catalyst for initiating staff performance.

The role client-consumers play in organization development involves giving the regulator as manager suggestions for improving key areas. These include allowing joint activity planning sessions between client-consumers, staff, management, and consultants whenever possible. Suggestions by client-consumers may also include ideas to support staff and the creation of innovative activities that sponsor client behavior change in settings that may involve establishing interagency partnerships.

The regulator as manager meets with all levels of management and board members. This is done to establish policies and resources to support staff management family members and community volunteer efforts to accomplish key objectives of the organization's mission. Since the board of directors is comprised of a collection of individuals with influence, formal authority, and power that is needed to shape all aspects of the organization, it is important that they be included along with other players to sanction and promote intra-system negotiations and decision-making on how to best implement organizational policies.

PERSONAL SUPPORT

The mentor as manager is responsible for providing personal support to all key people in the organization. For client-consumers, staff, and management (all levels), the mentor as manager serves as an advocate, an advisor, and a nonthreatening provider of performance feedback. Additionally, they may even provide the staff on-the-job training as a basis to enhance staff performance, career development, and personal growth.

Keys to Sustaining Organization Change Efforts

Highlighted in Table 6.2 as the guardian as manager, the main structural components that administrative practitioners need to keep in mind include vision, mission, conceptual model of service delivery, definition of structure, and care cycle. When they function as regulator, the administrative practitioner will need to be concerned with the structural elements of defining outcomes, planning intervention, and monitoring the process. Finally, as mentor, the structural features administrative personnel tend to include evaluation of outcomes and enhancement and development of functions and activities.

The associated relationship-based activities are defined and presented in Table 6.2 as data elements. Once collected, these data can be used to assess and evaluate organizational functioning, dynamics, and outcomes relative to the aims of cultural competence and family-centered and accountable community organizations.

VISION

The organization's vision is where it wants to be after the mission has been accomplished (Briggs, 2001). Culturally responsive organizations define their dream in terms of the healthy interconnectedness between client-consumers, families, and communities. Setting this broad goal up front is essential to the organizational change process. According to Briggs (2001), "In a multilevel family-centered urban community organization, the catalyst and process of change begins with a clearly stated vision, a measurable mission statement, and support for improved outcomes and services, all facilitated by interested and affected families, staff, management, community residents, and board members of an agency" (p. 385).

MISSION

The mission of the organization is the primary purpose in culturally responsive family-centered, accountable organizations. The guardian as manager works with the board of directors to sanction family participation as integral to the board and its policy-making function. The manager gets the board of directors to adopt an agency philosophy that sanctions full family participation in the planning, implementation, and evaluation activities of the organization. Thus, as the organization is planning to evaluate or revisit its mission, the guardian as manager works closely with the board of directors to include the input and feedback by family members in the modified or altered mission statement.

TABLE 6.2 } Multilevel family-centered perspective in urban community organizations

Definition of mission	Conceptual model of service delivery	Definition of structure	Care cycle	Definition of outcomes	Plan of intervention	Monitoring the process	Evaluation of Outcomes	Enhancement and development
Sanction family member participation on board. Facilitate modification of mission to reflect measurable objectives for family participation in planning, implementation, and evaluation. Adopt agency philosophy that sanctions family-centered participation in planning, implementation. and evaluation.	Define scope of organizational policies and procedures to reflect philosophical orientation, with disability groups, practice theories, and anticipated outcomes at family and organizational levels. Develop clear policy on methods and theoretical orientation used to deliver family-centered services.	Create board committee with families, professionals. and community residents. Set policy and review operations of organization to ensure 1) family participation.2) that services are available to meet family needs, 3) that fundraising plans are implemented to raise unrestricted service delivery. and 4) that time and resources are spent in accordance with family objectives.	Set policies on how families need to access services as well as the coordination of visible services and objectives of the organization	Define measurable objective in mission statement. Define job description for board committees. terms of family objectives. and outcomes Define measurable indicators for family. staff. and management performance.	Define plan of action to pursue short- and long-range family objectives. Assess/ plan fundraising needs. Assess/plan budget needs. Identify process for strategic planning with staff and family participation.	Assess the way services are provided via quality-assurance reports. Monitor financial practices.	Through program evaluation, track family responses to service delivery via satisfaction of service effectiveness. Track staff performance. Track board objectives.	Do needs assessment to determine relevance of current programs and service to address community needs. Review management recommendation for budget and plan in accordance with family needs and outcomes. Celebrate agency change and family- staff accomplishments.

(continued)

TABLE 6.2 Continued

Definition of mission	Conceptual model of service delivery	Definition of structure	Care cycle	Definition of outcomes	Plan of intervention	Monitoring the process	Evaluation of Outcomes	Enhancement and development
Educate/clarify mission within and outside of the organization. Expand participation of *staff, family* members. and board in defining mission. Meet with family members and staff in program to seek in about organizational focus. **Sanction family outcomes and mission statement.**	Management task staff ways to understand theories of human behavior and practice technology that promote family participation and family achievement.	Define infrastructure on team of major objectives. Promote participating management philosophy practices. Use team management group to get task and activities completed. **Use feedback from staff to facilitate service delivery**	Arrange case-management. therapy. and training process to facilitate enhanced independent functioning	Identify client outcomes in job description. in agency program plans. and in program operating policies and procedures.	Define family objectives and input in program plans. **Develop linkages with out-side agencies educating them about focus on family outcomes.**	Develop staff. family, and management quality-assurance review. **Learn to ensure delivery of services in focus of the family use of supervision.**	Evaluate service effectiveness in focus on family accomplishments and behavior change. **Evaluate staff performance in accordance with family behavior change and community adjustment-**	Plan activities to achieve objectives not previously met. Increase positive attention on how well staff and families are performing responsibilities. **Assess staff for training or supervision in context of promoting family behavior change and participation to service delivery.**
Identify service outcomes with family member outcomes and mission statement. **Adapt principles of family-centered practice.**	Staff and family collaborate on service methods and treatment approaches to promote family achievement.	Participate in committees with families and management to plan board organization, staff training, and activities and services.	Use policies and procedures to revise ways for families to enter and exit system.	Use time-management plan to identify service tasks and outcomes.	Use family service plans. treatment contracts. and joint family. staff and management committees to lay our activities to pursue family outcomes.	Use time management to evaluate tasks. activities. objectives, Use quality-assurance procedures to assess progress.	Track trend and frequency of service outcomes (family reaction to treatment) by individual and caseload.	Focus on family treatment gains. Provide more support to family in areas in which they have demonstrated small behavior change.

Arrange meeting between family member groups and management to get family input on primary purpose of organization.	Family members inform staff of the services they are seeking to promote family achievement.	Participate in board committees. quality-assurance committee and activity planning meetings with staff and management.	Participate in defining service plan to address family statement of problem.	Resolve outcomes in observable and measurable actions and behaviors.	Plan activities and services with staff to correspond with self-identified objectives. Learn self-reinforcement skills. **Identify reinforcement for task completion.**	Involve family in tracking staff activities. **Share feedback about staff and organization delivery treatment review.**	Use family member satisfaction. **Maintain log of family outcomes.**	Use self-reinforcement skills. **Increase contact with support system.**

The guardian as manager collaborates with all levels of staff, management, and other family members (non-board members) to obtain their input on the revised mission. The manager does this by having sessions with management to clarify aims and to secure measurable working definitions that are practical for use as performance indicators, broadly defined.

CONCEPTUAL MODEL OF SERVICE DELIVERY

The manager as guardian works with the board of directors to establish a theory of change that characterizes the organization's philosophy. By defining the scope of organizational policies and procedures, the board of directors, with the assistance of management, establishes policies that highlight the organization's philosophical and theoretical orientation, which is compatible with culturally responsive, family-centered, and scientifically based practice theories and methods.

Also, the guardian as manager works with management, staff, and family members to establish a shared understanding about the theories of human behavior and the practice methods needed to promote the achievement of organizational aims. To enforce a family-centered agenda through service delivery, staff and family members collaborate on service methods and treatment approaches to accomplish stated family-centered and culturally responsive aims.

DEFINITION OF STRUCTURE

To ensure desirable organizational functioning, the guardian as manager assists the board of directors in establishing a relevant operating structure. At the board level, the manager, with assistance from the CEO, creates a policy that enables board committees to include family members, professionals, and community residents. The guardian as manager assists the board to think through policy for reviewing the organizations' operations. These policies are designed to ensure (a) family participation in evaluation activities, (b) service delivery that is culturally responsive and available to meet the needs of families and people from diverse backgrounds, (c) fundraising plans that are implemented to collect funds and in-kind resources, and (d) resources and efforts that are directed to assist all levels of the organization in promoting culturally competent, family-centered, accountable organizational aims and related agendas.

At the management level, the guardian as manager is responsible for assisting other managers in defining a team management infrastructure. The manager encourages all others to promote the theories and philosophies and the practice methods that incorporate organizational objectives. The guardian as manager helps others see the benefits of using team management groups to complete the work of the organization. This infrastructure includes family members and former client-consumers who have accomplished their goals. These former client-consumers are encouraged to participate so that they can share information concerning what worked and what did not work for them.

At the staff level, the guardian as manager ensures staff participation on all teams. The use of staff feedback to facilitate responsive service delivery is essential to team management. Staff sensitive to or interested in promoting the organization's cultural responsiveness, competence, and family-centeredness participate in committees with family members and management through board representation. Their aim is simply to give input that will assist management in revising and designing the committee structure of the board of directors and planning staff training activities.

The guardian as manager works with family members to get input and assistance in planning the means for family members and community residents as organizational allies. In this context, operating policies and procedures reflect the values and tasks necessary for family participation in quality assurance, activity planning, training, and evaluation committees.

CARE CYCLE

The guardian as manager works with all levels of the organization to define and ensure implementation of the care cycle offered to client-consumers. The manager works with the board of directors to set policies for how client-consumers access direct case management and case coordination services. With other managers, the guardian as manager works to establish opportunities to review and evaluate the best evidence-based practice methods that can be adapted for use. This particular manager gets input from family members, management, and staff regarding which methods are more likely to be compatible and useful. The guardian as manager uses the feedback to establish operating policies and procedures. They define how the organization arranges case management, clinical services, and training processes to facilitate enhanced client-consumer functional capacities. As these mechanisms are implemented, the guardian as manager routinely assesses the feasibility of the care cycle and what, if anything, needs to be revised or changed.

DEFINITION OF OUTCOMES

The regulator as manager serves as a brain trust of expertise in community, evidence-based, and administration and management practices. This person helps all levels of the organization plan or identify tools for outcome evaluation, interventions, and monitoring processes. In this context, the regulator is responsible for designing opportunities for skill development for all levels of the organization's infrastructure in the previously mentioned areas. At the board of director's level, they assist the board in defining measurable process and outcome-based objectives that comprise the mission statement. The regulator helps the board by defining its job description for various board committees in terms of the aims of culturally competent, family-centered, accountable organizations. As a means for developing a shared perspective, before program plans and job descriptions are approved in policy, the board of directors provides input to the regulator about what they think the performance indicators should be for programs and services, which include, performance data on client-consumers, family member participation, staff, and management.

The regulator as manager assists other management personnel in identifying measurable client-consumer outcomes in job descriptions, agency program plans, and through operating policies and procedures. Also, the staff and family member involved with service delivery (such as providing personal support and problem-solving assistance to other families) are taught methods for combining case planning and time management schedules into a useful tool. This tool should allow staff to use time wisely and to define tasks, expectations, time frames, and responsible parties on a weekly basis. This same plan can be used to evaluate what actually happened and if planning done by staff is reasonable or unrealistic. Either way, the data collected will allow them to critically think through the next steps in the process.

PLAN OF INTERVENTION

The regulator as manager is involved with assisting all levels of the organization design and development of intervention plans. At the board of directors level, this involves assessment and planning interventions in areas such as strategic planning, fundraising, budget management, organizational capability, personnel, and new or creative policy initiatives that complement or are consistent with the organization's foci. At the management level, the regulator as manager is responsible for ensuring the design and development of measurable program plans, program policies and procedures, and job descriptions, which include tasks for changing behaviors or enhancing performance of staff. Sometimes, the work of the organization is done through interagency partnerships. Use of interorganizational arrangements present structural challenges and barriers because of lack of formal authority and accountability between agencies. So, the need to intensively scrutinize intersystem negotiations, joint decision-making, and working agreements between organizational players becomes paramount to ensure quality of services and intended outcomes.

In working with staff, client-consumers, and family members, the regulator as manager uses consultants or skilled staff to assist in planning out interventions based in best practices. These creative solutions are written into service plans, treatment contracts, and activity plans and are reflected through the program operating policies, procedures, and staff and management job descriptions.

MONITORING THE PROCESS

Managers who are successful follow a simple formula—they believe what is monitored gets done. This is precisely what the regulator as manager does to ensure use of therapeutically and empirically sound intervention methods. The regulator as manager works with all levels of the organization to perform quality assurance activities. These activities include internal fiscal audits, intra-agency peer program reviews, quarterly intra-program reviews, and routine supervision. The data collected on program review are used to share progress and to learn if what is planned needs to be modified, given the data responses.

EVALUATION OF OUTCOMES

The mentor as manager is responsible for annual program evaluation, enhancement, and development activities of the organization. The evaluation of the various programs, services, and support functions of the organization allows the mentor manager to find out how well various units and the whole organization have faired on stated aims and objectives. The extent to which objectives have been met informs the mentor as manager as to the positive results of the efforts of client-consumers, staff, management, and board members. It also tells the mentor manager what is working and needs to be maintained. An assessment of the evaluation data is done to maintain what has been accomplished, and the mentor as manager uses this opportunity to increase positive attention to individuals and teams for their desirable performance.

ENHANCEMENT AND DEVELOPMENT

For areas in need of correction, the mentor as manager works with all levels of the organization through teams or committees to assess objectives that were not accomplished. The need for additional supervision, training, and other environmental supports is assessed so that redress may stimulate the desired results. If any, all, or a combination of these approaches is needed, then the mentor as manager assists responsible parties in the design and implementation plan for correcting unmet objectives. The mentor as manager works with staff, family members, and the board of directors to provide support and encouragement for achieving approximations of desirable outcomes. This particular manager encourages people at all levels to use self-reinforcement skills and not to use a punishment approach or crisis orientation to manage difficult goals and objectives.

Conclusion

Establishing culturally responsive, family-centered, accountable organizations through the use of evidence will require the skills of a professionally trained social worker. The skilled practitioner will need to know how to integrate theory, evidence-based practice, evidence-based management methods, and evaluation methods. They will need to be able to perform these critical tasks within roles that are based in a cultural context that provides productivity incentives for employees as well as understanding and respect for clients. Accomplishing these objectives effectively requires flexibility, tolerance, and a different way of thinking. It involves normalizing the radical concept of organizations sharing their power with client-consumers, as well as encouraging, respecting, and supporting their input as legitimate internal and external stakeholders. In addition, it means we need to have a willingness for and commitment to eliminating oppression, institutional racism, ageism, sexism, and the like. We also need to acknowledge our interconnectedness in communities that are part of an expanding global economy.

7 }

Synthesizing Critical Thinking and Decision-Making in Program and Agency Management

PROBLEM- AND PERFORMANCE-ORIENTED
PRACTICE (POP) APPROACH TO PERFORMANCE
AND EVIDENCE-BASED MANAGEMENT

As the seventh integrative practice skill competency, the use of performance management, evidence-based practice (EBP), and evidence-based management (EBM) provides us with the curricula for teaching administration and management practitioners how to manage an agency through the use of evidence as well as through a learning organization lens. In this context, learning organizations that use the best available evidence to make practice decisions (administrative and clinical) are those that embrace different ways of understanding complex social problems. Leaders and managers of learning organizations are concerned with three types of learning: (1) lessons learned from the promising practices and evidence-informed programs used to address service needs, (2) lessons learned about the agency context and processes used to ensure service effectiveness, and (3) lessons learned from practice decision-making errors and omissions. To achieve learning of these varied types requires the sixth integrative practice skill competency: the skillful synthesis and use of EBP, knowledge of culture (previous chapter) and social policy, theory, performance management approaches, client voice, and community participation. This increases the leadership capacities of a social service agency to obtain successful client engagement and behavior change across multiple levels of an organization.

In this chapter, we hope to provide ideas that will enable management to (1) use synthesis and information literacy to draw upon and use different ways of knowing to gain a broader understanding of the contingencies that sustain the social problems that are addressed in larger systems; (2) use evidence to form a critical perspective about a social problem and what ought be done about it; (3) use evidence to form an answerable question or pose an administrative hypothesis about the root causes, correlates, consequences, and implications of a social problem; (4) use evidence to scan and comprehend the contingencies of the solutions to the social problem for management; (5) use evidence to investigate the costs and benefits of alternatives and options for problem-solving; (6) use evidence to make strategic decisions and critically think; (7) use evidence to track and monitor consumer reactions to services; (8) develop the capacity to evaluate program successes; and (9) use knowledge to engage in service coordination.

Sound program management involves *teaching* and *supervising* staff continuously in *critical thinking* and *decision-making skills*. The acquisition of these needed skills leads to the selection of better options for the implementation of a program or to manage an agency or a larger community system of care. Students of program implementation and agency administration seeking social work education as a route to developing competencies in effective and integrative organizational management will find this particular emphasis useful to their administration practice. They will find that critical inquiry and routine analysis of the by-products of responsible leadership are the cornerstones of an evidenced-informed and action-oriented manager (Rzepnicki & Briggs, 2004).

Perspectives on Critical Thinking

This chapter examines four perspectives on critical thinking. The first involves a theory of human behavior perspective on critical thinking. The second includes an evidenced-based perspective on critical thinking. The third involves a complex thinking framework of critical thinking. In the fourth, we highlight a comprehensive viewpoint of critical thinking. Finally, the chapter concludes with an examination of a decision-making approach to program implementation and enhancement.

Critical Perspective Theory of Human Behavior

In any general textbook on theories of human behavior by John Longres (1990), the subject of critical thinking is either chapter one or chapter two. He believes that, in social work, critical thinking allows practitioners to practice based on their formulation of critical perspectives regarding the goals, problems, or issues confronting the practitioner working within a client system. In this context, the practitioner is faced with having to (1) *identify* the social issue, goal, or problem that needs to be addressed; (2) *articulate* the reasons why the practitioner ascribes value to the issue, as well as doing something about it; and (3) *establish* a practitioners' functional hypothesis about what ought to be done to address the social issue or problem.

Evidenced-based Critical Thinking

Gambrill (1999) provides a model of critical thinking that involves the use of evidence which guides the selection of practice options available to the social worker. In this context, critical thinking is a function of research investigation into the claims and methods used to achieve stated results. It is also an examination and critique of alternative methodologies for changing behavior and the capacity to apply approaches different from the commonly used methods.

Complex Thinking

Netting and O'Connor (2003), citing Kroeger and Thuesen, believe that critical thinking involves stages of thinking that advance to higher order complex thinking. They see critical thinking as a process of thinking, beginning in the simplest form and leading to a complex thinking format. They believe that simple thinking begins with *copying* an existing approach. The next involves *comparing*, which involves using a second approach that is then compared to the existing approach. The subsequent step is defined as *computing*, which involves arriving at a judgment regarding the differences between the two alternatives. If each of them incorporate or share similar features to the other, then they are compiled. The next step involves arriving at conclusions as a result of *comparison*. The subsequent step includes the *coordination* of the information about both approaches to people who are making decisions about ways to act. The final step involves a synthesis of this information as potential future actions, which involves examining both alternatives within the context of resources, other priorities, and feasibility. They conclude that the ability to go from "concrete descriptions to synthesis is at the core of critical thinking in organizations" (p. 54).

Inclusive and Comprehensive Thinking

We believe that the basic ingredients of critical thinking are those fundamental questions every grade school student encounters as they are taught how to read. In an organizational context, these questions are: (1) What is our agenda? (2) When will I know that our agenda has been satisfied? (3) Where will our agenda begin and focus? (4) Why do we need this agenda? (5) Who will assist me in accomplishing our agenda? And (6) how will we approach the implementation of our agenda?

Decision-Making

The result of careful inquiry is a decision to either act or to do nothing. Acting on informed speculation, logic, and reasoning becomes the foundation by which the decision-maker functions, and these are subsequently used to make decisions. In an organizational context, this means that the actions of managers who use critical thinking are not mere guesses, nor are they actions based on uninformed hunches. Decisions that grow from critical thinking within an organizational context involve a series of sequential questions that begin with an emphasis on the overall organizational goal and its mission.

Making Decisions Through Problem- and Performance-Oriented Practice

To achieve the primary agency goal, leaders of agencies should be using an approach that is mission-centered and critical. Without the guidance and direction that mission statements provide as driving forces of an organization, staff generally act in their own interests, which often leads to chaos and crisis management.

A clear mission statement is needed to prepare competent leadership and management. It is the statement that gives the aims, direction, guidelines, and values and ethics by which they will achieve the agency's overall purposes and interests. Decision-makers can get buy-in at all levels of the organization by holding breakfast meetings, luncheons, or special cocktail hours between management and staff where the ideas of management and staff are interwoven through shared dialogue, participatory management, and internal capacity-building efforts.

Feedback from staff and program management provides an opportunity to improve and revise mission statements for board of director consideration. To enhance service effectiveness at each level of the organization, we recommend using a similar process in revising and updating program objectives so that they are incorporated and reflected as guideposts for tracking key aspects of the overall agency mission.

Getting stakeholders, such as family members, community, and funding sources, involved in giving ideas about the agency's mission as well as the aims of specific programs ensures the accountability of the agency in managing these various interests groups and their participation as agency allies. If there is a clear mission statement and the stakeholders are generally linked into some project or committee, then the next step would be to assess staff knowledge of and actions toward achieving the mission.

If the stakeholders' knowledge of the mission is assessed routinely, then maintaining periodic feedback about how well the agency and various program goals are being met will increase the staff members' attention to defining their roles and responsibilities. We believe that as the staff define their jobs in relationship to their problem-solving efforts with clients and other performance specific units that define the program and agency mission, they and management can systematically monitor individual job performance, as well as assess program and agency performance level data. Agency and program leaders can achieve these ends by implementing the problem- and performance-oriented practice (POP) approach.

Problem- and Performance-Oriented Practice Approach

The POP approach involves information gathering and assessment, staff selection, staff development, performance management, and intra-agency development.

INFORMATION GATHERING AND ASSESSMENT

Problem and Need Analysis

The frequency, duration, correlates, consequences, and impact of the particular problem behaviors are assessed by the social worker. To gain a fuller understanding of the problem and its sustaining components requires that it, as well as what precedes and follows it, be identifiable and subjected to further measurement and analysis. Such identification is not an easy information gathering task. A social problem can be as behavioral and concrete as a collection of staff not engaging in desirable performances. This particular problem can be described, classified, and tallied.

Alternatively, other problems involving internal phenomenon and processes, such as intentions and beliefs, escape visual modes of analysis because their chronicity has rules out the effect of tallying and their relevance defies observable measurement (Claghorn, 1927). The more reliable and valid the measurement tool, the greater the precision and capacity for problem identification.

Performance Analysis

The extent to which problems are defined as target behaviors allows for a definitive analysis of their functions and access to sustaining circumstances and conditions. In this context, the social worker is probing for the underlying hypothesis about the manifestation of the problem, the problem's features and characteristics, and the conditions under which the problem occurs and under which conditions it is maintained. The extent to which the information is obtained without hesitation and judgment impacts the credibly of the respondents' participation. The extent to which people are comfortable impacts the accuracy and dependability of their self-reports and overall participation in sharing data about their performance. Avoid punishment when engaging people in problem assessment. Always look for ways to both increase reinforcement and assess its access, degree, and sustainability of opportunities for occurrence in the person's environment.

The extent to which desirable performance is incentivized and reinforced and undesirable performance is punished and penalized is an important set of contingencies that should be carefully assessed upon problem identification. Ignoring the wrong contingencies that actually maintain nonperformance in people and programs contributes to the sustainability of the problem of undesirable performance or nonperformance.

FORMULATION OF THE CRITICAL PERSPECTIVE, OPERATING HYPOTHESES, AND EXPECTED OUTCOMES

The formulation of the critical perspective involves a number of important components. First, it describes what ought to be changed and by whom and why such change is beneficial, value-added, and time-sensitive. It concisely delineates a change process as well as the intended program outcomes and effects it seeks to establish as the problem lessens and no longer exists.

In this and future discussions through this book, a "hunch" and an "operating hypothesis" mean entirely the same thing for the purposes of clarifying definitions. The *operating hypotheses* explicates the logical sequences and arrangements of the target inputs, outputs, and expected performance. It depicts the outcomes as the expected performance, which is the obvious logical next step; it is the planned consequence of the proposed interaction, therapeutic effects, and what you want to occur. The contingencies of each of the key players in the agency and program that ultimately impact the outcome need to be continuously assessed, reviewed, and intervened upon.

STAFF SELECTION AND STAFF DEVELOPMENT, PERFORMANCE MANAGEMENT, INTRA-AGENCY DEVELOPMENT

The effectiveness of any program or system of care depends largely on the quality of care and the skill competencies and experiences of the staff. The management of an agency involved in the business of behavior change should be searching for staff with the capacity to assist others in a teaching and nurturing context of care provision. Staff who are effective change agents can implement an intervention and change process. They are able to incentivize and motivate the client-consumer through direct influence and management of the contingencies that govern the onset and sustainability of desired behaviors of the client system.

Screening and Selecting Qualified Change Agents

Criteria to use to determine the suitability of a person as a behavior change agent has been provided by Pinkston, Levitt, Green, Linsk, and Rzepnicki (1982). The staff person is able to engage, incentivize, and encourage the client's participation. The staff person is capable of relationship building and can be depended on and is accessible by the client system. The staff person is able to coach and socialize the client system's involvement in learning, skill development building, and taking responsibility for self, activities of daily living, and safely surviving, as well as for behaving as self-sufficiently as practically possible. Staff who are believable, instructive, and accommodating of diverse styles of learning and doing make successful behavior change agents. Staff who are able to create opportunities for client systems to perform desired behaviors, as well as to receive reinforcement, have skills that are invaluable for programs seeking effective care providers and behavior change agents. Staff proficient in teaching behavior management and problem-solving skills are the type of staff management that should be hired. Also, applicants who have experience proactively involving client-consumers' families as allies in the plan of care are a bonus and provide value-added to programs in need of effective behavior change agents. Staff capable of involving families in the assessment, planning, implementation, and evaluation of services as well as for family support to client systems are invaluable and an aid to the staff and management of a program. Staff who are capable of teaching client systems strategies to avoid police contact and threats to public safety are very useful for community-based programs for persons with high- and at-risk status.

Standard hiring practice should provide an opportunity for new staff to complete a knowledge of behavioral principles inventory. As criterion of employment consideration, applicants should be provided an opportunity to discuss their behavior change approaches through case study and virtual scenarios during the interviewing and selection process.

Training

There are two approaches to training staff as change agents, as described by Corrigan and McCracken (1998) and Pinkston et al. (1982). These include educational and organizational approaches, yet both emphasize group training of care provider teams serving people in need of behavior change agents. Educational approaches include didactic sessions which provide step-by-step instructions for implementing behavioral techniques and procedures.

For example, change agents seeking to elicit and maintain desirable behaviors and actions require training in each aspect of contingent relationships between what precedes and follows desirable behaviors. Staff as change agents need to understand operant theory and the technical explanations and reasoning of the antecedents and consequences of behaviors. To comprehend the importance of modeling, behavioral rehearsal, and role playing, they should be taught the principles of social learning as described by Bandura and associates, the coercive theory of learning by watching others as articulated by Patterson and associates, and the power and relevance of positive reinforcement from Skinner (1953); Baer, Wolf, and Risley (1968); and Pinkston et al. (1982). All of these were successfully used by Briggs (1994, 1996, 2001). He used task-centered practice and performance management strategies to achieve service effectiveness through agency and systemic developments. These planned changes instigated and supported clinical and therapeutic developments in furtherance of achieving service effectiveness. As expected, he achieved desired performance among the management, staff, client-consumers, families, funding sources, and community stakeholders of an inner-city community organization in an African American community in Chicago.

Supervision and Program Review

The use of a supervisory checklist is beneficial when assessing the contingencies expected to elicit the desired behavior change by the clients through the performance of the staff. The supervisory checklist incorporates the inputs, outputs, and anticipated results obtained weekly to track and monitor how staff implement their clinical and care management hypotheses, as well as the behavioral reactions by the client systems they are helping to achieve behavior change.

The program manager uses this tool in weekly supervision with staff and also in quarterly program review and continuous quality assurance probes to ascertain the fidelity and accuracy of pursuing the desired contingencies between management, staff, clients, and family systems through the coordinated multilevel service delivery implementation process. This process involves the use of information literacy as a framework for using critical thinking through the applications of EBM, EBP, and model development implementation approaches.

Intra-Agency Development and Intra-Program Development Teams

These teams' respective primary purposes are the diffusion of innovations, critical thinking, and problem-solving for program development. These teams help enhance and improve organizations through pilot demonstration projects and by testing best practices by trial and error. Staff and client-consumer voice aid in their governance. They aid the team responsible for planning new activities and events with program managers and other program development team members.

Program development and enhancement teams work closely and collaborate as partners with family allies, community groups, and trade and funding source technical assistance staff to assess the evidence of structural and environmental challenges to client acquisition of desired changes. They aid program management as a design team by helping to establish opportunities for client skill development, learning and reinforcement, community engagement, and resource development.

These specific within-program or within-agency teams represent the change champions and catalysts for a particular program or for the entire agency. They serve as watch dogs, technical assistants, and consultants. They are identified not through political favor, but by virtue of the skill and material clout they represent, which constitutes and legitimizes the value they contribute to the development effort. These teams can be characterized as the innovators, trainers, and the go-to guys for creativity, as well as creating a culture for buy-in, turnaround management, inspections, monitoring, and quality assurance investigators. The team will become known as agency critics and skeptics who lead the change management and development efforts of a particular program or for the entire agency. Some agencies have department development teams that assume the function of program development and enhancement.

Their value should not be underestimated because through these teams, what is planned gets monitored, and what gets monitored gets done! These teams aid the agency director of development in the procurement of funds to support innovations in the provision and delivery of services to a population. They aid all aspects of the agency because their chief function is to proactively test out and pilot changes through the strategic use of evidence and innovation for the overall improvement of care and service delivery. The recipients of this aid are the client-consumers, families, communities, and the staff dedicated to the organization's vision of improving access to the social determinants that sustain us all.

Planning

The extent to which the intervention is likely to occur means that the program manager has access to the problem areas and environmental contingencies that need to change. They also have access to the resources and contingencies needed to elicit and maintain intended results. It always seems helpful to work backward and ask "How do I plan to get to Z from X, given the contribution and impact of Y?"

Wandersman, Imm, Chinman, and Kaftarian's (2000) accountability questions aid leaders of agencies and programs to plan, implement, continuously review quality, and guide program evaluation. These questions are useful for administrators and managers pursuing the achievement of planned outcomes through the use of best practices and evidence-based interventions. They include:

1. What are the underlying needs and conditions that must be addressed?
2. What are the goals, target populations, and objectives (desired outcomes)?
3. Which science- or evidence-based models and best-practice programs can be useful in reaching the goals?
4. What actions need to be taken so the selected program "fits" the community context?
5. What organizational capacities are needed to implement the program?
6. What is the plan for the program?
7. How will the quality of program implementation be assessed?
8. How well did the programs work?
9. How will continuous quality improvement strategies be incorporated?
10. If the program is successful, how will it be sustained? (p. 393)

Organizational Capability and Health Assessment

As a standard course of action, organizations that operate within a culture of learning and organizational health promotion should always conduct periodic check-and-balance assessments:

1. Are we achieving our overall aims?
2. Is our vision and mission relevant to the community, board of directors, and the funders of the agency?

3. What are our competitive advantages and areas of distinction?
4. What are our successes?
5. What are our challenges, gaps, and limitations?
6. What do we need to do differently?
7. How are we structured and organized to pursue change?
8. What are our corrective plans of actions for these critical areas, and are they successful?

Systemic changes advance therapeutic changes in healthy organizations. Organizational improvement achieved through question-and-answer–based planning involves agency change as a scheme comprising a theory of a problematic situation that is subjected to a theory of change that is expected to have some influence and capacity to effect and obtain a desired result. The envisioned process and outcome is hypothesized as a set of inputs and outputs that activate behavior change and that will always need monitoring. Monitoring is a good practice to use because it allows you to track your assumptions, change process, and actual versus targeted behavioral responses to ensure the eventuality of organizational improvement.

Plan of Change Logic Model

As alluded to earlier, the accountability framework of Wandersman et al. (2000) articulates an accountability process represented in a logic model that captures the key components of planning inputs, the implementation of best and EBPs, and the continuous quality improvement assessment of the contingencies that sustain progress as well as those that sustain wrong and undesirable performances and issues.

This ongoing quality control process allows the tracking of errors as an opportunity to enhance risk and resource management. It also permits the tracking of successes to incentivize staff and management through reinforcing consequences and events. The program evaluation phase of the Wandersman et al. (2000) logic model includes the use of methodology for measurement, data analysis, and evaluation.

Resource Assessment

Establishing better functioning individuals, families, and communities requires resources. Administrators and managers may find it necessary, and of use, to conduct a resource assessment of agency materials, manpower, and community resources that are needed versus those that are available to support the implementation of evidence-based and best practice programs intentions.

Weekly time management analysis allows staff, program management, and agency administrators to evaluate the resources used, actions, events, and decisions planned during the previous week and to plot their projected and future resource needs, actions, and decisions for the upcoming week. Briggs (1994, 1996, 2001) successfully used this strategy to achieve service effectiveness and agency development.

Implementation

To modify the wrong contingencies that elicit and maintain undesirable behaviors requires that we modify conditions that trigger and/or sustain undesirable behaviors. It is recommended that staff follow a recipe of systematic interventions. They should be strung together through a well-thought-out implementation plan. To do so effectively will require the administrator and manager to span the areas of model development, EBM, and EBP for guidance and direction. The achievement of expected performance is complex and not straightforward. Administrative and service delivery problems that interfere with the smooth implementation of best and EBPs require the same attention that a clinical social worker would give to an individual sufferer or family in distress. The only difference is that the unit of attention is the agency, program, or service system as subject for analysis, modification, and change.

EBM Process

EBM is performed in three distinct ways. Each approach to EBM is data-driven and analytic in character and style, which means that the central focus is the use of evidence through the practice of trial and error by examining every action and reaction through critical thinking. The role and purpose for using EBM in agencies is to demonstrate and incorporate science and advance the use of other ways of knowing as a framework for the management and administration of organizations. EBM involves resolving administrative and service delivery issues that circumvent service effectiveness.

Five-Step Process. The five-step process is instigated by designing an answerable question that involves an administrative and/or service delivery dilemma or problem.

1. Create an answerable administrative-related dilemma or agency problem.
2. Gather data on question from electronic and internal documents.
3. Assess reliability and validity of information gathered.
4. Summarize and prioritize alternative intervention options and supporting data sources.
5. Make administrative decisions informed by the evidence.

DSAP Process. This approach to EBM involves four stages:

1. Stage 1: Do: The administrator and manager make incremental changes.
2. Stage 2: Study: View the behavioral reactions to the small scale changes.
3. Stage 3: Act: Report the results and what was learned.
4. Stage 4: Plan: Investigate the process further through research and evaluation.

Eight-Stage Decision-Making Process. The eight-stage decision-making approach to EBM involves eight strategically focused questions:

1. Identification of a problem
2. Identification of a decision
3. Allocation of weights to criteria
4. Development of alternatives
5. Analysis of alternatives
6. Selection of an alternative
7. Implementation of the alternative
8. Evaluation of decision effectiveness (Briggs & McBeath, 2009, p. 247)

Briggs and McMillan (2012) articulate seven important lessons for using evidence in administration and changing agency practice:

1. Utilizing EBP in agency cultures requires a commitment on the part of the social work administrators and managers to think differently about the organization and the role and uses of program data.
2. Despite the increase in additional costs, it is sensible to foster a culture of rigor, monitoring, training, consultation, and interdisciplinary collaboration with families.
3. Time and resource needs may tax agency capacity to independently use the EBP process as a driver of the agency's performance management culture. The agency may have to integrate researchers into field agencies to assist as scholars in residence.
4. Needs for workforce development for existing managers may far exceed agency capacity and may require assistance from faculty as trainers and student interns as temporary manpower and support resources.
5. Diffusing EBM to agency culture is challenging, but worthwhile.
6. Establish a culture of experimentation. Settings where EBM and the EBP process are effective are in the healthcare and medical industries, as well as in other nonprofits that value research culture and scientific rigor as drivers of improvement.
7. Write a glossary of EBM terminology that can create a common language for all participants and that encompasses EBM as (a) a quality improvement system, (b) a problem-solving method, and (c) as a rational decision-making process. (pp. 170–175)

EBP Process

EBP involves the transparent use of best available knowledge, client participation, and professional expertise in selecting and implementing effective services. Similarly to EBM, EBP involves five actionable steps:

1. Step 1: Develop a client-oriented practice evidence search question.
2. Step 2: Search the electronic database for answers to the client-oriented practical evidence search (COPES) question.
3. Step 3: Review the reliability and validity of the research-based options.
4. Step 4: Discuss options with client to determine preferences, fit, and choice.
5. Step 5: Implement the client selection.

Model Development Process

Model development research involves the use of research methods, problem-solving, and intervention development as a toolkit for resolving social problems. It involves four phases:

1. Problem analysis and selection of needs
2. Problem specification and initial program development
3. Initial program testing and improvement
4. Dissemination and tailored improvement.

Continuous Quality Improvement

Pinkston et al. (1982) developed a set of intervention revision guidelines that are questions to be included as standard practice for assessing the quality and behavior of the change approach that staff and program managers are implementing to achieve behavior change. The questions to use for probing to determine if there is any need for modification of the approach and change process and the key considerations and recommendations for revisions (Pinkston et al., 1982, p. 56) are highlighted here.

KEY CRITICAL THINKING QUESTION PROBES	KEY CONSIDERATIONS AND RECOMMENDATIONS
1. Are the targets of change behaving?	Use every opportunity to elicit and reinforce wanted behaviors and remove reinforcement of inappropriate behaviors.
2. Is the change process being implemented?	If it is not, breakdown the course of action into smaller achievable tasks and activities; restructure the environment to decrease barriers and challenges to implementing the change process.
3. Are the intervention procedures behaving as expected or are there problems?	Use replacement strategy to obtain preferred change.

KEY CRITICAL THINKING QUESTION PROBES	KEY CONSIDERATIONS AND RECOMMENDATIONS
4. Are staff doing what they should be doing to activate the change process?	Structure opportunities for positive and nurturing staff attention and feedback.
5. Does the change agent have direct control over the desired contingencies?	Consider increasing the degree of control of contingent reinforcers by the change agent in the environment?
	Or, substitute change agent or change settings to increase control of contingent relationships by change agent.
6. Is there a behavioral model and goals of the desired performance?	Arrange for role playing, modelling and opportunities to rehearse the components.
7. Are the goals and approach realistic for the client system?	Incrementally pursue goal attainment by pursuing smaller achievable milestones.
8. Are there disincentives that inversely impact the desired performance	Remove the disincentives from the setting or remove the client by changing the setting and behaviors?

Evaluation

Evaluation involves the use of research and data analysis methods to assess the extent to which a course of action is followed by the desired program effects and impact. The evaluation process involves three main components: (1) identification of the targets of change; (2) behavioral definitions, measures, and data collection process; and (3) plan of data analysis. It is lesser concerned with theory testing and more focused on the effectiveness of the problem-solving process (Briggs, Feyerherm, & Gingerich, 2004). Its unit of attention is the (1) program, (2) agency, and (3) interagency relationships.

Program. At the program level, the evaluation is concerned with the change in the functioning and behavior of individuals, families, and group participants. It is also concerned with the change in the precipitating factors and contingencies that give rise to the problem's frequent occurrence. It is also concerned with the establishment and ongoing contingencies that trigger and sustain the onset of new desirable behaviors. Finally, it is concerned with the assessment of the opportunities taken and used to arrange reinforcing consequences to increase the frequency of desirable behaviors that infrequently occur at low rates.

Agency. At the agency level, the evaluation is concerned with the assessment of the efficiency and effectiveness of the structure and organization of the service delivery process and the outcomes achieved. The agency evaluation is concerned with the financial and material resources used to date. It is concerned with the extent to which the agency has accumulated or lost respect and political clout and capital among players of the agency's task environment. The agency evaluation tracks the quality of the manpower resources as well as the professional development supports and resources used and needed in the future.

Interagency. At the interagency level, the agency is concerned with the health and outcomes of its associations and the activities that it performs in concert with other organizations of the task environment. The interagency assessment involves a review of the continuity and coordination between agencies as well as the extent of autonomy and flexibility used across agencies to address issues of policy and practices that deter successful collaboration. This kind of evaluation is usually done informally, and any threats to the viability of interagency arrangements are typically handled by the executive directors of the consortia. This approach is done to preserve political and professional accountability and to avoid legal and regulatory involvement. It is discussed further in Chapter 12.

Core Specialization Skill Competencies for Administration and Management

Section II presents chapters that aid administrators and managers in performance management skill competencies to use in larger systems. These five chapters provide guidance and lessons on ways and means for structuring support to staff and managers implementing a strategic performance management approach that enables effective agency and program governance. In Section II, the authors critically examine the role, benefits, and challenges of effective leadership. Additionally, this section includes chapters on staff development, interpersonal intelligence use by administrators and managers, human resource development, and issues of power and politics in intra- and interagency collaboration. The chapters in Section II provide strategies and tips to use in leading, supporting, and enriching the agency environment to enable staff and management to achieve a better functioning client-consumer, staff, and management workforce. In this context, the chapters in this section represent the structural form that should be established to enable the organization's bottom-line function (the achievement of the organization's primary purpose and objectives). The application of lessons learned about developing styles of effective leadership, enhancing staff competence and expertise, and appropriately using interpersonal intelligence builds trust within an organization to drive performance outcomes. Other strategies such as managing human resources and following guides for understanding and leveraging the use of power and the politics of collaboration will equip and prepare agency and program administrators and managers to address the myriad of challenges and obstacles that interfere with achieving improved performance and service effectiveness by all agency stakeholders.

8 }

Effective Leadership

MOVING AN ORGANIZATION FORWARD

Often, we hear someone say, "That person is a born leader." All of us have our own ideas of what a leader is. For some, it may be a person who has the skill to persuade others to follow a vision. No one event or set of actions qualifies as the single most important condition that distinguishes whether or not a person is a leader. There are those who believe leadership is motivating others to perform at their highest potential. Whatever your motivation for leadership, to think of it brings forth the question: What are those characteristics and qualities that drive us to trust and take direction from others? To achieve a concise explanation for why people follow others who are identified as a leader, first, we must get a clear picture of what is meant when using the word "leadership." Everyone has a mental model of leadership. So, we really want to know:

What Is Leadership?

Schall, Ospina, Godsoe, and Dodge (2004), infusing Gardner's vision, discuss their definition of leadership. As they see it, leadership is a social construction. They believe that "leadership is socially constructed over time, as individuals interact with one another. This means that people carry mental models of leadership and those groups of individuals come to mean the same thing when they use the term 'leader'" (Schall et al., 2004).

Leadership in this context is a political process influenced by sociological, psychological, and institutional factors and considerations. Leadership, from this perspective, also means that it is not a rational phenomenon. How a leader sustains formal authority and the respect and trust of others within an organization has more to do with their style of leadership.

Some Initial Thoughts on Styles of Leadership

On styles of leadership, Morris (2000) states "that leadership styles tend to be dichotomized between task focused and follower focused or direction and collaboration or democratic and autocratic" (Advancing Women in Leadership, para. 2). However one may choose to identify leadership, as Jones describes it, "leaders produce positive change under dynamic conditions" (Jones, 2002). We agree with Jones and further contend that in order for positive change to occur, the leader must actualize three essential skill competencies. First, they must nurture and build relationships. Second, and equally important, leaders must know how to engage and further develop individuals in the organization. Finally, they must spur excitement while setting and moving the work of the organization through a clear vision and desirable goals.

Actualizing those fundamental competencies will typically result in a commitment to leadership. There are those who would then say with an ardent degree of certainty that, yes, people who lead are born with leadership qualities. Still, there will be others who will only faithfully ascribe to the belief that leadership skills can be acquired and mastered. While this age-old debate over the origins of effective leadership remains a popular topic of contemporary discussion raising considerable controversy, in this chapter, we will explore effective and ineffective leadership, leadership communication style, and leadership's ability to create and sustain a diverse, collaborative, productive, and successful organization. We begin our efforts by first focusing on the value of serving people as a prerequisite for effective leadership.

Leaders as Servants

Aminu Kano, a Nigerian teacher and politician, once said, "Anyone who wants to be a leader must first be the servant, not the boss, of those he wants to serve." These servant leaders place members of their organization first; they are not in the leadership position for self-interest and self-satisfaction; rather, they serve to coach and support others. Only when a leader is secure within their own self can they truly serve others because it is then that they are able to relinquish power. "Power" is a critical word. True leaders realize that the organization's success rests with all members; it is only through them that the organization's vision and mission can be realized. Serving others comes naturally to effective leaders; they jump right in when a need arises without pretense and expect no acknowledgment of their contribution.

More About Leadership

A leader of an organization has the responsibility to lead with values and vision, build relationships, support staff in their development, seek opportunities for organizational improvements, and listen as well as communicate clearly and effectively. They are able to do all of these things while collaborating in creating formal structures and systems to achieve their vision. People become effective leaders over time: even if you exhibit leadership qualities, being an effective leader doesn't happen overnight (Maxwell, 1999; Tichy & Cohen, 2002). As we explore effective leadership, the question of characteristics, behaviors, attitudes, and core qualities of a leader are common themes that surface. Maxwell identified twenty-one indispensable qualities; in the next few pages, we will discuss those and other qualities core to effective leadership (Maxwell, 1999).

Leaders are consistently confronted with internal and external issues and situations that present challenges for their organization; it is how they respond and manage those challenges that provides insight into their leadership capabilities. The character of a leader was once expressed to the second author as having "below the line qualities," those qualities that are innate to the core of a person, while the "above the line" qualities are those that can be learned. Leadership is portrayed in many ways: as honesty, responsibility, humility, compassion, respect, fairness, and citizenship.

These portrayals of character are all critical in effective leadership. Often, the character of its leader reflects the character and integrity of the organization. When a leader's actions do not coincide with their intentions, then their character is called into question (Maxwell, 1999). Leaders with character are able to get things done in the right manner that honors the process and inspires others to engage in the same level of integrity as they pursue their work. In recent history, we have witnessed leaders whose lack of character marred the reputation of the organization and in some cases destroyed it. An example of this is Enron, whose leadership touted values and vision, yet their leadership lacked character and failed to follow and uphold the very values they professed.

The Organization's Mission and Vision: The Primary Emphasis of Leadership

Drucker (1990) tells us that, "The first job of the leader is to think through and define the mission of the institution" (p. 3). The purpose of having a mission is to clarify the purpose of the organization. The mission directs the actions of the organization. When an organization struggles for focus, its mission statement should be all that is needed to place it on the correct path. How does a leader know if they have an effective mission statement? Effective leaders typically have a singular purpose, which is the achievement of the organization's mission. Rarely are effective leaders driven to achieve transient or temporary missions. Short-lived missions are the purview of ad hoc committees, commissions, and task force groups. Clarity of vision, values, and purpose involves being crystal clear, precise, simplistic, intelligible, and transparent about your wishes, ideas, drive, determination, and commitment.

Executives trust that if they are doing their personal best to execute the direction of the organization, others will also do their very best to follow and implement the vision. Also, they consistently remind stakeholders by clarifying the vision and purpose of why the organization exists and why each person in the system does what they do and their added value to the entire organization. Without vision, an organization will flounder and the leader will be unable to lead. Effective leaders create, communicate, and inspire trust and unite staff around the vision.

Blanchard and Miller (2004, 2007) believe that "creating a compelling vision is" the single most qualifying characteristic of an effective leader (p. 37). It brands the organization. Also, it articulates the distinctive character of the organization's goods and services compared to other organizations that provide similar services. They are able to forecast where the business is going and why it is important for everyone in the organization to pursue and achieve performance and service effectiveness.

Characteristics of Effective Leadership

While there are those who believe character is one of the cornerstones of leadership, it is often confused with charisma. As a leadership quality, *charisma* is hard to "put your finger on." How often have we heard, "that person is a charismatic leader"? Martin Luther King and Gandhi were said to be charismatic leaders, yet this was also said of Hitler. In 1990, Peter Drucker stated that charisma is not enough. He cites three historic leaders, Stalin, Hitler and Mao: these were people who led by their charm. Being a leader is more than having charisma; it is having a mission. While we largely attribute charisma to being a positive quality, one that leads people in a constructive way, it has also had a negative leadership impact and outcome.

Maxwell (1999) describes charisma as "the ability to draw people to you" (p. 10). Leaders with charisma have a contagious persona and are able to lead an organization and affect its overall ability to perform. That affect can also be negative, as it was in the case of Enron. Some of their executives were rapacious and ethically bankrupt while all of this was masked by charisma. Who would want to follow a leader who is a negative person? The leader sets the culture of the organization and, in doing so, must behave and communicate in a positive manner. Having a positive attitude is important to a leader's success and necessary to motivate others. In most organizations, the leader is visible, both in person and in the press.

The *Merriam-Webster Dictionary* (2014) defines *courage* as "mental or moral strength to venture, persevere, and withstand danger, fear, or difficulty"; clearly, effective leaders have the courage to take a stand for what they believe in. It is the leader's responsibility to provide the vision for the future (Blanchard & Miller, 2007). When a leader provides the vision and moves the organization forward, they must demonstrate courage and conviction for that vision. Courage allows a leader to step out and take on difficult tasks such as organizational change. It takes courage to steer a ship, and even more courage is needed to change its course. Effective leaders seek knowledge and are always in the mode of continuous improvement; they are not satisfied with just the status quo. The proverb, "you're never too old to learn" holds true. Leaders have the desire to learn and grow, always striving to be the best leaders they can be, not afraid to show their vulnerability. There is no shame in leaders discussing the need for continuous improvement. These types of leaders set their sights on new levels of competency, always taking their organization to the next level. To facilitate improvements and increase competencies, they ensure that their staff have the tools necessary to meet the needs of the future. This competence comes with understanding your programs, services, and processes while also identifying the appropriate staff to implement these elements. The ability to lead is exacerbated by the complexity of this fast-paced and ever-changing economic environment.

Other Concerns of Leadership

Leaders take time to reflect and anticipate what potential problems could arise. They are forecasting what the environment is around them and the potential hurdles and road blocks that may affect the organization. They look for the signposts and have a plan in mind for the direction they need to go. They are strategic in thought, identifying all the potential risks. These competent leaders have the ability to utilize their extensive knowledge to analyze and make effective and timely decisions. The ability to analyze the situation and identify the core of the problem is a skill. These decisions are often ones that drive the strategic direction of the organization. While knowledge is critical in making decisions, there are also many factors involved, and often it is a matter of identifying priorities. There are those instances when a leader is not afforded the time to put all the parts and pieces together to make a decision; they must rely on the information they have and their intuition. Truly effective leaders are able to focus and prioritize in order to accomplish their goals. Scattered attention and no focus can lead an organization into total chaos.

Leading Change

No organization can afford to remain stagnant; with new technologies, an aging workforce, and changes in the overall economic environment, knowledge and courage are necessary. All too often we find leaders of organizations that are not willing to recognize the signs of change; they are unable to make informed decisions and take the risks necessary to move and grow an organization. Fear of change can negatively impact an organization. Leaders who embrace change encourage their staff to seek best practices and engage in continuous improvements. They recognize the need to involve everyone in the change process and are not autocratic in their style of governance. They demonstrate the ability to engage in robust discussions to learn from those who do not have formal authority. They see the value of seeking staff feedback on what are the best approaches to achieving the vision.

Effective leaders are responsible for introducing change to the organization; not change for change sake, but change for the endurance to compete with other organizations and to offer efficient and effective programs and services. When there is an increased level of change in an organization, more leadership is needed to motivate and energize staff to follow the vision and mission. Change management includes identifying sponsors, stakeholders, and change agents for implementing organizational change. When an organization institutes change, whether it is large or small, there are risks. With each change, leadership must decide on and implement a structure to support moving the change forward. Something that may seem as simple as a new database system requires executives to articulate the vision for the change and for management to provide the training and support to implement the change. No organization will reap the full expected benefits from change unless the executive staff engages in the following: (1) ensures that decisions for change were thoroughly researched and best practices identified; (2) articulates that the vision for change is clearly active and visible throughout the change process; (3) sees the value and puts in place the time and resources necessary to train, facilitate, and support the organizational change; and (4) listens for, recognizes, and manages resistance at the onset of change as well as throughout the change process.

While managing change, maintaining focus and propelling an organization in a strategic direction is the responsibility of leadership. This takes commitment. This means commitment to both internal and external stakeholders. In today's nonprofit environment, leaders must be committed to their client needs and to staff development. They must be willing to be in it for the long haul for the health and welfare of the organization.

When a leader has passion, they are able to engage and be committed to the leadership role. Passion is about caring for others, the desired overall success of the clients you serve and the staff that provides that service. Believing and possessing overall joy in what you do is what makes a great leader. When a leader has passion, they can be the driving force behind the entire organization. Leaders with passion also understand the importance of being involved, taking action, and following through on commitments.

Involvement of personnel across the organization is not only crucial, but an effective leader knows that in order to move an organization forward with change, involving staff in the process is critical. Covey (1989) writes, "Without involvement, there is no commitment" (p. 143). These leaders take action and make the right things happen. Great leaders initiate action all the while encouraging and supporting their staff, a process that is paramount to the overall success of the organization. Many use the words "trickle-down effect," where actions and behaviors exhibited at the top trickle down throughout the organization. As executives exhibit these leadership behaviors, they are also engaged in multilevel communication to ensure that their message(s) are disseminated throughout the entire organization.

Communication and Leadership

Effective leaders understand that their communication must be clear, concise, and frequent. Often organizations communicate at the executive and middle management levels without providing a standard process for disseminating important messages to the organization at large. Imagine strategic discussions and decisions being made at the executive level of the organization without a communication plan to ensure that this vital information is filtered down through the ranks for implementation. It is also critical that staff receive periodic communication from executive leadership; it is not enough for staff to hear from their direct supervisors or managers. If they are to understand and believe in the vision of the organization, the messages must also have the face of the executives. The way in which people communicate has vastly changed with the event of email, texting, and social media. It is important to have leaders at all levels of the organization enabling the dissemination of the organization vision.

A key responsibility of leadership is aligning their staff, so it is important to communicate both vertically and horizontally (Charan, Drotter, & Noel, 2001). Aligning the organization and getting staff to understand the vision and mission of the organization requires communication. This may require holding "town hall" forums where staff can both see and hear management convey the message. It is in these forums that staff are able to ask questions and receive answers. It is the staff that must carry out the vision and mission of the organization, so the importance of staff communication and engagement is key to the overall organizational outcomes. Often leadership is communicating several messages that include a short-term plan and future strategies to accomplish the vision (Kotter, 1996).

Although we place a premium on communication, the quality of listening is grossly underrated. It is amazing the information one can learn by simply listening. Leaders who understand the value agree that listening to others in the organization discuss issues and concerns provides them with the opportunity to ask probing questions and learn in real time the pulse of their organizations. The knowledge gained by listening allows them to assess the organization's climate and proactively set forth necessary changes to implement improvements.

Theories of Leadership Styles for Integrative Practice in and for Larger Systems

While leadership is fast becoming a important theme in the social work literature (Banks, Hopps, & Briggs, 2018; Holosko, 2009), it is a common staple in the business management literature (Brilliant, 1986). Until recently, the concept of leadership in social work was sparse. Definitions of leadership have evolved over time. Traditionally, leadership focused on motivating a group of people to set and achieve goals (Stogdill, 1974). Others, such as House (1971), define leadership as motivating both, individuals and groups to pursue and achieve setting- or situational-specific goals. Thus, influence is a central core of leadership (Holosko, 2009).

The extent to which leaders are successful in influencing others to act effectively is subsumed under three types of theoretical paradigms. These paradigms involve trait theories, behavioral theories, and situation theories of leadership (Brilliant, 1986). By definition, *trait theories* entail the specific characters and qualities that embody leadership (Brilliant, 1986). *Behavioral theories* explicate the contingencies that sustain desirable leadership performance, while *situation theories* consider the unique and peculiar context that requires a flexible and seamless form of leadership. Such views on leadership involve sociological, psychological, social work, political, and business administration characteristics.

With respect to trait theories, while no one or set of personal features and characteristics of leaders is universally applicable to all leaders (Brilliant, 1986), those who are able to galvanize the masses to work toward a strategic goal are leaders who park their ego at the door. They maintain healthy professional boundaries by always assessing (1) Why am I engaged in this event/relationship? (2) What is my responsibility to this person/situation? And, (3) how will what I am doing enable me to both achieve the strategic intent and vision of the larger system and result in the achievement of my own personal and professional aims?

These types of leaders are usually transparent and follow a mantra that they can better show you than tell you the style of leadership that they operate within. Due to their sincerity, authenticity, charisma, and respect for and by their followers, these kinds of leaders can depend on stakeholders to go above and beyond the minimum performance standard and consistently strive to exceed their personal best. They have an honest character, cultural humility, and social and emotional intelligence. These are the qualities of leadership that inspire and retain people in organizations.

Respected leaders are skilled in building relationships among their followers. They are also uniquely competent in getting individuals to actively contribute and invest in themselves and the larger system, which could be an organization as well as an entire community-wide system. By doing this, leaders of this kind (a) know the importance of maintaining higher standards while preserving faith and hope, (b) motivate everyone in the larger system to strive for their personal best, and (c) understand the need to encourage emotional intelligence, creativity, process improvement, and collaboration with their direct reports. Thus, leaders of this kind are genuinely reinforcing, have unimpeachable integrity, have a desire to seek further development and honing of their leadership skills, and are transparent and open to feedback and learning from people who report to them while aligning their personal performance goals with the performance goals of their direct reports and stakeholders to ensure the organization's performance outcomes.

With respect to behavioral theories, leaders who are able to get others to embrace and execute their direction-setting approaches are able to structure the supervisory relationship as an incentivizing professional development process for the direct report. In this session, the leader strategically coaches direct reports in executing and implementing strategies that will yield positive performance. These leaders ascribe to the mantra of "you can't manage what you can't measure." They rely on data as well as on active listening, collaboration, and a consult and decide decision-making process in aligning employee's performance expectations with the organization's aims and the leader's expected performance outcomes. These leaders draw upon a range of incentivizing mechanisms such as flexible work schedules, administrative support, and arranging additional resources to aid their direct reports in optimally and feasibly managing workload. Leaders of this type employ a contingency performance management approach based in reinforcement and supportive corrective feedback (See Chapter 7).

To avoid the onerous possibility of punishment and perverse communication practices, these leaders study and assess the strengths, weaknesses, limitations, and challenges of each function. These particular leaders share the results of strengths, weaknesses, opportunities, and threats (SWOT) analysis to achieve clarity and organizational buy-in and joint planning to pursue change management outcomes. In doing this, they achieve higher functioning staff, organizations, and communities (Briggs, 2001).

With respect to situational theories, leaders who ascribe to this perspective understand that everyone in the larger system shares a common fate. In this context, they realize that everyone is in the same soup together and that their survival and longevity is tied to group dynamics and norms (Brilliant, 1986). To others, situational theories may be viewed as the function of a sense-making leadership paradigm (Netting & O'Conner, 2003). The context drives and prescribes who leads.

As an emerging leader of a larger system, one will probably draw upon each of these leadership styles at some point of your career. We recommend that you consult *Reframing Organizations*, a text by Bolman and Deal (1997), to further explore the context and choices of leadership style to consider when leading as well as when reframing organizations. Also, you should read *Organization Practice* by Netting and O'Connor (2003) to further examine the role and diverging theoretical paradigms to use in macro practice with organizations and community systems.

The integration of clinical practice with performance management across functions will require the use of all of the aforementioned theories of leadership. In a larger system, your role is to administer the day-to-day operations, which requires a great deal of people as well as technical knowledge and behavioral competencies. Trait, behavioral, and situation theories of leadership will become a natural part of your repertoire.

Through frequent and strategic use of these theories in your practice, their application will become both instinctual and habitual. It may be prudent as you formulate your personal practice model for leading and managing larger systems that you begin developing your leadership and macro integrative practices by creating a perpetual life learning resource guide, guided by lessons learned.

An integrative leadership practice includes self-care as a part of management's daily routine. Self-care sets the message of focus and prioritization for the organization. The first lesson of integrative leadership is to lead by example while arranging resources across functions and providing vision and clarity for structure and sanctioned processes as well as quality assurances and process improvements to ensure that systems operate efficiently and effectively. The second lesson is to be genuinely reinforcing and listen to your stakeholders. This is where trait theories take center stage, leading the array of leadership skills and competencies that accompany assessing, listening, and building relationships across the organization. The third lesson is to assess and understand the structure of the day-to-day operations of the larger system's central administration. The fourth lesson moves the behavioral theories of leadership center stage while sustaining a culture of action, process improvement, and movement as a result of leading the environment through the application of trait theories which inspire, influence, and incentivize people to act on their self-interests as well as on the success of the larger system. Through behavioral theories, the contingency management framework is used to define the antecedents and incentivize the consequences of desirable and undesirable behaviors. The job description and annual outcome-based performance assessment is used to define expected performance, plan and implement job duties and responsibilities, and gauge and judge completion, partial completion, or noncompletion.

Throughout the course of your employment in larger systems, you will be faced with situations that have you draw upon situation theories of leadership. The fifth and final lesson of integrative leadership encompasses the application of situation theories of leadership. Situation theories involve the use of all three theoretical perspectives as an integrative framework. The leadership style used varies with the context and dynamics within the organization and the extent of the task (Brilliant, 1986). In short, some organizational situations, such as holding an employee accountable for sexual harassment behaviors, require a top-down approach, whereas others, such as preparing self-study for accreditation, may require a team management style of leadership (Brilliant, 1986). A third form of situational leadership can involve following the lead of the collective of consumers, families, lay peer professionals, or the bottom echelon of a larger system (Friesen, Koroloff, Walker, & Briggs, 2011).

Regardless of which theory of leadership you resonate with, at some point each one will prove of considerable value to you to include in your leadership development journey. Each of the above-mentioned theories of leadership will aid you as you undertake a process of thinking and synthesizing an array of administrative and management functions and tasks. Integrative practice in larger systems requires thoughtful coordination and collaboration across different stakeholders within and outside the larger system you lead. While no one leadership theoretical approach will be the best approach, each is critical in responsibly and effectively leading the system's vision and managing the array of functions encompassing integrative practice in and for larger systems.

Think of the program directors and program managers who report to you as people who may need either executive-level sanction, coaching, support and resources, feedback, or a combination of a few or all of these. Whatever the person and situation, you must be prepared to be involved and collaborate with them in seeking the best integrative performance management strategy that fits who they are, you, and the situation.

One way to ensure the achievement of the goals established is to arrange the supervisory session to provide a menu of coaching types. As a course of action, it might be useful to treat the goal as an innovation that will get the staff closer to operating more efficiently and effectively while pursuing predetermined outcomes.

Mager and Pipe (1970) have articulated a simple strategy for assessing and intervening on performance challenges that you might find an easy and quick solution strategy to use.

Leaders know the importance of building relationships and understanding what motivates and excites their staff. Organizations will not reach their full potential of success if their leadership does not build relationships and extend as well as earn trust with staff. Giving of oneself is a rewarding experience. A true leader isn't generous on occasion; they give because that is the core of who they are. Generosity in the second author's opinion is similar to servanthood, which is another of Maxwell's characteristics in that, to serve others as a leader, you are generous in your intent. Former Oregon State Senator Margaret Carter sees effective leadership as encompassing three essential qualities: (1) transparency, (2) trust, and (3) clarity of vision and purpose.

In contrast, ineffective leaders participate in power games, don't trust staff, and tend to micro-manage the organization. They lead their organization using a military style, not including others in sharing information and making decisions without input from other members of the organization. Many leaders began their careers as individual contributors to the organization, and their hard work was recognized and rewarded by the management by giving them the opportunity to lead. The transition from individual contributor to leader is where many individuals have difficulty. It is at this juncture that one ceases to be an individual contributor with "control" of the work; as a leader, one needs to be able to accomplish the same end through the staff. The leader's role is to set the vision and direction and delegate the work, remove barriers, and coach and mentor staff to achieve the organization's performance metrics.

Charan, Drotter, and Noel (2001) identify several indicators that reveal aspects of ineffective leadership. The ineffective leader (1) interprets staff questions as disruptions, (2) takes on the responsibility of "fixing" staff problems instead of

coaching and supporting their learning optimal ways to address problems themselves, and (3) does not take accountability for staff failures and problems.

All too often, leaders ignore their true role of mentor and coach and do not
invest the time and effort needed to identify the needs of their staff and how to
support them. Leaders must cease to identify their own importance and focus on
the development needs of staff. These leaders typically do not understand their
role and responsibility in leading. A leader's role is to remove barriers and provide
the technologies and resources for staff to succeed. All too often, staff is forced
to find the "work around" necessary to achieve results. This process is both time-
consuming and ineffective. Leaders who allow staff to function in an ineffective way
will, over time, experience system and process failures throughout the organization.
Ineffective leaders fail to understand the complexity of an organizational system.
They are unaware of the value and complexities of both the formal and informal
systems that run as threads throughout the organization.

An ineffective leader is short-sighted and only seeks to accomplish what he or
she believes will help keep the doors open and the money coming into the organization. This type of leadership over time will permeate an organization and negatively impact the programs and services delivered to external stakeholders. It is the
vision, values, and behavior of leadership that sets the tone and direction of an
organization.

Leadership is not a role for those who expect to be appreciated, admired, or held
in the highest esteem. It is a role that requires self-affirmation, forward and strategic
thinking, a caring heart, a thick skin, and a desire to support and motivate others.
In the previous pages, we discussed the characteristics of both effective and ineffective leadership. For those who are in leadership roles or aspire to lead, the following
list describes a few suggestions and recommendations for honing your leadership
skill competencies.

Getting to results through effective leadership includes:

Setting a clear vision and expectations:

- Identify existing and future challenges
- Identify your beliefs and values
- Be practical, concise, consistent, and inspiring•

Leading organizational change:

- Identify process improvements
- Provide clear, concise, and frequent communication
- Manage resistance
- Provide training and support

Build and transform relationships:

- Genuinely care for your staff
- Encourage, reinforce, and recognize performers

Communicate with clearly and with compassion:

- Provide clear and concise communication
- Communicate frequently, both verbal and written

Focus on getting to results:

- Set challenging goals for the organization
- Effectively utilize resources
- Hold staff accountable

Engage, reinforce, enhance, and further develop staff competencies:

- Involve employees in collaborative decision-making
- Provide timely and effective feedback
- Assess development needs
- Provide development training and opportunities

Leadership and Effective Organizational Behavior Management

In the preceding tips for enhancing leadership comptencies, leadership as a process for establishing credible and dependable organizational behavior among stakeholders is the result of adopting proven strategies and lessons. Readers now know that effective leadership is derived from how one can nurture others to stay the course and believe in the organization's direction and values; it requires a critical perspective and the overall skill competencies to manage a larger system. Effective leaders not only provide the vision and set direction and priorities to follow, but they add value to the organization. Effective leaders are not autocratic in their style of governance and administration. They set clear boundaries and model the behaviors they want to observe in their staff.

Attention to the issue of ineffective leadership in this chapter has been deliberately brief, but this issue is not unimportant. As we see it, ineffective leadership lets you know that the people in charge have failed to gain the respect, confidence, and allegiance to their mission and vision. Ineffective leaders engage in power games and almost always micro-manage the organization.

As stated earlier, former Oregon State Senator Margaret Carter sees effective leadership as encompassing three essential qualities: (1) transparency, (2) trust, and (3) clarity of vision and purpose. Their definitions and application to agency management are concisely delineated here.

> *Transparency.* Transparency involves the demonstration of clarity, sheerness, or being translucent or photographic, which all means that the vision, mission, or belief system is easily discernible, above board, and is no secret.

Trust. Trust involves faith, belief, hope, conviction, confidence, expectation, reliance, dependence, and custody.

Clarity of vision and purpose. Clarity of vision and purpose involves being crystal clear, precise, simple, intelligible, and transparent about your expectations and ideas, drive, determination, and commitment. In an organizational management context, effective leaders are transparent and authentic. They trust that if they are doing their personal best to execute the direction of the organization, others will also strive for their best. Also, they constantly remind stakeholders by clarifying the vision and purpose of why the organization exists and why each individual adds value to the organization at large.

Effective leaders are able to articulate the distinctive character of the agency's goods and services compared to other organizations that provide similar services. They forecast where the business is going and why it is important for everyone in the organization to stay the course while they pursue intended performance and service effectiveness. Effective leaders typically have a dual purpose, which is the achievement of the larger system's mission and the subsequent actualization of its vision. As students seeking to be leaders of an organization or a community, it will not be enough to know the characteristics and attributes of effective leadership. The continuous use of the recommendations presented in this chapter will give you the experience and competencies to handle and resolve the challenges that keep leaders up at night.

9 }

Staff Development

In preparing this chapter, I recalled a conversation with the second author, and we reminisced about the importance of a chapter on professional staff development and training to macro practice curricula in social work. I juxtaposed the ideas in it with the ideas in a paper I co-wrote with a social work colleague. In this paper, we critically examined the differences in the preparation of physicians receiving education in medical schools versus being educated in schools of social work (Briggs & McBeath, 2009). As I remember, in the former scenario, the quality and outcome of care provided as a student is tied to a proficiency standard, degree completion, and credentialing which grants a license and permission to practice with the expectation of continuing education for certification. However, in the social work education scenario, the achievement of service effectiveness is not a requirement for degree completion or professional practice. Additionally, while licensure is only needed for third-party billing and reimbursement in the social work scenario, it is a prerequisite for professional practice in medicine.

Thus, the way social work practitioners are educated for professional practice, what they learn, and the credentialing process to qualify them as fit for professional practice has nothing to do with achieving service effectiveness. Arguably, it has less to do with acquiring proficiency in the delivery of culturally specific services. In short, the social work academy has not addressed these as distinct formidable issues, their interrelationships, or the impact of their absence on the quality of the professional training of its practitioners and the delivery of effective social work services to historically marginalized individuals, families, and communities (see Chapter 2).

Sadly, academic schools of social work do not create curricula, qualifying exams, or placement aptitude tests that are tied to the achievement of knowledge or skill proficiencies across job classifications, roles, responsibilities, and skill competencies required in the professional arena of social work, broadly or specifically defined. Given the variety of arenas and fields of practice encompassing social work, the design of curricula to address all of the knowledge and skill proficiencies unique to the specialties and general practice of social work would dramatically change the way we educate and prepare our students for practice.

Nonetheless, staffers with jobs and careers in social and human services seeking to become and remain proficient need professional training supports and resources. To enable them to provide credible, dependable, and effective services to historically marginalized communities through social service programs in nonprofit organizations, they must have access to experts in effective social services as well as ongoing competent staff development and training programs. Therefore, to be effective, they must possess training and staff development in effective helping knowledge, which is comprised of both technical and general skill competencies and abilities.

Staff training models typically involve classroom-based approaches (Corrigan & McCracken, 1997). Given this context, usually the individual staff person is the unit of attention and the goal of training is to increase the staff's capacity to implement a best practice program or intervention. The limitations of educational approaches for organization personnel, as well as practice routines and practice environments, provide an opportunity to explore more sustainable solutions (Corrigan & McCracken, 1997).

To ensure that best practice innovations are adopted and implemented in agency practice, leadership needs to reject the use of traditional training methods and move to alternative staff interactive approaches. In this context, the training focus is on the team and their competencies to advance user-friendly program development (Corrigan & McCracken, 1997), program enhancement, and quality assurance (Briggs, 1994, 1996, 2001; Briggs & McMillan, 2012). Team building and ownership by the staff in program development are the two driving organizational principles that have been included in the interactive staff training facilitative team development perspective (Bowditch & Buono, 1994; Corrigan & McCracken, 1997).

Interactive staff training models include four phases: (1) introduction to the system, (2) program development, (3) program implementation, and (4) program maintenance (Corrigan & McCracken, 1997). This process is instigated by a training facilitator maintaining a schedule of monthly training sessions for a period of no less than six months through eighteen months. Along similar lines, Briggs (2001) spent seven years establishing and sustaining a performance and evidence-based management system in an inner-city community organization administered by graduate and advanced degree African American human service professionals.

Briggs successfully used an intervention design and development model in two separate and distinct service divisions (child welfare and residential services for adults with developmental disabilities) and a subsequent four-year organization-wide behavior modification approach. It included five distinct phases preceded by problem analysis and pre-project planning activities: (1) information analysis, (2) program development, (3) staff development,

(4) organizational development, and (5) coaching, mentoring, and personal support with direct care staff, managers, executives, and board of directors of a non-profit organization. Information analysis included interviews and discussions with staff, management, community residents, providers, and funding sources. While changes in the program procedures, staff performance and management, and agency-wide functioning were under way, there was also a change in the way client-consumers participated in and received habilitation programming. Participatory management, performance- and evidence-based management, and evidence-based practice along with cultural knowledge comprised the content knowledge and approaches used successfully by Briggs (2001, 1996, 1994) to achieve service effectiveness and to effect staff performance, staff management, and organization-wide transformation.

Senior leadership sanctioned as a requirement the training teams of direct care and service coordination staff to provide a series of positive youth development and family support programs and services to gang-involved youth and families (Corrigan & McCracken, 1997; Briggs, 2001). Senior management controls the employment contingencies of all stakeholders, with the exception of the board of directors. They not only oversee and manage all of the organization's resources, goods, and services, but they also are the keepers of the purse strings, the carrots, and the sticks. To that end, senior administrators are champions because they give credibility to the change management consultants and experts, and they speak on behalf of the CEO. They also provide instant approval of resources that increase the speed by which the team may act to change a program or service system's course of action.

When assessing the needs of staff for training, their perceptions in identifying gaps in knowledge, and what is needed to support them to drive for results are essential sources of data. This data can be used to motivate and provide incentives for staff participation. Simply put, if you want staff buy-in and ownership, then you have to reinforce their participation by recognizing the value added from the ideas and concerns they express (Briggs, 2001; Briggs & McMillan, 2012). In a review of the research evidence on effective staff training approaches, Corrigan and McCracken (1997) summarize current thinking best: "Line-level staff members are likely to implement intervention programs that reflect their perceptions of important consumer care and milieu management issues. Conversely, line-level staff is likely to resent program decisions that represent an outside expert's perceptions of their program" (p. 39).

Briggs (2001) and Briggs and McMillan (2012) report the importance of the perceptions and needs of staff and management to change management in organizations. They showed the success achieved when all layers of an organization use training and performance management consultation to enhance staff and management performance and role competencies to pursue social service effectiveness.

Develop the Staff That Drives the Success of a Larger System

The ultimate success of any larger system (e.g., organization or community system) relies on the performance, strength, commitment, trust, and loyalty of its staff. This certainty was also presented in the previous chapter on leadership; leaders must invest in the staff's professional development. In this difficult economy, each day there are more clients to serve and fewer budget dollars to provide the programs and services needed. Under those constraints, leadership is asking staff to assume more and more responsibilities. In some organizations, this is coined as "doing more with the same" or in some cases "doing more with less."

Typically, when there is a call by executives or boards for budget cuts, funding for staff development is the first to be minimized or cut all together. Management is often short-sighted on the needs for staff development and frequently give in to the pressures of budget shortfalls. They act too quickly, without stepping back and assessing the longer term impact that cutting staff development will have on the organization. When budgets are created, there is already a hesitancy to spend too many dollars in the area of staff development. When an organization does not invest in training, they risk losing talented staff and breeding mediocrity (Ulrich, 1997a, 1997b). With the right tools and supports, staff will stay committed to the mission and vision of the organization. Management should be aware of the roles and responsibilities of each staff member and their development needs. Those organizations that are highly successful believe having a trained and motivated staff positions you with a competitive advantage (Ulrich, 1997a, 1997b).

To ensure the health and welfare of the organization, management must have a plan to develop the skills of their staff. With such a complicated mission as staff development, where should one start? For the purposes of this chapter, we will focus on three areas: (1) assessment and planning; (2) building capacity through training, continuing education, and professional development; and (3) performance accountability to achieve results.

ASSESSMENT AND PLANNING

Staff assessment and planning serves as a valuable tool for an organization. Managers need to understand the value of maintaining and improving staff performance and positioning for future organizational needs. Every organization is striving for improved performance, and starting with an investment in your staff is crucial to your success. Staff may be succeeding by meeting expectations in their current role, and, because of their good performance, we assume they are ready to take on added responsibility without taking the time to consider whether or not they are fully capable of executing without additional training. Management often focuses on the task needed to be accomplished and not the training necessary to accomplish the task. Management ensures a disservice to staff when they do not consider the potential impact of adding work without assessment and training.

It is important for management to reflect on the current landscape: Are the positions identified able to meet current and future program and service needs? What are the triggers that would lead to a change in staffing? Triggers such as program changes and service needs, whether they be an increase or decrease, can prompt staff movement. Management should review the position descriptions of each staff member to assess the effectiveness level of their roles and responsibilities. The review may prompt updates and revisions to the position descriptions. Once the position description review is complete, create an assessment checklist listing the essential role and responsibilities. This tool will provide a baseline of staff performance effectiveness relative to their current position. This process enables management to assess the development needs of staff. There may be areas of staff performance effectiveness related to their function where they are still performing at a baseline level; in a specific area such as written communication skills (see Figure 9.1), this would be a development opportunity. The figure below is a tool to assist in understanding your staff and how to best support them.

The goal of management is to ensure that staff performance either meets or exceeds performance expectations. To this end, management must provide performance feedback. Feedback is best given in a timely, direct, and constructive manner. While feedback is often given in a more formal environment as it relates to performance, to truly be effective it must be provided periodically or on a day-to-day basis. Acknowledging staff successes as well as giving feedback when performance is ineffective is important (Pulakos, 2004). Providing positive feedback is important: staff should be acknowledged for the positive contributions they make. If staff doesn't feel valued, they may decide to seek employment elsewhere (Harms & Roebuck, 2010). Providing timely feedback allows staff to recall particular event and that will have the greatest impact. Feedback allows staff to make performance corrections and identify training needs to further enhance their strengths and improve in those areas that are their weakest, all while moving toward enhanced performance. Feedback from multiple sources, such as peers and stakeholders, will also assist in providing information on performance. Supporting the idea of feedback from multiple sources are authors Muniute-Cobb and Alfred who studied peer performance feedback as it relates to team primacy concept-based evaluations. This evaluation concept is characterized as a multi-rater evaluation with three characteristics: (1) self-feedback, (2) supervisor feedback, and (3) its distinguishing evaluation characteristic of face-to-face peer feedback (2010). The study capitalizes on Kolb's experimental learning model to articulate how staff learns from the evaluation and uses the information for their development.

In a study by Druskat and Wolff (2009), their research supports a facilitative context for peer appraisals. The peer appraisal had a greater impact when given in a

Staff Career Summary

Name: _____   Date: _____

Department: _____

Supervisor: _____

This document will be used as a communication tool. Please clearly complete this summary by responding to the questions below. Areas are provided for additional comments. Please express clear and honest responses.

1. Career Objectives	Comments
2. What are your short term career goals?	Comments
3. What are your long term career goals?	Comments
4. What developmental support do you feel you need in your current position?	Comments
5. What developmental support do you feel you need to achieve your career objectives?	Comments

FIGURE 9.1. Staff Career Summary

timely manner, so much so that it positively impacted the peer's personal interactions as well as the task outcomes. The study also states that when peer appraisals are used as a tool for development, the communication is more open and the feedback can be delivered face to face. Drexler, Beehr, and Stetz (2001) found in their study that while peer ratings are important, their validity may be challenged by the reluctance of peers to provide negative feedback. Often feedback must be provided on an individual level as well as a team level. Research by DeShon, Kozlowski, Schmidt, Milner, and Wiechmann (2004) from Michigan State University predicts that feedback provided to individuals will yield a stronger commitment and efficacy for achieving higher individual goals, and, conversely, this holds for feedback that is targeted at a team. In the study, those participants not provided individual feedback or team feedback had a reduced commitment to individual goals (see Figure 9.2). Feedback truly is a gift.

It is also important to understand how the staff views their own performance. To fully engage staff in the assessment process, management must have staff assess themselves. Self-assessment allows staff to reflect on their own performance and identify areas for improvement (Harms & Roebuck, 2010). This process positions both management and staff for an in-depth dialogue identifying gaps and opportunities that exist for staff development. Once both staff and management have had the opportunity to discuss the performance assessment, the next step is identifying those areas for development and planning the training necessary to address gaps (see Figure 9.3). The self-assessment checklist below allows staff to be reflective and identify areas of strength as well as development.

Planning the next steps for staff development is as important as the assessment itself. For the planning to be effective, there are three components to the planning process: (1) identify specific areas of focus for development in the current position, (2) identify future development needs and organization career objectives, and (3) identify specific areas for career development. Planning that is based on staff career objectives allows them to explore their interests and the type of work they want to do in the short and long term within the organization. It also provides a potential career path and assists management in understanding staff interest, which may be used in staff planning and development.

In providing a development plan for staff to support their current position, there may be multiple areas that require focus, and both staff and management must prioritize these areas in order to execute staff development training. This prioritization will maximize the staff's development plan, allowing them time to integrate training into their work schedule. Prioritization also allows management to forecast a budget for staff training.

Peer Feedback Assessment Form

Peer Name: _____   **Date:** _____

Department: _____   **Review Period:** _____

Feedback Provider: _____

Assessment Guidelines:

This form is to be used as a tool in communication of peer feedback. The preferred delivery of the peer feedback observation below is face-to-face, to generate a discussion regarding the observations.

Feedback Ratings- The following guidelines are to be used in selecting the appropriate rating:

1 Unsatisfactory	2 Marginal	3 Meets Requirements	4 Exceeds Requirements	5 Exceptional	N/A Not Applicable
Description		**Rating**	**Comments**		
Demonstrates required job skills and knowledge					
Has the ability to learn and use new skills and technology					
Uses available resources efficiently and affectively					
Demonstrates analytical and problem solving skills					
Demonstrates strategic and innovative thinking					
Demonstrates team behavior					
Completes assignments and agreed upon timelines					
Contributes constructive ideas and solutions					
Takes responsibility for actions					
Honors commitments					
Communicates effectively					
Demonstrates performance suitable to the generalist and specialization skill competencies, agency standards, methods, and value base appropriate to the position					

FIGURE 9.2. Peer Feedback Assessment Form

Staff Self-Assessment Checklist

Name: _____   Date: _____

Position: _____   Overall Rating: _____

Department: _____

Supervisor: _____

Please assess yourself by the definition that best describes your current behaviors or skills.

Ratings	1	2	3	4	5
Elements	Unsatisfactory	Marginal	Meets Requirements	Exceeds Requirements	Exceptional
Technical Skills • Demonstrates analytical and problem solving skills. • Demonstrates position knowledge and skill for critical and non-critical functions.					
Communication Skills Clear and concise written and verbal communications.					
Project Management Manages multiple projects simultaneously assuring each project priorities and timelines are identified and met.					
Time Management • Manages time effectively to spend appropriate time on each task. • Prioritize tasks so that all critical timelines are met.					
Working in a Team or Work Group • Establish good relationships with team/work group members and be willing to support others. • Actively seek out work and show initiative. • Effectively contribute to the team/work group goals.					
Achieving Quality Assurance Practice Results Consistently achieves expect performance outputs and outcomes.					
Professionalism Demonstrate performance suitable to the generalist and specialization skill competencies, agency standards, methods, and value base appropriate to the position.					

FIGURE 9.3. Staff Self-Assessment Checklist

TRAINING, CONTINUING EDUCATION, AND
PROFESSIONAL DEVELOPMENT

Staff training is as valuable as staff selection and retention. Effective staff training can result in positive change. As organizations downsize, combine, and repurpose positions to stabilize during a slow economy and still achieve continuous improvements, more demands are made on staff to perform. Effective organizations engage in process improvement and, in doing so, may invest in systems, practices, and procedures that require a different set of skills. The skills that management may need staff to utilize today may not be the skills required tomorrow. Bolman and Deal (1997) state that staff deficits in knowledge and skill will place an organization at risk on the basis of quality, service, and overall cost. For this reason, training must be an integral part of an organization's staff development strategy. Some training may be mandatory in order to meet organization policy or regulatory requirements. Staff training is useful and especially important to bring new theories and methodologies to seasoned staff, as well as giving younger staff an opportunity to learn and grow and put more tools in their tool belt. There are several ways to administer training to maximize time and budget. Management will find it critical for the training topics to be as diverse as their staff. It is also important to understand the diversity of your staff's learning styles (Hecht & Ramsey, 2002) as well as know what motivates and incentivizes them.

The human resources (HR) professionals of an organization are typically tasked with the development of general competence curricula. This training curriculum is made available to all staff to ensure that they have the resources necessary to acquire the skills needed to do the work. For those organizations that do not have an HR staff designated to develop and implement curriculum, management and staff must be creative. Many organizations utilize *mentors* as internal resources to assist in transferring knowledge from one staff member to another. Mentors are frequently identified by management as staff within the organization who are subject matter experts, continuous learners, and know how to achieve results. Often mentors are better trainers since they understand the organization and the skills needed to accomplish the results. Another advantage to having mentors as trainers is the opportunity for one-on-one engagement for learning. The downside of leveraging mentors for training is that it may take them away from their scheduled work. Considering their time, leveraging mentors for training must be planned carefully by management and staff.

Whether a mentor, an interactive seminar, formal presentation, webinar, or an interactive online workbook provides the training, offering a variety of options allows staff to be flexible in receiving new information. Ulrich (1997a, 1997b) discusses internships, cross-trainings, and collaborative projects as a structure for developmental experiences. Internships and cross-trainings are also an opportunity for staff to experience various work areas and either move forward, continuing to learn and grow, or decide that they are not interested or suited for that particular position. This also provides management an opportunity to see if the person is a good "fit" for the position. Collaborative group projects, while not skill-specific in their training, can provide a rich learning environment. Ulrich's recommendation for development training assumes that staff members are prone to "hands-on" learning and would benefit from these types of experiences. Building staff skills is a difficult challenge and one that takes time, money, and commitment from both staff and management.

Continuing education units and professional development hours provide staff the opportunity to keep their skill and knowledge current. While taking courses to obtain degrees may be offered by an organization as part of its benefit package, these courses are focused on staff's long-term career development objectives. With the changing economic marketplace, having a high school diploma and being able to continue to work your way up the chain from position to position within an organization is becoming increasingly difficult. In this case, the skills acquired are broader based in nature and not targeted on specific skills that one would receive in a focused training.

For an organization to become or remain dynamic, it must invest in technology resources and, above all, create a culture of staff development, training, and continuous learning. Building this culture of continuous learning leads effective organizations to achieving results (see Figure 9.4). Staff development is important to building competencies and achieving results.

PERFORMANCE ACCOUNTABILITY TO ACHIEVE RESULTS

We have discussed the importance of staff assessment and planning as well as the value of training. The expected result of these activities is enhanced staff performance. Management cannot expect to achieve results with staff that is not fully competent. When management identifies and addresses gaps in staff development, it is then that they begin to build staff competence. How will management be able to measure the effectiveness of the assessment, planning, and training process? The outcome must be staff efficiently and effectively achieving results. One may think that is an ambitious statement, in assuming the process will yield that level of achievement. Since leadership is ultimately responsible for the results, it is incumbent upon them to be good stewards of the talent that is entrusted to them (Drucker, 1990).

Drucker (1986) states that costs are not the only measurement for results, but instead, the relationship between effort and results. For staff to have a clear understanding of their role in achieving results, management must clearly identify and communicate performance expectations. Performance goals are signs of accomplishment that engage and empower (Katzenbach & Smith, 1993). Metzenbaum (2006) believes that goal-setting can be a driving force for motivating people. Staff

Staff Development Plan

Name: _____   Date: _____

Department: _____

Supervisor: _____

Areas for Development	Learning Action	Completion Dates
Generalist and Specialization Job Performance Skill Competencies	Identify and engage in appropriate on the job generalist and specialization skill competencies training webinars, seminars, workshops, or conferences	
Communication Skills	Join Toastmasters International Identify and engage in webinar, seminar, workshop in communication, both written and verbal	
Time Management	Develop tool for setting and meeting timelines Identify and engage in time management webinar, seminar or workshop	
Performance Management	Identify and engage in key generalist and specialization performance management on the job training workshops, webinars, seminars or conferences.	

FIGURE 9.4. Staff Development Plan

must participate in creating their performance goals and understand how their individual performance contributes to the team, the overall department, and the organization as a whole (OPM, 2001).

So, what is the key to staff achieving results? When setting performance goals, it is important to remember they must be clear, concise, and measurable. Performance goals should not be broad or easy to achieve; they need to be specific and challenging to motivate performance (Metzenbaum, 2006). Remember that old saying: what gets measured, gets done. While leadership is responsible for identifying the right results to achieve, staff must be accountable for meeting their performance goals.

Staff Performance Scorecard

Name: _____   Date: _____

Department: _____

Supervisor: _____

Focus	Goals/Objectives	Measures	Outcome Metrics
Client Perspective			
Delivers client centered services	Enhance client satisfaction through goal attainment	Client Surveys and interviews	Client responses reflects pleasure of services received and identifies satisfaction with the direction of treatment and services
Ensure Client access to needed services	Engage clients, complete service plans, deliver services identified in plan	Use progress notes to document client responses to services	Maintain expected staff/client caseload ratios as budgeted while ensuring that all clients established services plans are being fully implemented and pursuing positive behavior change
Clients are achieving service aims and objectives	Clients either achieve a portion, most, or all service plan objectives	Staff maintain weekly log of client goal attainment while documenting client progress as often as services are delivered and assessed for behavior change.	Staff record and demonstrate client goal attainment data for entire caseload and report percentage of goal attainment for each client in weekly supervision using self anchored data logs detailing client case management objectives /treatment goals met, partially met, still in progress, and not achieved status
Financial Performance			
Staff is maintaining budgeted caseload standards	Delivers services within budgeted guidelines	Staff documents services provided and timely completes all required paper work to support accurate billing statements generated by the business office to funding source	The progress notes and billing forms are consistent with monthly caseload projections and reimbursement requests generated to the funding source by the agency business office

FIGURE 9.5. Continued

Quality Assurances Practices			
Staff ensure daily record keeping by tracking and monitoring whether the correct forms and documentation has been performed to reflect expected staff performance as contracted between the funder and agency provider.	Ensure staff performance is performed as contracted and where skill competency deficiencies are observed then engage in a staff development modification program of training to eliminate staff skill deficiencies; where staff skills are not the issue but lack of timely supervision is the issue then arrange performance feedback weekly to adhere to the principle of what gets monitored gets done!	On Thursday afternoons staff should complete weekly time management plans by using job description on each Thursday late afternoon as time to check in and complete a checklist to assess what was done during the first 4 days of the week. As the week is evaluated the staff should plan what realistically can be done the next day (Friday) to end the week while completing a detailed job duties things to done schedule for the next week. This should be repeated weekly each Thursday.	Set a performance completion standard of 80% or better. Review the assessment data from the weekly evaluation of the time management performance management plan and determine if what you are doing is what is written as policy and procedure and adherence to best practices and agreements with supervision. Review the process in supervision for feedback and planning support from the program supervisor.
Staff Development			
Staff should use their job descriptions as a self assessment checklist to assess staff generalist and specialization skill competencies	Pursue supervisory support to arrange on the job training supports to enhance skill competencies and reduce staff performance skill competency deficiencies	Participate in a program of learning and training codified through a staff development plan that uses pretest and post test measures to assess for enhance of generalist and specialization skill competencies that supports the effective delivery of services and programs aimed at establishing positive and sustainable behavior change and service effectiveness with client consumers receiving agency and community based services.	Compare skill competencies assessed on pre and post tests while aiming for higher post tests performance ratings that would be achieved through implementing a staff development plan and series of trainings.

FIGURE 9.5. Continued

In setting performance goals to achieve results, Labovitz and Rosansky (1997) put it best:

> What managers decide to measure sends a signal to everyone that that is important. That signal drives behavior of employees and that behavior ultimately creates the business culture that we end up with. Our goal is to create a culture that is naturally self-correcting and self-aligning, therefore we need to be careful about what we measure. (p. 139)

Within some organizations, staff performance goals are often structured as both individual and team contributions to results, in which case those results are also

Service Coordination			
Ensure continuity of services for clients receiving services in multiple agencies	establish eligibility for each service and program the client is enrolled in and get a contact person who is responsible for the service the client is receiving through a community partner to establish a memorandum of understanding as to which provider will serve as the lead agency to coordinate the plan of multiple service accountability to avoid fragmented and gaps in services and to support the efforts of the client in pursuing wellbeing.	Include in the memoranda of understanding a joint provider checklist of both individual and shared agreements on activities and tasks by each provider.	Conduct weekly discussions with the client to gauge what kind of joint service efforts may maximize their motivation for engaging in services. Assess if clients seen by multiple agencies have agreed to an established memoranda of understanding that includes their voice and input. Also, assess if whether a one stop schedule of co-located service provision has been established between providers to share resources and build trusting alliances and nurturing support of the client efforts in navigating across service multiple providers.

FIGURE 9.5. Staff Performance Scorecard

linked to the department goals. Performance goals should be structured in a tiered format, from the executive level to management, to first-line supervision and individual contributor. It may also be necessary to include performance goals that span departments. One department of an organization may be responsible for a program or service design, while another is tasked with their implementation. The cross-functional performance goal should link design and implementation in the outcome. For example, a performance goal could require monthly collaborative meetings between departments to review expected milestones and identify a minimum of two program or service improvements each quarter. This cross-functional performance goal engages two different departments in investing in continuous improvement, which benefits the organization and the clients served. Kaplan and Norton (2001) describe this cross-functional performance as part of a *Balanced Scorecard*, which allows linkages across organizational silos. The idea of a Balanced Scorecard is used in many organizations. Utilizing a Scorecard engages management as well as staff to collaborate on how they will achieve the organization's overall strategic objectives. It is often clear that no one department or unit has complete influence over the outcomes: they are often bound by processes. Yet their accountability is not linked to the outcome. Metzenbaum (2006) believes that goals and measures are powerful and can drive behavioral change. Goals provide focus and affect attitudes and effort, while measures support goals and engage staff in seeking effective options (see Figure 9.5). The Staff Performance Scorecard allows individuals to focus on their outcomes and provides a framework to drive for results.

Staff Performance Scorecard Assessment

Name: _____   Date: _____

Department: _____   Rating: _____

Supervisor: _____

Assessment Ratings-The following guidelines are to be used in selecting the appropriate rating:

1	2	3	4	5	N/A
Unsatisfactory	Marginal	Meets Requirements	Exceeds Requirements	Exceptional	Not Applicable

Focus	Outcome Metric	Results	Rating (1 2 3 4 5)
Delivers client centered services	Client responses reflects pleasure of services received and identifies satisfaction with the direction of treatment and services		
Ensure Client access to needed services	Maintain expected staff/client caseload ratios as budgeted while ensuring that all clients established services plans are being fully implemented and pursuing positive behavior change		
Clients are achieving service aims and objectives	Staff record and demonstrate client goal attainment data for entire caseload and report percentage of goal attainment for each client in weekly supervision using self anchored data logs detailing client case management objectives /treatment goals met, partially met, still in progress, and not achieved status		
Staff is maintaining budgeted caseload standards	The progress notes and billing forms are consistent with monthly caseload projections and reimbursement requests generated to the funding source by the agency business office		

FIGURE 9.6. Continued

Staff ensure daily record keeping by tracking and monitoring whether the correct forms and documentation has been performed to reflect expected staff performance as contracted between the funder and agency provider.	Set a performance completion standard of 80% or better. Review the assessment data from the weekly evaluation of the time management performance management plan and determine if what you are doing is what is written as policy and procedure and adherence to best practices and agreements with supervision. Review the process in supervision for feedback and planning support from the program supervisor.		
Staff should use their job descriptions as a self assessment checklist to assess staff generalist and specialization skill competencies	Compare staff skill competencies assessed on pre and post tests while aiming for higher post tests performance ratings that would be achieved through implementing a staff development plan and series of trainings		
Ensure continuity of services for clients receiving services in multiple agencies	Conduct weekly discussions with the client to gauge what kind of joint service efforts may maximize their motivation for engaging in services. Assess if clients seen by multiple agencies have agreed to an established memoranda of understanding that includes their voice and input . Also, assess if whether a one stop schedule of co-located service provision has been established between providers to share resources and build trusting alliances and nurturing support of the client efforts in navigating across service multiple providers.		

FIGURE 9.6. Staff Performance Scorecard Assessment

Conclusion

The goal of any organization is to succeed in operating as efficiently and effectively as possible and to ensure that clients are provided the best programs and services available to meet their ever-changing needs. But, to do this, management must invest in its greatest asset: its staff. Hecht and Ramsey (2002) agree that financial, program, and service measures don't provide a clear picture of an organization's most important asset, its people. The three areas of assessment and planning, training and development, as well as performance accountability are an investment that management must make in order to realize the organization's strategic outcomes. Those organizations that believe only when staff, vision, organizational values, clients' needs, and infrastructure are in place then measuring performance by Balanced Scorecards will appropriately guide the necessary organizational priorities (Hecht & Ramsey, 2002).

As stated by Hecht and Ramsey, Balanced Scorecards developed by Kaplan and Norton focus on the past and present performance measures which are based on the organization's vision and strategy (2002) (see Figure 9.6). It is often said you can't manage what you can't measure and evaluating performance key to identifying areas of strengths and areas for improvements. The Staff Performance Scorecard Assessment below is a tool to evaluate and measure the teams overall performance.

Many organizations have strived for excellence and world-class status only to fail. Bolman and Deal (1997) site Collins and Porras (1994), who identified a vital characteristic of organizations that were extremely successful and established long-term success. Those organizations that guided and inspired their staff and perceived pure profit as a necessity, but not the sole purpose of the organization, were far more successful.

Bolman and Deal speak of an organization as having a "soul": a "soul is a bedrock sense of who we are, what we care about, and what we believe in" (p. 340). These authors believe that for an organization to have a "soul," it must believe and invest in its staff.

Interpersonal Influence

FUNCTIONS OF AN OFFENSIVE WIDE RECEIVER
AS A LARGER SYSTEM PRACTICE STRATEGY FOR
LEVERAGING POLITICS, COMPETING POWER BASES,
AND SOCIAL SERVICE DELIVERY

As far back as Burton Gummer (1990), politics and political behavior are value added to macro social work practice and play significant roles. It is our contention that politics in and of itself is not a bad thing. It is how people use it that makes for ineffective and unethical practices. The thoughtful use of influence, persuasion, and social, economic, and political capital to the integrative practice of social service delivery has received little attention in the social work practice curricula, broadly defined. In this chapter, we address that major omission by discussing the significance and contributions of interpersonal influence, social capital, and political networks on enhancing the design, implementation, and integration of effective social services in larger systems.

The role of a *liaison*, by definition, is to connect, link, forge relationships, be in the appropriate associations, have the right connections, and achieve cooperation between stakeholders and key participants. It is the responsibility of management and staff to use this role thoughtfully in order to use influence in professional practice in a way that benefits the organization and client-consumers alike. To be effective, the influencer needs to be fluent and competent inside and outside the system, as well as between the systems. Essential skills and capabilities of the influencer include the ability to conduct environmental scanning, information analysis and processing, problem-solving, quick decision-making, navigation, use of social and economic capital, and implementation. They represent features of a successful interpersonal influence management framework. Digestible, chewable, do-able, and actionable responsive tasks comprise the job description of the influencer. It is the influencer's chief job to use the political landscape of the task environment to get the job done as efficiently and effectively as practical.

Program implementation is as much a function of interpersonal influence as is any act of social interaction involving the interdependence of people, their skills, abilities, motivations, disincentives, and contingent actions. The extent to which people standardize a practice has much to do with the influence of the social network and the politics of the informal network in an organization. If the early adopters of a new procedure or practice find that it does not modify their professional sense of self, it requires very little interruption in what they do, and it is agreeable to their peer colleagues, then it is more likely that they will adopt and standardize an innovation.

In this instance, getting people to engage in a desired activity is getting them to believe in something that makes sense to them and that they hold as truth. The sociopolitical nature of this scenario requires that we understand the nature of informal network political participation and the clout of staff and management. The informal network determines the extent of resistance to change old habits and adopt newer and innovative approaches. In business, resistance to change is handled through what is now referred to as *change management*. It involves business coaches and consultants hired to help management assist employees in managing the chaotic nature involved in reorganization and organizational change.

In social services, change management, participatory management, and team management have become important due to the financial limitations imposed by hiring executive coaches and consultants for nonprofit executives. Change from within organizations involved change champions, change catalysts, and change processes (Resnick, 1978). It is a galvanizing experience to empower the lower echelons to join upper management as teammates and partners in organizational change, principally driven from within and from the bottom rung of the organization with administrative sanction (Briggs, 2001).

It will not matter if change is initiated from the bottom or top of the organization. In a culture of learning, organizational practices will require that managers and staff committed to transformation be cognizant of threats to change and the adoption of innovations. Independent of the motivation for change, which result from learning through continuous quality improvement, staff need to know ways to navigate the political land mines within organizations. These threats interfere with pursuing the implementation of sound management and prudent and well-established practices. The staff needs to be as calm as doves in their disposal of agency policy, but strategically intentional as owls and serpents. In this context, it is recommended that staff and the people who supervise them be mindful. They must carefully monitor barriers that need to be removed, while continuing to strive to improve ways of patterning how to do accountably perform their roles and responsibilities by watching others who are successful (refer to the section on Theories of Styles of Leadership for Integrative Practice in Chapter 8 for a further discussion).

Media and Digital Information Literacy

The retrieval of information required to perform duties and responsibilities comes in many forms. Yet, lately, information seems to be primarily accessible electronically through media and digital venues. Chief among the required skills is knowing the path of least resistance that lies between the information processes of idea generation and outcome achievement. Staff and management need a logic model conception of the plan of action that ultimately will result in their intended program effects. Failure to have it means that management and staff lacks a clear vision of what to expect as they pursue program implementation with the intention of achieving behavior change. At almost all points, it is the responsibility of staff and management to behave as informed skeptics. It is necessary to consider what could go wrong as you plan what to do and how to pursue its achievement. This is where the area of informatics could support the agenda of practitioners in larger system with access to a range of useful information. In this vein, a partnership between a school of social work and a college of engineering may prove to be useful as well as fortuitous.

Analysis and Processing

To ascertain where we hope to end, we pose a few important questions so that we may set a clear course of action. For example, given what I am supposed to do, is the road clear ahead for me to pursue what I need to do to achieve service effectiveness? If there is something blocking my way, what is it? Can we get around this challenge or overcome it so we can push on to do what is expected? In some cases, the obstacle can be direct care staff, co-workers, and management colleagues; lack or inappropriate use of resources; or the lack of executive management support and sanction of the change and next steps.

Environmental Scanning Through Use of Evidence

Environmental scanning allows a person to constantly survey and assess his or her situation prior to acting prematurely and ill-advisably. Any staff member in an organization, who is effective, draws upon a variety of information from their primary and extended social networks and key relationships with internal and external stakeholders. They do this to provide resources and supports to engage client-consumer systems as they pursue their primary duties, with the aim of achieving better functioning individuals, families, and communities. They also get information to navigate the organizational politics that interfere with their expected performance, process, intended outcomes, program effects, and impacts.

Recently, studies have shown the positive contributions of agency gossip on reducing organizational liabilities and missteps by employees in need of human resource sanctions. Feedback and information generated through informal networks
can also aid in giving information about certain issues, people, and conditions to
avoid when seeking to complete a task or gather support on a particular issue.

Implementation

The central question driving program implementation is: How can management
get the job done efficiently as well as effectively? Since many programs and services
are provided through interdisciplinary teams and groups, there is a certain degree
of cooperation, good will, and respect for diversity in passion and focus that comes
with the delivery of social and human services.

LEARNING THROUGH APPLICATION

Since everyone's task contributes to one holistic behavior change approach, it will
become increasingly important to learn while performing from the data collected,
which tracks the singular and additive contributions of staff to client-consumer
behavior change and client-consumer problem areas. Learning while applying
involves watching the staff and client reactions to programming, observing the
contingencies responsible for the desired client behavior changes, and noting the
impact of the client's behavior in the agency, among family members, and in community settings.

PROBLEM-SOLVING

Staff and management need to be competent in contigent thinking in order to
handle people, situations, and a lack of resources that may create barriers. To get
to where I need to be to achieve Z through doing X, how can I get X done, despite
the presence or lack of availability of Y, which is blocking me from achieving Z? In
another way of realizing and articulating the possible unattractive consequences of
a decision, the staffer or manager needs to predict catastrophic events or issues by
completing an "if-then" proposition. For example, "*if* I engage in X, despite knowledge of the presence or availability of Y, *then*, realistically, what do I expect about
the occurrence of Z, given the aforementioned realities?"

QUICK AND PRUDENT DECISION-MAKING

There are many instances where time is a luxury you cannot access, and in order for
you to get something done requires that you act now and judiciously. This is not a
new problem or set of scenarios unfamiliar to staff and management in nonprofits.

As a way of avoiding an unwanted consequence or disaster, staff and management are often faced with dilemmas which require that they choose the best alternatives and options available that would cause the least harm and risk.

NAVIGATION

It is hard to imagine anyone disagreeing with the assumption that if you knew better, you would do better. Navigating the terrain of social service delivery and implementation requires a fund of knowledge about people and their learning styles, their incentives and drives, their disincentives and punishers, as well as their reinforcers. What works for some will not work for others; this is a reality. Being an effective influencer is a characteristic of personal leadership that every member of the organization must possess, demonstrate, and rely on as they pursue the vision of achieving service effectiveness.

Establishing buy-in by others about a clear and concise vision and how that individual can contribute will determine the extent to which people will help you achieve your goals and outcomes. At times, people will join you if what you want to do aligns with their values. But, in other cases, it will require that you incentivize their behavior to gain their engagement, support, and participation.

USE OF SOCIAL AND ECONOMIC CAPITAL

Informal networks are chief among the many ports of information and transfer of knowledge, and they are a good place to exercise the development of personal leadership skills that enable the effective use of interpersonal influence in the workplace. Seeking innovation, improvement, and enhancement in programs and agency functioning through getting others to accept and promote your ideas about change is tied to how others view you, both as a dependable follower and skillful leader with respect to style and accomplishments. The staff or manager who effectively leverages political and economic clout is able to use persuasion and influence in a strategic and deliberate way. People with these skills negotiate agreements and settlements in times of conflict. These people have taken time to establish the political clout and experience needed to achieve successful personal leadership qualities.

Staff and managers with effective personal leadership skills use information and individual and group dynamics as they pursue and execute job duties and responsibilities. Agency leaders who are able to gain buy-in and commitment from others in the work place to adopt a particular way of thinking or improve job performance and engage in additional activities are rare and are keepers. Those who are skilled at getting staff to change well-established work routines and sustain effective staff performances, qualify as having essential performance- and evidence-based management skills. They possess the capacity to use evidence to lead teams, incentivize behaviors, and aid others in the development of participatory management competencies. Enhancing effective interpersonal influence and motivational skills among the team is the most efficient way to ensure that management and staff possess training in altering and modifying behaviors that are counterindicated to the goals of the organization.

Developing the team's competencies to become client-consumer and family-centered is an essential skill and agency asset (Friesen, Koroloff, Walker, & Briggs, 2011). Agency leaders who are able to coordinate and build healthy and productive work relationships, as well as being able to cooperate with others in the pursuit of agency aims, are invaluable, and these key competencies need to be included as training outcomes. They serve as important training aims to pursue when working with teams of staff and managers to improve personal leadership and follower skills. To be an effective personal leader, one must be effective in being a meaningful and successful follower. The ability to play fairly and squarely in the sand box is a good test of this important competency. In many academies, the faculty would fail this particular test. This is due primarily to popular opinion that what often makes an excellent scholar and university faculty member is their apparent failure as young children to play well with others in the sand box!

In agency practice, the ultimate achievement of service effectiveness, which is reflected in the better and optimal functioning of the people, families, and communities served, depends on building and fortifying mutual respect, cooperation, shared responsibility, and the implementation of a "getting to results" system of accountability (Wandserman et al., 2000). It has been the first author's experience that it is easier to achieve this in agency practice as opposed to academic units, departments, and universities. In agency practice, managers are not subject to the benefits of academic freedom, which contributes to the failed shared governance experiences of the academy. The "herding kittens" mentality is pervasive to academic cultures but not a typical experience in community based agency cultures.

Alternatively, the agency culture and the programs and services that are contained within them become embedded into the regulation and discretionary behaviors, the personality, and the help-giving behaviors of staff and managers. This co-dependency requires that everyone involved in those transactions that lead to service effectiveness learn ways to minimize obstacles and maximize the participation and full cooperation of all. Clarity of purpose, clear coordination, cooperation, and communicating effectively among all parties involved, from the initial engagement through follow-up processes, need to be emphasized as essential characteristics of staffers and managers successfully demonstrating interpersonal influence skill competencies. All in all, staffers and managers with useful and successful interpersonal influence and personal leadership skills have acquired the talent to work cross-culturally and understand that goal achievement is an interdependent set of processes that shape a series of strategically anticipated milestones and outcomes.

Establishing competencies in interpersonal influence and personal leadership behaviors requires a foundational set of organizing principles and agency values that must be upheld, both as personal and organizational mandates. This requires transparency, integrity, shared risk, and shared governance for driving team management. Staff and managers who hold these values and principles as guides learn how to artfully and authentically gain the respect of teammates through competent and regular use of policies and procedures. Also, these same hard-working employees know how to use the formal and informal networks of an agency to pursue and achieve their aims and daily responsibilities. These kinds of employees do not depend on random events and spurts of activities to demonstrate the care with which they pursue their tasks. Instead, they carefully achieve their intended program effects by engaging people and others in what they hope to accomplish by leveraging and sharing the benefits that will accrue. Tools used by them include, the skillful and frequent use of the five steps of evidence-based practice and the five steps of evidence-based management approaches to learn from the problem-solving and decision-making experiences that come with the pursuit of positive results.

Achieving interpersonal influence comes with gaining the respect of others and the belief that people will engage in tasks and follow your leadership. This responsibility comes with helping others achieve their personal and professional best in their job duties, responsibilities, and ultimate outcomes. Helping others by engaging in joint and teamwork planning, goal-setting, transparent quality assurance, and random focus group evaluation sessions, as well as carefully using and learning from previous performance, helps shape future performance. This makes the use of evidence for tracking and monitoring a standard practice routine.

11 }

Human Resource Development

Increasingly, workforce diversity has become a popular human resource theme in social work administration and management. The literature in this area highlights its contribution as broad-based and multi-faceted. Gummer (1998), in his review of management literature on diversity, states that the definition of diversity reaches far beyond the original Affirmative Action Program definitions. Currently, there are myths and misunderstandings about what has been reported regarding labor force diversity in the United States. Gummer outlines the first myth as being that workforce diversity will dramatically increase over the next decade, while the labor force participation of non-Hispanic white males will decline.

For more than a century, the participation of white women in the workforce has been steadily increasing while the participation of African American women has also increased, but at a slower rate. In recent years, overall women's movement into the workforce is slowing and the focus on immigration is more visible. Gummer points out that while there are problems regarding the diversity of the overall workforce, organizations are nonetheless faced with having to incorporate a means of working to increase diversity and diverse ways of thinking that reflect the diverse backgrounds and perspectives of client-consumers. Organizations that engage staff and incorporate their varied perspectives into the development of policy, programs, and goals establish an environment of diverse thinking that opens the doors to increasing diversity of all kinds. This review of literature observes two perspectives of leaders and managers of larger systems: (1) organizations and community systems are proactive in exploring diversity and its effect on the workforce and how work is done, and (2) organizations as well as communities are encouraging and allowing open discussions on cultural competence.

In exploring the concept of diversity as a human resource development theme in an organization, you must first look at the nature of an organization and its processes. Organizational processes are defined as group or team activities, decision-making, and access to vital organizational information and resources. The development of the inclusion-exclusion concept by Mor Barak and Cherin (1998) discusses a link between race, ethnicity, gender, and age that reveals how involved the employee is in the organizational processes. Mor Barak (2000), expanding on her original article, "A Tool to Expand Organizational Understanding of Workforce Diversity: Exploring a Measure of Inclusion-Exclusion," with co-author David A. Cherin, explains that "demographic changes in the American population, coupled with civil rights legislation and affirmative action programs have created an unprecedented diversity in the American workforce" (p. 7). With this diverse workforce, Mor Barak broadens her support of the inclusion-exclusion research to identify this theory as both personal and organizational in its outcome. The author identifies four workforce propositions: (1) individuals with diversity characteristics are more likely to experience exclusion than are those who belong to the "mainstream" in work organizations, (2) there are interaction effects among diversity characteristics with respect to levels of exclusion experienced—individuals with more diversity characteristics are more likely to experience higher levels of exclusion, (3) diversity characteristics and perceptions of inclusion-exclusion are correlates of personal outcomes, and (4) diversity characteristics and perception of inclusion-exclusion are correlates of the organizational outcomes (Mor Barak, 2000).

Although each of these workforce diversity themes is integral to the human resource agenda of social service human service agencies, they do not include an emphasis on the generational aspects of workforce diversity. In corporate America, the proliferation and concentration on generational diversity has been a human resource theme with a focus on research, skill development, and implementation as far back as the early 1990s. These, as well as other human resource strategies, such as downsizing, collaborative partnerships, reorganizing, and retraining of employees are important strategies used by social administrators to meet the needs of the client base they serve. All in all, these strategies have presented a few challenges to leaders of social service agencies. Often, the human resource changes just described are prompted by budget cuts and policy amendments. These changes affect the clients who are the beneficiaries of organization policies and practices, as well as the employees who provide services to clients and act as organization stewards. This crucial relationship points to the value of enriching human resources as an important strategy to use in preparing staff to skillfully navigate change and manage and enhance their overall performance. This chapter provides a perspective for leaders of organizations to consider as they organize their agency's human resources activities. Without careful attention to the support and resource needs of its greatest asset—the employees—leaders of social service agencies may not be equipped to arrest the hosts of issues which are certain to follow. In this chapter, we emphasize four crucial dimensions: (1) the correlates, (2) causes, and (3) consequences of effective human resources, and, (4) as a long-range investment and human resource strategy, age diversity is highlighted and its implications for workforce development in social service organizations are examined. Each of these key dimensions involves a discussion of unique and overlapping factors that contribute a practical knowledge base for administrative practitioners. We believe that a focus on these key dimensions and their associated factors is important to any effort aimed at sustaining a quality workforce in larger systems.

Correlates of Effective Human Resources

The strength and ultimate success of an organization rests strongly on the commitment and loyalty of its employees. Peter Drucker (1990) states that "People determine the performance capacity of an organization. No organization can do better then the people it has" (p. 145). The question is: How do you gain loyalty and commitment from your employees? The answer is simple: Meet the needs of your employees. Workforce commitment is influenced by five key factors, according to Educational Business Publications (2003). They are (1) benefits and compensation; (2) organizational culture, leadership (for further substantive discussion about the influence of leadership, see Chapter 8), and direction; (3) management of change; (4) employee selection, training, and development (see Chapter 9 on Staff Development for a detailed discussion); and (5) work–life balance.

Benefits and compensation are important, especially in times of economic uncertainty, rising unemployment, and fear. All of these factors motivate people to get as much as they can now. Employees expect their benefit package to be competitive and their salary commensurate with the market. An appropriate performance-based merit increase plan is also important in providing compensation. Benefit packages, especially for healthcare benefits, are often convoluted. Some healthcare plans offer dental and no vision; others require that employees meet at least a minimum individual or family deductibles prior to the medical benefits actually paying a claim. Employers are responsible for clearly communicating to their employees the plans that are offered. Employees, more often than not, count on their employer to provide their retirement and future savings. Some companies provide seminars for employees on financial planning. Enron and WorldCom taught people valuable lessons about diversifying investments and not having faith in the future of companies. Employees want their "piece of the rock" now, and if they can get some extra for the future, that is all the better. While the salience of and subscription to this perspective fluctuates across generations, if current trends continue, we will see more people trying to get the best salary and benefits and also looking to work a second job to meet increases in the costs of living. Money and healthcare coverage are not the only ways to keep employees, but they are certainly an important area that requires careful consideration and planning. Employers often struggle to identify the right healthcare packages that will meet the needs of their employees. Wise employers will conduct employee surveys prior to evaluating their current benefits package for changes. This is an opportunity to gain insight into the current needs of employees. This choice becomes even more difficult when the organization is small in size.

The organization should also consider other benefits such as childcare, flex schedules, commuting compensation, parental leave, and family care. It is also key for human resource specialists to understand the broad range of the ages of their employees when choosing benefit packages. While most employees value retirement benefits and healthcare, the group identified as Generation X (born between 1960 and 1980) would rather believe in the "the existence of UFOs than in the likelihood of a Social Security system to support them when they retire" (Hisey, 2003). This generation will not operate out of the same employment agreement that their parents used: loyalty to the organization; "work hard, long hours and your employer will reward you with a job for life and pay increases." Generation X's values are different. They have seen the aftermath of their parent's loyalty and have developed a new employment agreement: acquire skills needed to perform, perform at or above expectancy, promote company values, then invest in my development, recognize my contribution, and compensate me accordingly with a share in the company's success (Hisey, 2003). While the profession of social work may not have a structure that would support the concept of profit-sharing, Generation X employees' perceptions and expectations should be considered when outlining benefit opportunities.

The Role of Leadership in Developing Human Resources

As previously highlighted in Chapter 8, leadership is another key factor that impacts the quality and retention of employees. Effective leaders keep their focus on achieving results with few or no costly errors. They are aware of their own biases and judgments. They pay attention to different perspectives of staff and supervisors. They are able to convey the ideological as well as organizational factors that may be contributing to the opposite ways of viewing and addressing a particular responsibility. Also, these leaders depend on conflict to inspire the team to work collectively toward problem-solving and to hold each other accountable for maintaining higher standards as they pursue a shared vision (Lencioni, 2002). Open, clear, and direct communication from leadership is also critical. They must be able to communicate the mission and vision of the organization such that each employee understands his or her role and responsibility for the success of the organization.

Effective leaders understand that their role is also as a mentor. Chemers (1997) states, "One of the leader's most important responsibilities is the development and direction of subordinates' goal-oriented capabilities and activities" (p. 155). The development of employees is essential to the survival and success of the organization. Some managers direct their employees in a dictatorial manner that leaves employees feeling as if they are not allowed to contribute. Being able to contribute allows the employee to feel responsible and to take ownership. An ineffective leader is often the cause of an organization losing qualified and productive people. Drucker (1990) states, "The most important task of an organization's leader is to anticipate crisis" (p. 7). Employees expect leaders of an organization to communicate the onset of a possible crisis. This allows them to participate in preparing for action rather than respond to the damage.

Employee selection, retention, training, and professional development leading to career advancement are essential investments to staff performance, quality control, and staff morale. In the process of new hires, organizations start by screening the applications. In most cases, this process requires the screener to review the applications and attempt to match the job description and requirements with the potential candidates. This can be a painstaking activity. It is important that the screener have an outline of the specific characteristics critical to the position. All too often, staff is hired hastily to fulfill a need, instead of the organization taking the time to find the best fit. Some staff are political hires: this strategy can be useful in some respects, while in others, counterproductive. Staff as political appointments may increase leverage among funding sources, politicians, and key community players. Just having them connected to the organization may increase your fundraising outcomes as well as your bargaining and negotiation power in other important venues. As useful as they are, political appointments may be a manager's worst nightmare. If not seasoned team players, they create a toll on management. They can become involved in unproductive conflicts and may be more trouble than beneficial. Hiring good staff is not dependent on politics. It is driven more by experience and skills involving job search and job matching and, sometimes, good old fashion luck. Finding the right person for the job requires advertising an attractive and challenging job with lucrative benefits, and the feeling of a good match as perceived by management and the job applicant. Organizations today are realizing that more emphasis should be placed on the retention, training, and development of their employees. Replacing staff can be as costly as 150% of the salary of the person leaving (Branch, 1998). Why, you might ask? Sometimes, even with all the up-front effort in the hiring process, organizations still face the cost of the new staff member being unproductive in the first few months and the existing staff taking responsibility for on-the-job training, which causes lower overall productivity. Retention strategies are a way of keeping the cycle of knowledge moving in your organization. It is similar to passing on precious family recipes from one generation to the next: different cooks, but the same love and passion for the dish.

Staff training is as valuable as staff selection and retention, as thoroughly discussed in Chapter 9. For most organizations, staff development falls under the responsibility of human resources. They are charged with not only hiring staff, but, in partnership with management, they must ensure staff that are well trained to accomplish their performance outcome. Effective staff training can result in positive change, but what about instances in which training is inconsequential—when it achieves no observed changes to a performance problem? Sometimes employees need supervision and performance feedback, instead of wasting time and money in unnecessary training programs. Still, other employees benefit from training experiences. As previously discussed in Chapter 9, McCracken and Corrigan (2004) suggest two approaches to effective staff training and diffusion of innovations from theory to actual practice: educational and organizational approaches. Each of these perspectives provides staff with essential skill opportunities and administrative supports as resources to do a better job by learning practical ways of adopting evidence-based practices. Staff who are trained using the best knowledge available are rare and valuable commodities. Those trained in evidence-based management approaches are extremely hard to find in social services, as well as in other disciplines. Because of their result- and research-based orientation, these particular staff need to know that they can depend on leadership to be reciprocal. These staff raise the question: "If I do my very best, will everyone else around me be expected to do the same thing?" Trained staff keep management accountable as management keeps them on their toes, too! These are the staff that we invest in and depend on to be team leaders, demonstrating guiding and leading behaviors for others to see and adopt.

Staff training is useful and especially important to bring new theories and methodologies to seasoned staff, as well as giving younger staff an opportunity to put more tools in their tool belt. As organizations downsize and combine positions to stabilize during the present economy, more demands are made on staff to perform. What you may have been asked and were skilled to do today may not be what you are asked to step in and help with tomorrow. Ulrich (1997a, 1997b) discusses four types of staff development activities: (1) systematic management curricula, (2) developmental experiences, (3) action-learning training activities and (4) staff who work in teams, discussing projects and team mechanics. It is critical to have your training topics as diverse as your staff. Often, certain training is mandatory in order to fulfill a management objective. To balance mandatory training, offering a menu of diverse topics provides the staff with the opportunity to pick and choose.

Helping staff to establish a healthy balance between work and home life is just as fortifying and supportive. Teaching staff to balance the demands of the job and home life involves setting professional boundaries. Leaders who teach staff to protect themselves and who monitor them for burnout communicate a message to staff that has far-reaching implications. It informs the staff that they are valuable and admired by administration for their work efforts and talents. The encouragement by management to get sufficient rest and respite validates management's commitment to the staff's emotional health. In most organizations, human resources has an employee assistance program that supports staff with resources from crisis support, counseling, and work–life resources. This is certain to positively impact staff satisfaction. This balance allows staff to view home life as vital to their overall development as employees. It allows them to re-energize and approach their job rested and under less stress than staff who cannot get enough reinforcement for being workaholics.

If these conditions are addressed and continuously reviewed and updated, the impact will positively affect organizational factors and processes. Thus, human resources plays a principal function in sustaining as well as expanding organizational capabilities and experiences (Ulrich, 1997b). Since no two staff members are exactly alike, their unique talents and performances, as well as their individual merits, contribute to the organization's strengths. Also, what gives organizations a feather in their cap is their leadership capacity to manage a team of diverse people to produce desirable organizational outcomes. Although emphasized earlier, organizations that are run well and produce reasonable results are those that hire leaders with certain abilities and experiences. Chief among these talents are the capacities to self-regulate, lead and manage conflict, inspire organizational buy-in, and manage the assets and goals of the organization. They do this by using ethics, earning trust, and pursuing sound human resource practices.

Unfortunately, the concept of human resources has not been viewed with the same appreciation and as user-friendly by some organizational staff. For these staff, human resources engenders the same types of feelings and thoughts one gets when one is called into the boss's office without any prior notice of what is about to take place. It is like being called into the principal's office. This perspective on human services is not uncommon. Often in an organization, when the words "human resources" are mentioned, the initial reaction is typically negative. From the staff perspective, interaction with human resources is typically infrequent and necessary only when you have a problem. Management also considers human resources when they have a problem employee. To develop a strong organization and change the negative perception often experienced by staff and human resources, it is important they seek to form a proactive and collaborative partnership. Focusing on staff development and removing barriers enabling them to drive for results.

Age Diversity: Workforce Development Strategy

Since the 1990s, workforce diversity training has become an essential part of the American company's training portfolio. Bell (1997) states that, in 1995, two-thirds of American companies offered a form of diversity training. With the emergence of global markets, American companies have had to become aware of cultural differences and the appropriate way of transacting business with other cultures. Although the word "diversity" usually evokes perceptions of culture, gender, race, and sexual orientation, Sonnenschein (1997) also presents age and physical abilities as areas of diversity. Sonnenschein states that "diversity is the result of a broad range of complex social, political, economic, and other forces that have put in close proximity people who have vastly different orientations, frames of reference, backgrounds, and perspectives" (p. 2). This section explores diversity as it relates to age and its linkage to employee attitudes and how companies could leverage this human capital to improve their overall business performance.

Our workforce demographics are constantly changing and, with this change, is a growing awareness of how vast the misunderstandings and resentments are between the Veterans or traditionalists, the Baby Boomers, and the Generation X employees. This section will only address these three generational groups; Millenials are included in the next section. Data are still being gathered on their impact in the workplace and their influence on an organization. As companies continue to change their operations to remain competitive in today's global economy, more jobs are being affected. Staff are feeling the competition for those few remaining positions. Zemke, Raines, and Filipczak (2000) state that it is no wonder that "there is a growing sense of individual and generational enmity" (p. 2). This resonates in an "every man for himself and God for us all" attitude. The authors go on to say that Veterans and Baby Boomers hold on to what they have achieved through their years of employment and are having to fight to survive in organizations where Generation X employees are eager to make their mark in achievement and advancement. Generations are defined not just by their dates, but also by their collective experiences, thoughts, and feelings (Zemke et al., 2000). These generations must learn to value each other's differences. With this kind of dissension, how productive and competitive can a company be in the local or global market?

To further explore this dynamic, an overview of those making up the Veterans, Baby Boomers, and Generation X is important. First, the Veterans were born between 1922 and 1943, before the end of World War II. To truly understand these employees, you need to understand what experiences shaped their lives: the Great Depression, New Deal, World War II, and the GI Bill. These employees grew up in hard times and believe in hard work, teamwork, traditional values, discipline and obeying authority (Lackey, 2002). The Depression alone, with its bread and soup lines, unemployment, and economic failure, is enough to characterize the struggle that this particular work group had to endure. Zemke, Raines, and Filipczak (2000) state, "When you think of American values, civic pride, loyalty, respect for authority and apple pie," this is what the Veterans represent (p. 18). The Veterans did not have the luxury of television; they relied on radio and newspapers for their up-to-date information. The authors continue by saying that the Veterans' vision and hard work was responsible for rebuilding this country. This generation was the momentum behind the country rising out of the ashes of the Great Depression like a phoenix. They typically did not go to college, but instead figured out ways to make a living in order to take care of their families (Lackey, 2002). During the time of the Veteran, the space program was developed and the United States landed a man on the moon. Vaccines for tetanus, polio, and tuberculosis were created (Zemke et al., 2000). Given all that the Veterans have endured, it is no wonder they are often perceived by Baby Boomers and Generation X employees as being tight with the budget, not willing to take risks, uncomfortable with conflict, and preferring things to be standardized. They are also said to be extremely regimented, impersonal, conservative, focused on the past, in need of too much data, and slower at making decisions (Lancaster & Stillman, 2002). This generation strongly believes in working hard for what they get. Veterans aren't interested in "making waves" in the system; in their day, it was too hard to get a job and you were grateful for it. From a manager's point of view, the Veteran's tenacity, loyalty, and dependability are valuable work ethics (Zemke et al., 2000).

Next, the Baby Boomers were born between 1943 and 1960, after World War II. Boomers represents 32% of the population, are the most college-educated segment, and are considered the most influential generation in America (Briggs, Donovan, Foster, & Mendenhall, 2002). This generation was raised in an environment of opportunity, progress, color TV, sex, drugs, and rock and roll (Lackey, 2002). Baby boomers were the generation of the Civil Rights movement, the Vietnam War, and the concept of "buy now, pay later" (Heselbarth, 1999). Zemke and colleagues (2000) divide the Baby Boomer generation into "first half and second half." The second half is identified as being born in the mid- to late 1950s; they make up the largest population of that generation—3 million more than the first half. The first-halfers are said to be more idealistic, tend to put career first, and are considered workaholics. The authors continue to note that demographers identify that first-halfers born in the 1940s tend to make more money and own more homes than second-halfers. The idea of achievement and success for first-halfers was designer wear, BMWs, and ski trips to Aspen—all "yuppie" stereotypes. The second-halfers, on the other hand, are turned off by yuppie status; they look at the first-halfers as "greedy and materialistic." First-halfers tend to define themselves by their work; Zemke and colleagues state that their "work ethic" and "worth ethics" are synonymous (p. 77). Unlike the first-halfers, these second-halfers are focused on family and enjoy time off. They experienced the first wave of downsizing and tend to share more of a Generation X attitude. Since Veterans spent their time rebuilding America after the war, boomers were able to experience economic prosperity. They could focus on themselves, attend college, challenge authority, debate traditional values, and find out how they could have it all. Larson (2003) says that boomers are good at relationships, extremely driven, and team players. He goes on to say that they don't like conflict, are self-centered, judgmental, and reluctant to go against peers. From a manager's point of view, the Baby Boomers' valuable work ethics are that they work hard and are dedicated, and driven.

Generation X was born between 1960 and 1980. This generation was said to have grown up in the shadow of "The Boom" (Zemke et al., 2000). Generation X is known as the "slacker" generation. During the time of this generation, there was a 40% divorce rate; if they had both parents, then both worked. Their era is characterized by Watergate, MTV, personal computers, microwaves, and economic recessions (Heselbarth, 1999). Bray (2001) states that Generation Xers were our latchkey kids; they had to be emotionally independent and self-reliant. This generation is our most ethnically diverse generation, they are environmentally conscious, steeped in television, not afraid of change, and never take anything for granted (Lackey, 2002). This generation had to develop survival instincts; they witnessed downsizing, layoffs, and pension issues with their parents. They have a tainted view of company loyalty and tend to change jobs on average about every eighteen months (Jurkiewicz, 2000). Generation X is often characterized by Veterans and Baby Boomers as not having a work ethic, being too dependent on technology, and having no loyalty (Smith, 2003). Larson (2003) also states that this generation is impatient, inexperienced, cynical, and needs to develop people skills. He also identifies their assets as being adaptable, creative, technology savvy, and not intimidated by authority. From a manager's point of view, Generation X's technical savvy, adaptability, and creativity are valuable work ethics.

Lancaster and Stillman (2002) state that each generation brings its own set of ideas to a workplace. Each is motivated by events that influenced their life experience. Given the already existing generational issues in the workplace, coupled with today's changing market where staff are facing downsizing, layoffs, restructuring, mergers, and joint ventures, you will find that employees' attitudes of commitment, loyalty, and teamwork are definitely challenged (Educational Business Publications, 2003). The attitude of each staff member impacts the overall workgroup. Most employees have very strong attitudes or emotions about their work, as demonstrated in *Valuing Human Capital,* which discusses a study conducted in the Fall of 2002 (Educational Business Publications, 2003). The purpose of the study was to find out how emotionally connected employees are to their jobs. The workforce demographics of the Fall 2002 study are not discussed in the publication. The data were gathered from 1,100 randomly selected employees from mid- to large-size companies in the United States. The study showed that 55% of employees had negative feelings about their current work experience, 22% had intensely negative feelings, and 23% were intensely positive. The study also identified workload, at 15%, as the largest factor affecting employees' feelings about work (p. 120).

In another survey discussed in *Valuing Human Capital*, employee commitment gaps were explored; Generation X employees (age thirty and under) had a Workforce Commitment Index of 96.1, while their coworkers who were older than thirty, had a score of 102 (p. 8). Given the changing market, which can affect workload, employee commitment, and the Veterans and Baby Boomers who are fighting to survive in companies where Generation X employees are eager to make their mark of achievement and advancement, there is bound to be some modicum of conflict. Employee attitudes are crucial to the success of an organization.

Zemke, Raines, and Filipczak (2000) state that there are "two keys to creating a successful intergenerational workforce: aggressive communication and difference deployment" (p. 153). The authors go on to say that generational differences are based on assumptions. Each generation takes a biased and hostile view of the other. Aggressive communication is self-explanatory, and difference deployment is explained as "the tactical use of employees with different backgrounds, experiences, skills and viewpoints to strengthen project teams, customer contact functions, and at times, whole department units" (p. 154). Sonnenschein (1997) quotes Max DePree: "The simple act of recognizing diversity in corporate life helps us to connect the great variety of gifts that people bring to the work and service of the organization" (p. 65). Organizations that value their employees' differences by looking at them as strengths are generally more successful than those who desire to create a "pasteurized" environment (p. 155). The authors also provide an insight into the attitudes of Veterans, boomers, and Generation X and the world around them.

Table 11.1 is a snapshot of attitudes outlined by Zemke, Raines, and Filipczak (2000).

From a human resources perspective, knowing the demographics of your workforce is just the start to assist managers in developing strategies to manage generations effectively. These strategies should focus on minimizing conflict between generations, allowing each employee to contribute to the work group and positively impact the corporation's bottom line. Ulrich (1997a) discusses the role of human resources as a strategic partner working with front-line managers; this alliance is critical in the process of motivating and encouraging cohesive generational workgroups. Zemke, Raines, and Filipczak (2000) identify five strategies or "ACORN imperatives" that have been successfully used by the management of several companies who have had generational discord (p. 156). The ACORNs are as follows:

- *Accommodate employee differences.* "Treat your employees as you do your customers." Learn about the employees and work to meet their specific needs and preferences. Make an effort to support such issues as scheduling needs, work–life balance, language, and lifestyles.
- *Create workplace choices.* Create an environment that is not regimented, hierarchical, or stagnate. Implement casual dress policies and explore a shorter, less bureaucratic chain of command. Empower staff and allow for humor and a relaxed environment.
- *Operate from a sophisticated management style.* Management should be direct in their communication and approach. Management should be tactful and specific in communicating goals, vision, mission, and measurement. They give their employees feedback, recognition, and praise when appropriate. There are times when managers may ask for input, consultation, and/or consensus. At other times, they may need to make the decision on their own. Managers know how to make personnel decisions without inciting an overthrow by other staff. They

TABLE 11.1 } **Attitude chart**

	Veterans	Boomers	Generation X
Outlook	Practical	Optimistic	Skeptical
Work Ethic	Dedicated	Driven	Balanced
View of Authority	Respectful	Love/Hate	Unimpressed
Leadership by	Hierarchy	Consensus	Competence
Relationships	Personal/ Sacrifice	Personal/ Gratification	Reluctance to commit
Turnoffs	Vulgarity	Political incorrectness	Cliché/Hype

Source: Zemke, Raines, and Filipczak, 2000, p. 155.

are thoughtful in creating teams or giving assignments to individuals. Managers have genuine concern for their staff and for the tasks they are given. This management style works hard to gain the trust of their staff, and they are extremely good communicators.

- *Respect competence and initiative.* Management assumes the best of their employees. They try their best to motivate, support, and reward employees.
- *Nourish retention.* Management is focused on retention of their staff. They know that keeping their staff is important in the service of their customers. Training, coaching, and mentoring are keys to success. They encourage employees to move about the company, experiencing different opportunities.

Watkins (1999) advises managers to avoid stereotyping and using biases regarding age. She continues by stating that visions and expectations should be standard and made clear for all employees. Smith (2003) discusses having an open work environment and giving staff a sense of ownership. This allows staff to initiate new ideas and encourages them to contribute to the goals of the company. In today's changing marketplace, companies should make an effort to market internally. Many companies have spent thousands of dollars training their staff, so why incur the cost of training new hires? The cost of losing good talent is high (Kaye & Jordon-Evans, 2002). The question management and human resources should be asking is: How does a company become an employer of choice (Zemke et al., 2000)?

Truly successful companies understand the value of their staff and focus on their well-being, development, and growth. A workforce is energized and productive when staff feel valued by their management. A model of success would be human resources, management, and employees all working together to bridge generational gaps, which can only improve the overall attitude of the workforce and contribute significantly to a company's bottom line.

Additionally, four strategy-building probes were used to investigate the literature and identify the crucial employment interests, incentives, and motivational factors that impact employment retention decisions made by Generation X.

Strategy Building Probe 1: What Would Attract Generation X Employees to Long-Term Employment?

Generation X is the most transient of all the generations (Nagel, 1998). For Generation X, quantity and quality of career alternatives within their environment is important (Jurkiewicz, 2000). Typically, this generation has witnessed downsizing, layoffs, and pension issues with their parents. Their parents' experiences have definitely tainted their view of company loyalty, and they tend to change jobs on average about every 18 months (Jurkiewicz, 2000). Generation X's overwhelming reasons to stay are (1) autonomy, (2) good schedules, and (3) time off (Lancaster & Stillman, 2002). This generation does not commit themselves to a company, but rather to themselves (Jurkiewicz, 2000). Generation X doesn't believe their employers are loyal to them, and they don't believe they should risk being loyal in return (Arellano, 1999).

Strategy Building Probe 2: What Could Be the Limitations and Barriers to Working with a Particular Company?

Becoming stagnant in a company is a fear of most Generation X employees (Lancaster & Stillman, 2002). Many highly skilled young people leave positions because management does not understand their needs (Smith, 2003). Management's lack of understanding of this generation will contribute to diminishing a valuable resource (Tulgan, 2000).

Generation X needs to be provided with successful career paths that don't always move up. Management is too often fixed on the idea of upward mobility being the only way to challenge and motivate staff (Lancaster & Stillman, 2002). Career paths not being discussed with Generation X staff was one of the complaints identified on the BridgeWorks Survey (Lancaster & Stillman, 2002). Having to be employed for years with the same company to earn higher positions is a barrier for Generation X staff who don't share the same view as older folks on entitlements (Keller, 2000). Generation X understands the need to earn your way up, so they are not willing to "pay dues" in a system or club that used to mean "job security" when that system no longer exists (Tulgan, 2000).

Traditionally, companies use a longevity-based recognition and promotion program. Generation X staff are looking for performance-based promotions and rewards (Smith, 2003).

Strategy Building Probe 3: Describe Those Characteristics That Help Make a Good Work Environment?

Short-term rewards, autonomy, security, flexibility, ability to learn new things, teamwork, and feedback are what Generation X believes are values for a good work environment (Jurkiewicz, 2000). Generation X wants flexibility, respect, a balance between work and leisure life, opportunity to grow and learn new skills, and, last but not least, money.

Citing Neal in Arellano's article, "Marking the Spot for Gen X," she states that this generation is used to a more lateral management structure, rather than a traditional, top-down system (1999).

Strategy Building Probe 4: What Are the Reasons and/ or Incentives Used to Justify Staying with a Particular Company?

Generation X considers incentives or rewards that will make them safe in their employment now, not later. This generation is rewarded by funding their educational advancement and by providing employee pension plans that are portable (i.e., a retirement/pension they can easily build for the future without being committed to one organization). The key in rewarding Generation X is to keep in mind the word "freedom." For this group, freedom is important in dress codes, open office designs, flexible leave plan, paid time off, ongoing training, and, overall, a more open, flexible corporate environment (Lancaster & Stillman, 2002). This generation is interested in furthering their skills and wants opportunities for personal growth by attending seminars, workshops and off-site classes (Smith, 2003).

Millennials

The retirement of the Baby Boomers leaves quite a void in the workplace, and the Generation X population isn't large enough to fill the void. This brings us to millennials, who outnumber Generation X by 88 million to 50 million (Meister & Willyerd, 2010). With such a daunting hiring task, human resource departments in organizations across the country are familiarizing themselves with the characteristics and needs of this next pool of potential candidates. It is said that both Baby Boomers and Generation Xers are looking for security and structure in the workplace, while Millennials find it important to have flexibility (Brack & Kelly, 2012). Listed here are the areas of importance of a survey by Rigoni and Adkins (2016) of 1,700 US workers consisting of Boomers, Gen X and Millennials, identifying what they look for when they are applying for a job:

- Opportunity to learn and grow
- Quality of manager
- Quality of management
- Interest in the type of work
- Opportunity for advancement
- Overall compensation
- Organization encourages creativity
- Organization is a fun place to work
- Informal work environment

These results are consistent with the findings of another national study commissioned by CNBC (Pfau, 2016). In that study, six traits that Millennials look for in potential employers include: ethics, environmental practices, work–life balance, profitability, diversity, and reputation. Study participants also assessed the extent to which the potential employer provides opportunities for training and skill development (Pfau, 2016). Millennials understand that education and training are needed to succeed in a global knowledge economy. Brack and Kelly (2012) suggest positioning Millennials for learning by building intergenerational respect, providing soft-skill training, team building skills, and coaching and mentoring.

Given the projection that one in three Americans of the workforce will be Millennials by 2020 (Donston-Miller, 2016, managers will need to identify and embrace the concept of flexibility. Human resources managers recognize the need to re-evaluate their hiring, promotion, and retention strategies when it comes to Millennials. In order to attract them to your organization, you must communicate features such as technology, flexible schedules, cross-training programs, and staff development. A real case example may better illustrate this point of view. A human resource firm was hired by a multibillion dollar company to set up interviews for two candidates, both who happened to be Millennials. To their surprise, both candidates canceled their appointments. Instead of in-person interviews, each applicant requested an interview using Skype technology. Both applicants felt that the use of telecommunication technology offered a time and costs saving alternative to expensive and inconvenient travel across country to interview (Bisceglia, 2014). This is a perfect example of Millennials' reliance on technology and flexibility even in how they manage their time and pursue their career. Millennials are already experiencing the change in compensation packages as many organizations no longer provide a pension plan, and Millennials don't believe they will ever see a Social Security check. Their plan is to finance their own retirement fund, so if an organization is able to provide immediate eligibility into a 401k plan that would be considered a good benefit (Brack & Kelly, 2012).

Once an organization attracts Millennials, key to their retention is the opportunity to learn and grow. For staff, it is important for the organization to invest in their development. The wisest investment an organization can make is in its staff. Millennials value learning, growth opportunities, great managers, and work that will complement their talents and interest. As they enter the workforce, it is important to help them with soft skills which will help them build rapport with team members (Brack & Kelly, 2012). Millennials prefer a roadmap that provides a clear path to success within an organization. For these employees, acquiring new skills and remaining relevant in the knowledge economy is critical. Providing a program that provides mentors is a good way to allow them to learn various roles throughout the organization (Meister & Willyerd, 2010). Beyond hiring and providing a robust development plan for the Millennials in your organization, it is also important to provide open and honest communication, as well as a flexible and relaxed culture (Brack & Kelly, 2012). Human resources will have their work cut out in evaluating and improving the human landscape of the organization with the influx of Millennials. This is particularly relevant given recent best estimates from the US Department of Labor which reflect the positive employment outlook in social work. As of 2016, graduates of schools of social work are typically younger than thirty, which makes them members of the Millennial generation (Millennials are born as early as 1981 and as late as 1997; Pew Research Center, 2016). Millennials are a diverse generation driven by social causes; they identify with social media personalities and brands (Business 2 Community, 2016). They represent the "life is all about me generation." To engage Millennials involves *social listening* (Business 2 Community, 2016). Social listening can be accomplished by engaging social media outlets and following the narratives that comprise the discussions and overall focus of Millennials. Those who focus on self-care, well-being, and other social welfare issues and causes may follow local causes such as the Race for the Cure and the MS Walk and may volunteer during the holidays in organizations that feed, house, and clothe the homeless. What drives who they are is aligned with social causes (Business 2 Community, 2016). Their drivers include "happiness, passion, diversity, sharing, and discovery" (Business 2 Community 2016). Thus, leaders of larger systems seeking to hire personnel to deliver direct and clinical social services will need to consider these distinct generational values as probes to use in the planning workforce needs and in the hiring process. Understanding the population values and work ethics of applicants provides agency leaders opportunities to hire applicants whose skills enable them to implement the intra- and inter-organizational skills competencies required to provide effective services and further the development of the organization or community as a larger system.

12 }

Power and Politics of Organizational System Collaboration
IMPLICATIONS FOR SOCIAL SERVICE AUTONOMY, AUTHORITY, ACCOUNTABILITY, AND CONTINUITY

Keva M. Miller and Harold E. Briggs

Integrative macro social work practice and inter- and intra-agency collaboration are synonymous as the profession has historically been an advocate for social justice within and across collaborating systems. Collaborative initiatives are often well intentioned, but there is the potential for failure if social work professionals lack a clear understanding of organizational systems' complexities and the influences that power and politics have during the decision-making processes, goal formulation of service delivery, and implementation of services. This chapter explores the different types and purposes of collaboration. Organizational systems and power and politics theories are discussed because they potentially facilitate or impede organizational autonomy, authority, service accountability, and continuity of services in the context of inter- and intra-organizational collaboration.

Providing social and human services through collaborative work is not new to social work practice: rather, the terms "social work" and "inter-" and "intra-agency collaborations" are interchangeable as well as synonymous. The social work profession has been a leading advocate for the promotion of social justice through collaborative initiatives, which has increased social workers' capacities to effectively and efficiently address complex social problems for individual systems, family systems, organizational systems, community systems, and the broader society (Ivery, 2007). While collaborative initiatives are well-intentioned, often benefiting clients, there is the potential for failure if social work professionals enter into these ventures without a clear understanding of organizational systems' complexities and the influences that power and politics have in the decision-making processes, service provision goal formulation, and implementation of services.

This chapter synthesizes the authors' ideas about their shared experiences with inter- and intra-agency collaborations through personal narratives. Additionally, a conceptual framework that incorporates organizational systems and power and politics theories is presented for practitioners' consideration during the initiation and implementation of inter- and intra-agency collaborations. Four distinct aspects of service collaboration are highlighted: (1) a definition and delineation of the types of collaboration from a traditional and broad-based lens, (2) reasons for collaboration, (3) an overview of organizational systems and power and politics theories as they relate to the collaborative process, and (4) a discussion and conclusion concerning the conditions that facilitate or impede autonomy, authority, service accountability, and continuity of services within the context of inter- and intra-organizational collaboration.

Defining and Categorizing Types of Collaboration

There is no universal operational definition of "collaboration" as we lack consensus on the concept (Reilly, 2001). A broad-based conceptualization of collaboration is that it serves the function as both a process and an organizational arrangement (Sowa, 2008; Wood & Gray, 1991) in which distinct representatives of two entities interact as peers serving a common purpose (Page, 2003). A traditional view of collaboration is that of a professional province that promotes an opportunity for different individuals or agencies to join forces and pursue a shared plan of action (Brownstein, 2002). Ideally, there is comprehensive planning and communication in the initiation and duration of the collaboration. Collaboration in its purest form promotes consensus decision-making (Reilly, 2001). However, the definition of collaboration differs based on the structure, motives, and directives of the initiative. A number of key questions need to be answered to identify the varying types of collaborative initiatives. Is the collaboration occurring within or across a single agency structure? Does the collaborative initiative occur between two or more agencies? Is the collaboration occurring between individuals representing divergent professional perspectives? Within these queries, two primary collaborative types emerge—inter-agency/organization and intra-agency/organization collaborations.

INTER-AGENCY/ORGANIZATION COLLABORATION

As a practice model, an inter-agency collaboration presumes interdependence between two distinct organizations, with the joint pursuit or mutual goals that maximize the quality of service provision (Anderson-Butcher & Ashton, 2004; Graham & Barter, 1999; Mizrahi & Rosenthal, 2001; Smith & Mogro-Wilson, 2008). Collaborative participants in these joint ventures may share values and goals as well as resources, expertise, status, and political interests (Graham & Barter, 1999). Social workers who participate in inter-agency collaborations often partner with a host organization/agency (Brownstein, 2002). Social work partnerships that function in host settings include initiatives within educational systems, psychiatric and substance abuse facilities, hospitals, nursing homes, and criminal justice systems. The host agency usually does not view social work services as a primary function of the organization's mission (Jansson & Simmons, 1986; Netting & O'Connor, 2003). They have an agreed commitment to work jointly with social workers to supplement services provided to their clients. This type of collaborative initiative may operate in a moderately autonomous manner where each organization has its own independent set of policies and procedures with separate governance. Yet, there is an agreement to work as a unit within specified policy and procedural service provision guidelines.

INTRA-AGENCY/ORGANIZATION COLLABORATION

Conversely, delivering vital human and social services via an intra-organizational collaboration refers to service coordination efforts involving personnel from more than one division or department under the same umbrella. These types of collaborations are beneficial options to consider when an individual or family requires services that are provided from multiple departments within a single agency. Because agency departments often have different funding sources but similar eligibility, service duration, staff contact, goals, and objectives requirements, there must be attention to avoidance of costly and unnecessary service duplication. Thus, different departments with different funding sources have unique requirements for service delivery. Social workers involved in intra-agency collaborations, in particular, must be mindful of potential service fragmentation and competition for resources between departments. Examples of intra-agency collaborations are services for individuals with comorbid substance abuse and mental health issues or individuals on parole who need housing or employment services.

Reasons for Collaboration

Reasons for collaborations can seem infinite and largely depend on historical, political, and economic circumstances. Social workers and many other professionals find themselves confronted with the ecology of societal issues such as burgeoning poverty created by the lack of educational opportunities and decline in labor markets, noncohesiveness or dysfunctional family behavioral patterns, concerns over public safety and healthcare crisis, and social demarcation and discrimination (Bronstein & Abramson, 2003; Fraser, 2002). Efforts to address these issues are complex and difficult within the constraints of one agency. Collaboration is an approach many social work agencies ultimately choose to adequately and ethically address the myriad of contemporary individual and societal issues. This approach is also viewed as an effective way to take preventive measures for future problems. The more at-risk the larger population, the more collaboration may be necessary.

As evidenced by the collaboration literature, social work professionals are involved in various types of collaborative efforts (Anderson-Butcher & Ashton, 2004; Boettcher, Jake, & Sigal, 2008; Bronstein & Abramson, 2003). Many of these initiatives have been within the venues of both intra- and inter-disciplinary efforts. These ventures are interdependent and created to address one or more of the following issues: (1) to fill service delivery gaps, (2) to enhance or maximize service delivery, (3) due to competition over scarce resources, and (4) for innovation.

FILL THE GAPS IN SERVICE DELIVERY

The primary goal of an organization is to provide quality services to clients that are consistent with the organization's overall mission. Yet, within these systems, clients encounter multifaceted complex issues often outside of the realm of the organization's mission. An organization may attempt to go it alone and branch out to provide additional services, but risk sacrificing highly specialized services. The alternative, service collaboration, allows organizations to maintain a concentrated focus on specific services while contracting out for supplemental or complementary services. Thus, organizations look to one another to strive for optimum service provision that simultaneously addresses needs across several fronts (Anderson-Butcher & Ashton, 2004).

Case Example

Social Workers Serving Schools (SWSS) was a social work agency that provided services in a host school setting through an inter-agency collaboration using an interdisciplinary mechanism. Within this type of inter-agency collaboration, the role of the social workers was to assist school personnel to help students successfully learn, remain in school, and prepare for their futures. The SWSS's purpose was to assist school systems in providing services outside of the realm of student learning by providing counseling services that addressed psychoemotional and behavioral needs, outreach to the community as a resource for student mentors, and aid in the schools' efforts to enhance learning.

ENHANCING AND MAXIMIZING SERVICE DELIVERY

Collaboration for the purpose of enhancing or maximizing service delivery is similar to the purpose of a collaboration to serve the purpose of filling in the gaps of service delivery. The major difference is that when an agency makes the decision to enhance services, the organization already provides adequate services to meet clients' needs, but realizes that clients are better served if more comprehensive or variations of services were available.

Case Example

Supporting Family Network (SFN), a small social service program, and the State Division of Parole entered into an interdisciplinary interagency joint initiative. The inter-agency collaboration was a social service program in a host setting of the state parole office. The SFN was responsible for ensuring that clients met the conditions of their parole by assisting clients in accessing services that would alleviate the difficult transition from prison to society. This type of collaborative initiative was developed to maximize services for ex-offenders in an effort to secure resources to address their employment, housing, and basic needs.

COMPETITION FOR SCARCE RESOURCES

While many collaborative initiatives are pursued to fill the gaps or enhance service delivery, financial motives are a compelling reason for mutual inter- and intra-agency partnerships. The economic landscape has greatly determined the availability of resources. The upward turn of the economy during the 1990s created several funding opportunities for small and large social service agencies. The more recent downward spiral of the economy has left many of these same organizations scrambling for funding to maintain services. During this time of retrenchment, social service organizations have struggled to provide the same level of quality services as during good economic times. Organizations have also struggled to expand their services because there is competition for funding service expansion. Thus, an increasing number of social service agencies opt for collaborative partnerships to respond to market conditions and avoid competition for waning available funding. Smaller agencies are particularly interested in forming collaborations with larger agencies to maintain their existence. Moreover, funders are attracted to and often explicitly require evidence of collaborative proposals that emphasize resource sharing, inter-organizational cooperation, and service coordination.

Case Example

In an effort to access scarce resources, thirteen social service organizations serving persons with developmental disabilities each responded to a source for grant funding to promote a local comprehensive system of care for persons with developmental disabilities. Pairs of the thirteen agencies shared expertise in the same program areas; however, neither program had the expertise or capacity to deliver the total components of required service. Each of the thirteen applicant organizations requested funding to expand its service capability to include new service functions as a way of meeting the minimum qualifications to deliver required services defined in the funding opportunity. Instead of using limited dollars to grow and expand the service system capacities of any of the thirteen social service organizations, the funders encouraged a collaborative structure that allowed full participation of all of the applicant organizations. The organizations followed the funder's recommendation, and the grant was awarded. More agencies are finding that funders are interested in collaborative initiatives as a creative and innovative approach to direct social work practice.

INNOVATION

Organizations appear to be in constant pursuit of innovative methods to service provision. This trend moves from the traditional service provision to cutting-edge strategic models of service delivery. Rapid and emerging social problems require organizations to think differently about how services are delivered to clients (Graham & Barter, 1999). Additionally, when organizations think about how to set themselves apart in service delivery from competing organizations, the decision is made to expand by creating alliances with other organizations. Funding is a huge factor in this process, as creativity and innovation require resources that a single organization may lack. An example of innovation to service delivery is the inclusion of clients in the decision-making process. When one thinks about collaboration, clients as a potential collaborative partner are not routinely recognized (DeChillo, 1993). Clients are often the most knowledgeable actors, and they possess solutions to the issues they encounter. This innovative mechanism is consistent with a practice-based evidence model and is cost effective as it builds upon the expertise of clients who are already involved in the process (Walker, Briggs, Koroloff, & Friesen, 2007).

Case Example

In the field of children's mental health, the parent–professional collaboration approach to practice is an innovative mechanism for service coordination. As a way to deliver services to families of youth with serious emotional disorders, the views and expertise of family members are now included as key to service planning, service implementation, quality assurance, and service evaluation of children's mental healthcare systems. The use of family advocates and support people in service collaboration increases state and local funded service systems' use of low-cost, yet rich experiential community bases and indigenous support networks and resources. This nontraditional strategy promotes the use of natural healers, cultural and linguistic resources, and empowerment. This mechanism changes the role of families and provides training to professionals in the effective use of community-based resources that are consistent with family values and preferences. Additionally, this type of innovative joint initiative taps into the use of client expertise as an instrumental source for problem-solving.

Embedded within the parent-professional collaboration approach in children's mental health is an example of the evolution of influence and power exercised through families and youth voice, which has been accompanied by changes in children's mental health policy and practices (Friesen, Koroloff, Walker, & Briggs, 2011). Friesen et al. (2011) attribute French and Raven's (1959) and Raven's (1965,

2008) six types of influence and power that resulted in family and youth influence. The first of these include *reward power* granted by funders, which involves incentivizing behaviors that are aligned with a desired platform, such as a family-driven agenda. The second, involved the use of *coercive power* by punishing behavior that is out of alignment with desired platforms of partnering and collaborating with families and youth. The third, involves *legitimate power* used by funders that sanction and administer rules for grantees to use to adhere to desired platforms, such as partnering and including families and youth peer professionals in the governing structure of the grant-funded programs and services. The fourth, involves *expert power,* which involves establishing the evidence and research base to support desired platforms, such as partnering and collaborating with families as a promising practice in the planning and delivery of child mental health services. The fifth, involves *referent power,* leveraging relationships with key family and youth organizations as key reviewers of grants and contracts to assess the extent to which family and youth voice are authentically represented in funded programs and services as well as proposals for such funding. The sixth is *information power,* which involves the management of the desired platform's messaging and its dissemination, such as communicating the value added to systems of care through the strategic use of family and youth voice and participation as allies (Friesen et al., 2011). Of particular note, is the fact that the majority of the shapers and architects of the family and youth movement were white women and men. Thus, white women were privileged to exercise what Hopps (1982) refers to as "deferred power," which she likens to the power of a sleeping giant. White women opt to exercise their "derived power," acquired from their personal and social network relationships to white men and women in positions of authority and power, to sponsor system-wide adoption of desired platforms that incorporate youth and family voice, partnering, and collaborating with families and youth.

Theories of Organizational Systems, Power, and Politics

Buying into and sharing a common ideology by both organizations contributes to the overall success of service collaborations. Additionally, the success of the collaborative arrangement and processes largely depends on the ability of each participating organizations to be able to preserve its individual distinctiveness as a separate entity and be able to manage the experiences of interdependency, flexibility, and creativity in its capacity to work with others. When one system enters the realm of another, the potential for disequilibria are created for both systems, as each often has its own mission, purpose, values, and culture. Therefore, each organization must be open to incorporate differences in ideologies about goals and perspectives on the methods for service provision. Organizations that adapt, rather than remain stagnant or paralyzed, are the most likely to have productive collaborative initiatives. Systems entrenched in politics may produce a debilitating power of one organization over the other and create a dysfunctional process that will predictably fail. There are important considerations of organizational systems, power, and politics theories that are useful for conceptualizing a framework for successful collaborative initiatives.

ASSUMPTIONS OF ORGANIZATIONAL SYSTEMS THEORY

Collaborations have great potential to be dynamic, not static, when there is a sustained commitment to respect what each organization brings to the alliance, while working to function as an aggregate whole (cybernetic system) (Mizrahi & Rosenthal, 2001). The interconnected relationships within and between organizations are complex and can be unpredictable (Sankar, 2003). The organization still maintains the ability to adapt if it is an open system. *Open systems* promote the transfer of information and resources, while *closed systems* limit such interactions (Ivery, 2007). Adaptable or permeable organizations are more apt to grow and therefore are more receptive to the increased benefits of shared experiences, which in turn promotes a higher order of functioning (Netting & O'Connor, 2003). The collaborative is comprised of key staff representing each of the participating organizations. It benefits from the performance of specialized tasks by each entity, as well as their collective capacity to gather, process, interpret, and share information (Sankar, 2003).

While the two agencies must be willing to make changes, there is a natural tendency for agencies to maintain some sense of normalcy during times of transformation. This is referred to in the cybernetic literature as *self-regulation* or maintaining *homeostasis* (Netting & O'Connor, 2003; Sankar, 2003; Scott, 1961; Yollis, 2003). This tendency is expected and may be healthy to create "rational order." When changes are abrupt rather than being strategic, incremental, and made with a consensus, the organization is at risk for failure. Therefore, collaboration must be a process that is dynamic, yet systematic and gradual enough for each agency to adjust to the changes. The least disruptive processes are apt to foster greater productivity in each agency as well as in the overall collaborative organizational system's functioning.

ASSUMPTIONS OF POWER AND POLITICS THEORIES

Understanding the power and politics that are endemic in organizational systems is critical to the analysis of the overall functioning of an organization (Wilson, 1999). While most assumptions of power and politics within organizational systems are often discussed as separate functions, there is much overlap, making it difficult to apply one concept without the other. Power is a structural phenomenon that exists when there is a relationship between at least two agents (French & Raven, 1959). Neither power nor politics is inherently bad, as most functional systems have some level of each to create order and protocols that can serve as a source of strength within inter- and intra-organizational collaborative mechanisms. Power and politics become problematic when they are used to promote the self-interests of one collaborator at the expense of the other.

Traditional conceptualizations of power and politics focus on explanations of who has the power and/or about the processes involved in decision-making (Hatch, 1997). In an ideal situation, the power is distributed equally throughout the planning and decision-making process around the organization of the joint initiative. A shared role in planning ensures that the mission and the goals of both collaborating systems are reflected in the provision of services. Moreover, an equal voice further ensures that the two systems benefit from the financial and personnel resources needed to enhance service provision. Finally, equal power promotes equal decision-making around issues concerning the implementation of innovative methods of service delivery. Political agendas can prevent the collaborating organization from achieving rational decision-making, which in turn, negatively impacts clients. After the initial planning phase, it is desirable for the power structure to shift slightly, such that, each agency within the inter- or intra- agency collaboration has a level of autonomous control over the power to ensure that service delivery is within the purview of the specialized training of each agency. This is a delicate pursuit because having multiple authorizers competing for power can complicate the decision-making around organizational policies and procedures (Page, 2003; Wilson, 1999).

Some inter- and intra-agency collaborations are more amenable to equal power distribution and nonproblematic political interests because clarity around decision-making and the roles and responsibilities of the collaborators are established prior to the planning of services phase. In particular, intra-agency collaboratives have similar shared values, goals, and missions concerning delivery of services to clients. According to Jansson and Simmons (1986), inter-agency interdisciplinary collaborations within host settings are particularly vulnerable to grossly unequal power distribution. These systems may have limited say in the extent that policies and procedures dictate the autonomy and authority (the most obvious source of power) to deliver services. This dynamic, a "one-down" approach, often creates less resistance from the visiting or outside agency. Thus, giving the host agency more license to exert more power leads to greater formal authority and autonomy in times of disagreement.

Organizational Systems, Power, and Politics in the Context of Service Autonomy, Authority, Continuity of Services, and Service Accountability

AUTONOMY

While it is important for organizations within the collaboration to work together, under certain conditions, it is necessary that collaborating organizations have a level of flexibility and freedom to provide services that are unique to the independent agency's strengths. Service autonomy within collaborations demonstrates evidence of a multidimensional power structure (i.e., multiple entities) where there is trust among the collaborating agencies. Autonomy, at an organizational level, refers to the degree that an organization is an open system and that representatives of the system have the power to control its environment. Rogers and Whetten (1982) posit that professionals within organizations may experience tension and conflict when roles are ambiguous and autonomy is too limited.

Ambiguous and limited autonomy may occur when individuals perform more than one vital function (an internal and external) within an agency; such as a field liaison who has access to executive management and highly classified internal agency strategy and engages in frequent direct conversations with top policy and executive heads of partnering agencies. The successful collaboration liaison may be charismatic and capable of operating skillfully between the two agencies, but their chief internal function is that of unit supervisor. Their access from top to bottom may be considered highly autonomous, yet a well positioned move for their direct superiors. Unfortunately, and all too commonly, they will be perceived as a threat to others already higher up, but who want the same privileges accorded to those in the role of external liaison for the agency. It is the dual function that is embedded in their role as field liaison—which spans the boundaries of the agency's chain of command and provides direct access to the main source of power for them while denying these privileges to others—that creates the tension between co-workers. However, the personality of the liaison and how the liaison handles disputes may exacerbate conflicts associated with the multiple roles of inter- and intra-agency collaborations. Further, the manner in which decisions are made within a collaborative tells a lot about which perspective is operating at the time. If a systems perspective is used to make the decisions, an ecological/environmental scan will always be considered to avoid unduly hampering or creating a burden on one single system player. Whereas, if a power and politics perspective were used, the extent to which decisions are made becomes a function of who has the votes. Subsequently, being able to influence those who vote gives one unfettered control over any agenda.

The enhancing and maximizing service delivery scenario is an example of an interdisciplinary inter-agency collaborative initiative where the intentions were to assist ex-offenders' to successfully reintegrate into society. The venture provided employment and housing resources as well as other basic supports to clients and their families. In SFN's initial planning stages, social workers collaborated with the State Division of Parole as an extension of parole services. As the parole division personnel became increasingly challenged by the ability to perform criminal justice duties, the dichotomy between the two profession's expectations for service delivery—criminal justice versus social justice—became more apparent. The host setting began to mandate that social work professionals become agents of the criminal justice system. There were concerns that performing criminal justice duties would compromise the social workers' ability to uphold the National Association of Social Workers Code of Ethics. In the end, the interests of the host setting superseded the interests of the small social service program. Issues around the organizational system's structure and power of service autonomy were neither examined carefully nor defined clearly during the initial planning stages of the collaborative initiative. Friesen and Briggs (1995) suggest that attempts be made to develop written agreements that address potential discourse in values, ethics, and roles within inter-agency collaborations.

AUTHORITY

Authority is one of the greatest sources of power. Collaboratives with authority have the power to make decisions about the structure, motives, and directives within an organization or politically influence these decisions. The range of power held by individuals is defined officially through structural features such as job descriptions, contracts, and letters of employment. Each of them specifies the terms by which an individual or group is hired to perform and deliver a specific set of products and outcomes. With respect to children's services, the authority to consent to services is the responsibility of the parent or person with legal guardianship. While each of the previously mentioned examples of authority is tied to position or organizational structure, the extent to which collaborating organizations assume control or take the leadership role becomes a matter of either politics, what people agree to, or the extent to which one organization is more influential in certain matters than others.

Influence is just as effectual in altering behavior as a directive from management or instructions given by a direct supervisor. The main difference between the three is that influence is a function of "personal characteristics and expertise," while directives or instructions are related to one's organizational position (Friesen & Briggs, 1995, p. 73). Additionally, what gives the power and support to directives from management and instructions from direct supervisors is the "structural position and opportunity" and privileges that come with the rank they hold in the organization (p. 73). Influence, on the other hand, is not derived by organizational context but is comprised of incentives, threats, penalties, reinforcers, and other leveraging mechanisms to change behavior or course of action. The informal network is an example of a leveraging mechanism at the organizational level. The informal network is just as powerful in altering behavior as individuals who hold positions of formal authority (Ehin, 2005). If the informal network sanctions an idea or practice, it will be performed as routinely as if it were etched in stone or a constitutional right. If it makes sense and is favored by most, then it will have few implementation complications or adoption barriers. As long as there is little change to the social status of the group, there are no additional responsibilities incurred, and the idea is acceptable to the individuals who are agency supporters, then organizational changes or innovations are more likely to occur (Ferlie, Fitzgerald, Wood, & Hawkins, 2005; Gold, Glynn, & Mueser, 2006).

In the SWSS case, the social workers had equal authority, along with school personnel, to make decisions about how to enhance student learning. Social workers had nearly complete authority to make independent decisions concerning psychoemotional and behavioral services and to negotiate services through community outreach. SWSS possessed a structural position of power that was established in the initial planning of the inter-agency collaboration.

CONTINUITY OF SERVICE

In the context of service delivery, a primary benefit of collaboration is obtaining resources (Graddy & Chen, 2006). Continuity of service delivery is essential to the success of a collaborative initiative. This is particularly true as two agencies determine that the nature of services delivered by the organizational system will be somewhat altered under the new approach. Ideally, well-coordinated, uninterrupted unified services should be at the forefront of the organization's goals. During the collaboration process, it is essential that there is a smooth transition from service to service (Friesen & Briggs, 1995). As the collaborative mechanism is developed, changes must be incremental to avoid initial disruption of each collaborating agency's traditional functions. Further, due to clients' unique needs and circumstances, the collaborating agencies must be given the flexibility, discretionary power, and latitude to jointly determine how and when the transition of services will occur.

Case Example

Three months from Webster's fourteenth birthday, he had a day of explosive behaviors at home. He carried out his frequent outbursts and bullying behaviors until he was put into restraint and transported directly to a state hospital with extended residential care of severe emotional disturbance (SED). His mom, a nationally recognized family advocate and statewide family support leader, felt that the staff at this facility had an excellent reputation at managing difficult and aggressive youth mental health issues. By the age of sixteen, Webster's aggressive behaviors were managed by medication and behavior modification programs, which were transferable to community placements. His mother requested a family support team and successfully petitioned the state mental health director for wraparound services for her and her son so that his return home would be staffed with the supports needed at home, at school, and in their community. In her initial email to the family support team leader, she posed a number of questions: (1) Will the transportation, after-school tutoring, respite, therapeutic trips, youth mentor, and social companion programs that were available for Webster when he was under age twelve be available to address his emotional and developmental challenges in his teenage years? (2) Are these new youth services tied into the adult system? (3) At what age will these programs handle Webster's transition to adult services? (4) What gender and personal supports will the team assist her with, and will these supports continue and be available in the adult system? How is cultural diversity represented and addressed in the programs she is seeking to arrange for Webster in the community? How will his cultural values be included in the case planning efforts? The family support leader quickly replied that she had found a place that had a one-stop community agency that had a five-year grant to help racially diverse families of youth like Webster complete high school, attend and complete college, gain employment, and find housing.

SERVICE ACCOUNTABILITY

According to Walker (2002), accountability is complex and subject to various conceptualizations depending on the theoretical context in which it is interpreted. Within the context of organizational collaborations using systems and power and politics perspectives, accountability is the collaborating organization's responsibility to services. Service accountability within these theoretical contexts is multifaceted and involves multiple players: the client, the individual systems within the joint initiative, and the collaboration as a whole. Service accountability is both a value and a goal that prioritizes and respects the needs, preferences, and values of the clients (Friesen & Briggs, 1995). Additionally, service accountability occurs when each organization within the system and the system as a whole have the power to implement quality and ethical services. Under these conditions, the feedback between the two systems is fluid and subsequently can permit creativity, mobility, and productivity while fostering shared ownership in quality and ethical decision-making for client services. The feedback may come from measurement of the effectiveness of service delivery. Accountable organizational systems will implement evaluation that incorporates feedback from clients and measures how each organizational system, as well as the collaboration, provides service delivery effectiveness.

In the scarce resources case example of thirteen autonomous organizations forming a service collaborative arrangement, the issues that threaten or limit accountability are complex. In this context, accountability involves accountability to the other member agencies, accountability to each agency's contractual and verbal agreements with the collaborative, accountability to the consumers, accountability to the fiscal agency, and accountability to ethical mandates, professional values, and practice principles. Clearly, the lead agency that emerged had the political influence, incentive, power, and politics on its side. However, its chief auditor, though politically astute, lacked sufficient technical skills in performance management and continuous quality improvement methods. He also lacked the experience to lead external reviews, report pertinent information, and utilize formal sanctions to garner compliance with the contracts and memoranda of the thirteen agencies and meld them into a single point of entry, multidimensional service for persons with severe and profound developmental disabilities. The lead agency went into a period of reorganization and began using evidence-based management, performance management, and behavioral contracting as a basis for leading a culture of inquiry, problem-solving, and critical thinking among the thirteen-member agency collaborative.

Historically, social work professionals have sought effective mechanisms to assist vulnerable individuals during times of distress, hardship, and uncertainty. Often, agencies encounter complexities and difficulties concerning personnel and financial resources that place significant constraints on their abilities to adequately meet clients' needs. Thus, the social work profession has sought inter- and intra-agency collaborative initiatives for service delivery. While inter- and intra-agency collaborations present a number of challenges, these initiatives have great potential for success. The extent to which service collaborations achieve the stated aims and benefit the intended beneficiaries will largely depend on each collaborative's ability to adapt, as well as have a sustained commitment to function as an aggregate whole and effectively manage issues concerning power and politics during the decision-making process and goal formulation for service delivery. Flexibility around collaborative arrangements need not to be cumbersome nor threaten agencies' uniqueness or distinctiveness. To the contrary, the flexible nature of the collaboration can innovatively allow for combined personnel and financial resources and indigenous community supports to share scare resources for service provision. It is imperative, however, that social workers enter into partnerships where equal balance of power is present and the politics of the agencies do not hinder services rendered to clients. A commitment to a clear understanding of the collaboration's purpose and goals for service provision will enhance agencies' effectiveness in the facilitation and management of service autonomy, authority, accountability, and continuity.

SECTION } III

Core Specialization Administration and Management Enhancement Skill Competencies

Section III includes chapters on key enhancement skill competencies that support the capacity of agency administrators and program managers to improve their planning, implementation, and monitoring and evaluation functions. The chapters in this section amplify the enhancement skill competencies and capacity of administrators and managers; these include performance measures of organizational behavior, diffusion of innovations from research to practice, associated politics and organizational change issues, quality control management, program review, and program evaluation. In this context, the chapters that address enhancement skill competency capacity building for agency and program managers and administrators focus on key issues and strategies to ensure that the agency as well as its programs and services are driven by clearly defined measurable inputs, outputs, and outcomes that focus on performance attitudes, behavioral skills, procedures, and behavior change competencies. These competencies contribute to achieving the organization's bottom-line: better functioning client-consumers and staff, better agency management, and better overall community health and service effectiveness. Enhancement skill competencies are essential to the toolkit and arsenal of administrators and managers. These skills aid them in arranging assessment measures, selecting and adopting innovations and best practices, distilling a quality control mechanism, engaging in a continuous cycle of agency and program improvement, and adopting the evaluation function as a major feature of an ongoing and routine performance management capability. To obtain service effectiveness, enhancement skill competencies equip and prepare administrators and managers to prudently use evidence to leverage optimal incentives and facilitate the use of sound management and service provision results based contingencies and practices.

13 }

Performance Measures and Information Systems

The typical staff person, supervisor, manager, or administrator usually considers the measurement of how well they are doing right before they undergo a performance review. The use of performance measures in the program or service they are providing or managing is value added to the agency when it is subject to an accreditation assessment, program review, or program evaluation. All too often, many staff and some supervisors are not socialized and prepared to consider performance measurement or information systems as helpful to their roles and responsibilities. It has been observed that most social workers use intuition as opposed to physical data to evaluate their practice (Briggs, Feyerherm, & Gingerich, 2004). Often, for some, it (to evaluate practice) is more busy work or not aligned with their particular authority-based approach to social work practice (Gambrill, 2004).

People who endorse an authority-based approach to social work should read Gambrill (2004), who lays out the ethical obligation to practice with the best available evidence as well as the profession's code of ethics. People who endorse the cumbersome and time-constraint view need to know that the use of measurement to collect important data is not hard to understand (Bloom, Fisher, & Orme, 2009). The argument that information gathering and reporting is tedious and time-consuming is a reality, but not the end of the world. Nor should these key functions be relegated to the fringes of the social welfare agenda. These important functions and their associated tasks need not be considered a hindrance to staff or management of human service agencies. Measuring performance, tracking and monitoring everyone's activities routinely, does add value. Performance measures are invaluable as a means for management as well as staff to track their performance and client reactions to plans of care, and they can aid in assessing errors made in practice (Gambrill, 2004).

In this chapter, we discuss the value of performance measures as well as the key agency, management, and staff strengths, challenges, and critical issues involved with the use of performance measures and information systems in administrative

217

and program management practice. The major advantages and drawbacks to the use of performance measures and information systems will be emphasized and highlighted throughout the chapter. Implications for designing and utilizing performance measures and information systems in agency administrative, program management, and direct practice will conclude this robust discussion on their respective value to transforming systems of all sizes.

The Value of Using Performance Measures in Integrative Practice in and for Larger Systems

The following list of twenty-six items are skills that a problem-oriented integrative practice professional should be able to proficiently perform in small as well as larger systems (Briggs, 2001; Pinkston, Levitt, Green, Linsk, & Rzepnicki, 1982; Tolson, Reid, & Garvin, 2003).

1. Initiation, outreach, alliance and ally building, and engagement
2. Secure vital information to explore and establish initial clinical hunches and problem analysis
3. Pinpoint performance discrepancies
4. Be knowledgeable about the client population receiving services, the situations that present them challenges and that need intervention, and the larger systems that impede or promote change, including data on previous problem-solving efforts, behavioral strengths, developmental challenges, and crises
5. Be knowledgeable about contingencies that maintain performance problems and the potential resources to rely on for problem-solving and behavior change
6. Have the capacity to identify and focus on a problem situation
7. Have the ability to chart out the elements and severity of a problem's sequelae and being able to prioritize targets of behavior change
8. Define expected performance and measurable goals while pinpointing performance goal indicators
9. Have the ability to prepare and narrate a behavior change performance agreement or contract
10. Be able to modify and change performance contracts
11. Be able to conduct assessments of the problem and the goal behaviors
12. Be capable of modifying the assessment of the problem and goal behaviors when needed
13. Be able to aid the client to generate tasks and activities to achieve problem reduction and goal attainment
14. Be able to delineate and specify a plan of implementation for task and behavior change strategies

15. Innovatively arrange incentives, motivators, and other means to influences others to pursue positive behavior change
16. Capable of removing barriers to problem resolution and behavior change
17. Arrange and guide behavioral rehearsal of task and behavior change strategy implementation
18. Manage a behavior change process and nurture ongoing behavior change efforts
19. Operate within a time-sensitive problem-solving context
20. Be able to routinely assess and conduct a time series–based problem and outcome contingency analysis
21. Be able to partner with service beneficiaries and other larger system interagency stakeholders to preserve continuity, autonomy, authority, and accountability aspects of service coordination and collaboration (See Chapter 12 for further discussion in this area.)
22. Be able to secure and retain staff and management coinvesters in the change process
23. Have access to resources to aid in achieving problem resolution and goal attainment
24. Be able to prepare service beneficiaries for self-management
25. Be able to perform quality assurance and program review
26. Be able to conduct practice and program evaluations.

Performance measures of behavioral outcomes and desired performance at baseline aids management in a variety of ways. They help to determine the extent to which the intended outcomes are low rated and need to be established and sustained, which acts as a fundamental value by to the direct service workers, program supervisor, and agency administrators. The use of data from performance measures aids management in assessing both single performance and the contingent actions of a program. They allow management to inspect a time series of the actions and reactions of the staff, management personnel, and service beneficiaries. All of this establishes the "foundation of successful intervention" (Pinkston et al., 1982). Careful selection and assessment of the data and the manner in which they are identified, observed, recorded, and measured increases data reliability and validity. Data from performance measures allow the staff and management of a program and agency to specify and track desirable contingencies. They allow management to track the expected performance of the client-consumers and each participating layer of the social service agency.

Performance measures are very helpful to social service administration, management, and direct practice staff. Their value starts at the very beginning, at the point of conception and design. They aid immeasurably to the process of program and agency implementation and continuous quality assurance, monitoring activities leading to program evaluation. Performance measures allow you to examine the performance of a single aggregate, as well as a functional (contingent relationship) unit of attention.

The physical collection and measurement of data that characterize and represent the right contingencies of desirable behaviors help management set the trajectory for program goal achievement (Baer, 2004). Also, the routine use of performance measures aids in the assessment, tracking, and the subsequent elimination of the wrong contingencies, as well as the reduction of actual undesirable behaviors. Thus, the use of performance measures and data collection activities is essential to the problem-solving process, the achievement of intended program effects, and the accomplished performance and overall effectiveness of all agency stakeholders. This includes management, staff, consumers, families, communities, and program funders.

Performance measures allow management to identify, codify, classify, categorize, and electronically retrieve data elements. The ease with which they are available electronically increases their efficient use upon intake and assessment, during service delivery, and subsequently following the termination of services. These measures add immeasurable value to agency administrators, program managers, and the staff they supervise. All in all, the use of performance measures allows staff and managers to observe not only what they do, but also what every one else does, too! Data from performance measures aid different levels of management and staff to understand the strengths and challenges of the organization. The use of performance measures yields data about the populations being served and the host of needs and circumstances they present at service intake. Data from performance measures identify areas of client, staff, and management needs as well as the skill competencies needed to provide effective services. Data from performance measures that assess inter- and intra-agency collaboration and dynamics provide information that enables staff and managers to detect and resolves barriers to service delivery and the achievement of service effectiveness.

The Strengths of Performance Measures and Information Systems

Performance measures and information systems allow organizational leaders to actually track an agency's strengths. Data from such measures help determine what is good for them to keep and what to discard as waste. Organizations are in the business of maintaining the bottom line while sustaining its competitive edge, turf, and steady growth of revenues. They avoid unnecessary costs, inefficiency, and barriers to the overall bottom line. One underacknowledged goal of an organization is how it keeps what is good and distinct about it. This ultimately gives an organization clout in the task environment.

To achieve effectiveness and distinction requires an established baseline and proof that what you say you do actually works and how you are able to consistently produce the results better than anyone else. To be able to say that and back it up scientifically means that you know the right contingencies. The right contingencies maximize the interdependent relationships of staff and management that mediate the expected outcomes. To have effective staff management means that you know the people who work for you. You have information and intel from the staff and managers concerning their reinforcement menu. The reinforcement menu includes those events, conditions, and circumstances that sustain their interests and actions in doing the best job possible. Reinforcement helps staff and management stay the course until behavior change and goal attainment is achieved.

In for-profit industry, this phenomena is a departure from the rational management paradigm, which establishes the outcome as a function of the inputs and outputs that lead to outcomes. Incentives, motivation, interests, leverage, and the WOW factor replace the previously mentioned paradigm, which favors minimizing up-front and back-end costs and maximizing revenues. Global industries seeking to capitalize in the areas of organizational development and management expertise are exploring alternative methods. In one instance, a global company and major industry leader is consulting with a high-tech firm, university researchers of anthropology, and evidence-based practice and evidence-based management in their efforts in designing a WOW prototype.

WOW operates similarly to how data collection is included in weight loss programs; the more you track what you eat and how much you exercise, the greater the likelihood of your following the plan of change. Incorporating WOW, the effective contingent relationships between staff, management, and client-consumer as a standard organizational practice builds in immediate triggers and reinforcers of desired staff and management behaviors. The design and development of WOW includes using data as evidence to delineate the anticipated causal relationships between the outcomes that are expected and the control variables that arrange and sustain the onset of the desired outcomes (Baer, 2004; Pinkston et al., 1982). Control variables are environmentally and intrinsically available to the staff and management of an agency.

Establishing the WOW contingent relationship in the organization's culture through orchestrating change in the interdependent performances of staff and management provides agency baseline evidence that has significant value. Because of the multiple evidence of its effectiveness to the agency, WOW should become a standard practice via performance measures and information tracking systems.

Performance measures for administration and management include (1) recorded testimony and verbal reports; (2) indirect measurement indices, such as permanent product reports of supervision and administrative meetings; and (3) direct measurement of observations of behaviors, actions, and time series of actual events. Alternatively, information systems are mechanisms and vehicles by which information and data are organized for access and use by staff and management. On the other hand, information systems also serve the purposes of storage, retrieval, analysis, and update.

Performance measures and their regular and continued use provide empirical evidence of (1) the types of client-consumers who are mandated and seek agency services, (2) those who receive agency services, (3) the range of issues they present, (4) the scope of services provided, (5) the outcomes observed, and (6) the challenges experienced by the staff, the management, and the organization as a whole. They aid the direct care staff and program manager in pinpointing the client-consumers' reasons for receiving services, the sources of distress they are encountering, the impact and role of the environment as a trigger, issues that maintain the problem(s), and any and all previous efforts launched to resolve the problem(s). Also, they aid the staff in determining the units of attention for change, which ultimately spells out whose and which of their particular behaviors require change (Pinkston et al., 1982).

Performance measures allow the administrator and manager to track and monitor key agency functions. These functions include the supportive resources needed to address a particular set of client problems, supportive resources acquired, and supportive resources used to achieve the intended performance expectations of the staff, the management, and the client-consumers of programs (Pinkston et al., 1982). Performance measures aid the staff and management of a program to define positive behaviors and their contingencies (Pinkston et al., 1982).

The Challenges and Critical Issues of Performance Measures and Information Systems

It is almost a given that most social workers fail to collect physical data to determine the effectiveness of what they do unless they are mandated (Gerdes, Edmonds, Haslam, & McCartney, 1996). Instead, they use intuition. It is a known fact that many people do not like to record data (Pinkston et al., 1982).

Reasons vary for the avoidance and underuse of physical data and performance measures in the delivery and management of social services. There are some who blame the research phobia that people transfer from their student experiences to the workplace. Others, such as Briggs, Feyerherm, and Gingerich (2004), assert that barriers to the use of data in decision-making and organizational problem-solving are a result of the lack of organizational supports for sustaining a data-driven culture. Still, some five years later, Briggs (2009) continues to argue that too few aids and guides for integrating research designs into actual agency practice exist. He and others believe that there is not enough incentives to motivate staff to operate within a data-driven culture. Sadly, he and others report that there is insufficient evidence to show the positive effects of using data on the social worker's overall effectiveness. Thus, the lack of evidentiary support of the value added by using a data-driven culture may also contribute to its unpopularity in agency practice (Briggs et al., 2004, p. 328). Also, there is a lack of incentives and disincentives defined through legislative and funding source mandates that further obfuscate the automatic buy-in by staff to adopt a data-driven culture.

Nonetheless, Briggs (1994, 1996a) successfully incentivized the behaviors of management by defining its contingent relationship between service effectiveness and the effective performance and positive behaviors of staff. He taught the management and staff of an inner-city community organization easy-to-use approaches for using performance measures and physical data in their decision-making, problem-solving, and program management processes. Over time, the pilot use of a data-driven culture and the mechanics of skillfully using and managing it in two service divisions provided the case exemplars needed to advance diffusion opportunities for use agency-wide (Briggs, 2001a).

For these reasons, it is essential that administrators sanction the value of the use of data to all aspects of the organizations (Briggs, 2001). It is their responsibility to ensure that each staff and management employee learns to collect data as well as understand its value to them in a culture of learning and problem-solving. Staff and management always complain of not having time to adequately document what they really have to do to accomplish the service plan of clients involved with other organizations. As a standard practice, staff and management should be expected to narratively plan out their targets and courses of action and evaluate where they have been.

When teaching client-consumers and families to collect data and its value to them, it is important that social workers teach client-consumers the role that data play in documenting their self-determination, choices, and voices in sanctioning their active participation as an agency stakeholders and service beneficiaries. Reducing the complexities of participating in data collection will increase the likelihood that clients and families will collect data (Pinkston et al., 1982). It is important to emphasize that data collection is essential to the success of the intervention (Pinkston et al., 1982).

The approach used to teach staff and client-consumers data collection responsibility should be kept as simple and as straightforward as practically possible. Well-trained client-consumers and staff contribute to the overall success of the intervention (Pinkston et al., 1982). To be successful in data recording, staff and clients need to understand why they are recording certain behaviors, have a measurably and strategically linked set of procedures to follow during training, and have a routine appraisal of their data collection performances.

When competently assessing the client and staff skills for data collection, it is always a useful practice to behaviorally rehearse, role model, and provide performance feedback to clients and staff learning to record and report behavioral events (Briggs, 1996, 2001; Pinkston et al., 1982). The extent to which performance feedback and social praise is used has been shown to contribute to the eventual use of data collection procedures by clients and staff (Pinskton et al., 1982). There are occasions where data collection is impossible for client-consumers to perform, and those duties may have to be assumed by others such as family, friends, other agency staff, or collaborative partners (Pinkston et al., 1982).

Teaching the Client and Staff to Collect Baseline Data

The staff and client-consumers need to independently implement the use of a behavioral code and instructions. These help staff and management to track the occurrence or nonoccurrence of behavioral events. The use of additional training for client-consumers and staff between the days of recording increases the opportunities for reliable data recording (Pinkston et al., 1982). The opportunity to collect baseline data provides staff and client-consumers an opportunity to evaluate behaviors. Such data can be illustrated in the form of frequencies, duration, impact, and implications to the targets at baseline as well as during the change process.

Teaching Staff and Clients How to Check for Reliability and Validity

The stability and consistency of recorded behaviors is an indication of the strength of data's reliability. On the other hand, the extent to which a recorded or observed behavior is accurately measuring what you intend to measure is an indication of the validity of a performance measure. Pinkston et al. (1982) put it best: "valid data are representative measures of the behaviors the worker and the client intend to measure" (p. 48).

Teaching Staff and Client the Value and Use of a Functional Analysis

It is important to know the extent to which client's behavior change is in relationship to someone else's or to another set of circumstances. The extent to which the rate of behavior is observed to be a function of an environmental trigger or consequence of its occurrence is both an illustration of a functional analysis of behavior as well as an example of a behaviorally specific contingent relationship (Pinkston et al., 1982). In instances where the target behavior is low-rate or nonexistent, a functional analysis of past events helps staff understand the cause and effect between their inputs and client reactions. Such an analysis allows us to pinpoint what occurs that prevents the onset and maintenance of a desired behaviors or its opportunity to occur (Pinkston et al., 1982).

Information Systems for Administration and Management

The use of information systems is fast becoming increasingly popular in non-profit community social service agencies. Its skyrocketing importance can also be tied to the change from a service to a global knowledge economy. The surge of developments in the high-technology industry, the push for accountability, and the growing trend in the use of evidence-based practice across disciplines, as well as in business administration, justifies and contributes to the rise in information management as a career choice.

Information systems in nonprofit agencies consist of client-consumer records, financial records, program- and agency-specific tracking and monitoring systems, and internal reporting systems. Since the 1980s, use of computer hardware and advances in software development have made it more efficient to turn from manual to electronic information systems; added to that, the costs savings in physical storage and the infinite capacity that comes with electronic data storage has made electronic information systems approachable and necessary.

Funding requirements and compliance mandates drive the scope, content, organization, and structure of information systems in nonprofit organizations, not the broader achievements in medicine and the physical and natural sciences or even recent advances in social work's professional knowledge base and practice innovations.

CLIENT RECORDS

The client record is valuable to agency management on a number of key levels. It is a running diary and permanent product of the efforts to resolve problems and the progress and challenges to date within a client system. It memorializes the areas, services, and impact of care to the client within and outside the agency and those responsible for care management and direct services. It serves as a financial resource document, which justifies bills and requests for reimbursement for services provided and contracted.

Its structure, organization, and content varies depending on the scope of services and agency type. Yet, there are some common features that are included in client records and that serve vital forms and sources of qualitative information. These include signed releases of information from the client, referral records, and intake requests for services. This background information provides key data to current linkages and relationships between formal organizations and the client. It provides a descriptive chronicle of identification, confidentiality and informed consent agreements, and social and family history, and is a basic source of vital statistics. For example, birth date, residence, age, educational and occupational statuses, reasons for referral, and contact names, addresses, and telephone numbers of persons who can share information about the client are important items to record.

ASSESSMENT

For the purpose of assessment, data regarding performance measures, client and family interviews, direct observations, and narrations of case notes from meetings with other collateral sources need to be recorded. In the next section, the assessment summary and recommendations for services and initial service plans are also included. The progress notes make up the next section and should include the permanent service plan and a sequential record of notes detailing the client's reaction to programming as well as reflections and decisions made on behalf of the client in meetings or through case planning telephone and email exchanges with the staff of other participating service agencies.

The next section includes correspondence from other agencies, the client's family, and funding source requests. They also include any client evaluations and discharge planning notes and related documents. The final section comprises follow-up assessments and related notes and observations.

FINANCIAL RECORDS

The financial records of a nonprofit include all of the customary items, such as billing invoices for services provided, to instigate the accounts receivable function. The records of expenditures that encompass the account payables of an organization should be included under this rubric. Records of internal audits and bookkeeping records, as well as records of external audit statements, are vital financial records that nonprofits need to maintain on an annual and consistent basis.

The payroll record, including deductions and payments of employer-employee payroll benefits and related taxes, comprises an important set of financial records that must be maintained in accordance with state and federal statutes.

PERSONNEL RECORDS

The personnel records include employees' original application materials, copies of legal residence, and proof of US citizenship and immigration status to comply with I-990 legislation. (This law requires the employer to obtain proof that his or her employees are US citizens and satisfy immigration statutes or mandates for employment visas.)

PROGRAM COMPLIANCE

Each funding source requires its own standard set of program-specific forms, contact logs, and service record formats that it wants established and submitted in a timely manner. The approved scope of work and standard boiler plate contract between a funder and provider states specifically what should be included in record keeping systems to meet compliance and regulatory guidelines.

AGENCY COMPLIANCE

The agency typically requires its own set of records that staff and program management must maintain. For example, the employee time sheet is not a standard form; it varies in content from organization to organization. Another vital record is the mileage log, which includes the miles traveled by car on behalf of agency business.

The minutes of management and administrative meetings, including the areas of discussion, the decisions made, and the expected impact, are maintained in permanent and electronic record keeping systems. The storage of this chronology is a way to maintain institutional memory and longitudinal records of trends and discussions that pertain to conducting the business of the organization.

INTERNAL OPERATING INFORMATION SYSTEMS
DATA SOURCES

The internal operating information systems that are put into place include vital information and data that staff and program managers use on a daily basis. These include

1. Attendance sheets
2. Contact logs
3. Shift reports
4. Case planning
5. Time management
6. Employee identified task and activity logs
7. Records of staff meeting minutes
8. Project management software, objective specific timelines, and Gantt charts
9. Things-to-do checklists
10. Task analysis and process checklists
11. Weekly supervisory checklist
12. Staff performance checklist
13. Program manager monthly checklist
14. Monthly quality assurance assessments
15. Quarterly program review
16. Annual program evaluations
17. Quarterly organizational development assessment
18. Annual agency evaluation

Performance measures allows management to track

1. The conceptual targets for change
2. Specification of change targets through behavioral definitions and indicators
3. Systematic measurement systems that encompass performance indicators and problem severity
4. Other influences and possible explanations for behavior changes (Briggs et al., 2004).

Conclusion

As we see it, the use of performance measures can aid social workers in what Corcoran, Grinnell, and Briggs (2001) depict as the seven components to use in structuring the foundations of social work practice and change:

1. Performance measures aid social workers in setting goals for social services or planned treatment. They are useful in tracking and monitoring the reduction in problem severity.
2. Performance measures aid social workers in setting client objectives. They help social workers delineate measurable behavioral change indicators that systematically approximate the full actualization of the desired behaviors.
3. Performance measures aid social workers in selecting the targets of change from a bevy of change processes and a myriad of treatment events. They allow the social workers to track the target problems with the right contingencies included in the treatment approach.
4. Performance measures aid the program manager and the social worker in structuring the intervention. They aid in achieving compliance to fidelity of the intervention approach. Their regular use allows you to track the frequency of treatment plan and implementation errors by the program manager and staff.
5. Performance measures are useful to plan, implement, and evaluate a treatment/service contract. They aid the program manager and the direct care worker in identifying and targeting problem areas, tracking the frequency and dosages of the treatment strategies, and monitoring compliance with administrative rules and management standards for delivering quality services.
6. Performance measures aid the program manager and the social worker in supervising program effects and client system reactions to programming. They support the use of data in making treatment decisions and tracking treatment errors and treatment successes.
7. Performance measures aid the program manager and the social worker in managing the sustainability of treatment gains. Data from performance measures that track treatment gains are useful during the follow-up phase of program management. It provides opportunities for giving stakeholders and service beneficiaries positive performance feedback.

14 }

Diffusing and Adopting Evidence-Based Practice and Empirically Supported Interventions in the Social Work Academy and in Practice

A COMPARISON OF PRACTICE PROCESSES

Harold E. Briggs and Bowen McBeath

This chapter introduces the reader to the distinct contributions of the School of Social Service Administration (SSA) at the University of Chicago as well as to the historic and continuing conversation around evidence-based social work practice. We describe the historical underpinning of SSA's contribution to contemporary social work practice and then devote attention to a comparison of evidence-based practice (EBP) with task-centered practice and evidence-based medicine. We highlight some challenges to diffusing and adopting evidence-based innovations and discuss translational research strategies, organizational behavior management methods, and culturally sensitive roles for addressing barriers to the diffusion and adoption of EBP in the academy and in social work practice. We conclude with a discussion of the implications for future research that may assist social workers in understanding the role of client empowerment as one of the major distinguishing aspects of the diffusion and adoption of innovations in social work.

> If there is nothing about social work practice and research that distinguishes them, then how do we justify our profession? We need to say how we are different and why that difference is important. This position immediately creates tension, because similarity with dominant groups is the path to societal recognition. When we call ourselves social scientists and therapists, we claim membership in high-status groups and indirectly assert professional legitimacy. The problem with this "we're like you" strategy is that it ensures a second-class citizenship relative to those groups. There is a quality of apprenticeship,

of being an aspirant rather than an authority. Emulating other disciplines gives them power to define us and our difference. (Witkin, 1998, p. 483)

The tensions and themes alluded to in this quote from Witkin have influenced the pedagogy and practice innovations developed and used by SSA educators and alumni since the inception of the school. This quote serves to remind new SSA students and faculty—and indeed *all* professional social workers—that we must distinguish our efforts relative to the other helping professions. The quote also represents a call to action for social workers to differentiate their activities and values from other professionals. Thus, these words inspire social workers to honor our responsibility to the production and use of knowledge that is created by and unique to social workers.

In 2009, the centennial year of its founding, the SSA recognized the founders, faculty, and alumni of SSA's contribution to social work, scholarly traditions, and distinction as a world-class institution. Since its founding, SSA has been comprised of forward-thinking faculty using social science research to advance social work practice and effective problem-solving. One of the reasons we celebrated SSA's legacy as a leader in social work education is because its faculty and alumni have historically accepted the challenge of developing rigorous, carefully crafted innovations and cutting edge ideas. In her invited January 2005 symposium on EBP to the Portland State University social work faculty, Dean Jeanne Marsh observed that the fusion of critical thinking, science, and problem-solving is critically important to SSA and is a major driver in what its faculty attempt as social work educators. At SSA and through its alumni, we remain dedicated to the cardinal value of contributing to the profession's evolving knowledge base.

Practitioners utilize this critical knowledge in their effort to move society toward self-determination and social justice. SSA alumni and many other skilled practitioners accomplish these aims through accessing and utilizing the best available knowledge. The challenges Witkin (1998) alluded to are among the core stimulants of the culture of learning at SSA. They bind the faculty and alumni of the school with a humanistic tradition of applied social science. Finally, these challenges serve as motivation for SSA to remain an academic center of higher learning, a responsive and progressive institution committed to preparing its practitioners and researchers to develop practical technologies that effectively and ethnically aid disadvantaged communities.

The Historical Context of SSA's Contribution to Contemporary Social Work Practice

Since the inception of social work as a profession, challenges to its distinctiveness have included tensions that (a) test our authenticity and value base as social workers, (b) test our flexibility and elasticity, (c) challenge our sense of urgency and time management, and (d) ultimately test our very existence and relevance as a viable and dynamic profession. These tensions are among the principal reasons why the founders and faculty of the SSA have continued to pursue cutting-edge research agendas and successful teaching careers. They do this through a culture of learning that includes faculty whom often represent various disciplines, professional schools, and even competing points of view. A central theme among SSA faculty members is their careful use of theory and evidence, information literacy, research utilization, and critical thinking. These core competencies are principal characteristics of the rich foundation of knowledge taught to students by SSA faculty. Their dream and that of the alumni is that we remain proficient and able professionals who continue the profession's tradition of effective problem-solving and conducting research to use in the care that we provide as professionals and in the instruction that we provide to future social worker educators and practitioners. These themes have been popular topics since the beginning of social work as a profession (Claghorn, 1927).

In the late 1960s and early 1970s at SSA, William Reid and Laura Epstein combined their collective expertise and core aspects of problem-solving, science, client self-efficacy and empowerment, practitioner competencies, and judgment. This fusion resulted in the establishment of a year-long first-year sequence on task-centered practice. Additionally, a second-year concentration was implemented, referred to as Problem Oriented Practice (POP), which was originally conceived by Laura Epstein but adapted by Elsie M. Pinkston and co-taught by Pinkston and William "Bill" Reid. Note that while POP was framed as an applied behavioral analytic approach to problem-based learning using single-case research databases, task-centered practice is an atheoretical problem-based learning approach that qualifies as an empirically supported intervention.

In 1978, the students in the task-centered sequence received research training by former Dean Jeanne Marsh, who was then a new assistant professor. She contributed curricula on information literacy, decision-making, and practice evaluation through group and single-case design, inferential statistics, and time-series analysis to graduate and doctoral students learning to use the task-centered approach or POP. Interestingly, while social workers at SSA were designing and testing task-centered practice in the 1960s and 1970s, medical researchers at McMasters University in Ontario, Canada, were simultaneously using the precursor and early prototype of EBP in medicine to train medical students. Since 1991, EBP in medicine and healthcare has been termed *evidence-based medicine* (EBM).

Identifying What Is Unique to Social Work in EBP

Beyond its similarity to task-centered practice (which we discuss in more detail later), EBP in social work was developed to help practitioners understand client needs, inform decision-making, and contribute to improved client outcomes. EBP, which concerns the integration of available empirical practice knowledge, client preferences, and practitioner experience, has been associated with cost-effective service programming as well as improved clinical decision-making (Zlotnick, 2007). EBP has been proposed to be a corrective for nonempirical, authoritarian services provided in the major social work fields of practice, including child welfare, mental health, and substance abuse treatment (Gambrill, 2006; Gibbs & Gambrill, 2002).

In emphasizing its discontinuity with contemporary practice models, EBP has been deemed a novel, sensible approach for adoption by diverse social work practitioners. While researchers have noted that EBP has drawn considerably from the EBM model used by the medical profession (Walker, Briggs, Koroloff, & Friesen, 2007), little research has identified how EBP in social work differs from EBM in healthcare (for an exception, see Gambrill, 2006, 2007). More broadly, the facets of EBP that are distinctive to social work have not been identified.

Identifying what is special about EBP may help social work practitioners develop comparative advantages and sustain a commitment to the utilization of research and other social work values in competitive market environments. In some fields of practice, social workers must increasingly collaborate and compete with allied helping professionals (Gibelman, 1997; Specht & Courtney, 1994). Medicine, psychiatry, and nursing have over the past decade begun to develop evidence-based service models (Sackett, Stauss, Richardson, Rosenberg, & Haynes, 2000). Yet, it is questionable whether EBP in social work aligns well within a medical model. A reflective consideration of EBP in social work should not only identify its merits and challenges for social workers, but also elucidate why it is essential that social workers (and not other health and human service professionals) provide social services.

The *stepwise approach to EBP* constitute the original EBP process that originated roughly contemporaneously in medicine (Sackett et al., 2000) and social work (Gambrill, 2004; Gibbs, 2007; Gossett & Weinman, 2007; Jenson, 2005; Rubin & Parrish, 2007; Rzepnicki & Briggs, 2004; Shlonsky & Gibbs, 2004). The five-step process involves:

1. Using clinical information to create an answerable question about practice needs.
2. Accessing published research through electronic databases to search for the best available knowledge that will answer the question.
3. Evaluating the knowledge collected by assessing its reliability, validity, and suitability for the particular practice situation.
4. Integrating the scientific evidence with client knowledge and practitioner expertise, and selecting a course of action that is acceptable to the client.
5. Monitoring and evaluating client responses to the intervention.

STEP 1

Using clinical information to create an answerable question about practice needs, the first step of the EBP process, requires that the practitioner help the client formulate an answerable question that reflects the client's central needs and interests related to seeking help (Gibbs, 2003). The question that guides the EBP process should seek to identify the target population and problem area (i.e., who the practitioner is working with and the issue that needs to change), clarify a particular intervention method (i.e., what the practitioner believes would help), propose a comparison intervention approach (i.e., another approach that the practitioner believes would solve the issue), and define expected outcomes (i.e., what the practitioner hopes to achieve as a result of the change effort) (Gibbs, 2003; Gossett & Weinman, 2007).

EBP questions can be proposed to seek answers regarding *effectiveness* (i.e., gauging the benefits derived from a course of action), *prevention* (i.e., avoiding the onset of problems), *assessment* (i.e., identifying established protocols for tracking problems, strengths, and benefits), *description* (i.e., acquiring an understanding of client experiences, circumstances, and needs), and *risk* (i.e., determining the odds of encountering issues and problems). Shlonsky and Gibbs (2004) describe the common problems involved with developing answerable questions as (a) identifying intervention methods that are not available to the client or those not desired by the client; (b) poorly stated questions; (c) posing questions without all four key parts identified; (d) using the wrong terms and concepts to represent the practice issue, intervention, or anticipated result; and (e) confounding the question with more than one question stated as a single question.

STEP 2

Accessing published research through electronic databases to search for the best available knowledge requires an awareness of how to search for published research as well as access to electronic databases and computing technology (Gossett & Weinman, 2007). A number of databases exist that provide well-documented systematic reviews of research, such as the Cochrane Collaboration (www.cochrane.org) or those that are linked to the website created by Gibbs (2003). Gibbs (2003) suggests that the practitioner search for evidence that confirms and disconfirms the practitioner's expectations to preserve practitioner integrity, critical thinking, and scientific honesty.

STEP 3

Assessing the reliability, validity, and suitability of the gathered information for the practice situation comprises critically appraising the results of the electronic search. This is the next step in the EBP process. Gibbs (2003) recommends using rating forms to examine and assess the quality of research studies. Shlonsky and Gibbs (2004) recommend that practitioners have competency in basic research designs and statistics as prerequisite skills for performing accurate critical appraisals. These critical appraisals of research studies involve at least two main phases. Phase 1 includes assessing the internal and external validity of the experimental outcome data of a single study. The assessment of cause-and-effect relationships is done through examining the evidence across the experimental and control conditions to not only assess the relative difference in the effect of a clinical activity across the two conditions, but to also assess whether measurement biases and sampling biases are present. Phase 2 of conducting critical appraisals involves using meta-analysis skills to assess the strength of the evidence of multiple research studies on a particular intervention (Gossett & Weinman, 2007).

In this context, "evidence" refers to statistical analysis of direct observations collected using structured checklists by more than one observer and is aggregated across subjects, summed within each experimental condition, and evaluated for stability within experimental conditions, as well as to assess fluctuations between experimental and control conditions. Finally, evidence about the intervention is reviewed to determine that the information contributes in a meaningful way to explaining the client's situation.

STEP 4

Integrating the scientific evidence with client knowledge and practitioner expertise and selecting a course of action that is acceptable to the client involves several factors. In this step, the practitioner shares with the client the scientific evidence, their prior experience in addressing similar client problems, and an estimate of the potential value of each identified intervention to the client's situation. The practitioner then elicits the client's input and perception of the face validity of each prospective intervention. Additionally, the practitioner and client discuss how each identified intervention fits with the client's customs and expectations. This is done by comparing the client's "similarity to those studied, client access to intervention described in the studies, and consideration of client preferences" (Gossett & Weinman, 2007, p. 149). If some EPB models are not transparent in terms of how this integration is to occur, then that should also be documented at this stage of the EBP process.

STEP 5

Monitoring and evaluating client responses to the intervention is based on the practitioner's recommendations and the client's selection and acceptance of one of the interventions options shared by the practitioner. The client's choice is implemented, and, during implementation, the practitioner monitors the client's response to the intervention as well as assesses anticipated outcomes. If the intervention is not progressing as desired, the practitioner gauges whether the intervention should be adjusted or discontinued.

In summary, the EBP process reduces the practitioner's reliance on intuition and unsystematic clinical expertise as a framework for planning, implementing, and evaluating social work services (Gossett & Weinman, 2007). A culture of questioning and skepticism is helpful in using the process of EBP (Shlonsky & Gibbs, 2004).

Comparisons Between EBP and Other Practice Models: Similarities and Differences Between EBP and Task-Centered Practice

From a historical vantage point, the EBP framework was presaged by the development of task-centered practice (Reid & Epstein, 1972), which involved the following sequential steps: problem identification and a search for potential interventions to suit an identified client problem, the collection and review of literature related to each potential intervention, choice of the most appropriate intervention or development of a novel treatment approach, pilot testing and then full implementation of the intervention, and evaluation and further refinement of the intervention (Bailey-Dempsey & Reid, 1996; Reid, 1975). Considered alongside this model of clinical practice and similar program-level practice frameworks (e.g., design and development), the EBP model of social work practice appears largely redundant, although its focus on assessing the quality of evidence derived from systematic reviews is somewhat novel (Bailey-Dempsey & Reid, 1996). Both practice frameworks rely on client, cultural, scientific, and practitioner knowledge bases. Some elements of the task-centered model are not present in the EBP approach. The task-centered practice model involves client feedback and participation in each phase of the process, whereas, in the EBP approach, the client's participation is introduced in the fourth stage of the process. In task-centered practice, the task completed by the client can be derived from a number of different practice methods, and the dosages of the assigned task are planned and negotiated with the client. In contrast, in EBP, once the client selects the treatment from a number of options offered by the practitioner, they are expected to follow a particular course of action. Finally, the task-centered practice model is perhaps more easily disseminated for use by paraprofessionals or clients than the more technical EBP process approach (although one could argue whether practitioners in real-world practice implement all the steps as originally conceived by Reid and Epstein).

Similarities and Differences Between EBP and EBM

The rise of EBP as a social work practice framework has, to some extent, mirrored the development of EBM. EBM arose in the healthcare field in response to rising expenditures, unequal access to healthcare, and variability in service quality stemming from "overuse, underuse, and misuse of medical care" (Timmermans & Mauck, 2005, p. 19). The primary purpose of EBM is to use evidence to improve the quality, appropriateness, and effectiveness of patient care.

Early in its inception, researcher-practitioners developed two dominant EBM approaches: the *evidence-based guideline approach* and *evidence-based individual decision-making* (Eddy, 2005). Under the former, practitioners use generic practice guidelines, policies, and standards that have been developed based on evidence concerning the efficacy of a clinical procedure, as applied to a particular client population. In contrast, evidence-based individual decision-making involves identifying and critically appraising the best available evidence for use in decision-making with individual patients, integrating evidence with practitioner expertise, and using a "personal, educational, bedside orientation" (Eddy, 2005, p. 19).

This latter approach to EBM is most similar to the stepwise approach to EBP in social work. As with medicine, however, the diffusion of EBP in social work has been accompanied by practice frameworks that seek to develop general guidelines and identify efficacious clinical interventions. The ongoing pressure for performance accountability by state and federal funders has resulted in the spread of evidence-based guidelines in healthcare and evidence-based intervention approaches in social work (Zlotnick, 2007). As a result of the popularity of these evidence-based interventions or evidence-based treatment approaches with funders and policymakers, there has been a reduced emphasis on evidence-based individual decision-making in medicine and social work. These practice developments stem in part from the common misuse or interchangeable use of the definition of evidence-based interventions to refer to EBP (Walker et al., 2007).

EBP and evidence-based individual decision-making in medicine share many common features. Each provides a process for allowing individual practitioners to improve decision-making and client outcomes through the integration of client preferences, the best available evidence, and clinician experience. Timmermans and Mauck note that "improved efficacy should also promote greater efficiency by allowing doctors and hospitals to filter scarce resources away from ineffective clinical practices and toward practices whose effectiveness has been conclusively shown" (2005, p. 20). Similarly, EBP in social work seeks to increase client outcomes, program effectiveness, and accountability. It is assumed, though not yet demonstrated, that the use of research utilization, client knowledge and participation, current empirical knowledge, critical thinking, and practitioner expertise will result in greater transparency. EBP and EBM thus facilitate practitioners' use of evidence to guide practice in lieu of reliance on tradition, authoritative opinions, and/or the continued use of ineffective or even harmful service efforts (Gambrill, 2001, 2004).

In two key respects, however, EBP in social work differs considerably from evidence-based individual decision-making in medicine. In EBP, the practitioner is ethically and procedurally bound to support client self-determination and decision-making. Moreover, attention to client preferences, particularly as expressed in

TABLE 14.1 } **Comparison between evidence-based practice (EBP), evidence-based medicine (EBM), and task-centered practice (TCP)**

Type of approach	EBP	EBM	TCP
Problem-solving approach	Five-step process	Therapeutic process	Client statement initiates helping process
Types of evidence used by the practitioner	Single-case, experimental, client, and practitioner	EBG: experiments, quasi-experiments EBIDM: single case study, experimental, client, practitioner	Single-case study, experimental, client, practitioner, collateral knowledge
Place of practitioner knowledge	Weighted as equal to all other forms of knowledge but for clients' knowledge	Weighted as equal to all other forms of knowledge	Weighted as equal to all other forms of knowledge but for clients' knowledge
Place of client preferences and culture	Client-informed: the practitioner is charged with formulating the central foci of action in response to client preferences	EBG: Responsive to population average and group-based client differences in race/culture EBIDM: The practitioner is charged with formulating the Client-driven: the client's preferences, needs, and interests drive all aspects of the therapeutic process	Central foci of action in response to client preferences

EBG, evidence-based guidelines; EBIDM, evidence-based individual decision-making.

culturally different norms, expectations, and needs, is essential to the EBP framework. In contrast, client self-determination and attention to culturally sensitive practice are not specifically incorporated in the EBM approach (Eddy, 2005). Table 14.1 compares the therapeutic intervention process, types of evidence used, and place of practitioner versus client knowledge in EBP, EBM, and task-centered practice approaches.

Challenges in Adopting and Implementing ESIs and EBP

As alluded to earlier, the reasons why ESIs and EBP have not been overwhelmingly embraced in the social work academy and practice arenas are due partly to (a) lack of understanding among social workers on how each of them incorporates social work values; (b) lack of knowledge of their social work origins; (c) a mistaken perception of its high-tech, information literacy, critical analysis components as being only the province of allied professions with a pervasive research foundation; and (d) the preference for social workers to obtain practice knowledge from supervisors rather than from journals and research. These issues and the bevy of diffusion and adoption concerns that come with using EBP and ESIs become further justifications used by opponents to dissuade other social workers from using EBP, instead of being recognized as the common implementation irritants and challenges that arise in almost all innovation and change efforts (Ferlie, Fitzgerald, Wood, & Hawkins, 2005; Mullen & Bacon, 2003).

As we see it, the problem of preserving EBP and its historical origins and distinctive use in social work is tantamount (or becomes another complication that contributes) to the complexities of diffusing and adopting EBP and ESIs in the social work academy and practice arena. The spread of EBP and ESIs has been, in part, based on the assumption "that interventions showing beneficial effects in outcome research should be taught and used in preference to interventions that have not been tested and shown to be effective" (Weisz, Jenson-Doss, & Hawley, 2006, p. 671). Chaffin and Friedrich (2004) identify a number of obstacles and challenges to disseminating and implementing ESIs in child welfare service settings, including (1) issues involved with financing technology transfer, training, supervision, and monitoring; (2) too few consumers and providers of child welfare services advocating for ESIs; (3) too few or no incentives for utilizing ESIs to achieve better client outcomes; (4) a lack of a culture of learning among child welfare service organizations; (5) discrepancies in values and agendas between the "research and practice communities"; (6) a lack of preparation and investment by child welfare providers in their current activities; and (7) the presence of considerable resistance to ESIs (p. 1110). Other complaints state that ESI approaches are generally not developed to be (a) appropriate for difficult cases typically seen in psychotherapy, (b) used with clients with multiple issues, (c) used flexibly or as part of an individualized system of care addressing unexpected or extraordinary circumstances, (d) as a method to facilitate relationship building, and (e) used with nonmajority populations (Weisz et al., 2006).

CULTURAL CHALLENGES

Despite the introduction of ESIs into many child and family service systems, the cultural appropriateness of many ESIs remains unknown. A growing body of research raises caution about ESIs derived through pilot testing with Caucasian-only samples, in which no attention was given to analyzing the usefulness of ESIs on ethnically diverse populations (Blasé & Fixsen, 2003; Briggs, 2004; Hasnain-Wynia, 2006). Researchers have also indicated that too few culturally diverse researchers, treatment outcomes, theories, and resources have been considered in the design, implementation, and research on ESIs. Isaacs, Huang, Hernandez, and Echo-Hawk (2005) describe the conflictual relationship between ESIs and cultural competence. They argue that researchers and policymakers often believe that the development of ESIs "is best achieved through the application of scientific methodologies and that science trumps culture" (p. 19). Other researchers suggest that there has been insufficient attention paid to questions of how practitioners should allow for cultural adaptations, client collaboration, and client self- determination within ESI service frameworks (Gambrill, 2007; Hasnain-Wynia, 2006).

CHALLENGES ASSOCIATED WITH THE PRESUMPTION OF ESI EFFECTIVENESS

While the use of ESIs is premised on their clinical efficacy, their effectiveness is constrained by many interrelated issues. Gambrill (2007) argues that focusing on ESIs encourages "inflated claims" of effectiveness (p. 430). Also, the group design-based evaluations used to identify treatment efficacy prevents researchers from identifying how many people are needed in the treatment groups to obtain expected results. Without this information, it is not clear how practitioners and clients are able to identify whether a selected ESI will be appropriate for use. Additionally, the preoccupation with ESIs as opposed to the process-based EBP approach reinforces and normalizes the use of ecological fallacies. The presumption that "if X is effective with a specific group, then X will be effective with all individuals within the group" encourages a group orientation instead of an individualized approach to service planning (Briggs et al., 2007).

CONSUMER CHALLENGES

Consumer challenges that may limit the use of ESIs include a lack of knowledge of available effective services, limited advocacy skills of clients to request or access ESIs, and high consumer-borne costs for addressing the cognitive, family, social, and personal challenges that need to be managed during treatment (Gold, Glynn, & Mueser, 2006). Consumers may lack knowledge of the existence of ESIs, particularly if service providers or funding bodies do not inform would-be users of the existence and potential benefits of ESIs. Additionally, clients may not know how to access these services or may not be able to articulate what services and resources they need and that are available through ESIs. Furthermore, as Gambrill (2007) points out, a focus on ESIs may preclude attention to client values, experiences, and culture; informed consent; research utilization via electronic databases; and use of client values and choices in treatment selection and process.

AGENCY AND SERVICE PROVIDER CHALLENGES

Researchers have identified a number of political, professional, staff, management, and fiscal-related issues and contingencies that may need to be addressed before ESIs can be successfully adopted and implemented by agencies and service providers. Mandates from executive management, staff resistance, and negative attitudes towards change; lack of staff training and support; and fears of malpractice are among the many factors that prevent service providers from implementing ESIs (Gold et al., 2006; McCracken & Corrigan, 2004; Rzepnicki & Briggs, 2004). Furthermore, a focus on ESIs insulates the practitioner from having to address resource issues, the need for changes in professional education, and changes in the status quo of standard agency practice (Gambrill, 2007). Additionally, it has been argued that the reimbursement practices of managed care may interfere with the implementation of ESIs (Gold et al., 2006). Finally, the demands, values, and goals of the developers of ESIs may be different from those of administrators and community agencies, "which often makes transferring even a powerful, effective psychosocial intervention from the lab to the clinic almost impossible" (Gold et al., 2006, p. 214). Others have reported these same barriers in their discussions related to challenges to using EBP. McCracken and Corrigan (2004) and Rzepnicki and Briggs (2004) attribute many of the challenges to implementation of EBP to innovation, staff, and agency environmental barriers. An ESI may be too complex to implement without the aid of training and ongoing technical assistance to agency staff and management. Furthermore, staff may not be able to consume and correctly use the innovation, may not know when it is appropriate to modify and adapt an innovation, and may not be sufficiently skilled to define or implement a usable database for periodically assessing client reactions or the effectiveness of the innovation. An additional staff weakness is the lack of appropriate supervision and quality assurance by program management staff and independently by executive management as a basis to implement Step 5 of EBP. In particular, it is for the practitioner to collect and review data pertaining to progress and systematic errors of oversight or misjudgments in case supervision, planning, and treatment by staff and/or supervisor (Briggs, 2001).

Translational Research and Diffusion Strategies

The translation research literature provides a useful reservoir of lessons learned and practice guidelines to use in addressing the barriers and challenges to adoption and diffusion of EBP and ESIs just highlighted. Nutley and Davies (2000) identify a typology of innovations including (1) innovations in existing services through program modification or program improvement, (2) expansionary innovations in which new groups are exposed to existing services, (3) evolutionary innovations in which innovations (new services) are given to established users, and (4) total innovations, which involve new services given to new groups of agency service users. The authors also review the literature on the key characteristics that will result in innovation adoption: certain adopter characteristics, such as a tendency to adopt; experience as a successful organization; the presence of an adoption strategy, agency resources, and structure; and political considerations, all contribute to the likelihood that an innovation will be adopted. Other factors influencing innovation adoption include social network characteristics as well as the unique features of the agency champion and the external environment (Nutley & Davies, 2000). Finally, the authors note that audits, client feedback and input, and identifying lessons learned are three different types of knowledge that are useful in successful innovation adoption. Baker, Barth, Bradley, et al. (2004) lament the lack of funding for research on ways to ensure the effective adoption, diffusion, and implementation of scientific, medical and social science advancements and innovations. Through four case study illustrations, the authors report the following observations as lessons learned for adopting, diffusing, and implementing innovations in healthcare. They urge practitioners seeking guides and help with selecting and implementing innovations to acquire (1) senior administrative sanction for the innovation; (2) skilled, competent, proven leadership within the intended agency setting; (3) acceptable database infrastructure as a foundation for decision-making at all levels of start-up, implementation, quality assurance, and evaluation phases of innovation adoption; (4) capacity to strategically and expediently manage unintended consequence that result from innovation adoption; (5) formal authority or influence and persuasive capacity to ensure or address coordination issues between departments or people representing interdisciplinary roles; (6) infrastructure, resources, and a plan of sustainability for the innovation; (7) a healthy partnership between the people disseminating and the people adopting and implementing the innovation; and (8) belief in the evidence and capability of the intended innovation to eliminate or minimize external barriers and challenges. To diffuse and implement EBP and ESIs in agencies, there are a few agency-based social network, interprofessional, political, and education-related factors that need to be strategically considered as key drivers of agency change and innovation adoption and implementation.

SOCIAL NETWORK CONSIDERATIONS

Valente (1996) argues that social network characteristics, which include adopter characteristics and external considerations, influence the process of adoption, diffusion, and implementation of innovations. Informal networks have considerable influence and decision-making authority over what network members accept and agree to do in actual practice. Through two case studies concerning the diffusion of healthcare innovations, Fitzgerald, Ferlie, Wood, and Hawkins (2002) demonstrate that there is no single decision to adopt an innovation. The authors observe innovation adoption, diffusion, and implementation to be a result of debate, negotiation, and acceptance by the informal leaders in the organization. In some instances, the authors find evidence of copycat behavior. Other considerations influencing innovation adoption include whether people who avoid or fail to implement the innovation encounter consequences, such as poor evaluation, a penalty or fine by administration, or experience lack of honor, social respect, or acceptance in the agency.

INTERPROFESSIONAL CONSIDERATIONS

Ferlie, Fitzgerald, Wood, and Hawkins (2005) argue that the lack of diffusion of evidence-based innovations in healthcare is due to the potential threat that the change would compromise the different and locally established work routines along with the social roles, regulations, and cognitive/epistemological aspects of professional identity that serve to buttress individuals' professional identities. Professional status and legitimacy are tied to the functions that practitioners perform in collaboration with other professionals such as nurses, psychiatrists, and other healthcare professionals. That is, innovations that lead social workers to lose status within their interprofessional circle are unlikely to be adopted. In contrast, the diffusion, adoption, and implementation of evidence-based healthcare innovations is more likely to occur when different professionals share common identities and values, have a record of strong partnership, and believe that the change would be beneficial.

POLITICAL CONSIDERATIONS

Burton Gummer (1990) proposes that everything that social workers do is political. Indeed, one of the first adopters of EBP in the social work academy was concerned with *politicizing* EBP. Gambrill (2007) raises the political aspect of EBP when she identifies the lack of resources available to address the client-oriented practical evidence search (COPES) questions in Step 1 of EBP. She acknowledges that the resource issue is one for legislators to address. A short time earlier, she advised the first author, a parent advocate, and SSA faculty that family and consumer groups could learn EBP as a means for sharing the best available knowledge about the services they prefer with other family members, their legislators, and their service providers (Gambrill, 2006). In this manner, EBP could be used by those most affected and impacted by public policymakers and their decisions on funding social, health, and human services (Briggs, 2009).

EDUCATIONAL AND PROFESSIONAL CONSIDERATIONS

The Council on Social Work Education (CSWE) may also stymie early adoption of EBP and ESIs in undergraduate and graduate social work curricula. CSWE's Educational Policy and Accreditation Standards (EPAS) do not specifically mandate the use of EBP and ESI.

McBeath, Briggs, and Aisenberg (2009) describe the failure of professional social work practitioners to experiment in how they practice. The authors suggest that professional practitioners establish a learning organization approach that is the embodiment of a culture of questioning and skepticism while using science to achieve problem-solving. Dusenbury and Hansen (2004) argue that local agencies transferring research into practice will need to consider the merits and research supporting the fidelity of innovations as strict adherence to the original intervention methods designed by the researcher. Conversely, agencies need to consider the notion that buy-in and implementation of innovations depend on learners' needs to adapt innovations to fit their unique circumstances. There is research to support both perspectives.

Staff Development and Organizational Behavior Management Strategies for Diffusion of EBP

Gotham (2004) discusses the implementation components necessary for successful implementation of innovations; which can involve the faculty and staff of universities and private coordinating centers that aid in the adoption, diffusion, and implementation in local communities (e.g., the Coordinating Center of Excellence at Case Western Reserve helps local community groups adopt and implement ESIs). The author recommends a focus on (1) reinvention/fidelity (innovation adaptation versus adherence to manualized instructions), (2) consumer involvement, (3) staff factors, (4) incentives, (5) support of management, and (6) measuring outcomes as a formula for ensuring effective implementation. Educational and organizational strategies are available to address the myriad staff, internal, and external constituencies involved in accepting, adopting, and implementing innovations and organizational change.

Educational strategies involve methods and curriculum based in applied behavioral analysis approaches that are skill- and competency-based and aimed at improving staff performance. These strategies include didactic and experiential teaching methods like lecture, demonstration or modeling, role-playing, and feedback; on-site training; professionally prepared manuals and treatment modules with instruments to assess staff competence and fidelity to the intervention; and trainer-apprentices. Training methods based on the educational model have been demonstrated to be effective in training staff to use newly developed treatment methods; however, implementing these skills in practice requires attention to the organization (McCracken & Corrigan, 2004). Organizational strategies are more focused on the setting-based behaviors and contingencies operating within the internal and external environments of the social service agency.

One agency change model used successfully by Resnick (1978) is the "change from within the organization" approach to achieve better service effectiveness. It involves bottom-up leadership that incorporates the values, attitudes, and buy-in of all staff as change agents and leaders in partnership with the top echelon of the agency (see also Briggs, 1994, 1996, 2001). A complementary way of adopting and implementing innovations in agencies is to use the interactive staff training model proposed by McCracken and Corrigan (2004), which involves four phases: (1) system introduction, (2) program development, (3) program implementation, and (4) program maintenance. This framework is compatible with Resnick's (1978) because it involves facilitators of change; assessing organizational, staff, and environmental supports and mandates; and obtaining support from agency formal authorities as the initial phase of adopting and diffusing innovations such as EBP or

ESIs (Corrigan & McCracken, 1997; McCracken & Corrigan, 2004). In the second phase, program development is conducted and involves a number of approaches such as Socratic questioning, modeling effective decision-making, and providing additional learning opportunities to the team of change facilitators. Program implementation is the third phase and involves activation and continuous program enhancement. Phase four includes continuous quality improvement and sustainability training exercises with the team of agency change facilitators (Corrigan & McCracken, 1997; McCracken & Corrigan, 2004). Fixsen, Blasé, and colleagues (2010) have a similar approach, but include an emphasis on addressing external environmental influences that impact the agency's adoption and implementation of change experiences.

All of the methods described by Resnick, Corrigan and McCracken, and Fixsen and Blasé and colleagues are components addressed in the evidence-based management/performance management approach used by Briggs (1994, 1996, 2001) in achieving efficient service effectiveness through adopting and implementing EBP and ESIs in an African American managed system of care. Through case study methods, he demonstrated the successful use of a package of behavioral interventions to achieve agency change, service effectiveness, and improved client outcomes in child welfare services (Briggs, 1994), mental health (Briggs, 1996), and social service administration (Briggs, 2001).

FUSING ADOPTION AND DIFFUSION STRATEGIES WITH CULTURALLY ENHANCED ROLES FOR SOCIAL WORKERS

Social workers as educators, social service administrator, or direct service practitioners seeking to diffuse, adopt, and implement EBP and ESIs with inexperienced agency staff and family or consumer groups will need to consider the culturally sensitive roles articulated by Briggs (2009) as a framework to use or adapt. These include, guide, interpreter, researcher, translator, and advocate. The author successfully uses these functions in the training of an African American foster parent and child mental health advocate in using EBP. He effectively applied the steps with technical assistance and achieved positive results, and he recommends that these roles be used in the training of other inexperienced foster or birth parents. To summarize and recap the essential features of each role as it corresponds to each of the five steps in the process of EBP:

> *Guide.* In applying EBP, the guide helps develop the COPES question
> with client input and assistance by using a fill-in-the-blank approach to
> creating COPES questions. In using an ESI context, the guide performs
> orientation to the intervention and on-the-job training on how to use
> it based in the fidelity protocol or instruction manual provided. From
> an empowerment and culturally centered perspective, the guide serves
> as an aid or assistant who supports, reinforces, and secures the client's

ideas, values, and beliefs about his or her incentives and motivations for change.

Interpreter. In the context of EBP, the interpreter retrieves the output from the COPES question and lays out the array of options that are central to the client's change expectations. When applying a particular ESI, the interpreter is only there to help the client achieve mastery of the implementation steps through role-playing, behavioral rehearsal, or through behavioral cues or reminders of next steps that need to be performed. The interpreter is available for training and reinforcement of skill competencies and supports.

Researcher. In applying EBP, the researcher is the person who performs a critical analysis of the reliability and validity of the data pertaining to the intervention and evaluation methods. Though these steps are not needed when applying an ESI, the researcher could help construct an evaluation tool for tracking errors and adaptations that are generally frowned upon, but that naturally occur when the reality of client reactions are not what was anticipated.

Translator. The translator uses the "bedside manner" approach to deconstructing the science into digestible and consumable information. He or she also juxtaposes the client's cultural customs and the requirements for each intervention option so that the client may appreciate the potential benefits and challenges involved with each option. The translator helps the client choose the preferred course of action. In the context of implementing an ESI, the translator provides assistance to the client by helping the client adjust to the ESI, adapt the ESI, or abandon the use of ESI and start over by using EBP.

Advocate. The advocate assists in implementing the client's choice of ESI, EBP, or other options, while advocating for social justice in areas in which the client is experiencing disparities or mistreatment of any form. The advocate is a function that is available to all clients regardless of the evidentiary nature of the services they receive.

For social work practitioners to compete successfully with other allied health professionals, they must develop and use effective, unique practice interventions. The movement of EBP from medicine to social work has been sustained by interest in the development of cost-effective, efficient, and responsive human services. The potential benefits of EBP revolve around improved effectiveness and transparency in decision-making and the opportunity for greater client input into the intervention selection, implementation, and evaluation process.

This focus on client input is a unique facet of EBP and serves to differentiate EBP in social work from the evidence-based frameworks in medicine and nursing (which do not disallow client preferences from being integrated into service planning, but do not specifically require such activity). That is, EBP is unique because it presumes that service provision can be improved through the practitioner's integration of the best empirical evidence with client input. This blending of diverse types of knowledge (from the practitioner's experience, the extant literature, the agency milieu, and the client's perspective) lets the social worker focus on client needs and strengths; allows for client participation and self-determination in the assessment, intervention, and evaluation process; and facilitates service tailoring in line with cultural norms and expectations.

Moreover, EBP in social work attends to client cultural expectations and norms and thus, asks practitioners to develop culturally appropriate and culture-centered strategies in partnership with clients from diverse backgrounds. To do so coherently and consistently, requires culturally informed adjustments in how social workers practice and the roles they occupy. These are unique social work contributions to the evidence-based models currently in use in the helping professions. In comparison, EBM focuses more on scientific knowledge and less on eliciting client feedback throughout the service planning, implementation, and evaluation stages.

At this early stage, it is unclear what challenges face social workers and human service systems seeking to incorporate EBP approaches into their existing service programming. Social workers seeking to implement the stepwise EBP model may be particularly challenged since the search for critical review and use of scientific evidence requires additional research-related expertise, experience, and resources. Moreover, weighing and balancing different types of knowledge utilized in EBP and creating opportunities for shared decision-making with clients may be difficult for some social workers trained in more authoritarian practices (Rzepnicki & Briggs, 2004).

It matters how social workers view their role(s) in the EBP process. For example, social workers unable to act as coaches may overemphasize the research aspects of EBP and attend less to issues of client service and self-determination. The process used to coach people in the adoption and diffusion of EBP should allow for client participation and COPES questions derived through culturally informed expressions of healing and wellness. The prominent place afforded to client cultural knowledge is a further unique aspect of EBP in social work. Client preferences, as expressed through cultural norms and expectations, drive the therapeutic treatment process.

While EBP may serve to correct social workers' historic and nonempirical reliance on clinical experience and authority-driven practice (Gambrill, 2006), it is important to clarify that EBP is valuable inasmuch as it serves to improve the quality and appropriateness of care to individual clients. In this manner, the use of evidence—and the consequent training of social workers as researchers—is a means to improving service quality and client well-being. The other roles introduced in this book serve to help social workers retain their commitment to client advocacy and empowerment. This should remain the cardinal goals of social work practice and the profession itself.

This chapter concludes with suggestions for human service systems and social workers interested in transitioning to EBP and for social work researchers of EBP. First, policymakers and social workers should understand the differences between the major approaches to EBP and, in particular, the evidence-based intervention and the stepwise EBP process approaches. Second, systems seeking to adopt the stepwise EBP approach should assess the resources needed to implement the approach properly. Client, staff, and organizational resources should be inventoried and training needs identified. Finally, despite the focus of EBP on identifying empirical support for practice decisions and interventions, social workers in EBP environments should retain their commitment to client empowerment and education. These goals may be facilitated by social workers taking on the roles of guide, interpreter, researcher, translator, and advocate (Briggs, 2009) and implementing staff development and organizational behavior modification strategies and translational research approaches.

More research that tracks the overall effectiveness of staff fidelity to EBP in agency practice is needed in social work research. Future research that directs and guides the transformation from research to agency practice needs to employ case study and random clinical trial research designs. Utilizing these robust methods will provide guides and lessons that will enable social workers to use better precision, reliability, and accuracy in their estimation as to the best available implementation knowledge to use to aid them in competently utilizing research transparently to achieve client self-determination and overall service or program effectiveness.

As leaders of larger systems, you should remember "it sometime takes an incredibly long time before good ideas have much impact" (Bloom, Fischer, & Orme, 2009).

A Guide for Integrating Program Management and Continuous Quality Program Improvement

For many years, I taught the Program Management class while chairing the Advanced Social Service Administration and Program Management concentration at the Portland State University School of Social Work. In teaching second-year graduate students, I often found myself remembering in strategic detail how I evolved from clinical practice to program management to a nonprofit agency chief operating officer for a period of six years. Prior to joining the academy, my last professional administrative practice role was that of a community-based agency associate executive director in charge of agency operations and organizational development.

Serving in the role of chief operating officer of a major, culturally specific community nonprofit organization provided me the learning organization context to apply my knowledge and experience. An incubator to blend research, agency management, innovative practice, and cultural knowledge into an integrative management practice technology. The agency held national status and distinction in its University of Chicago partnership, its accreditation status, and its expertise in performance- and evidence-based management. It provided me with a treasure chest of lecture material with which to teach across the clinical and macro practice curricula as I entered the academy. It helped me shape the social service administration and management concentration curriculum. It served as a key case study to illustrate the importance and the rationale for hiring agency executive directors (with professional social work education experience and degrees) as course instructors for teaching the administration and management of larger systems. The real-life experience also served as case study data for a score of publications dating as far back as Briggs (1994). My methods have been used for take-home and in-class tests to assess student competencies.

Throughout the years as a professor of social service administration and management, and in this chapter on program management and continuous quality improvement, I will chronicle some important lessons. In my opinion, to be effective, these particular lessons will need to be learned by beginning leaders of larger systems as well as by experienced agency administrators and program managers. Here, I will document my professional program management and quality assurance skill development experiences.

This chapter serves two purposes. It models for new management practitioners and students of social service administration valuable tools and lessons to include in their macro practice toolkit for working in nonprofits and pursuing service effectiveness through the skilled and strategic use of evidence. It specifies the particular tools and discusses the value they add. It also lays out my personal journey and legacy in developing my own voice and a pilot program management and agency administration practice model through the systematic use of evidence.

As alluded to earlier, the influence of Hoshino's perspective on issues on accountability instigated my interest in creating an administration practice model. The model's central focus included transforming program and agency management through performance and evidence-based practice. In this context, effective program management hinges on the ongoing use of data elements as core probes for a continuous quality improvement process. Transformation is accomplished through the systematic use of evidence, critical thinking, and strategic decision-making.

My first job as program director involved managing a youth employment and training program and directing a foster care program. The agency executive director was an outspoken, politically involved community leader with a sense of charisma that was very entertaining and persuasive during interviews and that led me to accept the position. Yet, upon my arrival to work, what appeared to be an exciting and challenging endeavor turned into a daunting nightmare! The seemingly professional executive director quickly shed his outward persona of a supportive and caring agent and changed in to a villain who terrorized all who worked for the agency. He was verbally abusive, threatening, and, at worse, a funding predator with no regard for accountability. I quickly learned that he had no professional ethics and lacked a critical perspective of theory or caring about what ought to be different about the clients' situation, the agency provider, or community.

The executive director did not allow outside community volunteers to participate in any way to assist in organizational efforts. He did not administer the agency by any standards of civility. He discouraged family participation because as he thought, families were the cause of their children's difficulties and should not be trusted as agency volunteers. Finally, this was an agent who did not care about solving problems or achieving goals. He was uniquely savvy in and capable of building relationships. He demonstrated this by securing several government funding sources for work that were already contracted and paid for in advance through funds granted by an out-of-state settlement house.

He knowingly received fiscal support through foundation funding for the entire program and all of its expenses, but he was charging the state and city governments for the same expenses and programs. He was later investigated and found guilty of fraud and other felony and misdemeanor counts. Bizarre as it was, the experience always remains a lesson for me to remind my students of management and administration of what to avoid and what not to do.

During my second week on the job, I attended a manager's meeting where this executive confronted each manager, giving them no positive feedback, belittling and shaming them for their shortcomings and lack of attendance, which resulted in less money for the agency. As he turned to me, he remarked that, unlike the rest, I was very intelligent and stimulated, but that I would soon learn that my education from the MSW and PhD programs at the University of Chicago was less than adequate for the job before me.

Less than two weeks later, I met with the funding source director who funded my program and was told that an investigation was under way and that they would be discontinuing funding within ten days. I resigned my position effective the day funding ceased, but was harassed through telegrams, letters, and telephone calls regarding my decision to terminate employment. Shortly thereafter (within two months), I found another position with a hospital that was starting a new psychiatric unit for adolescents and adults suffering from mental illness. I was happy to work at the ground level with hospital administrators to get the social work department designed and developed for implementation. In this job, I provided social work services, but unofficially. However, I was administratively sanctioned to engage in planning program development, intra-agency coordination, and training of psychiatric nurses, physicians, and mental health workers in brief therapy techniques.

Through this positive experience and subsequent employment opportunities, I found that agencies that were seeking positive results based on the concerted efforts of staff and managers used common data elements as a foundation for effective program management:

- Ethics and standards that define expected performance for all (including the voices and expectations of individual clients and families)
- A vehicle for communication of expected performance.
- A method for structuring and organizing agency performance-based work and implementation plans
- The tracking and monitoring of expected performance
- Tools for performance appraisals
- Use of data from performance appraisals
- Use of evidence in critical program management decision-making

These factors are discussed in the business and healthcare management literature. They have been vetted throughout the social work administration and management literature. They have relevance to social service organizations, but are not organized as a coherently structured script for using evidence in program management. They form the conceptual basis of the remainder of this chapter on program management and planning continuous quality improvement.

Ethics and Standards as Guides for Program Management

It does not matter if you are supervising or managing a subsidized biddy basketball program, coordinating county block meetings, arranging fitness classes for the medically or psychiatric indigent, establishing an accessible fitness center in an inner-city area, or hold responsibility for program operations in a small agency; each of these unique circumstances requires the use of ethics and standards to guide all aspects of effective program management.

Gibelman (2003) identifies the ethical guidelines for organizational practice. She says, "many of the sections of the code imply an organizational base of practice and address worker-supervisor relationships, maintenance of client records, staff development and training, conflicts of interest, relationships with colleagues, and workplace issues such as sexual harassment and labor-management disputes" (p. 6). Obviously, these factors were not included in the standard organizational practice used by the executive director in the previous example.

Also, Gibelman informs us of the seven commitments that administrators and managers must follow in their organizational practice in social service agencies. First, social workers should comply with the agreements and understandings identified by employer and funding organizations and their grant procedures. Fulfilling the commitments, ethical obligations, and employment responsibilities ensures consistency among agency employees. Transparency about what we know and what we don't know guides the ethical use of evidence-based practice (Gambrill, 2004).

Further, maintaining commitments to ethical obligations ensures that administrators and managers possess the ethical framework for making critical decisions. Such a framework helps managers understand and address dilemmas and conflicts that occur between social workers values and organizational needs and practices. Second, to improve the efficiency and effectiveness of organizational practice, social workers should engage in behaviors that enhance agency operations, distinction, and overall effectiveness. In this context, social workers should engage in critical thinking, problem-solving, and decision-making activities that lead to better organizational functioning and use of sound management practices.

Third, social workers as managers or administrators should employ strategies that ensure the timely and proper undertaking of ethical guidelines, values, and proactive principles described in the profession's Code of Ethics. From this vantage point, managers need to provide orientation and training to staff in all aspects of the Code of Ethics. Fourth, social workers need to follow ethical guidelines as specified in the Code of Ethics and avoid areas and situations that may conflict with agency practices. In situations where conflict is imminent, social workers need to follow risk management protocols that permit the protection of the agency through strategic actions that maximize ethical organizational practices.

Fifth, social workers as managers should engage in behaviors that enforce antidiscriminatory practices and actions. In cases where discrimination is apparent, social workers need to act in a manner that facilitates the removal of and elimination of policies, procedures, and activities that support discrimination in the workplace. Sixth, social workers as managers should only secure employment in social service agencies that utilize and adhere to prudent and judicious personnel policies and procedures. Seventh and last, social workers as managers should act as guardians of agency assets, use them prudently and appropriately, and avoid their willful misuse.

Vehicles for Communication of Expected Performance

The social worker as manager should establish and use tools that ensure the timely and widespread promotion of clear behavioral expectations and measurable performance objectives. There are a number of venues managers use to facilitate communication of expectations. These include agency contracts, job descriptions, policies and procedures, mission statements, minutes of supervisory and management meetings, program plans, and performance evaluations. Communication of measurable expectations through agency contracts specifies the legally binding agreements that are agreed upon between the funding source and service agency. It is the means by which the agency is judged, evaluated, and measured for compliance.

Management and administrative meetings are effective channels for communicating and making decisions that are mission-based strategies, actions, and events within rule-governed parameters and procedures. They are also a place where decision-making analysis takes place. This involves the systematic review of evidence concerning issues, decisions made, subsequent actions taken, results, and the impact of decisions in relationship to agency mission and objectives.

Job descriptions provide another means for agency administration to explicitly specify the agency's expectations of each employee desired inputs, outputs, and outcomes as measurable performance indicators. The expected performance of staff and management in an agency that employs a culture of learning always emphasizes strategic goal attainment as a context for describing job roles and duties.

Expected performance is accomplished through implementing the practice of trial-and-error change methods and an ongoing assessment of data demonstrating their observed effects. Practice by trial and error involves the use of methods that incorporate behavior change objectives, tasks, activities, areas requiring environmental modification, and anticipated results of employees' performance.

As a way of self-managing expected performance, the use of task analysis methods by staff can be very helpful to them. Task analysis methods enable staff to engage in planning and evaluation in the same way that one plans and evaluates the items on a daily to-do list daily. Using task analysis methods such as creating things to do list are beneficial to staff as well as managers who are interested in planning and transferring the progress and treatment gains made to the client consumer and their natural support systems.

Policies and procedures lay out the purpose, reasons, steps, and guidelines that staff and management should take to perform assigned duties and responsibilities. Policies and procedures ensure the provision of social services in an agency and represent its administrative sanction. Mission statements are a sound means to use in conveying the expected performance of all actors involved in the work of the organization. They provide a framework for staff to use in gauging how close or far their performance is from the intended areas of the organization.

Using preplanned checklists in supervisory and management meetings with direct care staff provides a basis to express the desires and expectations of agency administration. They serve as both a reminder and a direction setting routine for staff and management.

Program plans set forth a structure of guidelines that specifically communicate the administrative rules and instructions for staff and management to follow as they pursue target objectives and the anticipated objectives of programs and services contracted by funding organizations.

Performance evaluations specify the progress and areas that need improvement by staff and management. They serve as a report card that includes balanced feedback and a list of strategies to implement for providing critical feedback for maintaining desirable performance.

Structuring and Organizing Performance-Based Work and Implementation Plans

Social workers as managers should consider useful ways to promote the best performance of its staff, programs, and services. Through a detailed planning framework, managers should be able to systematically identify performance goals, objectives, action steps, responsible people, anticipated outcomes, threats or barriers to goal achievement, and strategies for removing obstacles and achieving planned outcomes.

In this context, performance-based planning involves the manager organizing a performance plan that lays out the key measurable activities and the responsible people needed to complete assigned activities, work, and implementation plans. Identification of performance goals involves creating a vision that describes the character, nature, and functioning that is supposed to occur after the targeted goal has been realized. The identified goal reflects the hopes, anticipated functioning, and actions that are likely to occur in the future following its achievement.

Objectives are clear and measurable assumptions that include indicators that can be systematically evaluated on an ongoing basis. In this sense, objectives serve as milestones that guide the program manager and staff toward expected performance.

Action steps are fundamental tasks and activities used to accomplish specific objectives. In this context, they are the strategic theory of change that delineate the steps, turns, and signals that should be followed to arrive at a particular destination or achieve a particular objective. Responsible parties are the people who are both capable of and assigned to performing particular activities and tasks. Identifying and securing responsible staff and managers to implement a particular set of activities strengthens the capacity of the agency to pursue program objectives.

Anticipated outcomes are the aspirations, dreams, and possibilities staff and management hope to realize through their actions and concerted efforts. In this context, anticipated outcomes are those future benefits and gains we hope to accomplish.

Threats and barriers to goal achievement are those roadblocks, bumps, speed breakers, and barricades that are contradictory to the planned course of action. In this sense, threats to goal attainment are those obstacles and limitations that block the way of progress.

Finally, strategies that delineate remedies and solutions for the removal of obstacles to planned change in programs and management are similar to treatment plans for individual client behavior change. In this sense, these strategies serve as behavior modification for undesirable behavior.

Tracking and Monitoring

Tracking and monitoring programs involve routine review of problem areas, objective indicators, resources and materials, and reactions by client-consumers and staff. These reviews are essential to managers as they routinely assess the performance of staff and programs for quality control, periodic evaluations, and supervision.

QUALITY CONTROL

Whoever said "what gets monitored, gets done" certainly understood the importance and merits of quality assurance activities. Because social service programs are generally based on theoretical assumptions and working hypotheses, they are subject to a host of factors and circumstances that may impede the planned program of change or cause the work to veer away from its intended purposes. Factors that may hinder the progress and overall accuracy of a program may include staff performance-related issues or constant staff change or turnover.

Another factor that may adversely impact program progress is the nature and infrequent use of supportive supervisory staff. For example, an agency may have a goal to increase staff diversity. Yet the program manager responsible for supervising new recruits undermines them and creates opportunities for conflict between new staff and those who have been with the agency for several years. The lack of any systemic effort to retain staff of color and diverse managers, along with the apparent use of neglectful supervision, sows the seeds of conflict. When this conflict goes unmanaged, it leaves the agency with only superficial diversity, and new staff are like fish in a barrel, to be eaten alive by insincere management or senior staff threatened by the diversity agenda.

Another set of factors that could be counterintuitive to program outcome involves the lack of appropriate resources and materials to conduct the program as originally planned. The lack of tangible resources such as transportation, sufficient support of staff, training materials, petty cash, and money to reimburse staff for professional use of their vehicles undermines the program's integrity and sends a message to staff that they must spend their income to support agency efforts.

Quality control efforts must begin at the conception of a program. Quality control should be pervasive to all aspects of planning, implementation, and evaluation activities. Through planning, the architects of the program should include measurable visions of the program. In what way have the intended effects of the program been actualized following the successful completion of the program?

The articulation of a clear picture that provides details of the future actions involved in the program establishes a mental image that can be used over time. Such a visualization technique creates a guide for planning the actions, activities, resources, and personnel needed to reach the intended objectives.

During implementation, this visualization can be used to guide program supervision and break it into digestible activities, steps, tasks, and events that lead to actualization and goal attainment. The visualization can be used to answer key questions such as: (1) How did we get here? (2) What makes the difference in our achieving this result? (3) Who is essential to helping us achieve this end? (4) Why are they essential to this endeavor? (5) Where should we begin? (6) When will we know that what we have done is enough? (7) When should we change our approach? (8) What should we do with the resources we think we need?

QUESTIONS FOR PROGRAM TRACKING AND MONITORING

During monitoring phases, many of the preceding questions will be helpful to us in determining the overall health and status of the program at different points in time. Other important aspects to consider during evaluation include: (1) Are we doing what we said we would? (2) How consistent are we in applying tasks and activities? (3) What is the staff's reaction to the program? (4) Is their performance different from what we expected? (5) Are there areas of concern that we missed during planning? (6) Is the client's reaction to the program as expected?

THE USE OF EVIDENCE IN PROGRAM SUPERVISION

The use of evidence in program supervision involves opportunities for examining the effect of program management oversight on staff performance and its associated impact on clients and their subsequent behavioral reactions. Program supervision comprises a review of the administrative feedback for and sanction of staff actions, staff renewal, support, and training. Program managers conduct hosts of program performance reviews. Typically, these involve providing routine progress reports and data in program areas that require modification or change. Using evidence to provide staff support involves giving staff performance feedback and encouragement and aiding them in problem-solving in a nonthreatening manner. Booster staff training involves consultation, technical assistance, and formal education by the supervisor to assist employees in acquiring technical knowledge to enhance skill competencies and overall improved performance.

Data Gathering Tools for Program Performance Appraisal

The standardized use of checklists during supervision with program managers provides opportunities to review and discuss data collected from program manager self-reports and staff supervisory checklists. In supervising programs and services, the supervisory checklist allows program managers to independently review client progress notes. They help program management to structure discussions about the findings with staff. The supervisory checklist, along with the review of service plans and client satisfaction surveys, are additional data sources that are useful for appraisal of staff performance. Self-report tools are useful for assessing staff performance. Tools such as weekly evaluations of time management plans, verbal statements made in supervision, completed staff reports, service logs, and mileage reimbursement forms are useful data sources. They maybe used to examine how staff actually spends their time compared to how they plan to spend their time.

Supervisory checklists help managers examine the extent to which staff is engaging in expected performance. A task analysis review of staff records of client progress and service use will provide management with some evidence about the client's reaction to staff actions. Periodic telephone calls from the program manager to client's family members is another useful supervisory tool for appraising staff performance. These calls between program managers and families provide opportunities for the manager to share client progress. They also give families opportunities to discuss their experiences, input, and ideas for improving services to their relatives. The data retrieved during telephone calls with families is valuable information for supervision, quality assurance, and program evaluation.

Random focus group discussions with client-consumers and staff by executive management are a rich data source and effective turnaround management approach. Focus groups and direct interaction between the top and bottom agency echelons enable a level of direct and reciprocal marketing. These data-sharing opportunities motivate staff to buy in to the agency's vision and direction. Additionally, client satisfaction surveys will give insight into what client-consumers perceive as useful, helpful, and not so beneficial to the care as service recipients. If at all possible, direct observation of staff performance would only increase the validity and reliability of your appraisal system.

Using Data from Performance Appraisals

The data collected from supervision, quality assurance, and client feedback are helpful for improving service delivery. Data collected through multiple sources help the manager decide what aspects of the program seem to be working and what elements may need further attention. The data from staff allow management to understand the efficient use of time and resources by staff. These data allow management to compare what actually happens to industry assumptions about what it takes to work effectively with a target population. It also allows management to address the question: Does this population require more care and resources than previously anticipated and budgeted?

Data from staff activities can also help staff renegotiate allocated time and resources based on experiences over time. These data can be helpful in renegotiating contracts for funding, as well as help in justifying the agency's continued use as a funded service provider, as in the case of the agency reported by Briggs (1994). Data can help staff track client reaction to service over different types of clients to ascertain the dependability of the service with diverse clients with different needs and capacities.

These specific data-generating sources and functions span the five functions of management, which include, planning, organizing, implementing, monitoring, and coaching. These five functions have been central to the management of organizations and programs since the early 1900s. In effective organizations, each of these functions involves (1) decision-making, (2) critical thinking, and (3) problem-solving.

Decision-making involves three key components or properties: (1) the capacity to be self-aware of thoughts and actions, (2) the capacity to organize and follow a critical thinking process, and (3) the capacity to select a course of action and use it in problem-solving. Hence, decision-making skills are metacognitive skills that you need in order to select cognitive skills such as thinking and questioning to identify and solve problems.

On the other hand, critical thinking skills are higher order cognitive skills; when selected, they are the result of decision-making and the means by which problems and solutions are reasoned and thought out systematically. Thus, the targets and consequences of problem-solving are the subjects or the unit of analysis for critical thinking. The concepts of decision-making, problem-solving, and critical thinking have as a common core the 5 W's and 1 H, which are the basic comprehension questions that begin with why, what, when, who, where, and how. Research by Buckingham and Coffman (1999) point to twelve questions that effective managers in well-run organizations are always faced with on a daily basis and are illustrated in order of relevance and priority status:

1. Do I know what is expected of me at work?
2. Do I have the materials and equipment I need to do my job right?

3. As worker, do I have the opportunity to do what I do best everyday?
4. In the past seven days, have I received recognition or praise for a day's good work?
5. Does my supervisor or someone at work seem to care about me as a person?
6. Is there someone at work who encourages my development?
7. At work, do my opinions seem to count?
8. Does the mission/purpose of my company make me feel my job is important?
9. Are my co-workers committed to doing quality work?
10. Do I have a best friend at work?
11. In the past six months, has someone at work talked to me about my progress?
12. This past year, have I had opportunities at work to learn and grow? (pp. 43–45)

Answers to these questions help managers fortify their work environments, thereby promoting healthy and productive organizations (Buckingham & Coffman, 1999; Lencioni, 2004).

Using Evidence to Address Critical Program Management Decision-Making

KNOWLEDGE OF STAFF REINFORCEMENT MENU

The program manager and agency administrator will need to know the desired consequences and the contingencies that elicit and sustain optimal staff performance. To gain knowledge of what directly influences staff performance, reinforcement menus are helpful and beneficial to management.

KNOWLEDGE OF STAFF BEHAVIORAL CONTINGENCIES

Triggers to optimal behaviors among staff vary as do their consequences; these can be understood and identified by directly observing staff and their interaction with clients and family caregivers. Audiotapes of staff and client interaction can be helpful to management in assessing the extent to which staff is engaging in the right contingencies to evoke the correct client behavioral responses. Interviews, self-report inventories, and questionnaires concerning staff preferences, incentives, and motivations can also contribute a degree of aggregate knowledge about staff attitudes and interests.

KNOWLEDGE OF BEHAVIORAL PRINCIPLES

It is important to assess to what extent the management, staff, client-consumers, and families have knowledge of behavioral principles. These data will help you determine how much foundational education is needed. Such education is essential to get everyone on board and thinking about the right contingencies of optimal staff performance. Knowledge of behavioral principles will also aid management in identifying and disposing of the wrong contingencies that sustain problems that contribute to ineffective service delivery and negative client outcomes.

PROGRAM OUTREACH, INTAKE, AND ASSESSMENT

The major issues for program management in beginning outreach and intake are highlighted in the following questions: (1) As an agency, how are we equipped to successfully solicit and recruit the eligible program participants? (2) What client, cultural, and scientific knowledge do we have about the behavioral contingencies that motivate the client? (3) How are we strategically planning to ensure the availability and use of the client's behavioral contingencies?

The data to consider upon reaching out to an eligible program population include cultural knowledge of the wellness and rituals involved in buffering the experience of injury, harm, and attacks. Another set of knowledge is geographical and social-marketing in context. Where do people with X condition go to seek a prophylactic healing response? Briggs (2004) reported that African Americans would rather seek the counsel of a good friend or their pastor as alternatives to seeking traditional mental health services. Additionally, to avoid perceived racial discrimination in healthcare delivery services, African Americans in King County, Washington, would rather skip or not seek or use preventive healthcare services.

The data to consider upon program intake involve the definition of the client-consumer problem and its functional relationship to the client and others, as well as environmental circumstances. For example, distressed parents driven to distraction due to multiple stressors both model and reinforce noncompliant behaviors for their children. Although the science shows that parents have the most influence over the contingencies of a youngster under age 12, many parents with fragile situations confuse adult stressors with parenting stressors. They relinquish access to and control over behavioral contingencies to their children's discretion. This is the same as communicating to children that you do not have to earn anything; your privileges are not contingent on anything.

In other words, why work to buy the cow if you can get the milk for free? Thus, be it a child, an adult, an employee, or a client, if you want a person's work habits, performance, and overall effectiveness to be improved, then a functional assessment is imperative. To make it happen, the staff situation, expected and desirable behaviors, and the setting must be assessed for their interdependence and intersectionalities.

The data on the availability and control over staff behavioral contingencies are essential to management. These data aid them in determining the type of change techniques that are needed to enhance staff performance and their resulting impact on the client-consumer. It is possible that control over the right contingencies may not be within the purview of administration and management. This would necessitate the use of self-management techniques as the preferred behavior change strategy (Pinkston et al., 1982).

PROGRAM IMPLEMENTATION

Incentivizing staff behavior to elicit the desired client reactions to programming that ultimately leads to service effectiveness requires a multilevel strategic plan of action. It requires an ongoing supervisory process that includes a schedule of reinforcement and performance feedback within and across program levels. This reinforcement and performance feedback rests on the data provided by staff as well as others. Other sources of data collected and used by program management include direct observations and the perspectives of families and other stakeholders. These data provide management a status report on the health and experience of implementing strategic interventions.

In program supervisory meetings, management and staff go over evidence of client progress and any errors or missteps made by staff in providing services. This is done transparently and as a heads-up to program management. The more information staff shares with program management, the better and more reliable the decisions management ultimately have to make and are able to justify. Program supervision is also a place where staff present and review evidence of client- and staff-related dilemmas with program managers. In program supervision, staff receives consultation as well as technical assistance on matters that present as risk management-related issues and threats that impede client progress.

Program supervision is also used as an opportunity to coach individual staff in certain areas. The manager goes over inferior performance in a nonthreatening and supportive context. During these times, it is more prudent to offer additional behavioral rehearsal, role-playing, and performance feedback as booster training for staff with needs. Program supervision is the place where you can share evidence of successful staff performance and what it can lead to for staff in the future. During program supervision, you can mentor people to become leaders as well as encourage them to advance their education and career aspirations (Briggs, 2001).

Program supervision provides the initial investigation into the inner workings of the program and knowledge of the program's successes, challenges, and where the bones are buried. Program supervision allows administration to track the successive approximations of the program's goal attainment. Given what the data say, the administration may tinker around with the change process. If the data indicate it, the administration may decide to abandon its current efforts and course of action altogether if no change has occurred and is not expected in the future.

Plans for sustaining treatment gains by client-consumers through desirable staff performance and behaviors need to be built into the program implementation design and overall work and implementation plans. Program supervision presents a convenient opportunity to build in sustainability efforts for ensuring gains made in both staff and client performance. Both staff and client can be taught self-management reinforcement procedures (Pinkston, Levitt, Green, Linsk, & Rzepnicki, 1982). Staff can reinforce themselves following the completion of a set of tasks that lead to the accomplishment of a milestone. Program managers can teach staff how to self-administer reinforcement by teaching them which behavioral definitions and reinforcement schedules and procedures to use.

To avoid poor staff performance, program managers will need access to and be able to use penalties and disincentives for undesirable staff performance. They need to learn ways to punish the occurrence of undesirable staff behaviors while reinforcing occurrences of desirable performance. Program managers can aid staff access to reinforcers by rearranging their work habits to increase opportunities for reinforcement as well as actualize expected performance.

Program supervision provides an opportunity to teach staff how to (1) prepare measurable behavioral definitions for both self-management staff performance enhancement and program management-directed staff management intervention programs, (2) review before and during staff management intervention phases the behavioral reactions of client to programming and service delivery by staff, (3) use single-case design methods to track staff performance and client-consumer progress over short and longer baseline periods, and (4) use graphic and visual aids to report client behavioral progress and simultaneously provide indirect client feedback. Program supervision also allows for artful ways to use data to provide staff performance feedback. Through program supervision, the manager may use visual illustration to facilitate a discussion of staff behavioral progress. Graphic feedback provides program managers with data to use in appraising staff performance. It can also be a useful visual aid in articulating the functional analysis between staff inputs and outputs and client behavioral outcomes. Graphic feedback can aid management in delineating as well as explicating the co-variation between staff activities and client behavioral reactions. These illustrations can be created to show the high frequency of the problem before staff intervention. They can be used to show the deceleration of problem behaviors and the inverse relationship between problem severity and the concomitant increase and rise in desirable performance. Staff nonperformance can also be graphically depicted, which is useful for staff assessment and intervention purposes. It can also be used in making staff changes and in reaching other personnel-related decisions such as the need for training, reassignment, suspension, and/or termination.

16 }

Program Review and Program Evaluation

As a practice improvement strategy, the relevance of program review and program evaluation to social work dates as far back as the origins of the profession. Claghorn (1927) puts it bests:

> It is an American habit, when something goes wrong, to concoct a special plan for dealing with it—pass a law, form a committee. Adopt a scheme. But after the law is passed, the committee formed, the scheme in operation, our interest slackens, until something reminds us that the troubles are not, after all, remedied; when we again pass a law, form a committee, adopt a scheme, which again may prove ineffective. What we should do is to follow up our law, committee, or scheme, observe its operations, measure its results, and take our next action on the basis of past experience. This is especially necessary in the field of social work. How many plans have been adopted on the assumption that certain procedures would bring desirable results! How few have been tested to see how far the assumptions on which they are based has been verified! (p. 181)

As such, the tradition of employing program review and program evaluation is undeniably useful to social service program managers and agency directors. It involves the measurement of how accurate and whether or not the program is behaving as planned and if the staff and management are doing what they said they would do. By contrast, program evaluation involves the assessment of whether or not agency staff and management actualized the desirable program effects envisioned. Program reviews, like program evaluation, include an assessment of program fidelity. Program review, however, concentrates more on the regularity or interruptions in the schedule of deliverables and goods recognized as inputs and outputs, and thus focuses on consistency. Program review is interested in assuring accuracy through tracking treatment gains and program milestones that approximate or approach the targeted outcomes. It performs a quality assurance probe to ascertain if program implementation is actually occurring as anticipated. Program evaluation is an empirical snapshot concerned primarily with the agency's progress, effectiveness, and impact.

In this chapter, the distinction and interrelationships between the functions of program review and program evaluation are highlighted. The advantages, challenges, and critical issues involved with each of these important agency functions are delineated and critically examined. Emphasized throughout the chapter is the reality that, as more funding sources require the effective use of best practices in the delivery of human services, the relevance and need for education in program review and program evaluation increases. The extent to which program review is a punishing experience as opposed to a learning experience is highlighted. Also, the extent to which program evaluation is a sterile hypothesis-testing investigation into how successful staff and management performed their roles and responsibilities as opposed to a learning process, a theory building method, and an interactive theory of change confirmation exercise is juxtaposed to assess their relative costs and benefits.

Effective program review requires transparency and a commitment to track success as well as errors and missteps. It is not a process by which managers should hide or camouflage the reality of a program's health. To the contrary, this is where you invest resources to collect data, review it, and make strategic decisions to either stay the course or change the direction in which the program is headed.

Program review, program monitoring, and program tracking are often used synonymously; they are used to communicate the process of continuous quality improvement. There are a number of benefits to using program review as a standard practice in administration and management. Benefits of program review are accrued to everyone's level of the organization and constituency base when done within the spirit of pursuing better functioning service beneficiaries (i.e., client-consumers, families, community stakeholders, and funding sources). Another benefit to program review is the value of what it communicates to staff, which is that management will typically monitor what it expects to occur, so keep on your toes and do the job that you are paid to do.

An additional benefit of program review is the opportunity to reassess the value added and the adequacy of the program hypothesis to achieve service effectiveness. Incrementally changing a course of action, staying the course, or abandoning the original hypothesis and starting from scratch are possible consequences of conducting an ongoing process of program review. Thus, program review presents opportunities to tinker and manipulate the treatment condition. It is also helpful to ascertain the extent to which human subjects' protections remain intact.

A challenge to program review is the failure to use a feedback loop to recognize sustainable desirable performance and to supportively address areas that need corrective attention. No attention to staff leaves them to their own devices to determine whether or not they should continue on the same course of action or slack off, since there are no consequences for performing or not performing (Mager & Pipe,

1970). Thus, the lack of sufficient consequences for poor or no performance negatively impacts program performance and ultimately threatens the achievement of
service effectiveness. If some programs in an agency are reviewed while others are
not, this, too, can be detrimental to the health of the organization and contribute
to staff conflict. Such circumstances raise questions of fairness, favoritism, and administrative incompetence.

Due to budget cutbacks and dwindling financing of human service programs
and services funding, sources may not have the manpower to independently review
program quality and may leave the program review function to the funded agency.
Another threat to the value of ongoing program review is that the funding source
needs the service to be performed by the agency. This is because too few providers
or no other service provider is available to deliver goods and services in a particular
catchment area or district or to a particular group.

Underresourced agencies may not be able to perform program review and may
forgo undertaking it as a vital function because maintaining it would compete with
other agency priorities for shrinking resources. A program review function might be
considered unnecessary if it's perceived as a drain on the support that should be used
for providing essential direct services. In this scenario, the agency's management may
be placed in the situation of "robbing Peter to pay Paul." Also, agency leadership
might be ignorant of the importance of program review to achieving its desirable
outcomes and how it can serve as a boost to the agency's credibility. In this circumstance, management is prepared to ignore the necessity of the assessment of quality
control. They are willing to gamble with their agency's reputation even though they
do not have the capacity to achieve what they seek to accomplish. Thus, the extent
to which "what gets monitored, gets done" is subject to economic, political, and
management competencies, as well as resource dependency-related conditions.

Now that the relative merits and challenges of program review have been
delineated, in the remainder of this chapter, we turn our attention to the content
of what should get monitored, the how's of effective program monitoring, and the
next steps to take upon completion of program review.

Foci of Program Review

While budget restraints and political reasons are among the various factors that
lead to whether a funding source engages in internal as well as external program
review, providers seeking to remain effective in their service provision need to periodically and strategically review their programs. This review should examine key
critical contingencies of inputs, outputs, and their associated outcomes that contribute to or challenge the achievement of program objectives and overall program
goals and vision.

We always begin by asking what the inventors of the program envision as the
(a) intended program impact; (b) units of change anticipated versus actually

observed, (c) staff, management, and, community actions planned versus actually needed to actualize expected results; (d) intervention strategy or package of change processes planned versus those actually used; (e) organizational resource use assessment, (f) assessment of the actual program implementation experience versus the proposed work plan, (g) staff behaviors in actual practice versus what is written in job descriptions and program plans, (h) assessment of the client-consumer's reaction to services, and (i) assessment of the involvement of family as allies and supportive behaviors toward client consumers. Also, we must undertake (j) an assessment of the extent to which what was planned actually occurred or any deviations and departures from the work plan, as well as any approximations and/or resemblances to the proposed plan and course of actions; and (h) a thorough and concise review of staff and program administrations time management.

HOW TO CONDUCT PROGRAM REVIEWS

First, different types of program reviews ought to occur in nonprofit agencies. For example, executive management quarterly reviews, monthly managers; assessments, and weekly program supervisors' assessments of program implementation contribute to a nonprofit agency's sustaining quality programming. External reviews by funding sources are essential and serve as a reminder to agency personnel that the funder is invested in the expected outcome and shares liability if programs and services are not working or being conducted as defined in municipal statutes, regulations, and philanthropic foundation program guidelines. As we know from current research on organizational accountability, this is a judicious and prudent management practice to uphold.

Second, effective program review processes almost always include measures of internal consistency and accuracy, as well as indications for possible opportunities for enhancements and modifications. The use of internal consistency measures involves three phases. Phase 1 involves establishing clarity of purpose, program intent, and the program's expected performance. This often includes reading the program's plans, policies, and procedures to become familiar with what was proposed and planned. Phase 2 involves interviewing staff, management, and the board of directors, as well as collecting and reviewing minutes pertaining to the program at the board, administrative, and program levels. Phase 3 involves directly observing a board meeting and the program management, staff, and client-consumer behaviors.

The review team reconciles all data and formulates an informed program review response that often includes their assessment of all three phases of data collection. Typically, the review will include observations, questions, recommendations, and suggestions. The best program reviews are not accusatory and punitive in nature and context. Conversely, best practices for program review include a cultural context and style that incorporates the key aspects of a learning organization.

It is always best to write the program review report in draft form to allow staff and management to clarify any misinterpretations and misunderstandings. Meet with the program supervisor and manager and staff to go over the review team's observations and findings maintains transparency. It is best to always give the written report to the program director or manager and allow them time to prepare an informed response to the draft review before it is finalized.

In circumstances where the in-house program review team's findings and the staff and program manager's beliefs about their performance varies, it is the responsibility of upper management to make the final call. In our experience, it is better to engage in a preemptive strike. In other words, as management, you should internally know what is really happening before it becomes noticed by the funding source or other stakeholders, such as the agency's board of directors, donors, and sponsors. Inexperience and unskilled managers and agency leaders use intimidation and political pressure to maintain confidentiality around internal and external program reviews. Threatening and punishing staff to get them to not discuss the agency's dirty laundry is not empowering. It lessens staff's commitment to the agency and to ownership of change from within the organization. Threatening staff breeds contempt, disrespect, and deception that ultimately negatively impacts the agency's reputation and ability to retain staff.

NEXT STEPS

Program review need not be avoided; it should be educational, supportive, and meaningful for all involved, which typically includes people at every level of the organization. Arranging technical assistance and training supports to aid staff and management in achieving program improvements and enhancements is entirely possible and may need to occur over a period of time. Staff and program managers may need technical assistance, booster training, or a program of formal training to alter, modify, or acquire content, relational, technical, or clinical skill competencies.

Content-specific skill competencies may include the need to better understand the basis of individual client-consumer resistance or cultural customs of healing and wellness. This is commonly unfamiliar to program staff and management who lack training in providing best practices and culturally specific social services. The use of science and culture in practice need not be incompatible. An example may better illustrate the point. In its early formulation, a common procedure in the application of Assertive Community Treatment is the mandatory use of medication. This practice runs counter to the beliefs of many who ascribe to a culturally specific African American belief system concerning overreliance on Western medicine or the belief that the use of medications with African Americans is perceived as a form of social control.

Failure to address content-specific skill competencies interferes with the ability of staff and program managers to form therapeutic alliances and develop trust with client-consumers. This impacts the quality of treatment and relationship continuity, especially among service populations who are culturally different or involuntary and mandated client-consumers. To get beyond resistance and trust issues requires that staff be taught to understand the structure of client resistance, how to confront the barriers to treatment as they see it, and how to get client-consumers to share their experience and explain why they are negatively reacting to the services that are offered. One of the useful approaches embedded into the task-centered practice approach is the use of the client-consumer's own formulation of the problem as a basis from which to secure motivation and incentivize the client's ongoing participation.

This example of client-consumer resistance conveys the need for management to articulate what type of staff training needs are indicated at the completion of program review. For example, training in task-centered practice in dealing with client resistance includes (content) identifying and understanding client resistance and (relational) addressing client resistance through honoring client-consumer self-determination, but also (technical) redirecting the client's avoidance behaviors by actively exploring options and seeking ways to improve the therapeutic relationship and (clinical) effectively dismantling and removing barriers to client-consumer participation. This process highlights the interdependencies among a myriad of skill competencies required by staff so that they can effectively address client-consumer resistance to program participation.

Changes in management behaviors and performance may also be included as an observation and recommendation by the program review team. Management personnel may need a range of interrelated skill competencies that span the domains previously mentioned as core for staff (e.g. content, relational, technical, and clinical [in circumstances requiring the support of employee assistance programs for staff requiring accommodations]). The unit of attention for reviewing program management differs from the review for direct care staff. The program manager's understanding of the program theory and guiding hypothesis for achieving change is assessed. How do program managers use evidence to make program management decisions? How do program management and staff address problems? Do they strategically and productively resolve problems together or in isolation? How does the program manager supervise? Also, what is the type, duration, and frequency of supervision, as well as the regularity with which they are involved in the continuous quality improvement activities that are typically assessed during program review?

Another area to which program review should be directed on an ongoing basis is the manager's use and administration of agency financial and material resources. To ensure that program staff and managers do what they say they do, they should always be under the careful scrutiny of an internal or external program review team.

This raises a related point. The program review team should include at least one program manager or director. This allows management to directly communicate with their peers about the findings and recommendations made by the program review team. Given the political realities of agency culture and the power differential between staff and management, as a matter of sustaining the chain of command

and since rank has its privilege, it is better for people to stay within their own lanes when participating on program review teams.

A useful way to demilitarize the process of program review is to give as much information as possible to the manager of the program under review prior to the actual review. It would be helpful to all involved to send out in advance a letter and pre-program review checklist of required documents. Included in this package should be a concise discussion about the purpose of the review, a timeline for review activities, a thorough description of how the review and post-review activities will be conducted, and a clear discussion of everyone's role, expectations, and ground rules prior to, during, and after program review.

Participating in program review is expected to yield more benefits than risks as long as it is done in the manner just described. It is essential to place emphasis on the context of the review. To yield maximum benefit across layers of the organization, program review should be helpful. At all costs, it should be embedded into an agency culture of learning, while staff and managers are competently trained to actively solve problems and making strategic decisions to aid people to behave as independently and self-sustainably as practical. Program review should occur within a supportive culture of learning for staff, management, client-consumers, and their family allies, as well as for participating members of the board of directors.

Program review is key to sustaining agency health at the program level, and it reinforces the value added that comes from widespread agency review. The assumptions behind the usefulness of program review and its difficulties are not new to the profession of social work. According to Claghorn (1927), the measurement of the effectiveness of social services "and the study of causes and success . . . is perhaps the most important job before the social work profession at the present time" (p. 181). As we turn our attention to program evaluation in the remainder of this chapter, we should be reminded of Claghorn's historical and still timely and relevant message to professional social workers about the benefits of the study of service effectiveness.

The current use of program evaluation in social work to determine causes of success or failure is accompanied by the same complications noted by Claghorn (1927):

> But this is no easy job. Its difficulties are enormous. The object of study itself is not easily analyzed. What is "social treatment"? An indefinitely numerous, heterogeneous, and overlapping assortment of activities, ranging from simple acts which may be definitely described, named, and counted to intricate series of processes, involving motives and attitudes, which defy analysis and seem completely to bar out counting. (p. 182)

Program evaluation is also plagued by agency politics, even though evaluation is fast becoming a regular function in standard agency practice for services based in best and evidence-based policy and practice. Successful program evaluation depends on "a definition of program, which in turns requires a definition of problem" (Baer, 2004, p. 310). One problem Baer (2004) noted is the lack of acceptable behaviors and an abundance of the undesirable ones: acceptable behaviors aid people in obtaining the pro-social aims they pursue, while undesirable behaviors "bar people from the future they want or the one that others want for them" (p. 310). Yet even Baer admits "not everything is known about behavior or about the behavior changes that are problematic with social work clients . . . with the exception of what we do know about environmental contingencies and their effective contributions to behavior change" (p. 310). Baer goes on to say that "environmental contingencies are powerful in changing behavior and thereafter maintaining it, and that individual differences do not alter that behavior" (p. 310). Baer provides an answer to Claghorn's (1927) quest for undertaking the study of causes and successes of effective social work treatment by concluding the following:

> So, if a problem is an absence of the right behaviors and an abundance of the wrong behaviors, or of their stimulus controls, the cause might be the absence of the right contingencies and an abundance of the right ones. If the contingencies are changed, the right behaviors and their control might appear, and the wrong behaviors and their controls might disappear. (Baer, 2004, p. 310)

Turning our focus back to the unit of evaluation attention, the program, Baer (2004) defines it simply. As he sees it, "a program is a large recipe for solving a large problem. It explains how to decide who receives the program, who applies the program, and what they should do, and in what order they should do it" (p. 310).

Approaches to Program Evaluation

Contemporary social work agency practice involves the use of best and evidence-based practice, and, as such, we would expect a change in how program evaluation is now conducted. Kettner, Moroney, and Martin (1999) define program evaluation and a measurable assessment of the program's outcomes and impacts. Modern program evaluation is complex and ought to include six important and intricate steps, according to Baer (2004, p. 311): "(1) measuring the program effects, (2) evaluating program fidelity, (3) establishing the relationship between cause and effect, (4) probing for generalization, (5) measuring the costs and benefits of the program and its outcomes, and (6) assessing the social validity of the program" (pp. 311–312). According to Dudley (2014), program evaluation encompasses seven key steps. These include (1) identifying the evaluation's unit of attention, (2) engaging stakeholder participation in the evaluation, (3) defining the evaluation's purpose, (4) establishing the plan of evaluation, (5) implementing the evaluation plan, (6) preparing a report of the results of the evaluation, and (7) sharing and reporting the evaluation results. Juxtaposing Baer (2004) and Dudley (2014), Baer's view of program evaluations is that it serves different purposes with different units of attention, which incorporates numbers (1) and (3) of the steps of evaluation previously defined by Dudley (2014). Using a combination of Baer's (2004) and Dudley's (2014) definition of program evaluation, we define it along the steps described in the following sections.

STEP 1: UNIT OF ATTENTION

Step 1 involves articulating the program evaluation's unit of attention. The program evaluation's unit attention can vary. It may examine the behavior change consequences following the program's implementation. It can also focus primarily on monitoring the stability of the program implementation procedures to determine if the program was done consistently, as originally designed. The program evaluation may center on assessing and determining the specific successful aspects of the program that produced the achieved desired results. As a way to ascertain short-term and long-term effects, the program evaluation may focus on tracking whether the treatment gains observed as a result of program implementation are sustained following the program's termination. The program evaluation may also be guided by questions concerning the program's relative contribution by assessing and estimating the extent of its value added or lost in resource capacity as a result of program implementation. To assess the extent to which a program is needed or is justifiable hinges on evidence that supports its existence. Through program evaluation, it is possible to assess its strategic intent and necessity based on reasons of morality, professional ethics, and social acceptance.

STEP 2: INVOLVING STAKEHOLDERS IN THE EVALUATION PLAN AND IMPLEMENTATION

Step 2 involves identifying and securing the participation of people most affected by the program in its overall evaluation. The perspective of stakeholders is more likely concerned with the reduction in the problems' severity or its elimination. In this sense, their contribution tells us about the consequences of the program's implementation on the targets of the program. Its lesser emphasis on cause and effect and its greater emphasis on behavior change and impact justifies the importance of ensuring the participation of the individuals and groups most likely to experience and hopefully benefit from the services and activities that encompass a particular program of behavior change. The cause and effect of a program is more the purview of the researcher than the service beneficiary and other primary stakeholders.

STEP 3: DEFINING THE EVALUATION'S PURPOSE

Step 3 addresses the main purpose of the program evaluation. The purpose and its function help management decide on the type of evaluation to select and perform. Program evaluations can be formative or process- or outcome-centered. Formative evaluations are done in the early beginnings and throughout the development of a new pilot program or in the implementation of a well-established program to ensure its fidelity. With respect to process evaluations, they are also done on an ongoing basis for purposes of assessment, monitoring, and tracking the completion of program outputs. Outcome evaluations, on the other hand, are done at the beginning to establish a baseline of the target behavior prior to program implementation. Outcome evaluations are also done upon the conclusion of a program of services to ascertain if (a) new and desirable behaviors have been established, (b) the elimination of undesirable behaviors or rates of its occurrence has been observed, or (c) an increase in already existing behaviors that need to increase in frequency of occurrence has been achieved.

THE PLAN OF EVALUATION

The plan of evaluation is an organized methodology driven by questions, therapeutic hunches and assumptions, measurable objectives with specified outcome indicators, and expected claims that are testable and subjected to assessment and verification. The evaluation's question and testable propositions and objectives serve as the function of the evaluation, while the evaluation design serves as its form, which depends on its driver, the function of the evaluation. Designs can include baseline assessment only (pre), post program implementation only (post), or pre-post evaluation designs, with and without control groups. Pre-assessment evaluations allows you to get an empirical snapshot of the program, its intended beneficiaries, and its behavior change targets prior to exposure to the independent variable, the behavior change process. Conversely, the post-evaluation can provide an empirical assessment of the targets of change following exposure to a plan of organized and systematic behavior change. The pre-post evaluation allows you to look at the targets of change prior to implementation and following the termination of the program as a context for comparison. While none of these types of evaluations gives the staff and management of a program any idea of the primary reasons for change or the lack of it, these data are useful for assessing the behavior of the targets of change across a time trend.

IMPLEMENTING THE EVALUATION

To implement an evaluation you need to identify a behavior definition for the targets of change and the desirable program outcomes and impacts. This definition must be measurable to ensure that you are examining the behaviors you intend to observe and investigate. This necessitates clearly and definitively written instructions for evaluators to follow in collecting evaluation data on the targets of the evaluation. If these instructions convey the use of materials such as questionnaires, written self-report inventories, or interviews with an evaluator, then these instructions need to be understood so that they can be repeated and fully explained by the evaluator to the evaluation participants to achieve their consent for participation that includes a statement of the potential risk and benefits for participation and use of the information. If the program evaluation data contain identifiable information that is needed for internal supervisory purposes only, then this understanding and the limits of the use of the data should also be made clear. It typically helps the people observably recording or collecting the data to have and follow a script to ensure that they are measuring the same behaviors under the same conditions for the same period of time to allow for equivalent comparisons.

PREPARING A REPORT OF THE FINDINGS OF THE EVALUATION

An at-a-glance report should be prepared highlighting the key findings and explanations for unanticipated and unintended consequences of implementing a particular program. The report should include the basic talking points that are important for people such as stakeholders and funders to know. These points are based in the answers to four basic questions: Did the program achieve intended results? Did anything change that was different from what was charted out as expected? How does continuing the program benefit and contribute value to those who need it? What would be the repercussions and impacts if the program were to be discontinued?

DISSEMINATING THE FINDINGS

One important way to sustain desirable performance is to publicize its positive contributions both directly and indirectly. Informing the staff and management of a program that they have done a very good job tells them that what they do matters and how they did it is an investment worth commemorating and memorializing. Indirect feedback through sharing the positive contributions of an employee or group of employees to key people within and external to a program creates a culture of recognition and celebration of achievement and is very powerful in an organization that is governed through informal means and mechanisms. The marketing of a program's successes and its limitations increases the public's perception of credibility and reinforces a sense of good faith accountability that can be expected from a particular organization that transparently conducts its affairs.

Financial, Resource-Dependency, and Ethical Considerations

So far in this chapter, we have amplified the relevance and essential features of program evaluation that describes the ways in which it adds value. Still, there are unattractive and cumbersome circumstances that shape and influence the program evaluation process. These are the political, financial, resource-dependency, and ethical considerations and complications that compromise and complicate the evaluation of the problem as well as the program's fidelity (Baer, 2004). Politically speaking, the stakeholders of the program may be people who have a double agenda that can influence the process and outcome of an evaluation. A program's value to the community, its funding source, and the public opinion it captures are a result of what it symbolizes as a socially responsible action to take or to avoid.

There are financial considerations that influence the emphasis on program evaluation. It is almost a certainty that any public funding as well as private funding has made continuation of its grant-funding contingent upon evaluation data that affirm the integrity, legitimacy, and necessity of the program. In some cases, manpower shortages due to financial circumstances can limit the amount of time used in evaluating a program's success, limitations, and challenges. The time allocated to perform the evaluation may be used to ensure the provision of direct services that were left undone due to a reduction in available staff.

Whether the program works or not may not be the only reason why a program is valuable Resource dependencies by politically disenfranchised groups such children, the elderly, the poor, and the medically fragile, along with political pressure applied by interest groups to continue the provision of resources to these groups, can outweigh any evidence from program evaluation to counter political will and public sentiment. Ethical considerations compel social workers to evaluate their practice, monitor client progress, engage in critical thinking guided by best available evidence, and establish personal practice models based in their own knowledge as well the experiences of others (Briggs & Rzepnicki, 2004; Gambrill, 2004). Ethical mandates are only applicable to individual social workers and are not enforceable by agency policy and procedure. Other staff who are not social workers are not obliged to adopt the same standards as mandates or guiding behaviors.

Commonalities of Program Review and Program Evaluation

While the program review is centrally focused on the program's overall health and the program evaluation's chief concern is whether or not the program is effective, each shares a number of commonalities. Both program review and program evaluation are concerned with issues of reliability and validity, which encompass the issue of program fidelity. Each is concerned with monitoring and tracking targets of change, and each has a role for stakeholders and beneficiaries to play in the planning and the actual process of program assessment. Each uses both objective and subjective sources of evidence to assess program functioning. Both are concerned with the structure and organization of the program, the character and the process of service delivery, the resources used to deliver the program's goods and services, the extent of the program's reach, and the program's effects by tracking the outcome and impacts of the program's change process on its intended targets. The data from both the program review and evaluation are informative and useful in continuing feedback and in the quality assurance cycle. These data point to what should be maintained and what ought to be changed. Both program review and program evaluation are program functions that are subject to external review as well as oversight by the leadership of the larger organization's executives, funding sources, legislators, and accreditation authorities. Both are subject to the politics of the organization's informal networks and external task environment context and realities.

As highlighted by Baer (2004) there are problems that accompany the process of program evaluation. As we see it, these contaminants negatively impact the outcomes of both program evaluations and program reviews. Different views of the problem can affect the measure selected to assess, monitor, and track the program's success. Some measures may actually reflect a problem, and some are less robust. Less robust measures may not capture all of the program's functioning, whether good or less than favorable. At times, the measure is provided to highlight a lack of funding necessary to perform all aspects of the program, and this can be a way to document the need for funding (Baer, 2004). As soon as the program become sufficiently funded, then the staff are encouraged to give examples of how well the program achieves it intended purposes even though they may not operationalize and use the entire program as conceived. This leads to questions about program fidelity (Baer, 2004). If the program is evaluated and found to produce significant results, but unanticipated procedures were used, then the program evaluation is impractical because the genesis of the results obtained cannot be attributed to the portion of the program used or may be due to the presence and use of unanticipated practices. In this case, program evaluation will be impossible to conduct with any reasonable assurance of determining what was responsible for the changes observed (Baer, 2004).

In some circumstances, the use of randomization, control groups, and multiple baseline single-subject designs increases the quality of the program evaluation and the ability to discern cause and effect regarding the program's effectiveness (Baer, 2004; Dudley, 2014). Random assignment sorts people into treatment and control groups and neutralizes the effects associated with selection bias. Comparing people in the treatment program with those in the control group on a particular indicator allows the evaluator to assess the differences observed between the two. This is more scientifically prudent, but randomized experiments are very expensive (Baer, 2004). Another way is to use single-case designs across all people in the program; this is time-consuming but lends itself to a formal assessment of cause and effect. In each of these scenarios, there must be a dedicated staff person or persons capable of planning and assessing program effectiveness. Thus, if done correctly both program review and program evaluation can help managers achieve three results: (1) an assessment of the program's overall success, (2) an assessment of the suitability of the theory of change to achieve the desired effects, and (3) an assessment of insufficient or lack of program implementation and the achievement or lack of achievement of program outcomes (Kettner et al., 1999).

CONTRIBUTIONS OF PRACTICE EVALUATION AS A TYPE OF PROGRAM EVALUATION

While the twentieth-century brand of social service delivery did not depend on the use of program review and program evaluation, this is not the case in the twenty-first century. The academy and practice arenas of social work are each sanctioning and pushing the use of evidence and the roles of program review and program evaluation as vital to the field's sustainability, transparency, and overall accountability. In this chapter, we have examined the benefits, contributions, and challenges of each to managers and executives of social service programs and organizations. Next, we conclude this chapter by articulating other concepts, such as practice evaluation, which are subsumed under the author's strategic and broad use of the concept of program evaluation. Practice evaluation provides a means to motivate the client to stay on their path and follow their plans. "What gets monitored, gets done" helps everyone to remain a central driver and to influence others to act as planned. Practice evaluation is used to determine if a desired client behavior change goal has been achieved (Corcoran, Gingerich, & Briggs, 2001).

The function and process of evaluation are practice steps that are essential to the change process and inherent to best practice and evidence-based approaches (Corcoran et al., 2001). What separates practice and program evaluation from research are, fundamentally, purpose, rigor, and emphasis. As an evaluation activity, practice evaluation is a check-and-balance feedback loop that is used to re-collect and re-examine the evidence on the targets of behavior change over a time series to assess whether a desired result was achieved (Corcoran et al., 2001). In this sense, it is chief among the ultimate values of social work practice and socially responsible program evaluation. In practice, the emphasis on cause and effect is of lesser importance; it is more an issue for the researcher and not for the client to figure out. Practice evaluation is driven by three key interrelated functions: (1) identifying the target of change and the indicator that encompasses the desired outcomes or measurable behavior change goals, (2) selecting the best measure to systematically use to record the program beneficiaries' behavioral responses and reactions to program implementation, and (3) assessing whether behavior change has occurred and the impacts realized because of it (Corcoran et al., 2001).

The evaluation of social work practice is as much a major concern now as it was in the humble beginnings of the profession, as observed by Claghorn (1927) earlier. Given that innovations in social work practice have been established as best practice and evidence-based treatment programs, the role and usefulness of evidence for program or practice evaluation is fast becoming an ethical imperative, as reasoned by Eileen Gambrill (2004). Leaders of social service agencies are wise to incorporate program evaluation as a routine practice activity requirement that all staff need to do. Early on and throughout all phases of the service delivery process, program review and program evaluation are value-added processes for leaders of social service organizations. Each provides a database to investigate whether or not the hunches and directions taken were the right course of actions. In this sense, program and practice evaluation data inform the decision-making, implementation, check-and-balance, and outcome assessment program processes.

Core Specialization Development Skill Competencies for Administration and Management

Section IV includes chapters that aid in the shaping and facilitation of skill competencies that contribute to and ensure agency and program development. The chapters in this section on development contribute perspectives and strategies to facilitate organization and program health and well-being. Changes and external pressures in the larger outside arena of the agency and program, as well as internal changes in budget and other key organizational dynamics (such as an aging workforce and changes in workforce characteristics) may necessitate the discontinuation of a program or set of services, the addition of new programs and services, or the rethinking, restructuring, or modification of how the agency, its programs, and its service system conduct day-to-day functions.

The preservation of an organization's health depends on the extent to which the agency leaders as well as its stakeholders use evidence and various sources of information to fully participate in all aspects of the life of the organization. The chapters in Section IV illustrate the extent to which stakeholders from the bottom up and top down are empowered by involvement in the planning, implementation, continuous improvement, and evaluation cycles. This involvement increases organizational buy-in and sustainability. Achieving organizational buy-in improves the capacity of administrators and managers to make the necessary shifts and changes that ensure a culturally responsive agency and program health even during times of fiscal cutbacks and downturns in the economy. In Section IV, the authors lay out strategies for arranging and conducting organizational and program development that enhances overall accountability but also supports improved stakeholder performance and overall service effectiveness. They use real organizational examples to illustrate the positive consequences that are a result of agency leaders investing in organizational and program development as a means to enhance agency and program accountability to achieve service effectiveness.

Organizational Development

Agencies that grow in size by virtue of their tenure in the task environment or by default because there are no other providers available need to be cautious and recognize the drawbacks relative to their noncompetitive advantage. It would serve leaders of these types of agencies to heed these words: engage in an ounce of prevention, for it is certainly worth a pound of cure! Unequivocally, sustaining an ongoing organizational development process will aid in the agency remaining relevant and innovative as well as avoiding becoming unsuccessful, ineffective, and obsolete.

The reality is that getting an increased agency budget without having earned it sets the agency up as easy prey for poor performance. If performance does not matter and you still get an increase in your bottom line, it only serves as a disincentive to good performance. It sabotages the agency's efforts to organize its staff inputs and outputs and its client outcomes into any meaningful interdependent contingent reinforcement relationship.

Agencies that are not required to demonstrate overall effectiveness and impact but are held to the industry standard practice requirement of ensuring the delivery of units of services only are at risk. They are susceptible to the propensity of failing to ensure regular self-inspection of and reflection on related ongoing organizational development activities. In these agencies, organizational development and organizational improvement are treated as obsolete, forgotten, or underused practices and functions in agency life because agency growth has not depended on them.

The health of the agency and its programs depend on the extent to which it routinely engages in an organizational development process. A learning organization perspective engenders and contributes to the overall growth and development of the agency as well as its stakeholders. As we see it, a culture of learning, which involves strategic decision-making based on evidence, is a useful framework to employ to ensure ongoing organizational development as opposed to a one-shot reorganizational development approach.

In this chapter, organizational development is conceptualized as a simultaneous learning and problem-solving process that involves organizational buy-in and ownership from top to bottom. It involves bottom to top approaches, turn-around management, and participatory management decisions. Each of these important features is highlighted in this chapter. Additionally, effective organizational development is an ongoing process that requires transparency, peer review, shared accountability, shared risks, and shared governance between staff and management. These concepts and their associated benefits and challenges are also critically examined in this chapter.

Organizations seeking to achieve service effectiveness through programs and services should invest in the organization's health and future. They can do this by budgeting funds that allow them to operate at ongoing organizational development capability. Organizational development efforts by social work administrators and managers should always be concerned with organizational health, growth, and sustainability.

Organizational Health

Agencies seeking to achieve as their bottom line better functioning for individuals, families, and communities require competent social work administrators as well as program managers. Chief among the skill competencies that the administrator and manager must demonstrate is experience and training in evidence-based management as a framework for leading organizational development. They will need to know how to use skepticism and questions as management tools. These are helpful because they structure the examination, promotion, and actualization of healthy organizational dynamics that are outcome-oriented and embedded in the values, ethics, and best practices central to social work.

UNIVERSAL TRANSPARENCY AND ACTIVE PARTICIPATION

There is a mutual sharing of explicit and implicit assumptions about the theory of the threats to the organizations' health. The theory of the threats to the organizations' health and how to handle it comprises a well-reasoned perspective on the organizational dilemmas, issues, and the capacity of staff and management to adequately address it independently or with expert consultation and technical assistance. The key activity here is to establish channels to discuss the origins, causes, correlates, and consequences of the wrong contingencies that are maintaining the organizational problem. Subsequent to establishing a clear problem analysis is the need to understand the right contingencies, based in the best science available, needed to effectively address the organizational dilemma or problem.

CONTINUOUS IMPROVEMENT AND PEER REVIEWS

At the program level, supervisory review and time management planning and review is done weekly, while internal peer review teams conduct agency program reviews quarterly. Data collected during peer review and internal audits are used to assess what is working as expected versus the occurrence of unintended or undesirable events such as negative client reactions to programming or unacceptable staff performance practices. These data help management redirect resources and intervene in problem areas while maintaining behavioral gains made by clients and staff as a result of successful programming.

SHARING ACCOUNTABILITY WITH INTERNAL AND EXTERNAL STAKEHOLDERS

The implementation and use of compliance agreements and performance contracts between staff, management, and the board of directors increases the likelihood that legal and hierarchal accountability is established internally and observed externally. The more complex the objective and its dependence on multiple players for its achievement means that everyone directly involved must assume personal responsibility for the outcome to keep each part of the chain linked and responsible to the other.

SHARING RISKS AND RESPONSIBILITY FOR SERVICE EFFECTIVENESS

Everyone inside the organization and who funds the program is liable for the unintended consequences, risk, and harm involved with the change process used to modify, remove, or establish new behaviors. With sharing risk comes shared decision-making and resource sharing as a context for establishing a reciprocally supportive system of care.

PARTICIPATING ACTIVELY IN SHARED GOVERNANCE

It is always best to establish a personal work ethic; most people just want to know that you are being a good citizen and doing your part in sustaining the agency. Being available for meetings and establishing a schedule of regular and dependable access by managers increases the likelihood that staff who are always at work are people who the agency can always count on to demonstrate organizational buy-in and leadership, as well as help carry and do the heavy lifting.

To be able to actualize these competencies means that they must be trained in the creation and sustainability of active cultures of learning. The training objective should be that management and staff will acquire evidence-based management competency. If the training is successful, they will be skillful in the strategic use of evidence as a guide for assessment, planning and development, implementation, continuous quality improvement, and enhancement and development, as well as in facilitating internal organizational behavior modification processes.

Every player in the organization should be chiefly concerned with doing their jobs. They should be committed to do the very best they know how and in the most efficient and effective way to achieve the desired program effects. The actualization of program effects and intentions positively reinforces agency stakeholders and service beneficiary endorsement of the leadership's reputation. The agency's credibility as a provider of distinction, its capacity and experienced manpower, and its organizational improvement processes increase the value of its brand as a service industry standard of excellence to achieve. The clout derived from that status allows the agency's leaders to leverage to expand markets and grow in response to the growing needs of funders.

To ensure that everyone in the agency is doing what was envisioned as the theory of the threats to organizational health and targets of organizational behavior modification requires that managers monitor all aspects of the plan of change through investigating regularly the way it operates to achieve desired outcomes. Leadership sets the bar for organizational health because they are always advancing the bar for themselves. They guide as well as support others to surpass established expectations while always getting staff and management to work toward continuously raising the learning as well as the performance bar.

Effective leaders manage organizational health building efforts through teams and shared responsibility arrangements with other managers, staff, and board members. They do this as a way to leverage the completion of a series of complex interrelated activities that will increase the probability of achieving desired milestones and ultimately actualizing the sought after outcomes. In this way, everyone has a job to do that impacts, supports, and enables another to achieve his or her personal best in an organization as well as to keep each player transparently accountable to others.

Organizational health is a process that involves a strategic assessment of how well an organization is functioning and if there are harmful unintended consequences as a result of the way agency operations occur. Interviews with key staff and management are essential. Equally important are data from the direct observations made by administration. A third set of important data is derived from the reported judgments of client consumers, family members, and other stakeholders. These vitally important data sources provide evidence to assess the health of an organization. The more transparent administration is about receiving and using feedback and its relative importance to learning, decision-making, and problem-solving, the more capable they are to effectively managing an active culture of skeptics and continuous inquiry.

Continuously tracking and monitoring errors and omissions can have dramatic effects on reducing agency liability. Learning about those conditions that sustain agency liability or ineffectiveness constitutes added value. Healthy organizations track their standard practice errors and successes as a basis by which to make critical decisions about the future of the organization's goods and services. Healthy organizations that engage in these practices have credible reputations and trademarks such as a brand, a way of conducting business, and a way of growing new business that typically expands beyond the province of turf.

Healthy organizations devise and execute organizational behavior modification programs. These have a particular organizational behavior modification objective in mind. They lay out a learning and change process for a team of motivated staff, management, and other allies to undertake as the change champions for that particular behavior change goal. Different teams of staff, management, and other stakeholders, like agency board members, should address different objectives, so that the organizational change process is experienced with 100% buy-in and participation. Organizational behavior modification plans include the targeted change objective; the research supporting the procedure and process being used; and the content, process, and feedback loop used to track the particular change process and the rate of expected versus actual change. Organizational behavior modification plans must also address the coordinating team responsible for the change objective and process, the resources needed and actually used, the schedule of planned versus actual meetings, and the evaluation of the timeline for achieving the intended change target and effects.

An example may help illustrate the approach to organizational behavior modification.

As depicted in Figure 17.1 the focus on leadership as an essential area of organization behavior modification is illustrated in the following example of a ficticious agency named CSI Inc. As a way of contextualizing its importance, the policy-making board of directors and the executive leadership of this organization were "grandfathered in" as a result of old loyalties and political allegiances to a community member who started and aged out of the organization. Through political accountability, the organization has experienced a growth in size and stature. Yet, with respect to child, family, and legal accountability, it is not operating desirably.

An outside consultant experienced in working with troubled nonprofits with high visibility and political clout was able to secure the respect of the entire organization and a few board members. Through his charisma and knowledge of non-profit organizational health and effectiveness, he was able to help each layer of the organization buy in to the change and the need for their participation in bringing about the transformation needed to achieve both service effectiveness and better functioning client-consumers, families, and overall community development.

The goal was to aid in the retraining and retooling of the executive management's competence in both evidence-based management and the competent use of culture and science as a foundation for administering a community-based organization. This organization is pursuing effectiveness in the reduction of maladaptive and poor functioning of nonachieving young adults capable of accessing the social determinants of health through the use of education, habilitation, and economic participation. The organization has been in existence for more than forty years, but

Example of CSI's Behavior Modification Plan

CSI's organizational development team will begin working agency wide to design a organization behavior modification plan and process to address identified areas of concern as targets for change.

TARGET BEHAVIOR and CHANGE STRATEGY	PLANNED OUTCOME
Leadership. The Executive Director (CEO) and key managers will receive coaching/training in an evidence based/performance management specialized leadership skill competencies.	**Leadership.** The CEO and key management will be able to administer programs and services through the use of evidence and performance management methods.
Communication. Effective communication will be achieved through bulletin boards, newsletters, etc.	**Communication.** Vital information will be disseminated daily, weekly, and monthly through bulletin boards, reports, emails, secure intranet chat rooms and blogs
Organization. Organizational and departmental policies and procedures and cross department policies and procedures will be established.	**Organization.** Organizational policies and procedures will be used and enforced agency wide.
Infrastructure. Establish an infrastructure with coordinated roles and responsibilities.	**Infrastructure.** CSI will operate within a clear infrastructure with job descriptions defining roles and responsibilities that are coordinated within and between departments.
Professionalism. Management and staff receive training in professional codes of conduct that dignify and affirm each others contributions and performance	**Professionalism.** Management and staff will demonstrate code of conducts identified in the Social Work Code of Ethics.
Teamwork. Create an internal administrative group of key staff and program supervisors whose chief responsibilities involve meeting to plan, implement and evaluate organizational buy in and management turnaround organizational development and organizational enhancement activities.	**Teamwork.** There will be on-going intra and inter organizational development activities that will sustain opportunities for building a culture of teamwork.
Accountability. Each department will assist the organizational development team in designing/implementing an internal and cross department accountability plan.	**Accountability.** Measurable policies, practices, procedures, roles and responsibilities will be tracked and monitored agency wide, so that management and staff are able to be clear about their expected performance, autonomy, and formal authority within CSI and in service collaboration with other provider agencies.

FIGURE 17.1. CSI's behavior modification plan

it has not kept up with hiring staff who know how to teach while using both clinical and therapeutic aids that prepare its client-consumers for engaging with and participating in a knowledge economy. The employees are products of educational institutions that are highly reputable, but the population they are serving present a number of challenges that are outside of the training and skill competency of this talented staff. These staff were trained in silos, using deficit thinking-based approaches, which only serve to alienate them from their clients, as opposed to engaging and supporting their connections to the marginalized population who populate alternative schools and inner-city community-based programs.

Unfortunately, the population they serve are without the political advocacy and resources that would list them as a protected class of special education students. A number of them also have juvenile and dependency court system involvements, come from racially oppressed backgrounds, and live within historically marginalized communities. Almost all of them are poor and are unable to finish secondary school in a traditional public school setting. As highlighted in Figure 17.2, these staff and the administration of this organization need personal leadership training as a team, while program, upper, and executive management need training in staff management people skills. This training would help incentivize and motivate staff and program management on ways to keep hope and the dream alive, as well as provide technical training in the use of evidence to obtain the resources and supports

---

Organizational Behavior Modification Objective
Increase in reputation as an impactful and effective agency

Best Practice literature tips

See Chapters 8 through Chapter 20 in this textbook to incorporate as guides for conceptualizing and implementing specialization skill competencies to lead and administer integrative practice in community based programs and agencies.

Refer to Resnick (1978) for practice approaches to facilitate organizational change from within and bottom up.

See Briggs and McBeath (2009) for options for implementing evidence based management in organizational settings.

See Chapter 8 by Briggs and McMillin in Rzpenicki, McCracken, and Briggs 's (Eds) (2012) textbook, From Task-Centered Social Work to Evidence-Based and Integrative Practice for an example and an approach to implement evidence based management and evidence based practice in community agencies.

Content
Enhance performance of stakeholder base

Process
A bottom up and top down individual development plan

Feedback Loop
Annual and routine performance updates

Administrative Coordinating Team
Member from Agency executive committee,
Member from program management committee,
Member key staff champions committee, and
Two members from other key stakeholders
(Families As Allies to Staff and Management)

Resource Needs
Infrastructure assessment
Central administration support
University faculty, family allies, and staff champions

Schedule of Meetings
Develop schedule of administrative coordinating team meetings
Incorporate identified key content areas of organizational behavior modification plan objectives into meeting schedule

Timelines of Milestones
Plan timeline of specific organizational behavior modification milestones for each of the planned objectives

FIGURE 17.2. Organizational Development Process Leadership

needed to further enhance staff and program functioning and performance, as delineated in Figure 17.3.

The team of staff, program managers, and executive management need training in the development of guiding behaviors that allow them to use their ethical framework as a staging ground for thinking how to practice competently outside the box. Additionally, turnaround management should be utilized to change the organization from within (Resnick, 1978) to establish an authentic culture of trial and error and learning (Senge, 1990) as a way to standardize the practice of using evidence to improve personal and program performance.

In nonprofit organizations, the staff and managers who administer the goods and services provided, lack a clear way to establish and ensure accountability in the

---

Organizational Behavior Modification Objective
The executive and program management will receive coaching in the use of evidence to supervise and manage agency programs and services.

Best Practice Tips

see Briggs (2001a) and Briggs and McMillin (2012) as a guides and examples for:

The strategic use of evidence in decision-making by management contributes to a better functioning agency, programs, and client consumers.

Reviewing practice decisions, errors and success contributes to both transparency and learning.

Content
The management team will acquire coaching in the use of performance and evidence based management of AGENCY X

Process
Management team will meet monthly with training facilitator for coaching in performance and evidence based management.

Feedback Loop
Management team will employ interactive staff training approaches to achieve agency transformation

Administrative Coordinating Team
1. Selected members from agency administrative executive team
2. Selected members from program management committee

Resource Needs
Central administration support
University faculty training champions
Management Consultants
Consultation from key staff level champions

Schedule of Meetings
Develop schedule of administrative coordinating team meetings incorporate key content areas of organizational behavior modification plan objectives into meeting schedule

Timelines of Milestones
Through consultation the management team will identify leadership development pal and course of action through coaching, booster training, and technical assistance.

FIGURE 17.3. CSI Organizational Development Process Leadership

delivery of social services. This lack of understanding of the importance and having checks-and-balances in an agency that depends on critical thinking and monitoring of its assumptions as a basis for pursuing behavior change is antithetical to the achievement of service effectiveness as alluded to in Figure 17.4.

Staff and program management may not realize how competing issues of accountability can challenge program improvement in nonprofit organizations, as clearly articulated by Seok-Eun Kim (2005). He distinguishes the countervailing forces and threats of each type of accountability. As he sees it, negotiated, compliance accountability is comprised of legal and hierarchical accountability.

Organizational Behavior Modification Objective
To establish an on-going check and balance system involving program review, quality assurance, and program evaluation within and across departments

Best Practice Tips

Effective agencies track and monitor the activities of all levels of an organization. It is always important to remember that what gets monitored gets done!

Content
Create a multi-level supervision, program review, Quality assurance, and program evaluation schedule of activities.

Process
Establish a change champions committee to establish a draft policy and procedure for weekly supervision, monthly quality assurance, and quarterly program review and program evaluation.

Feedback Loop
Prepare monthly reports of the committee's progress in designing checklists that are cross department and department specific.

Quality Assurance Coordinating Team
Member from Agency executive committee, member from program management committee, member key staff champions committee, and two members from other key stakeholders
(Families As Allies to Staff and Management)

Resource Needs
central administration support and sanction, university faculty training champions, management consultants, and key staff level champions

Schedule of Meetings
Develop schedule of broad base quality assurance coordinating team meetings
incorporate quality assurance organizational behavior modification plan objectives into meeting schedule

Timelines of Milestones
The committee identifies quarterly aims and milestones that reflect their work on policies, processes, and procedures to ensure quality control within and between departments.

FIGURE 17.4. CSI's Accountability Process

Professional and political accountability, however, are comprised of connections to power relationships based in *quid pro quo*, personal clout, and capital arrangements which circumvent the scrutiny and purview of legal and hierarchical accountability (Kim, 2005).

When allegiance to professional and political accountability is high, the organization and its players need to have assurances and use standard practices, which includes administrative sanctions and enforcement protections. As highlighted in Figure 17.5, enforcement protections are the contingencies that trigger incentives,

---

Organizational Behavior Modification Objective
Establish an organizational transformation process that will create opportunities for all staff and management to buy in and assist in using turn around management approaches to engender an all hands on deck spirit at AGENCY X.

Best Practice Tips

The best results from teams occur when they know what and why they are doing what they do. According to Scholtes, Joiner, & Streibel (2003): A organization functions better when there is a common understanding of the organization's vision and values.

Content
To create team building opportunities for all staff and management to contribute to the organizational transformation.

Process
Let change champions meet with staff and management and assess where they want to join and participate in the agency change process.

Feedback Loop
Change champions will track and monitor staff and management experience in organizational change process to determine support and resource needs and reactions.

Administrative Coordinating Team
Member from Agency executive committee, member from program management committee, member key staff champions committee, and two members from other key stakeholders (Families As Allies to Staff and Management)

Resource Needs
Central administrative support, university faculty, family allies, and staff champions

---

Schedule of Meetings
Develop schedule of administrative coordinating team meetings Align the implementation of organizational transformation strategies with each of the organizational behavior modification plan objectives and establish a meeting schedule to address each implemented objective and related strategy

---

Timelines of Milestones
The agency wide change champions that serve on the administrative coordinating team will establish a check and balance approach and implementation process to track progress of organizational transformation

---

FIGURE 17.5. Teamwork

penalties, and negative reinforcers that elicit activities and channels to ensure the regularity of legal and hierarchical accountability.

Organizational Growth

Planned organizational growth occurs when the resources needed to match the demands of capability and expertise are established through a standard RFP process, sole source agreement, or other financial agreements. This results in a contract between a funder and the agency procurement officer and CEO. In a resource-limited environment where service providers are scarce, the funder must depend on who is available to provide a necessary service and may end up increasing the size of an agency's budget that would otherwise be passed over due to a track record showing no measurable results and/or the provision of poor-quality services. Agencies that flourish under this scenario and the people who reinforce this type of service delivery give human services a bad name and represent a blight on the character of those of us who are ethically and transparently committed to delivering appropriate, high-quality, and effective services.

Community agencies, like most municipal and federal funders of social services, are actively seeking new streams of revenue to finance the delivery of vital human services to the people who need them. Periods of economic recession amid booming real estate foreclosure, a troubled housing market, and downward trends in lending from banks have redefined and endangered the middle class. They, too, have become a new client stream for community agency emergency assistance. As more people become economically challenged, there will be a rise in unemployment and a surplus of human capital with idle unused energy. Meanwhile, there are venture capitalists, in the energy field in particular (the lighting and biodiesel technology markets) who want to become socially responsible businesses. However, these businesses lack knowledge about economically fragile people and how to incentivize them to become competent, motivated workers, ready and sustainable for employment and careers in the biotechnology knowledge labor economy. In this scenario, both seek an economic stimulus. All that is needed is to recognize that reciprocal co-investment of untapped human and energy resources is a leveraging opportunity for increasing additional revenue and enhancing social, human, and economic capital among clients and communities, as well as participating energy conservation and new technology venture capitalist groups.

Another resource for the economic stimulus of social service agencies and organizations is to consider partnering with financial institutions such as the agency's insurance and pension funds providers. The relationship between financial illiteracy, financial distress, and health costs for organizations is phenomenally exorbitant. Creating co-investment opportunities to reduce healthcare costs associated with financial distress and financial illiteracy is a preventive health and interventive public health approach. This will yield costs savings that can be realized through financial incentives from insurance and participating pension fund providers, as well as other financial institutions that transact business with the social service provider. Also, linking treatment or service plans to include a goal of financial literacy and wellness from a financial institution that engages in socially responsible business practices and provides significant financial support to aid the agency in achieving its mission may prove to be an additional set of financial and curricula resources that contributes to both the health and longevity of the agency and its direct service beneficiaries and staff stakeholders. Thus, as organizations pursue growth potential, they should also be concerned with maintaining their market distinction as a dependable and reliably prudent provider of vital stabilizing and therapeutically based programs and services to a particular population at risk.

Organizational Enhancement

Nonprofit organizations' policy-making board of directors, staff, and management seeking to address issues of racial disparities and disproportionality experienced by an agency's client-consumers could benefit from additional education and technical assistance training. This would benefit a number of key areas that impact their efforts in working with client-consumers, groups, and communities impacted by a culture of systematic racism and inequalities.

SUSTAINING PRIVILEGE THROUGH STRUCTURAL RACISM

Staff and managers need to understand how to use multicontingency analysis and incentives systems as conduits for preserving choices and preferences in organizations (see Briggs & Paulson, 1996). Participants learn how policies and procedures function as mechanisms to sanction race-based preferences and minimize individual decision-makers. Corporate and social service agency examples are highlighted as a context for establishing a culture for organizational change aimed at arriving at and establishing cultural universal principles that respect gender and culturally specific traditions as well.

UNDERSTANDING CULTURAL DIVERSITY AND MODERN RACISM: FRIENDS OR RIVALS

It is important to acquire an understanding and use of pedagogy on race, the knowledge of vocabulary, and the interrelationship between modern racism and cultural diversity (see Briggs, 2001). Staff and management need to learn about competing perspectives on social justice along with their relative advantages and challenges to their overall adoption. Social justice frameworks for addressing the issues of institutional racism are highlighted and critically assessed here.

ACHIEVING CROSS-CULTURAL COMPETENCE

Voluntarily seeking and providing time to support staff and management skill competencies in honoring and using the culture knowledge and values of employees is crucial (see Chapter 6). It highlights ways of improving employee relationships and getting the best performance out of diverse employees.

Types of Cultural Diversity. Implement a day-long session devoted to addressing cultural diversity and the importance of awareness within the agency. This one-day session reviews best practice principles. Participants learn ways to honor the richness of diversity as an organizational investment and community affairs strategy for advancing diverse workforce targets and achieving the agency's performance bottom-line. This session also addresses the various types of cultural diversity (e.g., acculturation, enculturation, and racial socialization) as a context for learning about within-group diversity and between-group cultural axiology.

Racial Respect. Learn the theory of racial respect and its linkage to the social determinants of health for African American men and women. It describes what African Americans perceive to be value added to them as racially different people in American society. This session presents a framework that includes (1) an analysis of the differential significance of racial respect for African American men and women and its relationship to black adaptive and maladaptive identity theory (Briggs, Kothari, Briggs, Bank, & DeGruy, 2015); (2) an analysis of the influences of gender socialization; (3) an examination of the threats to racial respect, such as victimization from heightened exposure to HIV, cultural beliefs, drug abuse, and relationship to antisocial outcomes such as corrections involvement, participation in a network of people with corrections involvement experiences, and risky sexual practices; and (4) a concise discussion of the developmental competencies and prosocial correlates of racial respect for adult African American men and women; as well as (5) a confirmatory factor analysis of gender-specific racial respect scales and their correlates. The implications for respect and how it differs for other racial and ethnic groups are explored as a context for non profit and corporate culture organizational development.

Adaptive and Maladaptive Identity and Health Outcomes. Learn the theory and supporting data on adaptive and maladaptive identity with black adult men and women. This theory describes the differences between prosocial and criminogenic adaptive identity, racial identity, and racial socialization and the importance of understanding these differences when working with black people. Employees will learn about a multitude of racial injustices. In particular, they will learn about the sources of differential treatment of African Americans and its resulting effects on endorsed character and perceived well-being, which in turn influences their primary health and mental health. To investigate this proposition, we have developed and tested the Perceptions of African American Experience (PAAX) scale (Briggs, Bank, Fixsen, Briggs, Kothari, & Burkett, 2014). This is a new measure of two maladaptive and two adaptive identities among African American men and women.

What adaptive and maladaptive identities look like in other cultures is explored as a basis for examining risk and resilience in a corporate culture.

Culturally Competent Roles for Administration and Management. Management needs to understand the intersection of performance management and the relationship typology for managers, which infuses ideas from both Harold Briggs (performance- and evidence-based management) and Joy DeGruy (management relationship model) (see Chapter 6 of this book). This is a context for teaching managers the roles and responsibilities necessary in the cross-cultural supervision and management of racially diverse employees. Three key culturally enriched roles for managers are highlighted as a context for supervising racially diverse employees.

Coaching Fusion of Culture and Evidence-Based Management. Learn ways to implement the three approaches to evidence-based management and the concepts and strategies involved in culturally centered organizations (Briggs & McMillin, 2012). Evidence-based management is emerging in the helping professions in response to heightened demands for public accountability and organizational performance. This session defines evidence-based management and reviews its origins in the healthcare and business sectors, as well as its recent incorporation into the social work profession. Consideration is given to the similarities between the dominant models of evidence-based management and evidence-based practice (EBP). It explores the challenges facing administrators seeking to incorporate evidence-based management processes into social service agencies and the implications of evidence-based management for social service agency practice and social work management.

Infusing Culture and Evidence-Based Mental Health Services. Staff and mangers learn how to incorporate culturally centered principles and practices with evidence-based approaches in an organizational context for solving social issues. Participants learn to achieve organizational transformation and cultural centeredness in addressing mental health issues among culturally diverse populations (see Chapter 19). The lack of culturally appropriate health and mental health care has contributed to the large number of African American youth and families involved in the child welfare system. This session reviews the consequences of insufficient access to culturally sensitive, evidence-supported interventions for African American foster youth. The presenter offers a framework for the development of culturally appropriate mental health interventions responsive to the needs of African Americans. A case example illustrates the integration of culturally sensitive care and EBP principles in caring for African American foster youth and their families (see Briggs, 2009). A guide for aiding racially diverse foster parents and birth families in the use of EBP is provided as an approach for increasing family participation as allies in service delivery (see Chapter 20).

Racial Disproportionality and Racial Disparities and African Americans. Staff and managers need to understand the role that structural racism plays in racial disproportionality and the racial disparities encountered by African Americans. The session highlights blacks' experiences in low-end prevention and early identification systems, along with why they end up and remain in high-end restrictive health and human service systems. Although this session for policymakers and practitioners involved in improving health, mental health, and human service delivery systems focused solely upon racial disproportionalities—essentially ratios of racial imbalance—is necessary, it is not sufficient to improve the well-being of African Americans involved in high-end systems of care, such as child welfare and juvenile justice. Rather, we posit that it is essential to understand the often unnoticed relationship between, on the one hand, racial disproportionalities in high-end systems and, on the other hand, racial disparities in service accessibility, appropriateness, delivery, effectiveness, and quality in low-end systems of care such as health and mental health care. Understanding racial disproportionalities and disparities in their entirety requires a comprehensive assessment of the African American experience within and across prevention and intervention systems, such as behavioral and primary health care, as well as high-end restrictive care systems like child welfare and juvenile justice.

Organizational Sustainability

Sustaining the organization involves teamwork (see Briggs, 2001). Teamwork involves linking each part of the whole to others in a transparent and reciprocal fashion. The lack of teamwork disenfranchises many stakeholders inside and external to the organization. It is important to avoid unhealthy practices and to create internal change organization policies and procedures that establish the interdependent nature of the agency's vision, mission, and program goals as a matter of standard practice.

Working toward goals involves using a collection of individual and relational skills that come under the scrutiny of others in a culture of learning. This means that everyone is held accountable to each other in achieving better ways of working together to accomplish intended service and program effects. To minimize the expense for implementing these themes into training workshops would be to tie together agency and community-based projects that would result in a permanent product and sustainable organizational enhancement strategy. Preparing grants for external funding for training, service learning, and diffusion of science into real-world application provides a perfect opportunity to strike up relationships with faculty of schools of social work with expertise in training, grant development, and model development practice research with larger systems providing services to smaller systems. It was the strategy used by the first author in testing out the strategies discussed throughout this book (Briggs, 1994, 1996, 2001; Briggs & McBeath, 2009; Briggs & McMillin, 2012) (see Figure 17.5).

Successful teams follow and use incentivizing behaviors as a framework for participating in committees that are focused on a particular organizational development task or are specifically driven by an outcome, such as internal continuous quality improvement audits and program review. *Incentivizing behaviors* include honoring contributions, styles, and diverse points of view; instilling confidence among team members; and being responsible for each person's contribution to the others and the outcome. Incentivizing behaviors also include eliciting desired performance from teammates through nurturing encouragement and approaching tasks with teammates from a strengths orientation and as positively as practically possible.

Honoring Contributions and Diverse Perspectives. Joint efforts are difficult enough given the differences in style, opinions, and perspectives that accompany the involvement of different people to complete a task. It may prove useful to canvass the group as to their particular interests, preparation, and experience with aspects of the outcome that the team seeks to accomplish. A good approach to team projects is to recognize and accept the reality that no one person will end up shaping or achieving the finished product.

Different people present different work ethics and structure tasks variously, which can challenge the order and stability in which a team operates. In considering the outcome and tasks needed to complete the desired outcome, it would be useful to allow people as much flexibility as resourcefully possible. All meetings need not be attended in person by all involved as long as there is the ability to conduct tasks via teleconference calls, televised conferencing, webinars, or email.

Instilling Confidence Among Team Members. The outcomes pursued through teams require a spirit of cooperation. The climate and culture of group tasks can often disintegrate and create a level of abstractness and uncertainty that produces tensions for clarity of purpose.

Being Responsible for Your Contribution to Each Other and the Outcome. Taking responsibility for your part of the whole and negotiating the way in which you make the contribution to the team needs to be clearly articulated in advance of the team's organizing and structuring the team's scope of work. Staff and managers need to be creative and innovative in how they work together to capture passion and momentum.

Eliciting Desired Performance from Teammates Supportively and Encouragingly. It is often the case that you will be able to get more from others if you incentivize the team members' participation through desirable prompts and consequences.

Enabling Teammates to Participate by Engaging Others Through Reinforcement. At all costs, avoid using styles of communication that attack and blame others, which elicit diatribes and punishment. In circumstances where a team member requires corrective feedback and you value them and what you hope to get from them, avoid the use of punishment. Balancing criticism about lack of performance with positive reinforcement about desirable performance is a preferred approach to sharing performance feedback with a colleague who is not contributing as frequently or as regularly as others.

All in all, guiding behaviors are fundamentally important to organizational development efforts. They incorporate the ethics, values, and practice principles of the profession. Also, they are a useful framework to facilitate professional communication and interaction between staff, managers, and other internal and external stakeholders.

18 }

Program Design and Development

First, to begin a discussion that distinguishes a skillful approach to transforming student or practitioner knowledge in using evidence in designing and developing effective programs is no easy task. Given such a tall order requires that we begin with Baer (2004). His scientific perspective on the definition of a program provides an excellent starting point. Baer says, "a program is a large recipe for a large problem. It explains how to decide who receives the program, who applies the program, and what they should do, and in what order they should do it" (p. 310).

Donald Baer's definition of a program should not be thought to embrace or be in alignment with current perspectives on the fidelity of empirically supported interventions (ESI). With the exception of task-centered practice, multisystemic therapy, and a few others, typically ESIs are procedural approaches that must adhere to strict standards of fidelity to avoid losing their potential effectiveness. Such prescriptive adherence to following a prescribed recipe requires very little discretion or autonomy by staff and management. It incorporates robotic or assembly line schedules and simulated events that must not be altered or modified. This use of the word "recipe" is contrary to Baer's usage of the word in his definition of the concept of a program.

In Baer's definition of a program, the practitioner has knowledge of applied behavioral analysis. Through a behavior analytic lens, knowledge of the triggers and consequences of desirable behaviors informs decision-making in practice. The use of contingency analysis helps managers decide who gets what, why they need it, and who does what and when they should do it. These are a few of the key comprehension questions that characterize sound program design.

Second, the importance of applied behavioral analysis to decision-making in designing effective programs is noteworthy. Practitioners require a fundamental understanding of and capacity to strategically use the principles of applied behavioral analysis. Administrators and managers who are knowledgeable and competent in its usage, support the furtherance of our aims: to educate them effectively and competently to use single-case and group-design research evidence to develop successful programs. In practical terms, this involves the practitioner being able to critically think through a contingency analysis. This involves articulating the reason for the program and the answers to the questions that inform the key steps of program design. All in all, a contingency analysis involves creating a hypothetical statement comprising an if-then proposition.

Logic modeling provides a pictorial rendering of the origins, causes, correlates, and consequences of a problem. It is a problem analysis format that allows the practitioner to examine hosts of interrelational stressors and needs at a glance. Logic modeling helps you plan out the rest of the assumptions and their logical consequences as well as essential next steps. It is a way to illustrate a behavioral contingency analysis. The content of a contingency analysis involves identifying as well as eliminating the problem and its associated needs. In this context, the contingency analysis of a particular problem and subsequent program methodology to address it is logically spelled out. It includes the needs analysis, plan of action, the implementation and work plans, the continuous quality assurance and program review probes, and the program evaluation cycle.

Critical thinking by the practitioner is essential to establishing and defining what is meant by the "if" statement, which constitutes the theory of the situation, and the "then" statement, which constitutes the structure and organization of the theory of change. Differentiating critical thinking as one of the chief prerequisites and skill competencies enables the practitioner to successfully design programs using Baer's perspective.

Critical thinking involves the acceptance of perspectives alternative to your original claims and perspectives. Columbo, Cullen, and Lisle (2001) describe the character of critical thinkers. "Instead of focusing on dates and events in history or symptoms in psychology, she probes for motives, causes—an explanation as to how things came to be" (p. 2). They go onto define the critical thinker as a person who possesses imagination and "points of view different from her own—then she strengthens, refines, enlarges, or reshapes her ideas in light of those perspectives" (p. 2). Using critical thinking then yields at least two types of knowledge that the emerging program developer will need to consider.

According to Hunsaker and Alessandra (1986), these two knowledge types have been likened to the functioning of the two wheels of a bicycle. The back wheel, technical knowledge, serves as the nuts and bolts of effective program design which allows us to plan "exactly what would be done by whom to whom and when that would happen, where it would happen, and how often it would happen" (Baer, 2004, p. 315). This kind of knowledge serving as the "back wheel . . . supplies the drive that you have to go anywhere" (Hunsaker & Alessandra, 1986, p. 3).

The front wheel, people knowledge, involves the understanding of the motives, incentives, and contingencies that comprise the realities of how things are: the way of life of a program. This essentially involves understanding the culture and politics of a situation and how to use this subjective data to get people to implement technical knowledge. According to Hunsaker and Alessandra (1986), "you can have all the back wheel expertise in the world; but if people won't cooperate or don't know where to go with it, you won't go anywhere" (p. 3). Thus, one drawback to using technical knowledge in the absence of people knowledge is that you are at risk of paralysis or sudden death. In this sense, the role of culture is a very powerful influence, one that can determine if a new idea based on evidentiary standards is implemented.

On the other hand, a major drawback to exclusively using people knowledge is the phenomena Columbo, Cullen, and Lisle (2001) describe as the "power of cultural myths." They argue that, universally, culture molds, defines, and prescribes what is true, what is right, and what is wrong. In this context, people knowledge involves the conditioning process by which we "internalize cultural values leaving us with a rigid set of categories for good and bad . . . they give us a helpful shorthand for interpreting the world" (p. 5).

Based on this interpretation, the role of culture may be one that discourages critical thinking. Briggs and Rzepnicki (2004) adapted eight guiding questions from the literature that can be used to avoid the drawbacks of total reliance on people knowledge.

1. What is the issue or claim (thesis) being made in simple and direct language?
2. Are there any ambiguities or a lack of clarity in the claim?
3. What are the underlying value and theory assumptions?
4. Is there indication of any misleading beliefs or faulty reasoning?
5. How good is the evidence presented?
6. Is any important information missing?
7. Is consideration given to alternative explanations?
8. Are the conclusions reasonable?

Ignoring the value of critical thinking can lead to what Columbo et al. (2001) refer to as "cultural blindness." The effects of the experience of indoctrination and acculturation to a system becomes invisible to us yet, when ignored, results in biases that, if used over time, reinforces our habits, cultural rituals, cultural myths, and beliefs in a system.

As program planners and designers, we ask you to think back on how your knowledge of a particular problem and its solution has evolved. How has your perspective changed about problem X, and how have your ideas about the solution to problem X changed over time? Applying the eight questions to your claim allows you to examine the evidentiary basis of your ideas for each aspect of program development. In other words, you can use critical thinking in each aspect of program design, beginning with (a) the problem statement leading to (b) a problem analysis, which includes a thorough review of literature documenting the need for an innovative program response; (c) a review of literature regarding program methods that are effective in addressing the problem; (d) a search of literature to support you in designing your program; (e) an identification of goals and objectives; (f) the creation of a program plan, and (g) the creation of an evaluation strategy.

These steps are a slight adaptation of the model used in *Designing and Managing Programs: Effectiveness-Based Approach* by Kettner, Moroney, and Martin (1999). Their model of effectiveness-based planning is a fine example of using evidence in the process of program development. In their text, students begin to learn about the issues of accountability, scarcity, and the need for innovation and change.

Expanding on these earlier ideas, this chapter embraces three main principles of program development:

1. Critical perspectives include a statement of the social issue or problem, value assumptions, and a summary of proposed plan of action that drives program design activities.
2. Knowledge development and knowledge diffusion informs the critical perspective and is a crucial element in establishing effective program design and development.
3. Practitioners developing innovative programs require a developmental research framework to assist them in planning innovation and change.

Critical Perspectives

Generally, in my experience of teaching program design and development, a few curious students may decide that checking out the literature is a waste of time. Horrified at such a response, I move the discussion to the central theme of the course: program design and development. I ask these learners what they envision as a statement of the problem they plan to investigate in designing their own program. I then extend the question to the entire class: What do you envision as a problem statement that you feel passionate about investigating in order to design a program response?

After they have had an opportunity to write their statements on one side of the black board, I offer three different examples of problem statements on the other side as illustrated below:

> *Example 1 problem statement*: Persons with developmental disabilities lack group homes that preserve their choices and provide them access to community survival skills programming, which ultimately leads to their semi-independence or lack of self-sufficiency.
>
> *Example 2 problem statement*: Troubled youth at risk of violence, substance abuse, and incarceration require a social investment program after school. This program supports their biopsychosocial and emotional development. It also facilitates critical thinking and academic skills and teaches relationship and networking skills with entrepreneurs.

Example 3 problem statement: Persons of color with a dual diagnosis lack access to agencies with program resources and staff sufficiently trained in evidence-based interventions aimed at reducing hospital stays and improving social functioning.

I then ask them to compare their list to mine. After comparing both lists, I then ask the students to tell me what is common in each of the examples I provide, based on five basic assumptions:

1. Practitioner has a value base for planning change.
2. Practitioner has knowledge of the population.
3. Practitioner has knowledge of what works with this population.
4. Practitioner has a well-reasoned plan or recipe based on previous knowledge.
5. Practitioner has articulated outcomes and an accompanying evaluation strategy to measure and verify results.

I then turn to the curious student who does not want to use the literature and ask them to tell me what information they are using other than library or original research in preparing their problem statements for program design. Most of these students start with the value assumptions that influence their idea generation and overall critical perspective. That is not a bad place to begin.

Social work practitioners as students are taught how to form a critical perspective in the first year of graduate and professional social work education. The critical perspective is an informed hunch that includes your values, beliefs, and ideas about the subsequent actions that need to be undertaken to remedy a particular social problem. John Longres (2000) defines a critical perspective as having three main components: (1) a statement of the social issue, (2) the practitioner's value assumptions about the issue, and (3) what the practitioner believes should be done to resolve the issue. In this context, the concepts of issue and problem are used interchangeably and mean the same thing: a condition that requires attention. Applying the notion of a critical perspective to one of the problem examples highlights where the novice is most likely to feel grounded. For example:

Social problem: Persons with developmental disabilities lack group homes that preserve their choices and provide them access to community survival skills programming, which leads to semi-independence and lack of self-sufficiency.

Value assumptions: The population at risk is capable of contributing as independent members of the community with support provided by effective behavioral and family support interventions.

Proposed plan of action: Community, agency, and family support intervention—based on behavioral and family support approaches.

Based on this framework, the value assumptions statement of the social issue or problem and the introduction of the proposed solution comprises an informed critical perspective for initiating the planning of effective program designs. This of course, assumes that the student has merged what they believe with what evidence they have gathered through the literature to support their particular point of view. Clearly, value assumptions drive or are woven into your ideas concerning social problems. Examine the following value statements and reflect on the underlying assumptions being made:

> *Increasing the rate of marriage for single mothers with children on welfare will increase financial security, socioeconomic status, and overall psychosocial stability.*

Clearly, what we are assuming is influenced by what we feel ought to happen. To increase marriage as a panacea for the problems of single mothers on welfare suggests that marriage will result in relief from poverty. Although the literature does support the assertion that two-parent–income families are a better arrangement than single parenthood, the literature also shows that one of every two marriages ends in divorce or annulment (Briggs, 2011). The statement assumes that increasing the rate of marriage rather than increasing the number of jobs and benefits for education will address the problem of poverty among single mothers on welfare. It appears to denigrate and pathologize the single-parent family option (Comer, 1980). Also, this statement assumes that the demand for income-generating male partners is available in large supply to meet the supply of single females with children. For black single mothers on welfare, that assumption is not correct. Many of the would-be male spouses are either incarcerated, dead, unemployed, or enjoy single life with multiple single mothers as partners (Gilder, 1995).

Increasing the marriage rate of black single mothers without other supports may create additional poor families and even increase the rate of divorce. This example was provided to show you how people develop ideas based on their own system without contextualizing the intervention. The point here is to draw your attention to the fact that many practitioners encounter the need for innovation and change. This should necessitate them using approaches that facilitate their thinking outside the box that they and others have created.

Knowledge Development

Practitioners who seek to propose program solutions need to not only be guided by their values about the social issue, but also to participate in knowledge development activities to inform their ideas and program planning. Gambrill (2004) describes the importance of advancing the social work profession's knowledge base as an obligation prescribed by the profession's code of ethics. In organizations, Patti, Poertner, and Rapp (1987) describe the role of knowledge development to practice as a key link to designing and implementing "something novel" for innovative and change-oriented activities. Patti et al. (1987) illustrate the key role of knowledge development to program design by drawing from Thomas (1984): "As used here, design is . . . the planful and systematic application of relevant scientific, technical, and practical information to the creation and assembly of innovations appropriate in human service intervention" (p. 106).

Briggs and Rzepnicki (2004) explain the crucial role of knowledge development in practice as threefold. First, sharing what you know with others so that they may have the benefit of your efforts can help others avoid mistakes you made and build upon where your earlier efforts fall short of accomplishing the goal. Second, participating in knowledge development activities as a consumer of information improves your understanding of the evidentiary basis of the usefulness of different approaches. Third, participating in knowledge development methods aids you in monitoring your practice assumptions and client reactions to treatment. Participating in knowledge development advances what we know in the field to help people effectively resolve problems that interfere with client self-determination.

Developmental Research and Model Development

Patti, Poertner, and Rapp (1987), Ed Thomas (1978), and William Reid (1978) have contributed significantly to our understanding of the developmental research function in human services. This is commonly referred to as the *model development approach*, which involves the use of current applied research transformed into a set of procedures that are pilot tested and improved upon until ready for dissemination. This is similar to evidence-based practice: both use existing research findings to inform practice decisions. The major exception in model development is that the procedures being developed are in their infancy stages, whereas, in evidence-based interventions, the procedures have been established, empirically validated by random control studies, and include a fidelity measure that guides program implementation. Briggs (2001) used a model development approach to the design of a planning, implementation, quality assurance, and evaluation strategy for working with persons with developmental disabilities, their staff care-providers, families, and management of a community organization.

The model design and development approach involves (1) problem analysis and project planning, (2) information gathering process, (3) design and development pilot testing, (4) evaluation and advanced development, and (5) dissemination and adoption.

PROBLEM ANALYSIS AND PROJECT PLANNING

As the initial step of the design and development approach through problem analysis, it is essential to articulate an assessment of the correlates, causes, and consequences as well as the implications of ignoring or inadequately addressing the problem. Evidence that informs this aspect of program design and development comes from a number of sources.

Human interest stories, sensationalized media coverage, professional experience, and empirical research, as well as the voices of clients, families, community groups, and grassroots leaders all inform the discovery process in which social issues are transformed into problems with priority status. Gang violence, police officer fatalities, and the rise in the foster care rate are major social policy debacles with which many cities, counties, and states are grappling on a daily basis. Too often, problems of this magnitude never get the type of comprehensive redress or the assiduous detail and attention needed because the scope of the problem is too narrowly construed. To avoid this onerous possibility, problem analysis should examine and describe the individual, social/cultural, and genetic factors to ascertain the problem's extent. It should also be informed by knowledge of the population cohort's values and norms; these are usually in conflict when intergenerational interests exist. Recently, African American men and male youth surveyed about the barriers to their success in Multnomah County, Oregon, reflected stark differences across most questions asked (Briggs, 2011). Whereas black youth identified education-related barriers as their chief obstacle, their adult counterparts selected discrimination as their chief obstacle to success. Solving the problem of discrimination is unrealistic and tantamount to swatting at windmills, given the federal court's definition of the types of evidence one would need. On the other hand, addressing the problem of education-related obstacles, though perceived as equally elusive, is much more specific and realistic than attacking a problem that is wide-ranging and unfeasible due to its scope.

Problem analysis should include an examination and description of the affected population, the catchment area, its indigenous resources, challenges, tensions, and needs for sustainability. Once collected and examined, these data form the basis of the significance of addressing the problem and its relevance and priority status to the affected population and community.

The problem analysis should include as much demographic information as necessary that will convey its gravity, extent, and broad-reaching impact; the interrelationships between the problem and other stressors; and the issues impacting the target population. To highlight the problem's severity, the problem analysis needs to include relevant literature and public documents. The relevant history of the origins of the problem within the community context and the community's collective voices are essential data to report as part of the problem inventory. This includes using published accounts and human-interest stories as featured in newspapers and on television and radio shows as well as testimonials and cultural communication venues that include the church and conversations in barbershops or salons. The problem analysis should include a well-constructed plan based on a thorough analysis of the needs of the target population and community. The data used to establish the problem, need, and potential solutions should come from a variety of sources, including local and epidemiological statistics. These data should establish a baseline of the needs, the problems, and the goals for the affected population and impacted communities.

INFORMATION GATHERING PROCESS

This step of model development involves interviews, direct observations, and a review of written materials from people in your task environment. The basis of your inquiry should include a focus on the problem specifics and the needs of the eligible population. Next, state the course of action envisioned, the best practices that have been used and their reported effects and impacts, and the program-specific hypotheses you seek to test and achieve through practice innovations and model development.

Information on the local context of the problem and critical needs, extent of the problem, and the consequences of not adequately addressing problems all can come from focus groups. These groups should be comprised of former and current clients, family members, or other care-providing and supportive sectors of the target community's task environment. Ideas for solving the problems and needs of a target population, as well as the organizational and community resources required, are also identified in the establishment of the model program.

DESIGN AND DEVELOPMENT PROCESS

This stage involves the creating the blueprint of the model program. According to Thomas (1984), design involves (1) selecting the intervention and its primary objectives, (2) inventorying the materials and supplies needed for program implementation, (3) gaining knowledge of the contingencies and best knowledge available on solving the problem and that will ultimately elicit desired behaviors and performance, (4) reviewing the research and references of the intervention's documented experience through academic publications, (5) initial testing of the pilot intervention, (6) undertaking evaluation and refinement, (7) doing advanced model development, (8) providing examples of the intervention that should work, and (9) formalizing intervention procedures and process via a curricula manual.

In this stage of model development, it is important to delineate the primary purpose, goals, and objectives of the model program or intervention. It is important to explain how the target population and community would look if the program was effective. In this context, it is important to describe the results you expect to obtain and the effects they will have on the target population and community. A logic model would help lay out the model program components.

Whether you plan to use an evidence-based practice or a method with less scientific support, you will need to identify the intervention or procedure method and provide a discussion about the literature that supports your claim. The literature review will need to include published materials from reliable sources which dispute

(1) the credibility of the findings and (2) the usefulness of the intervention for the target population. Clearly, it is important to provide a reasonable justification for using this intervention with the target population given their cultural context and customs. Thomas (1985) defines development as the next step after design. He refers to it as the implementation stage of model development. This stage of model development includes (1) formulation of an implementation and work plan for the intervention, (2) preparation for implementation, and (3) initial test of intervention.

In this stage of model development, it is important to use a timeline chart that reflects major activities, goals, objectives by staff, and timeframes. This schedule should be developed with input from members of the task environment and key staff and management of the proposal model program. Implementation plans should include agreements between other agencies and reflect evidence of planning and start-up activities. As all plans face potential obstacles and barriers, a discussion of these issues and how management addresses them should be included in the implementation plan. One major challenge or potential barrier is how to sustain project funding. This will necessitate a host of activities involving resource planning, grant development, fundraising, or contract negotiation with local municipalities.

Additionally, the implementation plan involves a discussion of responsible staff and key management concerning the planned use of facilities, equipment, and other material resources, as well as training materials, brochures, and published procedure manuals.

EVALUATION AND ADVANCED DEVELOPMENT

This stage of model development involves an appraisal of the implementation of the intervention, client reaction to the interaction, and staff judgments and behaviors. Procedures that appear to be useful are mentioned, and those that require modification or change are adjusted for retesting.

The evaluation stage of model development includes a discussion of the plans to link project goals and objectives to performance measures, data correction activities, data analysis strategies, a presentation of results, and the impact of the project on the target population. The evaluation plan includes performance measures and the behavioral definitions that represent key evaluation study variables. It also includes a discussion of the reliability and validity of the measures and their prior use and experience with the target population.

The evaluation plan examines the implementation process as well as the model program outcomes. In this context, the evaluation plan includes a detail discussion of the process of implementation. The unit of attention through evaluation activities involves assessing program fidelity as well as any unintended consequences or modifications to program implementation. Furthermore, the evaluation plan uses outcome data to track individual as well as group outcomes. Interviews, questionnaires, direct observations, and permanent client records are excellent data sources to use in assessing program outcomes and program implementation or to justify program changes based on the review of data.

DISSEMINATION AND ADOPTION

This stage of model development involves the transfer of the intervention internally to other areas of the organization or to another independent group seeking a plan of action to address a similar issue. Dissemination and adoption includes diffusion activities such as training, education, consultant, and the preparation of instruction manuals for public usage.

In this chapter, the use of developmental research is applied to the design and development model to establish an approach to the use of evidence and stages of practice model research development to frame and design effective social service programs. Through this perspective, the use of evidence aids in the design of planned change by advancing new practice models. These innovations are accompanied by careful scrutiny of their systematic implementation through a series of repeated evaluations. Data from these evaluations are used to make subsequent decisions that contribute to both service effectiveness and the establishment of an effective course of action and its subsequent adoption. Through the stages of model development, agencies can learn while engaging in problem-solving. Model development incorporates the strategic use of evidence for guiding the program design and implementation of innovative program practices. Much can be learned through program design and the systematic study of its implementation as staff and management strategically pursue the reduction in problems experienced by target populations.

Integrating Evidence, Culture, and Community-Based Participatory Program Design and Development

IMPLICATIONS FOR INCREASING STIGMA AWARENESS AND MENTAL HEALTH SERVICE USE AMONG AFRICAN AMERICANS THROUGH CULTURAL INJECTION VECTOR ENGAGEMENT (CIVE) THEORY

African Americans receive less and are given poor mental health care compared to whites (Snowden, 2001, 2012). In this chapter, we discuss the key root causes and conditions which contribute to (a) the lack of access by African Americans to high-quality evidence-based and culturally appropriate mental health care, (b) the underuse by African Americans of empirically supported interventions (ESIs) as current advances in mental health care, and (c) the insufficient numbers of African Americans in mental health intervention research designs to investigate the cultural appropriateness of ESIs with African Americans and the three key empirical questions pertaining to the use of ESIs with African Americans (Briggs, 2009; Briggs, Briggs, Miller, & Paulson, 2011; Briggs & McBeath, 2010). Part two of the chapter, defines evidence-based practice (EBP) and describes how it differs from ESIs and how it incorporates client and cultural knowledge in the process of making decisions given the best available scientific evidence and professional expertise. Part three, discusses the ways EBP can be used at the community level to launch the design of a culturally specific stigma reduction and service engagement approach with African American communities. Part four, includes a case study that illustrates the transformation of community norms and attitudes concerning mental health services and the engagement of mental health services by African Americans. The chapter's conclusion presents *cultural injection vector engagement* (CIVE) theory as a gateway to implications and next steps for increasing service engagement and use by underserved and culturally diverse populations (Briggs, Banks, & Briggs, 2014).

Introduction

While the prevalence of mental disorders is similar for whites and other racial groups, a score of disparities distinguish the experience of whites and racial minorities with mental health care in the United States. African Americans and other historically marginalized cultural and ethnic groups such as American Indians, Native Hawaiian and Other Pacific Islanders (NHOPI), and Hispanics are less likely to have access to, use, or achieve the benefits of quality mental health care. Sadly, this reality exists despite medical advancements, and its chief consequence is a longer life span for White Americans, while the health and mental health outlook for many African Americans remains dismal. Indisputably and regrettably, African Americans have a shorter life expectancy compared to whites (Hare, 2008). Among those living in poor communities, research evidence is available to show that they have a greater probability of experiencing major depression even if they live physically healthier lifestyles than African Americans who possess mental health, but live unhealthy lifestyles with limited access to health venues such as those that typically exist in white communities. These particular African Americans have greater access to fast foods restaurants, liquor stores, and drug dealers as neighborhood-based coping strategies for handling mental health-related issues (Hare, 2008). Thus, inner-city African American residents not only lack access to health-related venues (Williams & Collins, 2001), but they also remain chronically underrepresented in outpatient mental health statistics.

Notably, there is a rise in suicide rates of African Americans (Xanthos, 2008), especially among teenage African American young men and women within recent years (Joe, Baser, Neighbors, Caldwell, & Jackson, 2009). African Americans tend to experience less and poorer quality care in the mental health service system and are unlikely to seek, receive, and stay in treatment (US Department of Health and Human Services [DHHS], 1999). The Surgeon General's Report on Mental Health highlights recent advances in the effective treatment of mental disorders, but is concerned with the low utilization rates by African Americans of mental health care. As depicted in Briggs, Banks, and Briggs (2014), underutilization of mental health service use by African Americans is the result of (1) factors internal to the mental health system that serve as barriers and obstacles; (2) factors external to the mental health system that reduce the likelihood of their frequent service use; (3) factors that are individually based, which disincentivize mental health service use; or (4) a combination of (1), (2), and (3) and their respective correlates. Factors internal to the mental health system that impede frequent utilization have been reviewed by Briggs, Briggs, Miller, and Paulson (2011), identifying a number of cultural insensitivities that plague the service delivery functions of outreach, diagnosis and assessment, treatment, and evaluation. Factors external to the mental health system that contribute to low utilization by African Americans include (1) the low quality of care and no attention given to behavioral health assessments and issues by primary care physicians, (2) limited supply of competent African

American mental health professionals as a result of ill-equipped educational systems that fail to prepare high school students for college and careers in the health and mental health professions, and (3) the fact that state and local revenues are in short supply and the demand for public safety and care for the elderly and children take center stage.

Political interest group pressures and budget restraints leave fewer dollars available to address the growing mental health needs of the population. This has grave consequences for historically marginalized groups experiencing the chronic cumulative risks of substance abuse, homelessness, and incarceration as a result of structural inequalities that guarantee, through unenlightened social policy, lesser opportunities. Still, there are individual factors that also contribute to the low utilization rates of mental health services by African Americans. Chief among the many reasons that African American families opt out and do not voluntarily seek mental health care is stigma and mistrust as a consequence of cultural taboos, family traditions, shame, disrespect, and denial, as well as fear of having to take medications or lose freedoms and civil liberties. The totality of these cumulative challenges to the utilization rates of African Americans strongly suggests that more must be done to link them to effective mental health prevention and treatment services (Xanthos, 2008).

Arguably, the overall goal of increasing African American use of effective mental health care is a major priority and an important social determinant of health (Briggs, 2014). Given the challenges that contribute to the underutilization of mental health services by African Americans, it would seem plausible that, in this particular area, service use will need to be incentivized for African Americans. One way to incentivize the utilization of mental health services by African Americans is to include their cultural customs and knowledge and use market research about culture-specific age cohort interests, values, and norms as part of the engagement strategy. Although research on age diversity as a factor to consider in human service programming is virtually nonexistent, more has been done with respect to cultural diversity and competency in social work. Since McGoldrick, Pearce, and Giordano (1982) and Cross, Bazron, Dennis, and Isaacs (1989) published their pioneering and important works, discussions of the importance of culture in mental health has become commonplace (Pinderhughes, 1994). However, research on the effectiveness of cultural competency training on healthcare processes and outcomes has been derailed (Price et al., 2005). Based on a meta-analysis of research in this area (Price et al., 2005), the lack of methodological rigor in the study designs and other study-related flaws compromise any ability to reliably and accurately assess the empirical value and scientific contributions of the role of cultural competency training on health and mental health outcomes. Nonetheless, on the face of it, culture has come to be recognized as value added to social work practice, theory, and research endeavors. It is sanctioned as an important knowledge base for student practitioners of social work by the Council on Social Work Education's (CSWE) Educational Policy and Accreditation Standards (EPAS) as early as 1983 (Banks,

Hopps, & Briggs, 2018). It is also a cardinal value and practice principle described in the profession of Social Work's Code of Ethics.

Yet, it is about the intersection of culture, EBP, and ESIs that we have had too few discussions (Briggs, 2009). There are some who believe that we need to resolve the apparent disagreement over the relationship between culture and science (Isaacs, Nahme Huang, Hernandez, & Echo-Hawk, 2005), while others are eager to illustrate the compatibility of culture and science, in particular, the natural fit between culture, EBP, and ESIs (Bell, Wells, & Merritt, 2009; Briggs, 2009; Briggs & McBeath, 2010; Lau, 2006; Miranda et al., 2005). What has not kept pace until recently has been discussions on the fusion of cultural knowledge and EBP in and across fields of practice in social work (Blase & Fixsen, 2003; Briggs & McBeath, 2010; Isaacs et al., 2005; Wells & Briggs, 2009; Wells, Merritt, & Briggs, 2009). Three questions comprise the state of the art and areas in need of further investigation. First, do we use the existing science and apply these programs as-is to African Americans and then learn from the study of these experimental experiences? Second, do we compromise program fidelity and modify existing effective programs to add cultural components? Or, third, for the sake of fidelity, do we pursue a totally different option? This would mean, keeping an effective program as it was originally designed, but changing the context in which it is introduced and delivered to allow for the use of culturally sensitive venues that incentivize the engagement and sustainability of participation by African Americans. In this context, the culturally sensitive venue serves as an *injection vector* (a corrective measure to rid a computer program of a virus so that the computer may be operational) used to properly anchor or encapsulate the inclination and interest of the potential user as both an elicitor and reinforcer that sustains program participation. Answers to these and similar empirical questions hold the key to reducing the underrepresentation of mental health services and use of evidence-based programs by African Americans.

The Explosion of ESIs and EBP and Its Aftermath

In recent years, researchers and professionals in the field of children's mental health have given considerable attention to ESIs in their search for effective mental health interventions for children and families. The rapid dissemination and diffusion of ESIs characterizes the science-to-service strategy that is being adopted across federal and many state auspices to fulfill the promise of high-quality services. This was alluded to in the report of the New Freedom Commission on Mental Health (2003) as the means by which to achieve Goal 5: "Excellent mental health care is delivered and research is accelerated" (p. 12). However, concerns exist about the limitations of the current evidence base for practice with diverse cultural and linguistic communities and for populations with more than one problem (Littell, 2010; Wells, Merritt, & Briggs, 2009).

ESIs VERSUS EBP

The term "evidence-based practice" has come to be known as a noun and a verb (Rzepnicki, 2009). As a noun, it is a single-method intervention with a strong research foundation, recognized as an EBP or an ESI. As a verb, it is a five-step process that meets the original definition of evidence-based medicine (EBM) as defined by Sackett, Stauss, Richardson, Rosenberg, and Haynes (2000). "Evidence-supported interventions," commonly referred to as EBPs, refer to specific programs and interventions that were initially tested under controlled environments and subjected to highly rigorous evaluation procedures by at least two independent investigators using intervention research based on randomized clinical trials with similar positive results. ESIs are reputed to be cost-effective and to meet the highest evidentiary standards and tests of efficaciousness (under controlled settings) and effectiveness (in real-world applications) (McBeath, Briggs, & Aisenberg, 2009). As a result, requirements for the use of ESIs are commonly included in federal and state requests for proposals (RFP) and grant announcements (GA). At the federal level, the National Registry for Evidence-Based Programs and Practices (NREPP), which is used by the Substance Abuse and Mental Health Services Administration (SAMHSA) to evaluate and designate if a program meets federal guidelines and qualifies as an ESI. Alternatively, "evidence-based practice," as a verb, aligns more closely with the original definition and philosophy of the EBM model (Rzepnicki, 2009; Sackett et al., 2000). This original approach to EBP involves the integration of the best available evidence with other factors such as clinical judgment and client preferences in planning clinical care. This process-based approach to EBP involves the following five steps: (1) designing answerable client-oriented practice evidence search questions, (2) searching for the best available evidence, (3) critically appraising the evidence, (4) using clinical judgment and expertise in considering client preferences and the resources needed to implement each option, and (5) applying and systematically evaluating the services consistent with client preferences (Gibbs, 2003).

AFRICAN AXIOLOGY AND AFRICAN VALUES

Nichols (1976) is credited as being one of the early pioneers in delineating the premium placed on relationships in the African axiology. Others such as Akbar (1991) and Nobles (1991) and Corneille, Ashcraft, and Belgrave (2005) have reported similar characteristics, such as strong ethnic identity; religious foundations; formal and informal social networks; and respect for self, health, and well being as among the host of African values and customs observed by Nichols (1978). Due to the cultural disintegration that grew out of the American chattel slave system, African Americans may differ in their subscription to either an acculturated identity, an enculturated identity, racial socialization, or a combination of any of these factors as a context for identifying and expressing their individual perspectives about their black or African American experience. Also, it is possible that a black person may identify more with adaptive or maladaptive identities, such as (1) a person in recovery transcending the temptations of addictive contingencies and triggers; (2) a sheltered and insulated person living a safe and protected existence, avoiding risky alternatives; (3) a faith-based personality; or (4) a person who adopts a street personality and has middle- and upper-class values and customs as opposed to claiming any allegiance to racial or ethnic identities (Briggs et al., 2009). To illustrate the importance of combining EBP and culture, the following case example highlights the interrelationship between them splendidly.

A Case Study Approach to Stigma Reduction and Service Engagement of African Americans

There is strong evidence that supports the fact that African Americans are at greater risk to experience mental disorders, yet they are less likely to be consumers of mental health services, to understand mental disorders, or to be aware of available services to make informed health promotion choices. Access is a major problem for African Americans with mental health needs. This issue is complicated because best practices and evidence-based treatments that represent the best knowledge available to address a particular disorder and its related complications are less likely to be available in African American communities (Briggs, 2009). This further exacerbates the disparate mental health experiences of black and white Americans in this country. In Oregon, State Senator Avel Gordly knew all too well the consequences of not having mental health services available for African Americans in her state. The following is a model development account that encompasses the first author's collaboration with Senator Gordly (see Briggs et al., 2014).

KEY ASSUMPTIONS AND PURPOSE

Drawing upon EBP and a cultural philosophy that integrates attention to an oral tradition, community choice, strengths and empowerment, beliefs about healing and wellness, and social justice, it was decided to use a culturally centered approach derived through a community-based participatory research (CBPR) development model as step five of an EBP program. EBP design and development approaches would ensure the preservation of community values, community ownership, and community partnership with university researchers working as a team to develop a stigma awareness and service engagement model. An African American mental health researcher worked with the community elders and community organizers to develop an intervention process to educate the community about mental health issues and about the state mandate involving ESIs and EBPs to address these issues. Involving the voices of the community and people directly affected by mental health issues was expected to result in a consistent increase in mental health service use. The overall goal of this project was to develop and demonstrate the effectiveness of a process that would change community mental health care-seeking norms while increasing awareness of stigma, the brain and its relationship to health and mental health care, and the importance of prevention and regular mental health care, which is relevant to all communities of color.

CONTEXT

Since its beginnings in February 2008, a newly formed outpatient mental health clinic for African American adults had a problem: low numbers of African American citizens of Oregon utilizing the mental health programs and services available to them. During its first ten months of operation, it barely attracted 6% of African American service users. During this same time, the mental health researcher worked with the African American Mental Health Commission (AAMHC) using participatory research methods, EBP, and a task-centered model at the community level.

THE PROBLEM AND CHALLENGE

In 1999, the North East African American Alliance, comprised of the African American Leadership of Portland, established the AAMHC, presided over by Senator Avel Gordly. She and key African American community leaders met with two mental health researchers and a key faith-based community leader to acquire funding from Multnomah County to conduct a CBPR assessment of the behavioral health needs of the African American community in Portland, Oregon. The study investigated the perceptions and knowledge of mental illness, awareness of mental health service availability, and preferences for culturally specific mental health services for African Americans in Portland. Focus groups of parishioners and pastors were held by the key faith-based leader to study the faith-based needs of persons with mental illness. Individual interviews were held with denominational heads of various faith groups to identify different faith perspectives used by African Americans in Portland, such as Baptist, Baja, Muslim, Catholic, and nondenominational churches. In addition to pastors and parishioners, African American leaders, community residents, and social service workers were surveyed by one of the two mental health researchers who was also a well-respected leader in her community. In order to conduct the assessment, the female mental health researcher developed instruments for use in the inner-city community and with faith-based communities. She pilot tested the instruments with the North East African American Alliance community leadership, community residents, and members of her church. She met with the male mental health researcher and faith-based leader to interview them for input and further development of instruments.

The male mental health researcher used what was available in the mental health literature regarding African Americans. He uncovered that African Americans are less likely than whites to seek and receive mental health treatment. In general, African

Americans view depression as a personal weakness and typically engage family and friends instead of mental health professionals for assistance with their emotional and psychological needs. He further found information that suggested the belief by some African Americans that prayer and worship are effective treatments of depression and that African Americans are as suspicious of psychiatrists as they are of police contact. To assess the extent of what African Americans in Portland knew about mental illness, how they would handle it if they had it, and what suggestions they had for planning systems of care for African Americans with mental health needs, the male mental health researcher wrote a grant proposal, seeking funding to complete the needs assessment process and to develop materials designed by local African American researchers and community leaders.

INFORMATION FROM THE NEEDS ASSESSMENT

Many respondents (60%) did not know that the brain had any relationship to mental functioning. Sixty percent of pastors and parishioners tended to believe that prayer and talking to a close friend can cure mental illness. More than 70% of the community respondents and almost 60% of the pastors and parishioners tended to agree that, among African Americans, there seems to be a cultural belief that too much stress can lead to a nonspecific disorder commonly referred to as a "nervous breakdown." Many community, pastors, and parishioner respondents did not recognize manic depression as bipolar disorder. Most of the respondents (90%) expressed a strong desire for additional information and education on mental illness. The majority of survey respondents tended to want more accessible and culturally enhanced services for African Americans. Many of the survey respondents were dissatisfied with the current skill set of non-African American providers serving the African American community. Many of the respondents (70%) felt that African American mental health needs were unique, and most (85%) tended to prefer having African American mental health professionals work with the African American community. Most respondents (90%) were not comfortable with the mental health services available to African American communities, and most expressed dissatisfaction (92%) with the number of available African American mental health professionals serving African American communities.

This data established the need for an accessible and confidential location, African American clinicians as direct service providers, and education about mental health diagnosis and service. In the 2004 report by the AAMHC to the Multnomah County Commission and an in-person meeting between members of the AAMHC and the Multnomah County's Division of Mental Health and Addiction Services, the male mental health researcher described the findings of the mental health needs assessment conducted in the African American communities in Portland (Briggs, 2004). These findings are consistent with findings in national studies on African Americans and barriers to receiving mental health services by Lonnie Snowden (2001) and others. After hearing the presentation of the findings of the needs assessment study, one well-respected African American professional stated that it is no surprise that African Americans prefer receiving services from black professionals given the apparent hostility toward African Americans in Oregon. According to this unnamed source, "the citizens of Oregon would rather hug a tree than an African American."

Since no model was available to address this community's stigma reduction and service engagement concerns, the male mental health researcher met with members of the AAMHC and community leaders to design a change strategy. This strategy was designed to increase learning about mental health, reduce stigma associated with mental illness and mental health treatment, and encourage an overall increase in African American service users. The strategy, which will be discussed following a brief background description, fuses cultural values and customs with information literacy and decision-making for problem-solving and goal attainment.

CLINIC DEVELOPMENT AND START-UP

Guided by the culturally specific value of key relationships comprised of teacher, parent, and mentor (Leary, 1996) and the evidence collected in the needs assessment mentioned earlier (Briggs, 2004), the AAMHC met to forge a partnership between the local Portland African American community and a world-class university-based healthcare system. The goal of this relationship was to share responsibility for the governance and development of the organization's capacity to address the unique needs of African Americans and continue its capacity-building efforts to reach other diverse groups of people in need of mental health services. The organization provides services to people with issues such as addiction and depression, panic attacks, posttraumatic stress disorder (PTSD), and generalized anxiety disorder (GAD).

Between 2004 and 2007, the male mental health researcher used five culturally specific functions (Briggs, 2009) to teach the Executive Committee of the AAMHC the five steps of EBP (guide, interpreter, researcher, translator and advocate; Briggs, 2009). As a guide, he taught them about the client-oriented practical evidence search (COPES) question. He modeled for them the question he used to create his practice-based evidence model. The male mental health researcher posed the question, "Will an Afro-centric approach to community outreach and service engagement versus information and referral result in increased service use by African Americans with mental health related issues, as well as increase their knowledge about mental health diagnosis?" In step two, as interpreter, he received no research to aid him in addressing the knowledge and utilization problems of the Center staff of the Avel Gordly Center for Healing. In step three, as researcher, he revisited the needs assessment data that were discussed earlier with the involvement of the leadership of the AAMHC. The AAMHC includes a nationally recognized Commissioner appointed by former President George W. Bush to serve on the national President's New Freedom Commission on Mental Health. Other leadership included the Chairman of the Commission, who is a pastor and previous consumer of mental health services; a Circuit Judge; two attorneys; and this writer, who served three functions—that of consumer, researcher, and practice expert in EBP and ESIs. All of these individuals are African American.

CHALLENGES

With this group's assistance, in step 5, the male mental health researcher translated evidence from the needs assessment to aid in the creation of the workshop's content and process. He developed a stigma reduction approach to address the educational and training needs of the community as well as the service engagement concerns of the clinic's administration. As an advocate, he introduced the African American communities to a training workshop on behavioral and primary health care and its importance to African Americans.

Ensuring strong community attendance at workshops was handled through using local community leadership as social marketers and event planners. They used their own contacts with various groups in specific neighborhoods and communities. The community-based workshops included training by clinic staff about the brain, health, mental health, and mental illness and treatment. Prior to each training session, a pre-test was administered. The pre-test measured information across a number of key domains. These included (1) knowledge of the brain, (2) the brain's functions, (3) knowledge of mental disorders, (4) knowledge of service availability through the clinic, (5) attitudes about the role of stigma in serving as a barrier to mental health service use, (6) intentions to use or refer someone to clinic, (7) knowledge of anyone who would benefit from the clinic, and (8) relevance and timeliness of addressing mental health issues as African Americans.

Training and education included an introduction to the session by a mental health researcher. This speaker set the occasion and provided a thorough review of the data collected during the needs assessment phase (Listening to the Community). Given the community's interests in and lack of knowledge about the brain, the second speaker was a world-class psychiatrist. The psychiatrist captured the audience's attention by integrating animation and talk-story methods with highly sophisticated charts, graphs, and pictures of the various areas which comprise the human brain. His analogies to common themes that the audience could relate to as he carefully delineated brain functions and their interrelations with primary health and mental health were well received by session participants. The third speaker, a clinical psychologist, skillfully illustrated the role of mental health issues throughout the tapestry of everyday life across home, work, and community, using street vernacular and analogies of interception in emotional and clinical functioning to the mechanics of an engine and its interrelationships to the distributor, carburetor, electrical system, and starter of an automobile. The fourth speaker was the clinic director and graduate-level social worker who described the cultural context for addressing mental health issues in a predominately white environment and how the daily stressors of denying racism wears and tears on one's capacity to manage health adjustment. The first speaker then wrapped up the next session with a request for the completion of the post-test and the dissemination of brochures and cards to reach people if additional information was needed. This session was repeated in African communities across various African American social and civic group venues and clubs and after three productions of a satirical off-Broadway theater performance. The play depicted themes that show how stigma and misinformation about mental health, culture, and medical advancements could lead African Americans to adopt cultural beliefs and taboos about mental health disorders that would make them wary of and refuse to use mental health services.

RESULTS

The pre/post data highlighted changes in knowledge of the brain, mental health disorders, and services. The behavioral intent to use or refer others for services increased, as did actual service utilization statistics during the seven-month pilot. Ten months prior to the intervention, the actual number of African American and other non-white service users was always less than 6%. The organization projected a total of 12% African American service users as their intended objective as an average for their first year of operation. Instead, during the intervention period, the numbers of African American and Somali service users were 24% for each of the seven months of the pilot intervention period. The clinic staff and administration observed the change as proof of success for the intervention. They were able to use the service engagement data and community support to restore state funding to the clinic, which had received a 50% cut in funding due to the county's broader problems resulting from failures in housing and lending institutions and the broader market. With the pilot data and information collected, the clinic staff was able to continue the stigma reduction and service engagement intervention, which is now under the direct control of clinic staff.

LESSONS LEARNED

Establishing a partnership between a community advocacy entity and a world-class university-based healthcare provider is not always a simple task to achieve. The values, orientations, and governance structures are often incompatible and require education and negotiations. In the example given here, there should have been discussions about the challenges to shared governance over the stigma reduction and service engagement program between community advocates who planned the clinic and intervention versus the professionals with noted community experience who were hired to administer and implement clinic services and serve as sole workshop presenters. The clinic staff did not want help from the community as presenters, even though the community hired the researcher to help them design the stigma awareness and service engagement intervention as well as participate as a presenter. The clinic staff vetoed that request because they wanted the researcher to design the quality and integrity of the session's content and the pre- and post-instruments that would track session knowledge by each session participant.

Also, these two groups had other challenges such as resolving the tensions between when the community meetings could be scheduled versus the clinic staff's insistence that they present the content of the sessions because of organizational liability and issues of truth in advertising. Similarly, the styles of some of the staff who were purely clinical, traditional, and detached—as a way to preserve professional boundaries—did not mesh well with the variable, organic, and hard marketing and community outreach strategies that went into ensuring attendance at workshops by different community groups. There were personality clashes and disagreements between the community event planners and clinic staff about scheduling flexibility. The clinic staff wanted to staff the workshop with one or two clinic staff who could also carry a caseload responsibility during regular office hours. They would have preferred limiting the number of staff involved because of time constraints. Clinic staff had to strike a balance between being out all day and late at night during community workshops and the need to stay in the clinic to increase clinic revenues. By increasing the number of paying clients, the clinic staff was able to offset the costs of care they provide to people who cannot afford to pay for services. Nonetheless, to ensure sufficient time off and to protect time for clinical work, the staff presenting the workshop was reluctant to spend late evening hours (later than 7 P.M._ throughout the week. Staff kept all scheduled sessions that were arranged between 7 A.M. and 7 P.M. during the weekdays and a few hours on the weekend to accommodate theatre-based sessions.

Next Steps

The next phase of model development and implementation involves four parts: (1) conceptualizing a practice theory based on case study experience, (2) transferring the engagement strategy to the clinic staff taking ownership of the project, (3) replicating this approach with other adult groups and with youth and families, and (4) subsequently tracking the African American participants in adult and youth treatment to assess their issues, outcomes, coping capacities, and adaptive identities and their linkage to primary health services.

THEORY DEVELOPMENT

The use of cultural customs, experts as workshop teachers, and culturally specific community leaders as social marketing and event planners, and the occasional use of theatre, was a result of critically thinking through five engagement planning steps:

> **Step 1**: Accepting cultural groups' definition of injury and wellness.
>
> **Step 2**: Engaging African Americans in underused system by emphasizing education, skills for success, and economic/employment impact.
>
> **Step 3**: Fusing behavioral health treatment with cultural customs, such as the use of a cadre of cultural experts as researchers, event planners, professional practitioners, and mental health consumers, as well as community meals and talk-story and oral traditions to incentivize the attendance of African Americans in mental health service use.
>
> **Step 4**: Using the cultural value of relationships as a therapeutic tool for designing community engagement workshops.
>
> **Step 5**: Using market research to inject age-/race-based interests to incentivize and engaged the age-specific target population.

Hare (2008) argues for an inverse relationship between adaptive coping and behavioral health and primary health. The approach used by the AAMHC participants included a focus on the brain and its interplay with primary and behavioral health domains. Future studies of this approach to stigma reduction and service engagement will need to involve an assessment of the treatment gains and therapeutic process and experiences from a client voice and cultural perspective. Questions to raise can include: (1) Describe how useful therapy was for you. (2) What is different now as opposed to when you first entered into therapy? (3) How were race and culture used in therapy? (4) Did having an African American therapist help you? If helpful, how so? If no, explain your answer in more detail with as much description as possible. (5) How were issues of primary health addressed in therapy? (6) Does your primary health provider inquire about your emotional and mental health during your visits to the doctor? (7) Has your physical health improved or remained the same as it was prior to receiving mental health care?

Future studies involving the application of the stigma reduction and service engagement intervention among African American youth will yield important data about the types of youth (youth identified as antisocial or resilient) who changed their mental health care norms and beliefs as a result of receiving the intervention. Such an investigation could also inform us about those youth who remained unaffected and did not respond as expected to the intervention. Future studies may even inform us of ways to adapt and improve upon the intervention to reach people across the life cycle and cross-culturally.

Through this study, we have learned that access to mental health care by African Americans can be enhanced through cultural values of empowerment and listening to the cultural messages and evidence provided by the community and through building on existing relationships, respect, and the use of experts and elder African American health providers and educators in community-based venues. Future studies by researchers with other diverse groups will need to factor in the community's participation, cultural values, and community norms about mental health and primary health as they embark on service engagement and stigma reduction efforts. Integrating the described EBP and community-based participatory methods as a strategy for increasing mental health service use included the use of client knowledge, scientific knowledge, practitioner knowledge, cultural knowledge, and implementation knowledge. This study showed how the use of EBP at the community level could facilitate the design and implementation of a culturally specific stigma reduction and service engagement intervention as well as the transformation of community norms about mental health.

Future research on community transformation of African Americans through practice-based evidence may want to examine the role of adaptive and maladaptive identities of young and adult African Americans in health and mental health outcomes. It is quite possible that adaptive identities will moderate the extent to which these youth and adults sustain health maintenance lifestyles and avoid risk-related outcomes. We further speculate that young African Americans who avoid the lure of maladaptive identities and the unhealthy venues and associations that come with risky behavioral practices will experience better health-related outcomes and life-sustaining resources. Alternatively, we speculate that African Americans who sustain a lifetime of risky behavioral practices have established a narrow path by which they pursue life. As a result of their pessimism and the reality of the uphill battle ahead, they erect barriers to achieving prosocial goals and objectives and avoid trying all together. The data will show that these people are less likely to use formal social service agencies and are less likely to experience self-respect or be valued, honored, and recognized by their peers, family, or society. Transforming primary and behavioral health care practices among these particular African Americans remains an empirical question.

20 }

Transforming Administration and Management Through Blending Science, Community Voice, Family, and Consumer Participation

A CASE EXAMPLE OF DIFFUSING EMPIRICALLY
SUPPORTED INTERVENTIONS AND EVIDENCE-BASED
PRACTICE TO CHILD WELFARE SYSTEMS SERVING
AFRICAN AMERICAN FOSTER YOUTH

Harold E. Briggs and Bowen McBeath

The problem of accessing mental health services by African American foster youth and their families can be eliminated by diffusing evidence-based interventions to service providers serving black families. First, the authors highlight challenges in adopting and implementing empirically supported interventions (ESIs). Next, the authors discuss consumer issues that impede service access, and then delineate the key cultural considerations that need immediate attention. The authors then include a detailed discussion of blending principles of cultural competence with lessons learned from implementing evidence-based practice (EBP) in a culturally specific context. The next to last section provides a case illustration that demonstrates a way to infuse culture and scientific knowledge into mental health practice with African American foster youth and their families. The final section represents the authors' ideas for next steps in the design, implementation, and evaluation of culturally centered mental health services for child welfare-involved African American youth and families. As Claghorn stated,

> It is an American habit, when something goes wrong, to concoct a special plan for dealing with it—pass a law, form a committee, adopt a scheme. But after the law is passed, the committee formed, the scheme in operation, our interest slackens, until something reminds us that the troubles are not, after all, remedied; when we again pass a law, form a committee, adopt a scheme, which again may prove ineffective. What we should do is to follow up our law,

321

committee, or scheme observe its operations, measure its results, and take our next action on the basis of past experience. This is especially necessary in the field of social work. (Claghorn, 1927)

Changing and transforming larger human and social service systems, especially state, county, city, and nonprofit community-based organizations in the twenty-first century requires the same prescription for the field of social work detailed by Claghorn some 75 years ago. Such change will include the unique knowledge bases and voices of the consumers and families, as well as community participation.

It will also entail using cultural knowledge along with scientific evidence to build and sustain the agency system and its task environment, as well as its partnering communities capacity, infrastructure, and the skill competencies of its targeted beneficiaries, families, and community residents. Reverend Martin Luther King Jr. (n.d.) said it best: "Forces that threaten to negate life must be challenged by courage, which is the power of life to affirm itself in spite of life's ambiguities. This requires the exercise of a creative will that enables us to hew out a stone of hope from a mountain of despair." In our more than forty-year experience, as we see it, to effectively accomplish this ambitious agenda will involve (1) the assiduous attention to details that come with consumer, family, and community marginalized experiences, voice, participation, and knowledge, and (2) the strategic use of consumer and family voice along with EBP and evidence-based interventions such as task-centered social work by key stakeholders.

Most Americans would agree that life in the United States for African Americans compared to whites represents vastly unique experiences. Andrew Hacker, in his seminal work, *Two Nations: Black and White Divided*, describes the black and white worlds in the United States as two foreign cultures co-existing on an unequal footing. For whites, he describes the properties and characteristics of well-organized systems of benefits and transfers, what many describe as white privilege. For African Americans, he sketches out a landscape of structural, economic, political, and social inequalities that resemble the lives of people in Third World, under-developed nations. Snowden (2001) and others such as Briggs, Briggs, Miller, and Paulson (2011) and Briggs and McBeath (2010) describe the major access barriers to mental health services that accompany broad based inequalities for African Americans, especially among black youth living in high-end juvenile justice and foster care settings.

Additionally, the Surgeon General's primary and supplemental reports (US Department of Health and Human Services [DHHS], 1999b) delineate that, while the prevalence of mental disorders is similar for whites and other racial groups, there are a score of disparities that distinguish the experiences of whites versus racial minorities in mental health care. African Americans and other cultural and ethnic groups, such as Native Americans and Hispanics, are less likely to have access to, use, or achieve the benefits of quality mental health care. "This supplement finds that racial and ethnic minorities collectively experience a greater disability burden from mental illnesses than do whites. This higher level of burden stems from minorities receiving less and poorer quality of care, rather than from their illnesses being inherently more severe or prevalent in the community" (DHHS, 1999b, p. 3). Due to their apparent marginalization and differential treatment, until recently, African Americans often declined to participate in mental health research that seeks to improve care. Currently, however, research on ESIs, which are single intervention approaches with strong research foundations for adults with mental health- and addictions-related disorders have been able to attract large enough samples of racially diverse people and have been found to be effective with African Americans (Hien, Cohen, Litt, Miele, & Capstick, 2004).

A way of effectively decreasing inequalities in service access by African American foster youth to innovative best practices is to diffuse evidence-based mental health interventions to child welfare service providers working with African American families. To achieve this aim, child welfare service providers will require the knowledge and skills to dismantle the hosts of programming-related barriers that sustain underutilization of mental health services by African American foster youth. Chief among the access barriers to evidence-based mental health services that foster care service providers can impact are (1) adopting and implementing ESIs, (2) consumer issues, (3) cultural considerations, and (4) incorporating information literacy and effective problem-solving methods into a culturally specific context for agency use.

CHALLENGES IN ADOPTING AND IMPLEMENTING ESIs

Chaffin and Friedrich (2004) identify several obstacles and challenges to disseminating and implementing ESIs in child welfare service settings. These obstacles and challenges include, but are not limited to, (1) issues involved with financing technology transfer, training, supervision and monitoring; (2) too few consumers and providers of child welfare services advocating for ESIs; (3) too few or no incentives for utilizing ESIs to achieve better client outcomes; (4) a lack of a culture of learning among child welfare service organizations; (5) discrepancies in values and agendas between the "research and practice communities" (p. 1110); (6) a lack of preparation and investment by child welfare providers to abandon what they currently do to adopt ESIs; and (7) the presence of considerable resistance to ESIs. Other critics of ESIs identify barriers to these approaches as (1) not being appropriate for difficult cases typically seen in psychotherapy, (2) only useful for addressing a single issue and not tested among people with multiple issues, (3) requiring strict adherence to fidelity with no flexibility to individualize care or to address unexpected or extraordinary circumstances, (4) interfering with relationship building, and (5) not normed against non-white people (Weisz, Jenson-Doss, & Hawley, 2006).

CULTURAL CHALLENGES

The cultural appropriateness of many ESIs remains unknown, despite the growing number of ESIs in many child and family service systems (Huey & Polio, 2008). Promoting ESIs derived through pilot testing with Caucasian-only samples, in which no attention was given to analyzing the usefulness of ESIs on ethnically diverse populations, is a major limitation, yet there is opportunity for experimentation (Blase & Fixsen, 2003; Hasnain-Wynia, 2006; McBeath, Briggs, & Aisenberg, 2009). Researchers have also indicated that too few culturally diverse researchers, treatment outcomes, theories, and resources have been considered in the design, implementation, and research on ESIs (Bernal & Saez-Santiago, 2006). Yet, the extent to which ESIs should be tested without modification or with cultural modification in ESI service frameworks remains debatable (Gambrill, 2007; Hasnain-Wynia, 2006; Lau, 2006, Miranda et al., 2005).

CONSUMER CHALLENGES

Consumer challenges that may limit the use of ESIs include a lack of knowledge of available effective services, limited advocacy skills of clients to request or access ESIs, and high consumer-borne costs for addressing the cognitive, family, social, and personal challenges that need to be managed during treatment (Gold, Glynn, & Mueser, 2006). Consumers may lack knowledge of the existence of ESIs, particularly if service providers or funding bodies do not inform would-be users of the existence and potential benefits of ESIs. Additionally, clients may not know how to access these services or may not be able to articulate what services and resources they need and that are available through ESIs. Furthermore, as Gambrill (2007) points out, a focus on ESIs may preclude attention to client values, experiences, and culture; informed consent; research utilization via electronic databases; and use of client values and choices in treatment selection and process.

INTEGRATING EBP AND CULTURAL COMPETENCE

EBP with culturally diverse populations involves the simultaneous use of two compatible processes: the process of EBP and the process of cultural competence. These processes share a focus on client choice, collaboration, and empowerment. The client's expression of their unique values, expectations, and issues serves as the driver for the use of the client-oriented practical evidence search and change process. This step is followed by the practitioner's use of available evidence and expertise, including knowledge of culturally specific realities, protective identities, and practices to aid the client in choosing treatments that incorporate the client's expectations, lifestyle, sociocultural realities, and sociocultural protective factors. This is accomplished by building relationships that reflect culturally specific practices with individuals and by cultivating resiliency (Bell, 2006; Sue & Zane, 1987). Each of these strategies is consistent with the EBP process (Briggs, 2009).

EBP in a cultural context parallels and incorporates generalist task-centered practice (Tolson, Reid, & Garvin, 2003) with diverse clients, and both approaches involve practice principles, including the following: (1) validating and empowering clients to pursue their choices and values; (2) incorporating the clients' view of the problem to provide opportunities to explore the incentives, motivations, and commitment to change; (3) using individual cultural differences and values as drivers of client-oriented practical evidence search questions; (4) cultivating resiliency as the practitioner assists the client in gathering all necessary supports connected with health promotion and protection; (5) using active listening to client needs and minimizing therapist bias; (6) exploring education in clients' culturally specific practices; (7) using cultural differences as an opportunity for practitioner learning; (8) being critical and suspicious of labels and their consequences for client resiliency and recovery; (9) modifying care settings to reflect the customs, rituals, and expressions of diverse clients; (10) celebrating commonalities across human diversity; (11) supporting a family- or client-driven advocacy agenda for improved services and decreases in health, economic, social, and political disparities.

DIFFUSION OF INNOVATIONS TO AFRICAN AMERICAN SERVICE PROVIDERS

Also, to achieve successful management of and change in agencies serving African American clients, Briggs and McMillan (Briggs, 1994, 2009; Briggs & McBeath, 2010, in press) delineate lessons for diffusing and using evidence-based approaches in direct, administration and in changing agency practices:

1. Agency staff, management, and administration will need to think differently about the organization, its role, and the uses of cultural and scientific knowledge.
2. Agency management needs to know what EBP and ESI can and cannot do.
3. There is controversy as to the definition and scope of EBP; some see it as a grab bag of best practices with a robust research foundation, while others view it as a process of transparency that empowers the client to be knowledgeable and involved in the process of identifying, selecting, implementing, and evaluating treatment options.
4. A team approach to adopting and diffusing EBP is preferable and should be based in a culture of learning, training, and partnership between service providers and families.
5. The agency will need to leverage resources to maintain the involvement of university researchers.

6. Faculty and students may provide training and manpower supports to agencies as they serve as field agency sites and field instructors.
7. Agencies need to adopt a trial-and-error evidence-based medicine (EBM) approach.
8. Agencies need to engage in experimentation with approaches they believe will generate desired results.
9. Agencies can use EBP to sustain quality control, solve problems, or aid in critical decision-making.
10. Agencies should incorporate different ways of knowing in their management and should document their agency change efforts.

All in all, the research to guide social workers in selecting the optimal methods to achieve the sustainability of diffused and adopted evidence-based interventions is mixed. There are those who follow the traditional views of Rogers about the rational order in which innovations become diffused, adopted, and standardized through elaborate implementation schemas (Fixsen et al., 2010), routines, and typical operating practices. Alternatively, there are others, such as Ferlie et al. (2005) and others, who view the diffusion and adoption of innovations into agency practice as a messy nonlinear process with a number of political and intra- and interpersonal social network considerations. Briggs and McMillan (2012) concur with the relative merits and contributions of both perspectives on diffusion and further highlight the field-based lessons alluded to earlier within a case example based in an agency culture of learning that incorporates each of the previously mentioned perspectives on diffusion research.

Integrating Culturally Sensitive Mental Health Care into Evidence-Based Child Welfare Practice with African Americans: A Case Study

The integration of the science of diffusion, cultural knowledge, ESIs (e.g., task-centered practice), and EBP provides a segue way to the following case study, which embodies such integration and describes an actual case study of an agency's transformation into an evidence-based, culturally competent service provider. Parents and Children Together (PACT) is a private nonprofit agency serving African American families in the metropolitan Chicago area. Its nine service divisions offer child welfare, mental health and substance abuse treatment, housing, and employment programming for youth, adults, and families. Responding to growing numbers of youth entering foster care in the early 1990s, the Illinois Department of Child and Family Services (DCFS) expanded its existing service contract purchase with PACT, so that the nonprofit agency could provide culturally specific and integrated child welfare, mental health, and substance abuse treatment services to difficult-to-serve foster youth and biological parents. An agency-wide transformation process was undertaken in preparation for the anticipated influx of foster care cases and to eliminate agency-related implementation issues consistent with the following barriers to implementation of ESIs in child welfare settings reported by Chaffin and Friedrich (2004):

- insufficient financial resources to absorb costs involved with the transition to ESIs;
- the lack of sufficient political support for the adoption of new treatment approaches from service providers and consumer groups;
- the beliefs that agency funding is not tied to client outcomes and that few incentives to pursue client outcomes exist in the child welfare service system; and
- little support for adopting new treatment approaches because such practices may not be consistent with child welfare agencies' current programming and service delivery cultures.

Ultimately, through a university–agency partnership aimed at training staff and management in the EBP and ESI approaches and by obtaining the support of the board of directors and executive staff to dismantle a series of financial, organizational, and practitioner barriers to culturally appropriate service provision, the agency was able to develop and provide culturally sensitive mental health services that drew on established ESIs and involved strong community partnerships. PACT underwent an organizational development intervention to improve the effectiveness and cultural appropriateness of its foster care programming. These efforts were organized around a self-assessment of the organization's experience, staff capability, and competence with key aspects of client programming that were hypothesized to contribute to positive service outcomes, which is summarized in Table 20.1. Administrators and staff used this question-based template to gather internal information concerning the expected appropriateness of various innovative programs for African American foster youth and families; these internal data were then compared with information gathered from literature reviews and conversations with consultants, DCFS administrators, and researchers around the country with expertise in African American child welfare and mental health service provision. Programs that were perceived by administrators and staff to be supported by internal and external information were preferred over those that seemed suitable for PACT clients, but were unsupported by empirical research. Similarly, programs with proven efficacy with majority populations, but that did not appear to be appropriate for PACT clients, were viewed by the agency as containing future promise, but were not adopted initially. After answering the questions in Table 20.1, PACT administrators developed client feedback forms to collect client-level data. Staff designed these forms, and the information gathered from them was used to inform decision-making about the suitability of programs being considered for adoption.

This process led to initiating substantial programmatic changes in PACT's foster care department. To more accurately assess the strengths and needs of foster youth

TABLE 20.1 } **Organizational experience with cultural difference as context for intervention selection**

What have we learned from our clients about serving African American children and families in a culturally appropriate manner?	What have we learned from others about serving African American Children and families in a culturally appropriate manner?
• Why do we believe that our existing staff have the ability and desire to work with our clients? • What evidence do we have to justify the belief that our program innovations are appropriate for our clients? How strong is this evidence? • Are our service approaches congruent with the cultural values of our clients? To what extent are these models compatible with their language, norms, beliefs, and values? • To what extent are these program models responsive to our knowledge concerning our clients' disability status, sexual orientation, gender, age, literacy, income, and within-group diversity? • Do our clients do appreciably better when served by our programs? Why or why not? • What needs to be added or removed from these program models to ensure that they are culturally appropriate for our clients?	• What information exists to identify the staff characteristics necessary to work with African American children and families? • What evidence exists to suggest that our program models are appropriate for African American children and families? How strong is this evidence? • Are these program models congruent with the cultural values of African American children and families? To what extent are these models compatible with their language, norms, beliefs, and values? • To what extent are these program models responsive to population factors such as disability, sexual orientation, gender, age, literacy, income, and within-group diversity? • Is there evidence to suggest that African American children and families do appreciably better when served by these program models than when served in other ways? • What needs to be added to or removed from these program models to ensure that they are culturally appropriate for African American children and families?

Briggs and McBeath (2010).

and their biological parents and develop need-responsive service plans, program supervisors and frontline staff were trained in task-centered foster care direct practice and a problem-based learning methodology called "problem-oriented practice." These approaches were chosen based in part on literature reviews suggesting that they had been used effectively to organize clinical case management on behalf of African American families in foster care (Briggs, 1994). A nationally recognized consultant was also put on retainer to train staff on methods to expedite family reunification and permanency planning and to help PACT staff develop culturally appropriate parent training classes (Briggs, Leary, Briggs, Cox, & Shibano, 2005; Smagner & Sullivan, 2005).

Staff was also trained in the relationship model (RM; Leary, 1996), a culturally specific practice model that is designed to facilitate culturally competent service provision and improve foster care permanency outcomes. Developed for use with African American youth and families at risk of family disruption, academic failure, and corrections involvement, RM seeks to facilitate the growth of healthy parental, peer, and mentorship relationships as a basis to facilitate problem-solving and goal achievement. Based on the RM philosophy that youth, parents, and families need a healthy relationship with a community ally, foster care clinical caseworkers took on roles as parents, teachers, and mentors of at-risk youth and families. Carefully selected community volunteers were also trained in the fundamentals and principles of African axiology, developmentally appropriate methods for building and sustaining healthy relationships, and an overall framework that was respectful of differential gender- and race-based socialization (Nichols, 1976).

To increase client access to in-agency mental health and substance abuse treatment services, caseworkers from the foster care, mental health, and substance abuse treatment divisions were required to jointly complete the intake process for each new foster care case. It was hypothesized that this process would expand the type and appropriateness of support services provided to foster youth and their biological parents, thereby increasing opportunities for parent–child visitation and reunification. Additionally, PACT implemented living in balance and seeking safety to augment its culturally specific mental health and substance abuse treatment service programming. Each of these programs had been shown to be efficacious in treating African Americans with substance abuse and mental health issues and each has been used successfully with urban foster care populations (Hien et al., 2004; Najavita, Weiss, Shaw, & Muenz, 1998). These were primarily manualized ESIs seeking to reduce internalizing and externalizing mental health disorders through a focus on stress reduction, interpersonal communication with family and peers, and planning for sobriety and relapse prevention. Each could be tailored in response to client needs and interests through the provision of supplemental sessions on topics including problem-solving, positive attitudes, child development and parenting, educational and vocational goal setting, dealing with grief and loss, nutrition, exercise, and spirituality. Thus, each ESI allowed for client self-direction in treatment planning and content.

PACT sought to ensure that its frontline worker–client interactions, parenting classes, and mental health and substance abuse programming approaches were compatible with the language, norms, beliefs, and values of its African Americans clients. Additionally, each intervention approach included opportunities for some client self-direction, had been developed for use and tested with African Americans of different ages and genders, and was appropriate for clients with different mental health conditions and substance abuse treatment needs. Finally, each intervention approach was adapted for use in individual and group formats and in combination with other treatment methodologies.

These changes in organizational structure and programming complemented the efforts of foster care caseworkers to deliver services in a culturally accessible manner to adults and foster youth. To promote client engagement during assessment, PACT caseworkers used motivational interviewing techniques to elicit information on family conditions and strengths. Client-oriented practical evidence search (COPES) questions were employed to identify material needs related to housing and financial support; physical and mental health care; and strategies for parent training, managing parent–child conflicts, and culturally appropriate child-rearing techniques. Caseworkers were trained to view the development of service plans as a collaborative process in which clients were to be given access to all PACT programs as well as appropriate referrals for community-based services in which clients were to be dignified with choices about service options and treatment formats (e.g., individual versus group-based counseling). Service planning was intentionally completed in a broad-based manner so that biological parents and foster youth could identify services to improve mental health outcomes as well as facilitate parent–child reunification. By shaping the micro-interactions between caseworkers and clients in this manner, PACT managers hypothesized that parents would express more hope in the possibility of reunifying with their children and engage more fully in the reunification planning process.

This multifunctional and multilevel organizational development intervention resulted in improved family stabilization rates and a decrease in the number of placement changes experienced by foster youth. In coordinating service provision to biological parents, foster care caseworkers increased access to and the use of mental health and substance abuse services. In terms of foster care permanency outcomes, there was an increase in the number of African American foster parents adopting youth placed in their home; however, the number of parent–child reunifications did not improve substantially, possibly due to the contemporaneous emergence of a crack cocaine epidemic affecting inner-city African American neighborhoods in Chicago.

Despite its efforts, the agency remained unsuccessful in returning some foster youth to households experiencing severe mental health or chronic drug dependency issues. While ancillary to the major program goals, an unanticipated consequence of the agency's increased focus on culturally competent service provision was a substantial decrease in frontline staff turnover. When supervisors and administrators left the agency to become administrators of other child welfare agencies, direct care staff were promoted within the agency. Functionally, the agency decided to incorporate the pilot programs it had initiated for the child welfare division, such that the focus on culturally appropriate service provision and continuous quality improvement was adopted across other program divisions. As the agency invested more resources in its service coordination function, it strengthened its formal linkages with other community providers and its informal ties to various community partners. The agency also strengthened its existing partnerships with major universities and collaborated with researchers on federal- and state-funded evaluations of its major child welfare and mental health programs. The agency developed pilot projects involving high-tech equipment and software as teaching tools for school-age youth and adults with developmental and persistent psychiatric illnesses.

As long as African Americans underutilize mental health service systems, more should be done to assure their knowledge about and access to effective care. Research that documents effective approaches to increasing access and service use among African Americans is needed. Such research will need to assess the extent to which African Americans are aware of and ways in which their service use and understanding of mental health-related issues are negatively impacted by stigma and other related culturally insensitive service system barriers (Briggs, Briggs, Miller, & Paulson, 2011). It is doubtful that policy developments such as healthcare reform will usher in a plethora of African American mental health service users. The cultural considerations and needs addressed in this chapter raise a much broader set of issues that beg the question of the impact of structural racism on the sustenance of culturally insensitive mental health care service systems. The high dropout rate and a shortage of African American students entering colleges and graduate schools majoring in social work is a direct result of economic and education-related circumstances. These conditions have their origins in racially segregated school districts with inferior curricula and resources preparing urban and inner-city African Americans to compete for higher education and advance study. It is quite possible that service providers encountered frustrations in addressing these broad social structural issues and ultimately gave up because of the cumbersome and elusive character of structural racism (Briggs & McBeath, 2010; Briggs & Paulson, 1996). Nonetheless, they do have direct control over the cultural relevance, integrity, promise, ethics, and transparency of their programming and social service responses in addressing the consequences that accompany African Americans experiencing vulnerability and marginalization.

As African American foster youth begin to utilize evidence-based mental health services, will we be able to assess the nature, context, and impact of the vitally needed services to youth in child welfare custody? Until we learn more about how African Americans respond to established ESIs or culturally modified approaches, utilizing ESIs is a matter of personal judgment. The science that is needed to help service providers give advice to African Americans of any age has not been established. Researchers and program evaluators seeking to assess the extent to which African American youth benefit from evidence-based mental health care will need to do a thorough assessment. They need to assess the extent to which current fidelity measures of ESIs include all facets of healing, wellness, relational growth, and intrinsic change that comes with experiencing balance, harmony, racial respect, and other relevant psychosocial and behavioral determinants of healthy functioning across different experiences of being African American.

21 }

Conclusions and Summary

Integrative Practice in and for Larger Systems involves the horizontal (interconnections across generalist knowledge areas) and vertical (sequencing of specialized social service administration and management core responsibilities, roles, and functions) synthesis and strategic applications of the core generalist and specialization competencies of social service administration and management practice in real larger systems (Reid, 1994). In social work, Reamer (1994) defines the foundations of social work knowledge as "social work practice, social welfare policy and services, human behavior and social environment [theories], research and evaluation, field education, values and ethics, oppression and social injustices, and diversity and populations at risk" (p. x). Section I chapters covered the foundations of social work knowledge needed for integrative practice.

Alternatively, social service administration and management knowledge bases represent key generalist and specialization curricula to use to prepare students seeking macro practice skill competencies. The chapters of Sections II, III, and IV presented social service administration and management practice knowledge bases. The combination of foundational knowledge base and social service administration and management knowledge base rubrics form the conceptual framework used in this book to educate clinical and macro practice students on the skillful use of integrative practices in and for larger systems.

The culminating integrative multilevel practice technology comprising the foundations of social work and advanced social service administration and management knowledge bases are contained within the chapters of this book. Integrative practice technology is designed to trigger a process of multilevel critical thinking, hypothesis development, planning, implementation, quality assurance, process and outcome measurement, and practice and program evaluation activities by leaders of larger systems. As emerging leaders of larger systems, you need the multilevel knowledge foundations that comprise the integrative social administration and management practice technology to do your jobs effectively within organizational and community service systems. Reading and applying the strategies depicted in this book will prepare you to strategically administer larger systems. It contains lessons learned and strategies to use to direct the provision of meaningful evidence-informed social services by direct care workers who want to achieve their intended targets of change: improved functioning and well-being across systems of all sizes (Briggs, 2001).

Introduction

The introduction of this book highlighted a unique approach in connecting a multifaceted strategic use of culture, science, and information literacy to best inform social work policy and practice. It emphasizes the importance of administrators and management practitioners' attentiveness to increasing the competency and functionality of their agencies by utilizing a multilevel macro practice curriculum that best reflects the core competencies that have proved efficacy in service provisions, community engagement, reflexivity, and effective program diversity. It addresses the importance of sensitizing administrators, staff, and students to embracing culturally competent, collaborative, and empowering skills that engage client-consumers and communities alike. We have emphasized the role of each change agent, from administrator to direct care provider, in assuring quality care and successful outcomes of policies and programs.

Chapter 1: Incentivizing Mechanisms: Transforming Administration of People, Organizations, and Communities Through Evidence-Based Management

The first chapter identified the pivotal role that social workers and social work administrators play in the delivery of quality services through attentiveness to social justice, cultural competency, collaborative organizational relationships, and client self-determination. Through program development and management, social service administration, and hands-on service delivery based on evidence-based practice (EBP), information analysis, culturally informed service implementation, and critical thinking practitioners can best achieve agency effectiveness.

We identified a multilevel approach that involves ten crucial skill competencies needed to manage staff, programs, and the overall agency in an effective way. These skills include:

- Engage in cross-cultural practice and evidence-based perspectives.
- Use transparency and information literacy to expand knowledge bases and broaden the understanding of social issue complexities.

- Utilize evidence to critically analyze ways to improve agency and program functioning and service effectiveness.
- Develop informed hypotheses about the root causes of agency-, program-, and client-related issues based on evidence.
- Use evidence to assess the contingencies of various solutions to resolve the problem.
- Investigate the costs and benefits of alternative options based on evidence.
- Make strategic decisions based on critical thinking about differential response systems of care and options utilizing evidence.
- Track and monitor client reactions to planned interventions as qualitative evidence to inform program efficacy.
- Critically assess the agency's capacity to evaluate program successes and weaknesses and the capacity to modify a course of action to assure quality service delivery.
- Use cultural knowledge and effective collaboration techniques to implement service coordination mechanisms within and across service delivery systems.

Various ecological domains, as well as the internal and external systems that an organization interfaces with, impact organizational practice, and curricula must focus on strategically establishing cultures of learning focused on enhancing program development, service delivery, and the related outcomes as they pertain to clients. We detailed the necessary steps that agency administrators and management practitioners must take to develop, implement, manage, critically assess, and coordinate services; oversee and guide staff to carry out service delivery collaboratively and effectively; and navigate the complexities of external and internal influences that affect service delivery outcomes. Chapter 1 highlighted the importance of making decisions that are guided by evidence, interagency coordination, cultural knowledge, sound management skills, and a multilevel approach to engaging the plethora of interacting systems found in social services. The information presented in Chapter 1 prepares students for social administration and program management practice by providing a curriculum that is current, culturally reflexive, empirically supported, outlines the use of political skills both within and outside of agencies, and provides a strong guide for developing, planning, and managing programs that effectively address the agency and service needs.

Chapter 2: Unraveling the Covert Aspects of the Culture of Oppression in Larger Systems: The Influence of the Culture of Silence, Culture of Power, and the Structural Determinants of the Culture of White Privilege

In Chapter 2, we discussed the relevance of deconstructing the culture of oppression by discussing the influences of the culture of silence, culture of power, and the structural determinants of the culture of white privilege on integrative practice in and for larger systems.

To actualize the social justice mission of social work for racially diverse groups in larger systems, we chronicled the state of knowledge in cultural competence education in social work. Next, we highlighted the culture of the conspiracy of silence. We presented an additional examination of structural social work and five structural determinants of culture, then we articulated the culture of power and its influence on the structural determinants of the culture of white privilege. We presented "next steps," which detail the education in social action and civil and human rights that is needed by social workers to realize the competencies needed to enable the systems they work with to realize and experience the social determinants of well-being.

Chapter 3: Interface of Social Policy and Social Administration and Management

Understanding social policy and the social/political realities for clients is imperative for social service agency management and staff. Chapter 3 outlined systemic problems in policy development both within and outside of an organization. Paying close attention to the way social policy issues are identified, socially perceived, prioritized, and regulated is important in grasping racial disproportionality and its impacts on marginalized client-consumers, families, and communities. Forming a critical lens by which an organization and its team members evaluate existing agency and political policies, as well as how they work toward social justice through changes to and development of policy, encourages culturally aware problem-solving. We pointed out racial residential segregation, exposure to high-end restrictive services, lack of support system and services that improve client self-sustainability, social welfare, and lack of access to services that fully address the broad scope of needs for historically marginalized people.

We presented ten core dimensions that must be a part of evaluating social policy effectiveness: (1) ethics, (2) efficaciousness/effectiveness, (3) efficiency, (4) equality, (5) equity, (6) ecologically based, (7) ecumenical, (8) empowerment-based, (9) economic participation, and (10) enforcement protections. We carefully deconstructed each of these dimensions as critical elements to establishing sound policy and service performance based on evidence, science, research, and community input that best addresses issues of inequity, racism, and ineffective services. We argue for a critical look into social work education as an origin to developing stronger organizational structure and practices and assessing the weaknesses of educational programs. The concepts of accountability, cultural competency, and multicontingency behavioral analytic perspectives that help to dismantle systemic, structural, and institutionalized racism norms and raise the performance and delivery standards of the organization are addressed by implementing into the organization's structure these ten accountability questions. By having continuous assessments of organizational health, an organization is better able to remain relevant, alter dysfunctional and problematic practices, progress with behavior modification plans, review outcomes, and assure service efficacy that helps to reduce social injustices and empower client-consumers.

Chapter 4: Theory and Service Effectiveness

The use of theory is important to guide behavior change in direct and management practice. Michael Holosko's leadership perspective (2009) is a practical performance management framework that includes the strategic use of applied behavioral analysis methods and organizational behavior modification techniques. This perspective entails five primary leadership competencies: vision, incentivizing others to act, team collaboration, facilitation of critical problem-solving, and promotion of positive change. Administrators carry out functional analysis at different levels of the organization in order to make necessary changes, which are promoted by the integration of behavioral modification techniques, in order to improve program functionality and client outcomes. The emphasis on a multilevel performance management methodology entails linking management practices and direct practice grounded in theoretical approaches. Applicable theories to enhance performance include the operant theory, which details a stimulus approach of manipulating antecedents and consequences to augment the process of events and desirable behavior, and social learning theories, which states that people learn by observation, modeling, and mimicry.

Enhancing staff performance entails a few crucial steps in the systemic behavioral change model that help to connect administrators and management to the daily operations of an agency. Task analysis enhances staff performance and desired behavior change through data tracking and program evaluation. Performance feedback provides a direct line of communication between staff and administrators to affirm strong performance and encourage behavior change for ineffective practices. Developing weekly residential time management schedules and work performance contracts streamlines daily operations and builds into protocol staff incentives. Supervision provides consistent review of staff issues and concerns and program operations. Procedural elements such as policies, procedures, program planning, individual habilitation plans, and program implementation procedures are also important elements. Finally, the system needs to have in place stimuli and environmental contingencies that generalize and sustain positive new behaviors.

Practice evaluation inclusive of theory entails assessing client outcome and incorporating the perspective and voice of clients into program development. Incorporating scientific procedures for collecting, reviewing, and disseminating data is crucial to improving service efficacy and increasing positive client outcomes.

This includes both quantitative and qualitative data and evaluation and can involve randomized controlled clinical trial investigations or practice-based experimental designs with control features, quasi-experimental experiments, direct observation, self-reports, and oral data from clients.

Pinkston's Problem-Oriented Practice (POP) was also outlined. POP combines the use of behavioral theory, a theory of human behavior, and a behavior change practice theory in the framework of a single-case design methodology that can act as a tool for social workers to use in the assessment, intervention, evaluation, and follow-up stages of practice. This combination of applied behavioral analysis and empirically supported single-subject design methodology encourages social work practice to be more rigorous and yet continues to tap into the unique problem-solving perspectives and use of behavioral interviews that define social work. The premise of the intervention is to assess the client's definition of the problem, define why the client is seeking assistance, gain insight into the various systems the client is involved in, and identify previous attempts to resolve the problem. This process guides clients toward the functional elements of their behavior and redefines problems as behaviors that can be adjusted to promote a supportive environment of participatory change focused on client strengths.

In the first phase of the POP approach, there are seven important steps, including (1) the initial assessment, (2) specifying desirable outcomes, (3) assessing available resources, (4) defining target behaviors, (5) selecting measurement techniques, (6) orienting client or significant other(s) to data recording, and (7) collecting baseline data. In the second phase of this approach, the social worker conducts design, training, and evaluation interviews to review data with the client through steps including (1) functional analysis of data, (2) determining intervention strategy, (3) implementing an intervention and drafting a clear intervention contract, (4) evaluating intervention procedures, and (5) revising the intervention. The third phase entails conducting maintenance interviews to expand and extend the impact of the intervention and make necessary adjustments for increased results. Follow-up interviews in phase four allows for the worker to evaluate the intervention's effectiveness and long-term results. A follow-up includes (1) evaluating the client, the intervention, the data, and the existing resources and systems at specified times; (2) returning to baseline; and (3) terminating worker participation.

The POP approach can also be used to enhance the effectiveness of service delivery at the organizational level. This entails engaging in a problem-solving framework, including (1) problem identification, (2) assessment, (3) planning, (4) application, (5) mastery, (6) evaluation and adoption, and (7) enhancement. This can help to evaluate staff performance and program effectiveness, and it involves clearly identifying and defining the problem in order to use appropriate and concrete problem-solving techniques. This is highlighted using a case example.

Chapter 5: Using Evidence-Based Management to Transform Multiple Agency Levels

In Chapter 5, we explained the key components of the unique framework developed by Briggs and colleagues to assess the individualized and collaborative roles of administrators, management, and staff within an agency with the goal of increasing efficiency and effective service delivery. By carefully examining seven core steps, we introduced the most purposeful means for managing multiple layers of an organization for accountability, efficacy, performance, and culturally relevant service delivery. The seven steps include (1) defining the mission that clearly states the organization's purpose; (2) defining the structure, including the framework and staff relationships within the organization; (3) setting goals for expected performance that are observable, measurable, and specific; (4) establishing behavior strategies to assure efficiency, including continuity of care and time management; (5) incorporating reinforcing events that provides staff affirmation, proactive direction, and communicative space for staff to ask questions and discuss issues; (6) evaluating outcomes; and (7) undertaking a final enhancement and development step to refine service and service delivery to improve the organization's functioning and best meet the needs of clients.

By implementing these seven steps, the organization aligns itself with the aim of unifying the work of management and staff to enhance performance, address problems, and create an environment of positive behavior change in each aspect of the organization; this assures the growth of the organization and its services for client-consumers. We provided EBP experience from the Afrocentric community social service organization Habilitative Systems, Inc., in Chicago. This organization set the bar in using data collection methods and theories to strategically deliver services for individuals, families, groups, and communities with the goal of client self-determination and sustainability. In utilizing a behaviorally based seven-step management system based on field-tested methods and protocols, this organization accomplished carefully planned strategies for addressing the behaviors of managers, staff, and clients, with constant attention to outcome goals of self-sufficiency. Furthermore, this organization is an excellent example of organization and client collaboration in that case management and coordination involved the service system and client based on the needs and expectations of both entities. The organization's valuing of the "experience as knowledge" of client-consumers and continual assessment of service delivery and outcomes using this seven-step system that has resulted in its strong twenty-five-year success.

Chapter 6: Infusing Culture into Administrative/ Management Practice

Chapter 6 addressed the importance of balancing management strategies with attentiveness to the nuanced complexities of social service programs that collaborate with clients and communities. Such balance can be acquired with the implementation of the comprehensive and yet flexible management practice methodology we proposed in this book. Ideally, organizations are culturally responsive service delivery organizations that are led by a management practice methodology that is based in relevant theories, adaptable intervention methods, and evaluator processes that result in an organizational culture that is responsive to its staff, stakeholders, and client-consumers. Incorporating core principles such as cultural competency, empowerment, and self-determination in an organization based on a family-centered, strengths perspective and evidence-based social work practice strengthens the functionality of the organization. The organization must value competence and capacity building in order to develop strong staff expectations for carrying out the organization's objectives. Each member of the organization must understand thoroughly each of the organizational objectives in order to establish reliable standards and best practices for effective service delivery that elicits positive responses from client-consumers.

Accountability happens at multiple levels within an organization. Understanding Maslow's hierarchy of needs in human behavior helps to establish a baseline of service delivery that is focused on addressing the physical and psychological needs of clients in a culturally responsive and accountable manner. Cultural competency is crucial in developing best practices that effectively meet the needs of client-consumers, facilitate a sense of connectedness and collaboration, strengthen clients' problem-solving skills, and increase overall self-sufficiency. Organizations that strive to remain culturally responsive must do so at the micro, mezzo, and macro levels and incorporate these practices within the administrative, management, and service delivery interfacing roles of the organization.

The concept of multilevel organizational cultural competency to guide effective service outcomes is based on Nichols's *axiological perspective*, the study of nature and criteria of values in his philosophical aspects of cultural difference theory. Historical survival adaptations by cultural groups influence the development of primary value systems and become the basis for how future members of a given cultural group seek to meet their needs. Four primary axiological constructs exist: (1) Member-Object, the European axiology in which the highest value is within the acquisition of the object; (2) Member-Member, the African, Arab, and Latino axiology in which the highest value is within the relationship between people; (3) Member-Group, the Asian axiology in which the highest value is within the cohesiveness of the group; and (4) Member-Great Spirit, the Native American axiology in which the highest value is within the relationship with the higher power. The Member-Member axiology emphasizes interconnectedness, the balance of internal and external factors, and the importance of each member of the group. Such a strengths-based empowerment approach is essential for an organization in order to provide a culturally responsive and collaborative infrastructure and services.

This strengths-based empowerment approach should happen at the micro, mezzo, and macro levels of the organization. At the micro level, administrators need to develop a participatory work relationship with staff that motivates them to carry out the organization's objectives, think critically to understand problems and goals, conduct themselves professionally and competently, be attentive to the fiscal restraints of the agency, and understand the external political factors that affect the organization and client-consumers. At the mezzo level, clients, families, and communities interact with the organization to inform programs, objectives, and interventions. This can entail clients, families, and community members attending organization trainings, meetings, social interactions, and agency development initiatives and participating in committees for agency quality assurance. Transparency and inclusivity connect the community and clients to the organization and additionally permit staff to interact with the clients, families, and communities outside of the immediacy of service provisions. At the macro level, the organization becomes a part of the larger community and reflects the political, social, and cultural systems that impact client-consumers.

Administrators and managers encapsulate various roles within the organization. They act as mentors, regulators, and guardians. As mentors, administrators, and managers they strive for efficient and effective staff work performance by providing guidance, incentives, awareness, motivation, feedback, and stimuli while also modeling performance expectations and the value of self-awareness. As regulators, the administrators and managers provide information to staff regarding job skills, behavioral guidelines, organizational expectations, and methods for using policies and practices. Regulators encourage staff to invest in the organization and draw from their strengths to best utilize their performance skills in an accountable and efficient manner. They assist with the development of intervention plans based in best practices and identify tools for monitoring service processes and measuring outcomes.

As guardians, administrators and managers ensure environmental safety and provide conflict resolution processes that protect open and empowering working environments. The guardian oversees the rules and rights that pertain to employees. They provide assistance, advocate for employees, and provide critique to improve work performance. Furthermore, guardians interface with client-consumers to better understand desired services, interventions, and gather feedback. The guardian as manager interacts with the organization's guiding committees and board of directors and planning committees to reflect connectedness, teamwork, and reciprocity. Together, the guardian and board of directors develop a theory of change and the scope of the organization's policies and practices and work with management, staff, and clients to achieve these organizational aims.

Chapter 7: Information Literacy, Critical Thinking, and Decision-Making for Agency and Program Management: Problem- and Performance-Oriented Practice Approach Through Evidence-based Management

EBP and evidence-based management employs the skillful application of cultural knowledge, science, client voice, and community participation to increase the agency's ability to provide exceptional programming that benefits the clients and communities in question. This means that program management needs to establish a culture of both learning and teaching. Management needs to also establish supervisory and evaluation methods to promote critical thinking and decision-making skills among staff. Critical thinking can be viewed from four perspectives: a theory of human behavior perspective on critical thinking, an evidence-based perspective on critical thinking, a complex thinking framework of critical thinking, and a comprehensive viewpoint of critical thinking. Any of these perspectives can be applied to the process of critically processing the agency's agenda, evaluation methods, procedures, service delivery, staff roles, implementation of program/intervention, and anticipated outcomes.

Decision-making involves utilizing informed speculation, logic, and reasoning based on critical thinking and evidentiary foundations. The organization's clear and measurable mission statement acts as the overall framework. Inclusive and participatory modes of input from staff, clients, families, the community, and stakeholders deepen the pool of informed speculation, logic, and reasoning, as well as provide additional evidence to guide decisions. Utilizing the POP approach provides the necessary tools for staff to carry out the program and provides a framework for formulating a critical perspective. Yet an organization is only as strong as its mission and staff capabilities. Developing strong staff hiring procedures and screening processes help to place the strongest and most skilled people on the job. Staff members need to conduct themselves within the expectations of their role and establish strong rapport and motivational relationships with clients. Staff members need to teach behavior management and problem-solving skills to clients, establish client participation, and troubleshoot potential problems and barriers that may negatively impact client outcomes. Strong training procedures are important in developing staffs' understanding of program policies, expectations, procedures, theoretical underpinnings, intervention techniques, and data collection, and to emphasize the organization's mission.

Intra-agency development and intra-program development teams assist in the dissemination of innovations, testing best practices with pilot demonstrations and trial and error, eliciting critical thinking and problem-solving for program development, and working closely with the clients' families, community group, stakeholders, and trade and technical staff. They are the catalysts of change within an organization as well as a set of critical eyes to challenge organization inefficiency and faulty program development. With these teams, a strong administrative and managerial staff, and skilled staff matched with quality control and established data collection processes, systemic changes can be properly implemented to the benefit of therapeutic effectiveness and client improvement. Evidence-based management approaches resolve administrative and service delivery issues. In Chapter 7, we outlined various evidence-based management and EBP approaches and the various steps to establishing best practices and improving service effectiveness.

Chapter 8: Leadership and Organizational Behavior

Leadership is a social construct based on political/social interactions and is influenced by sociological, psychological, and institutional factors. The style of leadership is at the core of leadership sustainability. Sustainable and successful leaders must encompass three key skills: (1) they need nurture and build relationships, (2) they need to engage and assist in developing individuals in the organization, and (3) they must motivate and promote the vision and expectations of the organization.

Chapter 8 detailed effective and ineffective modes of leadership. Successful leaders recognize that they serve first and put self-interest aside. Leaders need to embody honesty, responsibility, humility, compassion, respect, fairness, and citizenship and remain true to the mission of the organization. The effective leader creates a compelling vision and makes that vision paramount to every approach within the organization. Having and maintaining a passionate vision separates effective leaders from merely charismatic, and potentially negative, leaders. Effective leaders courageously guide the mission of the organization using their vision while also constantly learning, exploring, and improving in order to encourage the organization to meet and even surpass established goals. They represent and establish expectations of competency and anticipate potential problems in order to be adequately prepared. They are intentional with their priorities and remain focused on tasks as well as on changes to the environment that impact the organization. Such attention allows the leader to adjust to necessary changes, adapt to new needs, and implement new technologies that can help the organization to improve upon service delivery and programming. Strong change management includes involving team members in identifying the need for and implementing change, developing a supportive change structure, and referencing evidence-based research and best practices.

Active, consistent, and clear communication to all levels within the organization is important to strong leadership. An executive leader must speak directly to team members at all organizational levels. Hosting "town hall" forums is a manageable way to disseminate information, encourage staff participation, open the lines of communication, and address prevailing issues. It also sends a strong message of executive listening and helps to unite staff and leadership. Leaders can reaffirm that their primary roles are to represent the organization's mission, delegate work, remove barriers, and coach staff to achieve the organization's expected performance and goals. Ineffective leaders place their own needs ahead of their staffs' needs and fail to remove barriers that hinder productive and effective work. We provided a detailed outline for fine-tuning effective leadership skills and highlighted three primary qualities: transparency, trust, and clarity of vision and purpose.

Chapter 9: Staff Development

In Chapter 9, we pointed out social work's lack of an established prerequisite of proficiency standards, qualifying exams, and credentialing to practice and achieve service efficiency, as compared to medicine. Curricula that address the vast knowledge and skill proficiencies unique to social work and a system of aptitude assessment would assure more effective service delivery. Once in the profession, staff and management need to continue training and resource development. Innovative and interactive staff trainings that encourage the application of best practice and up-to-date program development are valuable to increasing knowledge and effective services. There are four phases to interactive staff training models, including (1) introduction to the system, (2) program development, (3) program implementation, and (4) program maintenance to be carried out over a six- to eighteen-month span. Trainings should reflect the perceptions and critical thinking modes of the staff in order to foster participation and motivation. This promotes staff inclusivity and investment and helps to guide training to work within the established culture of the organization. We detailed an example of a proven performance- and evidence-based management system that incorporated interactive staff trainings in an inner-city community organization as developed by the first author.

Staff development encompasses three primary areas: (1) assessment and planning; (2) building capacity through training, continuing education, and professional development; and (3) performance accountability in order to reach ideal results. Management needs to assess the need for specified trainings in order to address performance deficits and support staff in sharpening the skills necessary to advance or take on new tasks. Staff positions need to be relevant, and therefore assessments and capacity building enhances performance and effectiveness.

Providing daily feedback helps to create an environment of adaptability aligned with the goals and mission of the organization and helps staff to make necessary adjustments as well as affirm their successes. Furthermore, it helps to address issues and successes when they are recent. Implementing team primacy concept-based evaluations, designed to provide self-feedback, supervisor feedback, and face-to-face peer feedback, helps staff to draw from evaluation data to aid in development. Peer appraisal and team feedback are other proven methods of providing feedback to aid in staff development, personal interactions, and improving outcomes. Staff self-assessments permit staff to review their performance and their perceived areas for needed improvement. This helps management to identify training opportunities that will tap into staff-identified deficits in which staff are motivated to change.

Planning for staff development entails identifying specific areas of focus for development in a staff member's current position, identifying future organization career objectives and relevant development needs, and identifying specific areas for development in the staff member's overall career. Training keeps staff knowledge and service delivery current. Utilizing mentors as trainers can help to bridge the relationship between staff and training sessions. Other means of training include webinars, presentations, interactive workbooks, internships, collaborative projects, continuing education, and seminars. Regardless of the method, trainings enhance staff performance and improve the ability of the organization to remain fiscally responsible, deliver quality services, and attend to the needs of client-consumers in an efficient and competent way.

Management needs to clearly establish performance goals, which are active motivators for driven staff and provide expectation clarity. Multidepartmental processes can collaborate on performance goals by using a Balanced Scorecard. Inter-departmental collaboration and overall investment in the staff and their performance leads to organizational success.

Chapter 10: Interpersonal Influence: Functions of the Wide Receiver as Administrator and Manager

Political behavior and politics are an innate aspect of social work, and agency personnel need to be aware of the influence, both economic and political, that social capital has on the design and implementation of effective social services. Change management strategies help to invest and motivate staff to changes by addressing sociopolitical factors that can help to create an environment of team collaboration. Having a logic model plan of action helps to achieve assessment, new program implementation, and behavioral change to assure smooth transition into a new protocol. This involves using existing social and economic capital, digital and media information sources, environmental scanning, research regarding EBP, careful monitoring of the implementation process, contingent thinking, succinct problem-solving, and strategic navigation. Being able to work with staff and draw from them the motivation to adopt new strategies and improve performance by using these skills help to move the organization in the right direction and promotes positive attitudes about change and accountability.

Reinforcing interpersonal influence, personal leadership, and motivation is the most cost-effective and practical way to assure that management and staff are trained in effective change skills. These devoted staff and managers model intentionality, gain the trust of fellow staff, and utilize the five steps of EBP and evidence-based management skills to make competent decisions and solve problems critically. Drawing from performance assessments and outcomes allows these staff and managers to proactively engage in planning sessions to develop and implement EBP and empirically supported interventions (ESIs) that are most likely to have effective results for clients, families, and communities.

Chapter 11: Human Resources

Workforce diversity is undergoing a multitude of changes, and organizational development and sustainability relies on keeping current with trends, competency, and inclusivity. In Chapter 11, we explored Mor Barak's theory of inclusion-exclusion and its four workforce propositions and their relationships to organizational outcomes. At its core, an organization needs to have a well-honed human resource agenda that is attentive to the four dimensions discussed in this chapter: (1) the correlates, (2) causes, and (3) consequences of effective human resources, and (4) age diversity and its implications for workforce development.

In regard to correlates of effective human resources, meeting the needs of employees is crucial. This includes compensation and benefits, leadership style, training, organizational culture, the management of change, and the focus on work–life balance. We took into consideration the influx of Generation X employees into the workforce and their new perceptions of work ethics, compensation, and employee relationships to the organization. We encouraged managers to remain attentive to the power of leadership styles, the method of communication, and the role of leaders on conveying the organization's mission into day-to-day operations, organizational change, and development strategies. Careful and thorough hiring practices ensure that motivated and skilled staff are brought into the organization's fold and allow management to focus on appropriate employee training, performance feedback, staff retention, and development, which are financially more beneficial to the organization than the cost of high turnover.

Best practices and evidence-based staff training has many benefits, including organizational investment, developing uniquely skilled staff, and improving the quality of services to clients. Training provides experiences for staff to access new theories, update practices, and undertake innovations on service provisions as well as orient newer staff to the goals and expectations of the organization. Another supportive dimension to the organization is addressing the balance between work and home life. Establishing healthy boundaries is an important element to social work and human services and can help to prepare staff to avoid burnout as well as send a strong message that the personal experiences of each employees are important to the overall health of the organization. Additionally, well-rested staff are more productive, more motivated, and can better reflect a positive and empowered image to client-consumers.

Diversity training needs to also address age diversity, especially considering the immense differences between the three predominant age groups in the workforce: traditionalist, baby boomer, and Generation X employees. This chapter outlined the generational characteristics of each of the three primary workforce employee generations, which are in competition for workforce placement, stability, and advancement. We discussed Zemke, Raines, and Filipczak's (2000) ACORN strategy for managing generations effectively, which includes accommodating employee differences, creating workplace choices, operating from a sophisticated management style, respecting competence and initiative, and nourishing retention. Understanding generational motivations, workplace loyalty, desired incentives, and work ethics are important to gaining insight into employees' operational locus, which can help to develop management strategies, development plans, and effective workforce propositions. Incorporating the different perspectives of intergenerational employees can be an asset to the organization, one fostered by strong, nurturing leadership.

Chapter 12: Power and Politics Within Collaborations

Inter- and intra-agency collaboration is an integral aspect of social services, and attention must be paid to collaborations that are beneficial to the delivery of effective and quality services and that enhance organization functioning. Four different facets of service collaboration include (1) a definition and an indication of the types of collaboration, (2) reasons for collaboration, (3) a general overview of organizational systems and power and politics theories as they relate to the collaboration process, and (4) a discussion regarding the conditions that enhance or hinder autonomy, authority, service accountability, and service continuity within the context of inter- and intra-organizational collaboration. This is an informed approach that taps into the various resources of multiple organizations or departments of a single agency to create a full scope of care and service delivery. It also address the common problem of adequate funding that an organization or department on its own could fail to attain in order to fully meet the scope of services that clients need.

Inter-agency collaborations pair together social services organizations with host agencies that, in many cases, do not primarily operate in the social services, and so organizational autonomy must be balanced with shared collaborative efforts. Intra-organizational collaboration involves service allocation from different divisions or departments within an organization. Due to the various funding sources, policies, and protocols in different departments within an organization, this type of collaboration needs to be sensitive to departmental competition for funding and management hierarchy issues. Collaboration helps to bring together multidisciplinary approaches to systemic and complex issues. This is an invaluable way to increase the quantity of services provided or help to address multifaceted issues and/or systems impacting client-consumers. Reasons for collaboration are (1) to fill service delivery gaps, (2) to enhance or maximize service delivery, (3) undertaken due to competition over scarce resources, and (4) to promote innovation.

Intra- and inter-organizational collaborations have to remain open to incorporating standing differences in vision and approach. Open systems allow for adaptation and growth in the collective exchange, but strategies and communicative spaces must be in place to maintain a level of homeostasis and individuality.

Incremental and strategic unification in the collaboration process allows for adjustments and for staff to ease into the relationship. Concepts of power and the politics of the agencies or departments need to be carefully assessed. In a healthy organization, forms of power have been distributed throughout the agency and a culture of collaboration has been established, thus allowing for a more natural adaptation to intra- or inter-organizational collaboration. When engaging in collaboration, equal power and shared input is expected from both collective realms during the planning stages. Differentiation of power once the collaborators establish the relationship and implement change can occur in respect to their different service provisions, provided it is carefully monitored for effectiveness. That being said, once the collaboration is in motion, the differing agencies or departments need to have a level of flexibility and autonomy that permits the extension of service expertise in a way that wholly benefits staff and clients. This is best carried out when roles and expectations are clearly identified and appropriate management plans and performance and behavioral change plans are established. It is important for collaborating agencies to have written agreements that address potential disagreements in values, ethics, and roles, as well as clear conflict resolution strategies to process issues that may emerge.

Collaboration will result in a combination of services and resources that help to address complex social service issues for clients, families, and communities, and assuring a smooth transition without disrupting the existing services provided by each of the organizations or departments is fundamental for service effectiveness. Service accountability through a collaborative arrangement needs to be responsive to clients as well as to the other organizations. A commitment to accountability combined with clearly established protocol, power, and participatory input helps collaborating organizations to reap the benefits of working collectively to increase and diversify services.

Chapter 13: Performance Measurement and Information Systems

Performance measures built into programs and services are a critical enhancement and time saver when an agency undergoes accreditation assessment, program review, or evaluation, and also for ongoing tracking of staff performance and client reactions to plans of care. It can be equally beneficial to management as well as staff to visualize inputs, outputs, performance, and outcomes, and measurement is a valuable investment of time and energy. We outlined twenty-five skills that problem-oriented practitioners need to proficiently perform. Establishing performance measures of behavioral outcomes and desired performance at baseline helps to develop an anticipated trajectory of outcomes and outcome improvements, thus directing staff toward goals. Continuous use allows for more careful assessment and tracking of misplaced or wrong contingencies and the contraction of problem behaviors. Performance measures are an integral facet of problem-solving and are directly correlated to increasing program and service effectiveness. Furthermore, they provide clarity to the collection and analysis of data throughout all phases of programming and service delivery.

The concept of the WOW factor, in which organizations and businesses seek to go above and beyond the regular scope of service and programming without compromising the financial integrity and growth of the organization, was discussed. WOW involves clearly established performance measures and thorough investigation into the more effective and desirable services. In practice, the more an organization tracks the elements of a program and client behaviors, the more mistakes and weaknesses can be fleshed out, thus leading to improved performance and predictable outcomes. These performance measures include reports, recorded testimony, meeting records, direct observation, and information systems, and they allow management to track primary agency functions. While there is historic resistance for practitioners and staff to collect data and numerous realistic barriers to the practice of data collection, such as the lack of evidentiary support, the benefits to the organization and clients are plentiful. For the advancement of programming and careful documentation for future funding, growth, and expansion, as well as for increased efficiency in client interventions, the implementation of data collection and performance measures is a necessary step for modern agencies.

To assure efficient and effective interventions, staff, clients, and families need to be trained in the process of data collection to help track their steps toward established goals. This aids in the assessment of the effects of the intervention, the occurrence or lack thereof of essential behaviors, and revisions that need to be made, and it provides data for the overall evaluation of program and service delivery for the agency to evaluate. This also means training participants to collect valid and reliable data and using functional analysis of behavior to account for history, environment, and external impacts on behavior change or the lack thereof. To carry out data collection, an organization needs to have in place information systems that aid, and do not hinder, the process of collection and application of performance measures. This includes electronic methods for maintaining client, assessment, financial, personnel, program compliance, and agency compliance records, and internal operating information systems data sources. Performance measures are beneficial for social workers to (1) set goals, (2) set client objectives, (3) select an appropriate intervention(s), (4) structure the intervention(s), (5) establish a contract, (6) monitor and evaluate the effects of the intervention, and (7) establish a process for maintaining outcomes of planned change.

Chapter 14: Diffusion, Organizational Politics, and Organizational Change

The Social Service Administration (SSA) at the University of Chicago is an example of an innovative and progressive organization that implemented task-centered practice and eventually EBP methodologies as problem-based learning approaches for ESIs. EBP is an important approach in assuring quality, informed services based on sound clinical decision-making that directly correlates to client improvements. The Stepwise Approach to EBP includes (1) using clinical information to create an answerable question about practice needs; (2) utilizing published research through electronic databases to search for the best available knowledge to answer the question; (3) evaluating gathered information based on its reliability, validity, and suitability for the particular practice situation; (4) integrating the scientific evidence with client knowledge and practitioner expertise and selecting a course of action that is acceptable to the client; and (5) monitoring and evaluating client responses to the intervention. This process can be used when seeking the best approaches for effectiveness, prevention, assessment, description, and risk in developing and implementing an intervention that is most likely to be appropriate and desired by the client.

In comparison, task-centered practice involves client participation at all stages of the decision-making process, can be derived from various practice methods, and is more accessible to paraprofessionals and clients, whereas EBP involves client participation in the fourth step of the process, is more likely to follow one course of action once decided upon, and is more technical and therefore more appropriate for trained experts to implement. We drew a comparison between EBP and evidence-based medicine (in which EBP has its roots) and saw that both approaches seek to increase critical thinking, competency, and transparency. EBP is unique in that it is rooted in the core social work principles of client self-determination and cultural competency.

Implementing EBP and ESIs can be difficult in social work due to resistance, uncertainty, and the demands of research. Furthermore, there are additional difficulties in implementing ESIs into child welfare settings due to feasibility, resources, and a disconnect between research and practice social work settings. ESIs are often viewed as not being fully developed for marginalized or culturally diverse populations and multi-issue clients, as being irrelevant to psychotherapy settings, or as being not flexible enough for systems of care that address extraordinary circumstances. The use of ESIs in lieu of EBP can reinforce ecological fallacies and be too linear and universally presumed in some instances. There may be questions about the ability of agencies to provide the necessary resources, adopt new practices, train staff, overcome staff resistance, provide clinical supervision, or implement a navigable database for assessment. To aid in the adoption of effective and innovative EBP and ESIs, an agency needs to follow several manageable steps to assure adoption and sustainability; these steps are rooted in agency-based social networks and interprofessional, political, and education-related factors. These steps are outlined to highlight the benefits and challenges of transparent and thorough implementation of innovations in order to most effectively establish valid and reliable practice and interventions.

Management strategies for creating an organizational environment open to change and implementing innovations include a focus on reinvention/fidelity, consumer involvement, staff factors, incentives, management support, and outcome measurement. Additionally, educational and organizational strategies, such as experiential teaching methods, well-designed manuals, and on-site training, can help to introduce and train staff to innovations in a supportive and informative manner. Combining agency change models such as Resnick's (1978) "change from within" and Corrigan and McCracken's (2004) interactive staff training model with Briggs's evidence-based management/performance management approach can best assist in the implementation and diffusion of EBP and ESIs. Attention must be paid to the culturally sensitive roles of guide, interpreter, researcher, translator, and advocate and the assumption of a nonauthoritarian role due to the collaborative nature of EBP. The benefits of EBP and ESIs, including greater client input and preferences, client participation, and cultural responsiveness in social work organizations devoted to the principles of self-determination, social justice, and advocacy, are crucial elements of innovation in our profession. The use of evidence in practice demands that practice is relevant, appropriate, and attentive to individual client needs in order to improve service quality and client well-being.

Chapter 15: Program Management and Quality Assurance

Chapter 15 chronicles the professional development of the first author, Harold Briggs, in nonprofit agencies, which later culminated in a career in academia. His personal experiences shed light on the horrors of poor executive management skills that disrupted his and other staffs' ability to perform their jobs effectively, repelled collaboration and client participation, and practiced fiscal irresponsibility to the extent of breaking laws. This experience was followed by a positive position in mental health that involved intra-agency coordination, professional development, and proactive program management. Such experiences reinforced that key foundational elements need to be in place for effective program management, including (1) instituting ethics and standards that clearly define performance standards that are inclusive of input from client-consumers, (2) clearly communicating expected performance, (3) structuring and organizing agency performance-based work and implementation plans, (4) tracking and monitoring methods, (5) using tools for performance appraisals, (6) undertaking a strategy for using performance appraisal data, and (7) utilizing evidence in critical decision-making within program management.

Maintaining ethics and standards at all levels of the organization impacts staff performance, agency outcomes, service effectiveness, practice reliability, and overall functioning. This also provides the groundwork for culturally competent and responsive care. Clear communication of expected performance depends on strong management involvement and proactive vehicles for providing and eliciting communication. Job descriptions and agency contracts help to provide staff and management their expected roles, input methods, and boundaries. Task analysis methods provide transparency and clarity to goals and expected performance, which are further reinforced with well-established policies, procedures, and a mission statement. Supervisory and management meetings need to utilize preplanned checklists that assess all levels of agency administrative tasks and service protocol/delivery and should have recorded minutes. Performance evaluations should be built into the running of an organization to provide necessary critical feedback, establish a flexible and receptive culture of change, and affirm the staff's strengths. These elements are further supported when organizational performance-based work and implementation plans are in place and tracking and monitoring are consistently enacted for quality control, staff retention, diversity enhancement, and program visualization. Such steps should be documented using reports and supervisory checklists for reference. These data, along with direct observation, self-reports, and feedback from client families, is important in reviewing the steps necessary to improve service delivery and reinforcing strategies that are proving effective. These data impact the organization's planning, organizing, implementing, monitoring, and coaching functions by addressing the core components of evidence-based decision-making, critical thinking, and problem-solving at each level of the organization's functioning. Conducting program outreach, intake, and assessment demands that management and staff are truly tuned into the nuances of the community and client-consumers in question, and should be fundamentally based on a proficient understanding of the culture, evidence-based scientific approaches that have proved effective, and the behavioral contingencies of the clients. In order to assure participation in an organization's programs and services, clients have to trust that the services offered are both worth their time and can speak competently to their needs.

Chapter 16: Program Review and Program Evaluation

Program reviews focus on the schedule of services and goods (inputs and outputs) and the consistency of these deliveries. It tracks for accuracy, feasibility, and the process by which outcomes are reached for quality assurance. Program evaluation is empirical in nature and looks closely at agency progress, service effectiveness, and program impact on clients. Both assess program fidelity and are learning processes by which organizations can grow and thrive.

The focus of the program review is to examine critical contingencies of inputs/outputs and outcomes related to the achievement of program objectives, goals, and vision. To be effective, reviews must be transparent and carried out with an attitude supporting organizational benefit and improvement. Reviews allow for reassessment of the program hypothesis and alterations to improve staff functioning, quality of service delivery, and transmission of goods. Reviews are also an opportunity to redirect staff, issue critiques, and even impose consequences for poor performance. Reviews can be internal or external to the organization, and they serve as a check for accountability and internal consistency. Review teams should include one program manager or director for streamlined communication and dissemination of the culture and practices of the organization to the remaining review team. To do so, program reviews should collect data by following the detailed steps, reviewing all details of a program, such as plans, program policies, and procedures. Next, reviewers need to interview staff, management, and board of directors, and then process meeting minutes pertaining to the program. Reviewers should attend and observe meetings and programs to assess staff, management, board of director, and client-consumer behaviors. Disseminated reports include an overview of the data collected, observations, suggestions, questions, and highlights of successes. Any discrepancies or disagreements with findings are handled by upper management in an appropriate and proactive manner. Training, program change, and correctional actions related to content, relational, technical, and clinical realms can then be implemented.

Program evaluations look closely at service effectiveness and outcomes and impacts as they relate to client-consumers. There are various ways by which to carry out a program evaluation, and we conclude that the following steps will assist in an effective, detailed, and culturally informed evaluation approach: (1) articulating the program evaluation's unit of attention; (2) identifying and securing the participation of people most affected by the program in its overall evaluation; (3) defining the main purpose of the program evaluations as either formative or process- and outcome-centered; (4) establishing the evaluation plan based on questions, measurable objectives, and expected claims that can be verified and tested and that utilize pre- and post-program implementation assessments or a combination all stages of implementation; (5) identifying a measurable behavior definition of the targets of change and the desirable program outcomes and impacts and establishing clearly written procedures for the implementation of the evaluation; (6) drafting a report of findings, including the anticipated and unanticipated consequences of a program; and (7) sharing the findings along with critiques, feedback, affirmations, and suggestions.

Additionally, program evaluations must take into consideration the fidelity of the program as related to political, financial, and resource dependencies, and ethical considerations and complications, particularly for social workers bound to the Code of Ethics. These factors can complicate or complement evaluations. Reliable measures need to be in place to assure valid data and relativity to the program in question. Methods such as control groups, randomization, and multiple baseline single-subject designs can be used to measure outcomes and increase the quality of the program evaluation to properly assess the appropriateness and efficacy of the program to achieve desired outcomes. Evaluations assure an achievement of client goals and that clients are motivated to follow treatment plans by assuring that plans are effective, appropriate, and culturally informed. In order for organizations to maintain adherence to ethics and accountability, program evaluations need to be built into consistent organizational practices and culture.

Chapter 17: Organizational Development

Preventative organizational development should be a key priority for an agency. Implementing a culture of strategic evidence-based decision-making, participatory management processes, organizational transparency, checks and balances, shared accountability, and cultural competence helps to meet the goal of providing effective service delivery and program functioning.

Crucial to the healthy management and outcomes of an organization is the issue of accountability. Effective organizational management requires attentiveness to tracking errors and issues, developing a participatory culture of establishing goals and reviewing outcomes, and implementing organizational behavior modification plans to achieve staff, board, management, and client-consumer buy-in and necessary change processes. Developing cultural competence within the organization also requires assessing the structural, institutional, and systemic racism of the organization, the community, and collaborating institutions. Developing a social justice framework and identifying the multitude of cultural diversity concepts aids in staff cross-cultural competency as well as assuring that supervisors are maintaining culturally competent practices. This includes highlighting the importance of racial respect as it pertains to health, mental health, and issues of well-being for people of color and individuals who belong to marginalized communities.

In Chapter 17, we detailed the role of understanding adaptive and maladaptive identity theory in order to raise staff knowledge of racism and social injustice. These concepts identify the rampant disparities that African Americans face in accessing culturally relevant health and mental health services; the inequities of service provision; decreased legal and political protection; and the increased frequency of interfacing with high-end restrictive health and human service systems, such as foster care and correction facilities. Furthermore, the fusion of culture and evidence-based management and practices enhances the ability of the organization and its staff to address social issues as they pertain to clients, families, and communities in an empathic, empowering, and effective manner.

Organizational sustainability includes using guiding behaviors as a framework for creating an environment of participation and inclusivity for staff, management, and client-consumers alike. This includes instilling confidence and accountability, reinforcing management styles, and using an open means of communication that invests staff with the organization and its established goals.

Chapter 18: Program Development

Programs address large issues and practitioners must possess knowledge of applied behavioral analysis to best inform decision-making for effective programs. In Chapter 18, we explored how logic modeling helps to proactively prepare for potential consequences and assess related stressors and needs quickly by using behavioral contingency analysis. This plan of action approach involves a needs analysis, implementation plans, and instilled quality assurance and program evaluations to assure efficacy. At the core of effective programs, critical thinking is the primary factor for practitioners to know and incorporate. By balancing technical knowledge with the cultural and practical knowledge of programs and the people they serve, an organization can develop programs that have a check-and-balance system that incorporates a full circle of knowledge and the critical thinking skills to make changes as needed.

Program development includes three primary principles. First, critical perspectives include developing a statement of the social issue, culturally relevant value assumptions, and a plan of action proposal that acts to drive program design. Critical perspectives entail stating the social issue, being clear about the practitioner's value assumptions about the problem, and stating the proposed plan of action and system support to address the social issue. Second, the critical perspective needs to be informed by knowledge development and dissemination to establish effective program design. Drawing from practitioner knowledge introduces experiences that reflect an evidentiary basis of the effectiveness of planned approaches. Also, knowledge development helps to eliminate program design elements that interfere with client self-determination. Finally, planning innovation and program change requires that practitioners utilize a developmental research framework. We cited the model development approach as a practical framework in which current research is used to develop a set of procedures that are pilot tested and adapted as needed until ready for dissemination. The model development approach includes conducting a detailed problem analysis; gathering information from various sources; pilot testing design and development, evaluation, and advanced stages of development; and finally, disseminating and implementing the solution.

Chapter 19: Community Engagement Through Evidence-Based Practice and Community Participatory Model Program Development

In Chapter 19, we examined the existing disparities in the delivery of services, with African Americans receiving fewer and lower quality mental health services than whites. In addition, the low percentage of African American practitioners is an alienating factor for clients who need to feel connected to and trust service providers. A major factor in these disparities is the lack of culturally informed, evidence-based services that both address the cultural needs of African Americans and address the direct needs of the community through empowering community participatory approaches to better inform service delivery. Cultural stigma, a history of systemic health and mental health abuses resulting in distrust, also impacts the utilization of services. Juxtaposed with the growing health and mental health issues that historically marginalized groups face, it has become a public health crisis stigma is best addressed by taking a culturally informed approach to connecting African Americans to effective preventative and treatment services.

There are questions regarding current EBPs and ESIs and their limitations to being applied universally to diverse cultural population or populations experiencing numerous service needs. EBP entails five steps: (1) designing answerable client-oriented practice evidence search questions, (2) searching for the best available evidence, (3) critically appraising the evidence, (4) using clinical judgment and expertise in considering client preferences and resources needed to implement each option, and (5) applying and systematically evaluating the services consistent with client preferences. Yet little progress has been made in identifying EBPs and ESIs that are grounded in the cultural experiences and multiple identity classifications of black individuals. As a result of enslavement and deeply rooted discrimination, black and African American identity is nuanced and dependent on factors related to acculturated identity, enculturation identity, racial socialization, or a combination of any of these aspects that shape the cultural orientation of a black individual. Further, with low participation in mental health services and few services to choose from, little effort has been put forth to develop an understanding of culturally relevant EBP and ESIs.

Experience has shown that community-based participatory action approaches tap into the knowledge base of diverse localized communities and help to design services based on the presence of disparities and the needs stated by community members. Effective services that speak the language of the client-consumers and draw directly from their cultural and environmental experiences, values, social justice issues, beliefs, strengths, and styles are more likely to be utilized and sustainable. Community-based participatory research models are also better able to flesh out an authentic understanding of and beliefs about mental health care and the particularities of mental health issues as the community understands them. This is done by using culturally relevant research teams made up of academics, mental health practitioners, and even community residents. These teams help guide the development of respectful interventions and services through local capacity building, social justice, and advocacy based on the voices of residents. This approach was highlighted through a detailed case study of an African American mental health initiative in Portland, Oregon.

Chapter 20: Transforming Administration and Management Through Blending Science, Community Voice, Family, and Consumer Participation

The unique and nuanced perspective of community members is crucial to evolving human and social services. Partnering community knowledge and scientific evidence will assist in developing services and capacity building. Considering the vast disparities of African American, Native American, Hispanic, and other historically marginalized groups in accessing quality healthcare and mental healthcare and the reduced likelihood that individuals in these groups will seek services, there are numerous challenges to implementing ESIs, particularly in child welfare services. Traditionally, there is a lack of incentives for innovations and learning, as well as resistance, differences in the values and priorities of practice and research communities, and limitations to using ESIs in psychotherapeutic settings for multiple-issue clients. There is also the risk of interfering in practitioner–client relationship building, and the dominant-cultural normative nature of the evidence must be considered. Furthermore, there is a dire need for diversification within research and among those carrying out research in ESIs. Integrating EBPs and ESIs requires attention to clients' cultures and values, informed consent, and client self-determination. Attention needs to be paid to establish strong practice principles based on cultural competence and that foster client resiliency, reflect the customs and expressions of clients, and are supportive of advocacy need to reduce disparities.

It is also imperative that organizations working with diverse clients prepare to diffuse innovations by following detailed steps to integrate the necessary resources, training, cultural competency, assessment and tracking methods, and behavioral management for staff while being fully aware of the extent and limitations of utilizing EBPs and ESIs. This entails developing relationships with universities, maintaining transparency, using a trial-and-error method to assure the right fit, and putting into place the appropriate resources and financial support associated with the innovations. In Chapter 20, this was detailed in a case study involving EBP with African Americans in a child care welfare setting in Chicago.

REFERENCES

Abrams, L. A., & Moio, J. A. (2009). Critical race theory and the cultural competence dilemma in social work education. *Journal of Social Work Education, 45*(2), 245–261.

Adams, G. L., Tallon, R. J., & Rimell, P. (1980). A comparison of lecture versus role-playing in the training of the use of positive reinforcement. *Journal of Organizational Behavior Management, 2*(3), 205. doi:10.1300/J075v02n03_06

Akbar, N. (1991). Mental disorders among African Americans. In R. L. Jones (Ed.), *Black psychology* (3rd ed., pp. 339–352). Berkeley, CA: Cobb & Henry.

Alexander, M. (2010). *The new Jim Crow: Mass incarceration in the age of colorblindness.* New York: New Press.

Alvidrez, J., Snowden, L. R., & Kaiser, D. M. (2008). The experience of stigma among black mental health consumers. *Journal of Health Care for the Poor and Underserved, 19*, 974–893.

Anderson, L. M., Scrimshaw, S. G., Fullilove, M. T., Fielding, J. E., Normand, J., & the Task Force on Community Preventative Services. (2003). *Culturally competent health-care systems: A systematic review.* Ipswich, MA: Minority Health Archive.

Anderson-Butcher, D., & Ashton, D. (2004). Innovative models of collaboration to serve children, youths, families, & communities. *Children and Schools, 26*(1), 39–53.

Arellano, K. (1999). Marking the spot for Gen X. *Denver Business Journal, 51*(3), 23A.

Au, C. (1994). The status of theory and knowledge development in social welfare administration. *Administration in Social Work, 18*(3), 27–57.

Bacon, D. L., Fulton, B. J., & Malott, R. W. (1983). Improving staff performance through the use of task checklists. *Journal of Organizational Behavior Management, 4*(3/4), 17. doi:10.1300/J075v04n03_03

Baer, D. M. (1999). *How to plan for generalization* (2nd ed.). Austin, TX: Pro-Ed.

Baer, D. M. (2004). Program evaluation: Arduous, impossible, and political. In H. E. Briggs & T. L. Rzepnicki (Eds.), *Using evidence in social work practice: Behavioral perspectives* (pp. 310–322). Chicago: Lyceum Books.

Baer, D. M., Wolf, M. M., & Risley, T. R. (1968). Some current dimensions of applied behavior analysis. *Journal of Applied Behavior Analysis, 1*(1), 91–97.

Baer, D. M., Wolf, M. M., & Risley, T. R. (1987). Some still-current dimensions of applied behavior analysis. *Journal of Applied Behavior Analysis, 20*(4), 313–327. doi:10.1901/jaba.1987.20-313

Bailey-Dempsey, C., & Reid, W. J. (1996). Intervention design and development: A case study. *Research on Social Work Practice, 6*, 208–228.

Baker, D., Barth, M. C., Bradley E., Inouye, S. K., Koren, M. J., Lapane, K. L., . . . Webster, T. R. (2004). Translating research into practice: Speeding the adoption of innovative health care programs. *Issue Brief (Commonwealth Fund), 724*, 1–11.

Bandura, A. (1969). *Principles of behavior modification.* New York: Holt, Rinehart & Winston.

Banks, J. A. (2003). Teaching for multicultural literacy, global citizenship, and social justice. *The 2003 Charles Fowler Colloquium on Innovation in Arts Education.* College Park, MD: University of Maryland.

Banks, J. A. (2004). Teaching for social justice, diversity, and citizenship in a global world. *The Educational Forum, 68*, 297–305.

Banks, J. A. (Ed.). (2009). *The Routledge international companion to multicultural education.* New York: Routledge, 2009.

Banks, L., Hopps, J. G., & Briggs, H. E. (2018). Cracks in the Ceiling? Historical and Contemporary Trends of African American Deans of Schools of Social Work. *Research on Social Work Practice, 28*(3), 288–299.

Barker, R. L. (1995). *The social work dictionary* (3rd ed., p. 354). Washington, DC: National Association of Social Workers.

Barlett, D. L., & Steele, J. B. (2012). *The betrayal of the American dream.* New York: Public Affairs.

Baron, H. (1969). The web of urban racism. In L. Knowles & K. Prewitt (Eds.), *Institutional racism in America* (pp. 134–176). Englewood Cliffs, NJ: Prentice Hall.

Bartholet, E., Wulcyzn, F., Barth, R. P., & Lederman, C. (2011, June). *Race and child welfare* (Harvard Public Law Working Paper No. 11–27). Retrieved from http://ssm.com/abstracts=1889239

Bell, A. H. (1997). *The practical executive and workforce diversity.* Lincolnwood, IL: NTC Business Books.

Bell, C. C. (2006). *Exposure to a traumatic event does not automatically put a person on a path to develop PTSD: The importance of protective factors to promote resiliency.* Retrieved from http://www.giftfromwithin.org./html/ptomote.html

Bell, C. C., Wells, S. J., & Merritt, L. M. (2009). Integrating cultural competency and empirically-based practices in child welfare services: A model based on community psychiatry field principles of health. *Children and Youth Services Review, 31*, 1206–1213.

Bell, D. (2003). Diversity's distractions. *Columbia Law Review, 6*, 1622.

Bent-Goodley, T. B., & Hopps, J. G. (2017). Social Justice and Civil Rights: A Call to Action for Social Work. *Social Work, 62*(1), 5–8.

Bernal, G., & Saez-Santiago, E. (2006). Culturally centered psychological interventions. *Journal of Community Psychology, 34*, 121–132.

Bisceglia, S. (2014). *Outside Opinion: Millennials frustrated HR execs.* Chicago Tribune, September 5.

Blackman, D. K., Howe, M., & Pinkston, E. M. (1976). Increasing participation in social interaction of the institutionalized elderly. *Gerontologist, 16*(1), 69.

Blanchard, K., Miller, M., (2004, 2007). *The Secret. What Great Leaders Know and Do.* Berrett-Koehler Publishers, Inc., San Francisco.

Blasé, K. A., & Fixsen, D. L. (2003). *Consensus statement on evidence-based programs and cultural competence.* Tampa, FL: National Implementation Research Network, the Louis de la Parte Florida Mental Health Institute.

Bloom, M., Fischer, J., & Orme, J. G. (2009). *Evaluating Practice: Guidelines for the Accountable Professional. 6th Edition.* Boston: Pearson/Allyn Bacon.

Boettcher, R. E., Jakes, L., & Sigal, L. M. (2008). An evaluation of a community collaboration approach to psychosocial rehabilitation. *Journal of Community Practice, 16*(2), 165–181.

Bolman, L. G., & Deal, T. E. (1997). *Reframing organizations: Artistry, choice, and leadership.* San Francisco: Jossey-Bass.

Bowditch, J. L., & Buono, A. F. (1994). *A primer on organizational behavior.* New York: Wiley.

Bowen, E. (2004). Aging in a diverse society: The role of cultural competency in mental health care for older adults. *Advocates' Forum,* 31–41. School of Social Service Administration, University of Chicago.

Bowles, D. D., Hopps, J. G., & Clayton, O. (2016). The impact and influence of HBCUs on the social work profession. *Journal of Social Work Education, 52*(1), 118–132.

Brack, J., & Kelly, K. (2012). Maximizing millennials in the workplace. *UNC executive development.* Retrieved from https://www.kenan-flagler.unc.edu/executive-development/custom-programs/~/media/files/documents/executive-development/maximizing-millennials-in-the-workplace.pdf.

Branch, S. (1998). You hired 'em. But can you keep 'em? *Fortune,* November 9, 101–104.

Braveman, P., & Gruskin, S. (2003). Poverty, equity, human rights and health. *Bulletin of the World Health Organization, 81*(7), 539–545.

Bray, S. (2001). Managing Generation X. *Executive Excellence Magazine, 2001.*

Briggs, H. E. (1994). Promoting adoptions by foster parents through an inner city community. *Research on Social Work Practice, 4*(4), 479–509.

Briggs, H. E. (1996a). Enhancing community adjustment of persons with developmental disabilities: Transferring multilevel behavioral technology to an inner city community organization. *Journal of Applied Social Sciences, 20*(2), 177–190.

Briggs, H. E. (1996b). Creating independent voices: The emergence of statewide family networks. *Journal of Mental Health Administration 23*(4), 447–457.

Briggs, H. E. (2001a). Working with organizations serving people with disabilities. In H. E. Briggs & K. Corcoran (Eds.), *Social work practice: Treating common client problems* (2nd ed., pp. 371–390). Chicago: Lyceum Books.

Briggs, H. E. (2001b). Cultural diversity: A latter day Trojan horse. *Psychology and Education, 38*(1), 3–11.

Briggs, H. E. (2004). *African American mental health commission report: Assessment for cultural specific mental health service systems of care* (pp. 1–60). Portland, OR: African American Commission on Mental Health.

Briggs, H. E. (2005). Preface: Special issue honoring Elsie M. Pinkston, PhD *Research On Social Work Practice, 15*(6), 429–430.

Briggs, H. E. (2009). The fusion of culture and science: Challenges and controversies of cultural competency and evidence-based practice with an African American family advocacy network. *Children and Youth Services Review, 31*(11), 1172–1179. doi:10.1016/j.childyouth.2009.09.001

Briggs, H. E. (2011). *Governor's task force on disproportionality in child welfare.* Retrieved from http://www.oregon.gov/dhs/children/docs/tf-report.pdf

Briggs, H. E. (2014). Note from the editor: What do we really know about the role and impact of culture as a social determinant of mental health? *Best Practices in Mental Health, 10*(2), 96–99.

Briggs, H. E., Bank, L., & Briggs, A. C. (2014). Behavioral health and social-cultural determinants of corrections involvement among vulnerable African American females: Historical and contemporary themes. *Journal of Forensic Social Work, 4,* 176–202.

Briggs, H. E., Banks, L., & Briggs, A. C. (2014). Increasing knowledge and mental health service use among African Americans through evidence-based practice and cultural injection vector engagement practice approaches. *Best Practices in Mental Health, 10*(2), 1–14.

Briggs, H. E., Bank, L., Fixsen, A., Briggs, A. C., Newell, S., & Hood, B. (2009). *Perceptions of African American experience (PAAX): A new measure of adaptive identities among African American men and women.* Unpublished manuscript.

Briggs, H. E., Bank, L., Fixsen, A., Briggs, A. C., Kothari, B., & Burkett, C. (2014). Perceptions of the African American Experience (PAAX): A New Measure of Adaptive Identities Among African American Men and Women. *Journal of Forensic Social Work, 4*(3), 203–233. doi:10.1080/1936928X.2015.1029660

Briggs, H. E., Briggs, A. C., & Leary, J. D. (2005). Promoting culturally competent systems of care through statewide family advocacy networks. *Best Practice in Mental Health, 1*(2), 77–99.

Briggs, H. E., Briggs, A. C., & Leary, J. (2006). Family participation in systems change. *Best Practices in Mental Health, 2*(1), 42–58.

Briggs, H. E., Briggs, A. C., Miller, K. M., & Paulson, R. I. (2011). Combating persistent cultural incompetence in mental health care systems serving African Americans. *Best Practices in Mental Health, 7*(2), 1–25.

Briggs, H. E., & Corcoran, K. (Eds.). (2001). *Social work practice: Treating common client problems* (2nd ed.). Chicago: Lyceum Books.

Briggs, H. E., Feyerherm, W., & Gingerich, W. (2004). Evaluating science-based practice with single systems. In H. E. Briggs & T. L. Rzepnicki (Eds.), *Using evidence in social work practice: Behavioral perspectives* (pp. 323–342). Chicago: Lyceum Books.

Briggs, H. E., Holosko, M. J., Banks, L., Huggins-Hoyt, K., & Parker, J. (2018). How are African Americans currently represented in various social work venues? *Research on Social Work Practice, 28*(3), 275–287.

Briggs, H. E., & Koroloff, N. (1995). Enhancing statewide family networks: An analysis of the roles of sponsoring organizations. *Community Mental Health Journal, 32*(4), 319–333.

Briggs, H., Kothari, B., Briggs, A. C., Bank, L., & DeGruy, J. (2015). Racial Respect: Initial Testing and Validation of the Racial Respect scale for Adult African Americans. *Journal of the Society for Social Work and Research, 6*(1), 269–303.

Briggs, H. E., Koroloff, N., Friesen, B. F., & Walker, J. (2007). Promoting and sustaining evidence-based practice: Special Issue. *Journal of Social Work Education, 43*(3), 361–496.

Briggs, H. E., Koroloff, N. M., & Carrock, S. (1994). *The driving force: The contribution of family advocacy organizations in system change* [Monograph]. Portland, OR: Portland State University, Research and Training Center for Family Support and Children's Mental Health.

Briggs, H. E., Koroloff, N. M., Richards, K., & Friesen, B. J. (1993). *Family advocacy organizations: Advances in support and system reform* [Monograph]. Portland, OR: Portland State University, Research and Training Center on Family Support and Children's Mental Health.

Briggs, H. E., & Leary, J. (2001). Shields and walls: The structural and process of racism in American society. *Psychology and Education, 38*(2), 2–14.

Briggs, H. E., Leary, J. D., Briggs, H. E., Cox, W., & Shibano, M. (2005). Group treatment of separated parent and child interaction. *Research on Social Work Practice, 15*, 452–461.

Briggs, H. E., & McBeath, B. (2009). Evidence-based management: Origins, challenges, and implications for social service administration. *Administration in Social Work, 33*(3), 242–261.

Briggs, H. E., & McBeath, B. (2010). Infusing culture into practice: Developing and implementing evidence-based mental health services for African American youth. *Child Welfare, 89*(1), 31–60.

Briggs, H. E., & McMillan, S. (2012). Implementing evidence-based management. In T. Rzepnicki, S. McCracken, & H. E. Briggs (Eds.), *Evidence-based practice: An integrative approach to practice* (pp. 156–178). Chicago, IL: Lyceum Books.

Briggs, H. E., & Paulson, R. I. (1996). Racism. In M. A. Mattaini & B. A. Thyer (Eds.), *Finding solutions to social problems: Behavioral strategies for change* (pp. 147–177). Washington, DC: American Psychological Association.

Briggs, H. E., & Rzepnicki, T. L. (2004). *Using evidence in social work practice: Behavioral perspectives.* Chicago: Lyceum Books.

Briggs, V., Donovan, J., Foster, M., & Mendenhall, D. (2002). *Boomers Vs Gen. X.* A presentation for Marylhurst University Marketing Class.

Briggs, H. E., Miller, D. B., Sayles, R., Tovar, D., & Dozier, C. (1997). Correlates of substance abuse among youth: A note to professionals, service providers, and families. Community Alternatives. *International Journal of Family Care, 9*(2), 109–142.

Bronstein, L. R., & Abramson, J. S. (2003). Understanding socialization of teachers and social workers: Groundwork for collaboration in the schools. *Families in Society, 84*(3), 323–329.

Browder, D. M. (1987). *Assessment of individuals with severe handicaps: An applied behavior approach to life skills assessment.* Baltimore, MD: P. H. Brookes.

Brown, K. M., Willis, B. S., & Reid, D. H. (1981). Differential effects of supervisor verbal feedback and feedback plus approval on institutional staff performance. *Journal of Organizational Behavior Management, 3*(1), 57. doi:10.1300/J075v03n01_05

Brownstein, L. R. (2002). Index of interdisciplinary collaboration. *Social Work Research, 26*(2), 113–123.

Buckingham, M., & Coffman, C. (1999). *First, break all the rules: What the world's greatest managers do differently.* New York: Simon & Schuster.

Burg, M. M., Reid, D. H., & Lattimore, J. (1979). Use of a self-recording and supervision program to change institutional staff behavior. *Journal of Applied Behavior Analysis, 12*(3), 363–375. doi:10.1901/jaba.1979.12-363

Burgio, L. D., Whitman, T. L., & Reid, D. H. (1983). A participative management approach for improving direct-care staff performance in an institutional setting. *Journal of Applied Behavior Analysis, 16*(1), 39–53. doi:10.1901/jaba.1983.16-37

Burns, B. J., Hoagwood, K., & Mrazek, P. J. (1999). Effective treatment for mental disorders in children and adolescents. *Clinical Child and Family Psychology Review, 2*(4), 199–254. doi:10.1023/A:1021826216025.

Business 2 Community (2016). https://www.business2community.com/branding/what-we-can-expect-from-generation-z-implications-for-branding-02169841

Calman, N., Ruddock, C., Golub, M., & Le, L. (2005). Separate and unequal: Medical apartheid in New York City. Bronx Health REACH. www.institute2000.org

Carville, J., & Greenburg, S. (2012). *It's the middle class stupid.* New York: Blue Rider Press.

Chaffin, M., & Frederich, B. (2004). Evidence based treatments in child abuse and neglect. *Children and Youth Services Review, 26,* 1097–1113.

Charan, R., Drotter, S., & Noel, J. (2001). *The Leadership Pipeline. How to Build the Leadership-Powered Company.* Jossey-Bass, Wiley Co.: San Francisco, California.

Chemers, M. M. (1997). *An integrative theory of leadership.* Mahwah, NJ: Lawrence Erlbaum Associates.

Christian, W. P. (1984). A case study in the programming and maintenance of institutional change. *Journal of Organizational Behavior Management, 5*(3/4), 99. doi:10.1300/J075v05n03_06

Claghorn, K. H. (1927). The problem of measuring social treatment. *Social Service Review, 1*(2), 181.

Clarke, M., & Drudy, S. (2006). Teaching for diversity, social justice and global awareness. *European Journal of Teacher Education, 29*(3), 371–386.

Coates, T.-N. (June 2014). The case for reparations. *The Atlantic Monthly,* May 21, 2014.

Coles, E., & Blunden, R. (1981). Maintaining new procedures using feedback to staff, a hierarchical reporting system, and a multidisciplinary management group. *Journal of Organizational Behavior Management, 3*(2), 19. doi:10.1300/J075v03n02_03

Collins, J., & Porras, J. I. (1994). *Built to Last: Successful Habits of Visionary Companies.* Harper Collins Publishing, New York.

Colombo, G., Cullen, R., & Lisle, B. (2001). *Rereading America: Cultural contexts for critical thinking and writing* (5th ed.). Boston: Bedford/St. Martin's.

Comer, J. P. (1980). *School power: Implications of an intervention project.* New York: Free Press/Collier Macmillan.

Commission on Social Determinants of Health (CSDH). (2008). *Closing the gap in a generation: Health equity through action on social determinants of health.* Final Report of the Commission on Social Determinants of Health. Geneva: World Health Organization. Retrieved from http://whqlibdoc.who.int/publications/2008/9789241563703_eng.pdf

Conrin, J. (1983). A comparison of two types of antecedent control over supervisory behavior. *Journal of Organizational Behavior Management, 4*(3/4), 37. doi:10.1300/J075v04n03_05

Corcoran, K., Gingerich, W. J., & Briggs, H. E. (2001). Practice evaluation: Setting goals and monitoring change. In H. E. Briggs & K. Corcoran (Eds.), *Social work practice: Treating common client problems* (pp. 66–84). Chicago: Lyceum Books.

Corcoran, K. C., Grinnell, R. M., & Briggs, H. E. (2001). Implementing the foundations of change. In H. E. Briggs & K. Corcoran (Eds.), *Social work practice: Treating common client problems* (pp. 3–14). Chicago: Lyceum Books.

Corneille, M. A., Ashcraft, A. M., & Belgrave, F. Z. (2005). What's culture got to do with it? Prevention programs for African American adolescent girls. *Journal of Health Care for the Poor and Underserved, 16*(4,Suppl B), 38–47.

Corrigan, P. W., & McCracken, S. G. (1997). *Interactive staff training: Rehabilitation teams that work*. New York: Plenum Press.

Corrigan, P. W., & McCracken, S. G. (1998). An interactive approach to training teams and developing programs. In P. W. Corrigan & D. F. Giffort (Eds.), *Building teams and programs for effective psychiatric rehabilitation* (pp. 3–12). San Francisco: Jossey-Bass.

Council on Social Work Education (CSWE). (2008). *Educational policy and accreditation standards*. Alexandria, VA: Author.

Covey, S. R. (1989). *The 7 Habits of Highly Effective People*. Free Press, a division of Simon & Schuster.

Cox, W. H. (1982). *Behavioral group training of single parent/child dyads* (Doctoral dissertation). University of Chicago.

Cross, T. L., Bazron, B. J., Dennis, K. W., & Isaacs, M. R. (1989). *Towards a culturally competent system of care: A monograph on effective services for minority who are severely emotionally disturbed* (Vol. 1). Washington, DC: Georgetown University Child Development Center.

Cross, T. L., Friesen, B. J., Jivanjee, P., Gowen, L. K., Bandurraga, A., Mathew, C., & Maher, N. (2011). Defining Youth Success using Culturally Appropriate Community-based Participatory Research Methods. *Best Practices in Mental Health, 7*(1), 94–114.

Danieli, Y. (Ed.). (1998). *International handbook of multigenerational legacies of trauma*. New York: Plenum Press.

Daniels, M. C. (2015). *New refugees and immigrants: Social work's responsibility and response*. Opening remarks, Parham Policy Day 2015, School of Social Work, University of Georgia, Gwinnett Campus. Retrieved from http://ssw.uga.edu/events/ParhamPolicyDay2015.html

Daniels, M. C., & Patterson, V. C. (2012). Education: (Re)considering race in the desegregation of higher education. *Georgia Law Review, 46*, 521.

Davis, A. (2007). *Angelea Davis on race in America*. PBS. NOW. News Broadcast.

Davis, L. E. (2016). Race: America's grand challenge. *Journal of the Society for Social Work and Research, 7*(2), 395–403.

DeChillo, N. (1993). Collaboration between social workers and families of patients with mental illness. *Families in Society: The Journal of Contemporary Human Services, 74*, 104–115.

DeGruy-Leary, J. (1998, April–June). *The relationship model of managerial intervention*. Unpublished presentation: Strength-based case management, Multnomah County Department of Community and Family Services, Portland, Oregon.

DeGruy-Leary, J. D. (2005). *Post-traumatic slave syndrome: America's legacy of enduring injury and healing*. Milwaukee, OR: Uptone Press.

Delpit, L. (1995). *Other people's children: Cultural conflict in the classroom*. New York: The New Press.

DeShon, R. P., Kozlowski, S. W. J., Schmidt, A. M., Milner, K. R., & Wiechmann, D. (2004). A multiple-goal, multilevel model of feedback effects on the regulation of individual and team performance. *Journal of Applied Psychology, 89*(6), 1035–1056.

Donston-Miller, D. (2016). *Workforce 2020: What You Need to Know Now*. Forbes, May 5, 2016.

Dougherty, R. H., Friedman, B., & Pinkston, E. M. (1982). An analysis of time-out and response-cost procedures in a special education classroom. In E. M. Pinkston, et al. (Eds.), *Effective social work practice* (pp. 320–341). San Francisco: Jossey-Bass.

Drexler, J. A., Beehr, T. A., & Stetz, T. A. (2001). Peer appraisals: Differentiation of individual performance on group tasks. *Human Resource Management, 40*(4), 333–345.

Drucker, P. F. (1964, 1986). *Managing for results.* New York: Harper Collins.

Drucker, P. F. (1990). *Managing the non-profit organization: Principles and practices.* New York: Harper Collins.

Druskat, V. U., & Wolff, S. B. (1999). Effects and timing of developmental peer appraisals in self-managing work groups. *Journal of Applied Psychology, 84*(1), 58–74.

Dudley, J. R. (2014). *Social work evaluation: Enhancing what we do.* Chicago: Lyceum Books.

Dusenbury, L., & Hansen, W. (2004). Pursuing the course from research to practice. *Prevention Science, 5*(1), 55–59.

Eddy, D. (2005). Evidence-based medicine: A unified approach. *Health Affairs, 24*, 9–17.

Educational Business Publication. (2003). *Valuing human capital.* Retrieved from www.educationalesystems.com

Edwards, R., Cooke, P., & Reid, N. (1996). Social work management in an era of diminishing federal responsibility. *Social Work, 41*(5), 468–479.

Ehin, C. (2005). *Hidden assets: Harnessing power in informal networks.* New York: Springer.

Feagin, J. (2010). Review of the book *Blurring the color line: The new chance for a more integrated America*, by R. Alba. *American Journal of Sociology, 116*(1), 285–287. doi:10.1086/655633

Feder, L., Jolin, A., & Feyerherm, W. (2000). Lessons from two randomized experiments in criminal justice settings. *Crime &Delinquency, 46*(3), 380–400. doi:10.1177/0011128700046003007

Ferlie, E., Fitzgerald, L., Wood, M., & Hawkins, C. (2005). The nonspread of innovations: The mediating role of professionals. *Academy of Management Journal, 48*(1), 117–134.

Fischer, J. (1978). Does anything work? *Journal of Social Service Research, 1*(3), 215–243.

Fitzgerald, L., Felie, E., Wood, M., & Hawkins, C. (2002). Interlocking interactions, the diffusion of innovations in health care. *Human Relations, 55*(12), 1429–1449.

Fixsen, D., Blasé, K., Duda, M. A., Metz, A. J., Naoom, S. F., & Van Dyke, M. K. (2010, February). *Piecemeal is no meal: Implementation science and practice.* National Implementation Research Network. University of North Carolina at Chapel Hill Frank Porter Graham Child Development Institute, University of North Carolina Chapel Hill.

Foxworthy, R., Ellis, W., & McLeod, C. (1982). A management team system. *Journal of Organizational Behavior Management, 3*(4), 19. doi:10.1300/J075v03n04_03

Fraser, M. W. (2002). The ecology of childhood. In M. Fraser (Ed.), *Risk and resilience in childhood: An ecological perspective* (pp. 1–9). Washington, DC: NASW Press.

French, J. R. P. Jr., & Raven, B. H. (1959). The bases of social power. In D. Cart-wright (Ed.), *Studies in social power* (pp. 150–167). Ann Arbor, MI: Institute for Social Research.

Friedman, B. S. (1979). *Analysis of participation in a training program for single parents* (Doctoral dissertation). University of Chicago.

Freire, P. (1970). *Pedagogy of the oppressed.* New York: Herder and Herder.

Frederiksen, L. W., Richter, W. T., Johnson, R. P., & Solomon, L. J. (1982). Specificity of performance feedback in a professional service delivery setting. *Journal of Organizational Behavior Management, 3*(4), 41. doi:10.1300/J075v03n04_05

Friesen, B. J., & Briggs, H. E. (1995). The organization and structure of service coordination. In B. J. Friesen & J. Poertner (Eds.), *From case management to service coordination for children with emotional, behavioral, or mental disorders: Building on family strengths* (pp. 63–94). Baltimore: Brooks Publishing Co.

Friesen B. F., Koroloff, N., Walker, J., & Briggs, H. E. (2011). Family and youth voice in systems of care: The evolution of influence. *Best Practices in Mental Health, 7*(1), 1–25.

Galbraith, J. K. (1960). *The liberal hour*. Boston: Houghton Mifflin.

Gambrill, E. (1999). Evidence-based practice: An alternative to authority-based practice. *Families in Society, 80*(4), 341–350.

Gambrill, E. (2001). Social work: An authority-based profession. *Research on Social Work Practice, 11*, 166–175.

Gambrill, E. (2004). Contributions of critical thinking and evidence-based practice to the fulfillment of the ethical obligations of professionals. In H. E. Briggs & T. L. Rzepnicki (Eds.), *Using evidence in social work practice: Behavioral perspectives* (pp. 3–19). Chicago: Lyceum Books.

Gambrill, E. (2006). Evidence-based practice and policy: Choices ahead. *Research on Social Work Practice, 16*, 338–357.

Gambrill, E. (2007). Review of the book *Evidence-based practices in mental health: Debate and dialogue on the fundamental questions. Research on Social Work Practice, 16*, 338–357.

Gambrill, E. D. (1977). *Behavior modification: Handbook of assessment, intervention, and evaluation*. San Francisco: Jossey-Bass.

Garran, A. M., & Rozas, L. W. (2013). Cultural competence revisited. *Journal of Ethnic & Cultural Diversity in Social Work, 22*, 97–111.

Gates, B. L. (1980). *Social program administration: The implementation of social policy*. Englewood Cliffs, NJ: Prentice-Hall.

Gerdes, K. E., Edmonds, R. M., Haslam, D. R., & McCartney, T. L. (1996). A statewide survey of licensed clinical social workers use of practice evaluation procedures. *Research on Social Work Practice, 6*(1), 27–39.

Geronima, I. (2011). Systemic failure: The school-to-prison pipeline and discrimination against poor minority students. *The Journal of Law in Society, 13*(1), 281–299.

Gibbs, L. (2007). Applying research to making life-affecting judgments and decisions. *Research on Social Work Practice, 17*, 143–150.

Gibbs, L. E. (2003). *Evidence-based practice for the helping professions: A practical guide with integrated multimedia*. Pacific Grove, CA: Thomson/Brook/Cole.

Gibbs, L. E., & Gambrill, E. (2002). Evidence-based practice: Counterarguments to objections. *Research on Social Work Practice, 12*, 452–476.

Gibelman, M. (1997). *Who we are: A second look*. Washington, DC: NASW Press.

Gibelman, M. (2003). *Navigating human Service organizations*. Chicago: Lyceum Books Inc.

Gil, D. G. (1994). Confronting social injustice and oppression. In F. G. Reamer (Ed.), *The foundations of social work knowledge* (pp. 231–263). New York: Columbia University Press.

Gilder, G. (1995). Welfare fraud today. *American Spectator, 5 September B*(6).

Glahn, T. J., Chock, P. N., & Mills, D. L. (1984). Transitional teaching homes for individuals with developmental disabilities. *Mental Retardation, 22*(3), 137–141.

Gold, P. G., Glynn, S. M., & Mueser, K. T. (2006). Challenges to implementing and sustaining comprehensive mental health service programs. *Evaluation and the Health Professions, 29*, 195–218.

Goldiamond, I. (1974). Toward a constructional approach to social problems: Ethical and constitutional issues raised by applied behavior analysis. *Behaviorism, 2*(1), 1–84.

Goleman, D. (1998). *Working with emotional intelligence*. New York: Bantam Books.

Golembeski, C., & Fullilove, R. (2008). Criminal (in)justice in the city and its associated health consequences. *American Journal of Public Health, 98*(9 Suppl), S185–S190.

Gotham, H. J. (2004). Diffusion of mental health and substance abuse treatments: Development, dissemination, and implementation. *Clinical Psychology: Science and Practice, 11*(2), 160–176.

Gossett, M., & Weinman, M. L. (2007). Evidence-based practice and social work: An illustration of the steps involved. *Health and Social Work, 32*, 147–150.

Graddy, E. A., & Chen, B. (2006). Influences on the size and scope of networks for social service delivery. *Journal of Public Administration and Research Theory, 16*(4), 533–552.

Graham, J. R., & Barter, K. (1999). Collaboration: A social work practice method. *Families in Society, 80*(1), 6–13.

Grant, C. A., & Gibson, M. L. (2013). "The path of social justice": A human rights history of social justice education. *Equity & Excellence in Education, 46*(1), 81–99. doi:10.1080/10665684.2012.750190

Grasso, A. J., & Epstein, I. (1988). Management by measurement. *Administration in Social Work, 11*(3/4), 89. doi:10.1300/J147v11n03_08

Greene, B. F., Willis, B. S., Levy, R., & Bailey, J. S. (1978). Measuring client gains from staff-implemented programs. *Journal of Applied Behavior Analysis, 11*(3), 395–412. doi:10.1901/jaba.1978.11-395

Gummer, B. (1990). *The politics of social administration: Managing organizational politics in social agencies*. New York: Prentice Hall.

Gummer, B. (1998). Social Relations in an Organizational Context: Social Captial Real Work and Structural Holes. *Administration in Social Work, 22*(3). The Hayworth Press, Inc.

Hacker, A. (1992). *Two Nations: Black and White, Seperate, Hostile, Unequal*. New York: Simon & Schuster.

Hare, B. (2008). *Shorter life span of African Americans linked to mental health coping strategies*. Retrieved from http://news.medill.northwestern.edu/chicago/news.aspx?id=109701

Harms, P. L., & Roebuck, D. B. (2010). Teaching the art and craft of giving and receiving feedback. *Business Communication Quarterly, 73*(4), 413–431.

Harris, M. S., Jackson, L. J., O'Brien, K., & Pecora, P. J. (2009). Disproportionality in education and employment outcomes of adult foster care alumni. *Children and Youth Services Review, 31*(11), 1150–1159.

Hasnain-Wynia, R. (2006). Is evidence-based medicine patient-centered and is patient-centered care evidence-based?. *HRS: Health Services Research, 41*, 1–8.

Hatch, M. J. (1997). *Organization theory: Modern symbolic and postmodern perspectives*. New York: Oxford University Press.

Hecht, B., & Ramsey, R. (2002). *Managing nonprofits.org: Dynamic management for the digital age*. New York: John Wiley & Sons.

Heldke, L., & O'Connor, P. (2004). *Oppression, privilege, and resistance: Theoretical perspectives on racism, sexism, and heterosexism.* New York: McGraw-Hill.

Herbert, E. W., & Baer, D. M. (1972). Training parents as behavior modifiers: Self-recording of contingent attention. *Journal of Applied Behavior Analysis, 5*(2), 139–149. doi:10.1901/jaba.1972.5-139

Hersen, M., & Barlow, D. H. (1976). *Single case experimental designs: Strategies for studying behavior change.* New York: Pergamon Press.

Heselbarth, R. (1999). Good managers must cross-millennial generation gap. *Contractor, 46*(7), 10.

Hien, D. A., Cohen, L. R., Litt, L. C., Miele, G. M., & Capstick, C. (2004). Promising empirically supported treatments for women with co-morbid PTSD and substance use disorders. *American Journal of Psychiatry, 161*, 1426–1432.

Hisey, S. (2003). Employers must adapt to meet the needs of Generation Y, or risk losing serious talent. *Career Development International Bradford, 8*(5), 262.

Hoagwood, K., Burns, B. J., Kiser, L., Ringeisen, H., & Schoenwald, S. K. (2001). Evidence-based practice in child and adolescent mental health services. *Psychiatric Services, 52*(9), 1179–1189. doi:10.1176/appi.ps.52.9.1179

Hodge, D. R. (2010). Social justice as a unifying theme in social work education: Principles to realize the promise of a new pedagogical model. *Journal of Comparative Social Welfare, 26*(2/3), 201. doi:10.1080/17486831003687600

Hollis, F. (1970). Brief and extended casework. *Child Welfare, 49*(9), 531–532.

Hollis, F. (1972). *Casework: A psychosocial therapy* (2nd ed.). New York: Crown Publishing Group/Random House.

Holosko, M. J. (2009). Social work leadership: Identifying core attributes. *Journal of Human Behavior in the Social Environment, 19*(4), 448–459. doi:10.1080/10911350902872395

Holosko, M. J., Winkel, M., Crandall, C., & Briggs, H. (2015). A content analysis of mission statements of our top 50 schools of social work. *Journal of Social Work Education, 51*(2), 222–236.

Hopps, J. G. (1982). Oppression based on color. *Social Work, 27*(1), 3–5.

Hopps, J. G. (2016, August 1). Personal communication.

Hopps, J. G., Pinderhughes, E. B., & Shankar, R. (1995). *The power to care: Clinical effectiveness with overwhelmed clients.* New York: Free Press.

Hoshino, G. (1973). Social services: The problem of accountability. *Social Service Review, 47*(3), 373–383.

Hudson, W. W. (1981). Development and Use of Indexes and Scales. In R. M. Grinnell (Ed.), *Social Work Research and Evaluation.* Itasca, Ill.: Peacock Publishers.

Huey, S. J., Jr., & Polo, A. J. (2008). Evidence-based psychosocial treatments for Ethnic minority youth: A review and meta-analysis. *Journal of Clinical Child and Adolescent Psychology, 37*(1), 262–301.

Hunsaker, P., & Allessandra, A. (1986). *The art of managing people.* New York: Simon & Schuster.

Iguchi, M. Y., Bell, J., Ramchand, R. N., & Fain, T. (2005). How criminal system racial disparities may translate into health disparities. *Journal of Health Care for the Poor and Underserved, 16*(4,Suppl B), 48–56. Retrieved from http://dx.doi.org/10.1353/hpu.2005.0114

Ikard, D. H., & Teasley, M. L. (2012). *Nation of cowards: Black activism in Barack Obama's post-racial America.* Bloomington: Indiana University Press.

Isaacs, M. R., Nahme Huang, L., Hernandez, M., & Echo-Hawk, H. (2005, September). *The road to evidence: The intersection of evidence-based practices and cultural competence in children's mental health.* Presented at the National Alliance of Multi-Ethnic Behavioral Health Associations Consensus Meeting, Chicago.

Ivery, J. M. (2007). Organizational ecology: A theoretical framework for examining collaborative partnerships. *Administration in Social Work, 31*(4), 7–19.

Jansson, B. S., & Simmons, J. (1986). The survival of social work units in host organizations. *Social Work, 31*(5), 339–343.

Jenson, J. M. (2005). Connecting science to intervention: Advances, challenges, and the promise of evidence-based practice. *Social Work Research, 29*, 131–135.

Joe, S., Baser, R. S., Neighbors, H. W., Caldwell, C. H., & Jackson, J. J. (2009). 12 month and lifetime prevalence of suicide attempts among black adolescents in the National Survey of American Life. *Journal of American Academy of Child & Adolescent Psychiatry, 48*(3), 271–282.

Johnson, Y. S., & Munch, S. (2009). Fundamental contradictions in cultural competence. *Social Work, 54*(3), 220–231.

Johnston, J. S. (2009). Prioritizing rights in the social justice curriculum. *Studies in Philosophy and Education, 28*(2), 119. doi:10.1007/s11217-008-9100-8

Jones, T. G. (2002). *July Leading Organizational Change Class Lecture.*

Jordan-Evans, S., & Kaye, B. (2002). Retention in tough times: Here's what 25 global talent leaders say about keeping good people—especially now. (Retention). *Training & Development,* January 2002. Retrieved 3/17/2004 from www.findarticles.com.

Jurkiewicz, C. (2000). Generation X and the public employee. *Public Personnel Management, 29*(1), 55.

Kanfer, F. H. (1979). Personal control, social control, and altruism: Can society survive the age of individualism?. *American Psychologist, 34*(3), 231–239. doi:10.1037/0003-066X.34.3.231

Kanfer, F. H., & Goldstein, A. P. (1975). *Helping people change: A textbook of methods.* New York: Pergamon Press.

Kaplan, R. S., & Norton, D. P. (2001). Transforming the balanced scorecard from performance measurement to strategic management: Part II. *Accounting Horizons, 15*(2), 147–160.

Karl, K. A., O'Leary-Kelly, A. M., & Martocchio, J. J. (1993). The impact of feedback and self-efficacy on performance in training. *Journal of Organizational Behavior, 14*, 379–394.

Katiuzhinsky, A., & Okech, D. (2014). Human rights, cultural practices, and state policies: Implications for global social work practice and policy. *International Journal of Social Welfare, 23*, 80–88. doi:10.1111/ijsw.12002

Katzenbach, J. R., & Smith, D. K. (1993). The discipline of teams. *Harvard Business Review, 83*(7/8), 162–171.

Keller, H. (2000). Work ethic of teachers: A comparison of teaching levels, genders, and generation X and baby boomers (Master's thesis). University of Tennessee, Knoxville.

Kestenbaum, J. C., Hoyos Ceballos, E., & del Aguila Talvadkar, M. C. (2012). Catalysts advocacy. *NYU Clinical Law Review, 18*(2), 459.

Kettner, P. M., Moroney, R. M., & Martin, L. L. (1999). *Designing and managing programs: An effectiveness-based approach.* Thousand Oaks, CA: Sage.

Kim, S.-E. (2005). Balancing competing accountability requirements: Challenges in performance improvement of the nonprofit human services agency. *Public Performance & Management Review, 29*(2), 145.

Knitzer, J. (1982). *Unclaimed children: The failure of public responsibility to children and adolescents in need of mental health services.* Washington, DC: Children's Defense Fund.

Komaki, J. (1982). Managerial effectiveness. *Journal of Organizational Behavior Management, 3*(3), 71. doi:10.1300/J075v03n03_08

Koroloff, N. M., & Briggs, H. E. (1996). The lifecycles of family advocacy organizations. *Administration in Social Work 20*(4), 23–42.

Kotter, J. P. (1996). *Leading Change.* Harvard Business School Press.

Kroger, J. (2012). Personal communication.

Labovitz, G., & Rosansky, V. (1997). *Power of alignment* (p. 139). New York: John Wiley & Sons.

Lackey, L. (2002). *Demographic differences.* Instructors notes from Marylhurst University marketing class. Class lecture Spring of 2002 (April 18).

Lakin, K. C., & Bruininks, R. H. (1985). *Strategies for achieving community integration of developmentally disabled citizens.* Baltimore: P. H. Brookes.

Lancaster, L. C., & Stillman, D. (2002). *When generations collide: Who they are. Why they clash. How to solve the generational puzzle at work.* New York: Collins.

Larson, V. (2003). The Omaha World-Herald Company, Omaha Nebraska, March 17, 2003, Monday Sunrise Edition.

Latessa, E. J., Cullen, F., & Gendreau, P. (2002). Beyond correctional quackery-Professionalism and the possibility of effective treatment. *Federal Probation, 66*(2), 43–49.

Lau, A. S. (2006). Making the case for selective and directed cultural adaptations of evidence-based treatments: Examples from parent training. *Clinical Psychology: Science and Practice, 13*(4), 295–310.

Leary, J. D. (1996). A dissertation on African American male youth violence: "Trying to kill the part of you that isn't loved" (Doctoral dissertation). Portland State University, Oregon.

Leary, J. D. (1996, September 15). The relationship model. *Personal Communication.*

Lee, K. H., & Hines, L. D. (2014). Racial disparity: Substance dependency and psychological health problems among welfare recipients. *Social Work in Public Health, 29*(3), 207–219. doi:10.1080/19371918.2013.776322

Lee, O. E-K., & Priester, M. A. (2015). Increasing awareness of diversity through community engagement and films. *Journal of Social Work Education, 51,* 35–46.

Leitenberg, H. (1976). *Handbook of behavior modification and behavior therapy.* Oxford: Prentice-Hall.

Lencioni, P. (2002). *The five dysfunctions of a team: A leadership fable.* San Francisco: Jossey-Bass.

Lencioni, P. (2004). *Death by meeting: A leadership fable about solving the most painful problem in business.* San Francisco: Jossey-Bass.

Levitt, J. L., Young, T. M., & Pappenfort, D. M. (1981). Achievement place: The teaching-family treatment model in a group-home setting. *Reports of the National Juvenile Justice*

Assessment Centers (pp. 1–64). Washington, DC: National Center for the Assessment of Alternatives to Juvenile Justice Processing, National Institute for Juvenile Justice and Delinquency Prevention, US Department of Justice.

Linsk, N. L., & Pinkston, E. M. (1984). Training gerontological practitioners in home-based family interventions. *Educational Gerontology, 10*(4-5), 289–305. doi:10.1080/0380127840100402

Littell, J. H. (2010). Evidence based practice: Evidence or orthodoxy? In B. L. Duncan, S. D. Miller, B. E. Wampold, & M. A. Hubble (Eds.), *The heart and soul of change: Delivering what works in therapy* (2nd ed., pp. 167–198). Washington, DC: American Psychological Association.

Littel, J. (2009, November 17). *Power, privilege, and racism: Understanding racial disproportionality in child welfare.* Invited presentation, Symposium on Social Injustice and Racial Inequality, Portland State University, School of Social Work, Portland, Oregon.

Longres, J. F. (1990). *Human behavior in the social environment.* Itasca, IL: F. E. Peacock Publishers.

Loury, G. C. (2002). *The anatomy of racial inequality.* Cambridge, MA: Harvard University Press.

Luthans, F., & Martinko, M. J. (1982). Organizational behavior modification. *Journal of Organizational Behavior Management, 3*(3), 33. doi:10.1300/J075v03n03_04

Magee, J. C., & Galinsky, A. D. (2008). The Self-Reinforcing Nature of Social Hierarchy: Origins and Consequences of Power and Status. IAMC 21st Annual Conference Paper. https://ssrn.com/abstract=1298493 or http://dx.doi.org/10.2139/ssrn.1298493

Mager, R. F., & Pipe, P. (1970). *Analyzing performance problems.* Belmont, CA: Fearon Publishers.

Maguire, D. C. (1980). *A new American justice* (pp. 129–130). Garden City, NY: Double Day.

Maher, C. A. (1981). Improving the delivery of special education and related services in public schools. *Journal of Organizational Behavior Management, 3*(1), 29. doi:10.1300/J075v03n01_03

Maher, C. A. (1982). Performance feedback to improve the planning and evaluation of instructional programs. *Journal of Organizational Behavior Management, 3*(4), 33. doi:10.1300/J075v03n04_04

Maher, C. A. (1983). Description and evaluation of an approach to implementing programs in organizational settings. *Journal of Organizational Behavior Management, 5*(3–4), 69–98.

Maher, C. A. (1985a). *Professional self-management: Techniques for special services providers.* Baltimore: P. H. Brookes.

Maher, C. A. (1985b). Resolving problems of mainstreaming. *Special Services in the Schools, 1*(4), 83. doi:10.1300/J008v01n04_07

Marsh, J. C. (2004). Theory-driven versus theory-free research in empirical social work practice. In H. E. Briggs & T. L. Rzepnicki (Eds.), *Using evidence in social work practice: Behavioral perspectives* (pp. 20–35). Chicago: Lyceum Books.

Marsh, J. C. (2005). Social justice: Social work's organizing value. *Social Work, 50*(4), 293–294.

Marsh, J. C. (2012). Learning by intervening: Examining the intersection of research and practice. In T. L. Rzepnicki, S. G. McCracken, & H. E. Briggs (Eds.), *From task-centered social work to evidence-based and integrative practice: Reflections on history and implementation* (pp. 3–14). Chicago: Lyceum Books.

Maslow, A. (1970). *Motivation and personality* (2nd ed.). New York: Harper and Row.

Mattaini, M. A., & Moore, S. E. (2004). Ecobehavioral social work. In H. E. Briggs & T. L. Rzepnicki (Eds.), *Using evidence in social work practice: Behavioral perspectives* (pp. 55–73). Chicago: Lyceum Books.

Maxwell, J. C. (1999). *The 21 Indispensable Qualities of A Leader: Becoming the Person Others Will Want to Follow.* Thomas Nelson, Nashville, Tennessee.

Mazrui, A. A. (1985). African archives and the oral tradition. *Unesco Courier, 38*, 12–16.

McBeath, B., Briggs, H. E., & Aisenberg, G. A. (2009). The role of child welfare managers in promoting agency performance through experimentation. *Children and Youth Services Review, 31*, 112–118.

McCracken, S. G., & Corrigan, P. W. (2004). Staff development in mental health. In H. E. Briggs & T. L. Rzepnicki (Eds.), *Using evidence in social work practice: Behavioral perspectives* (pp. 232–256). Chicago: Lyceum Books.

McGoldrick, M., Pearce, J. K., & Giordano, J. (1982). *Ethnicity and family therapy.* New York: Guildford Press.

McMahon, A., & Allen-Meares, P. (1992). Is social work racist? A content analysis of recent literature. *Social Work, 37*(6), 533–539.

McPherson, J., & Cheatham, L. P. (2015). One million bones: Measuring the effects of human rights participation in the social work classroom. *Journal of Social Work Education, 51*, 47–57.

Meister, J. C., Willyerd, K. (2010). Developing Employees. Mentoring Millennials. Harvard Business Review, May 2010 Issue.

Metzenbaum, S. H. (2006). *Performance accountability: The five building blocks and six essential practices* (Report). IBM Center for the Business of Government.

Miranda, J., Bernal, G., Lau, A., Kohn, L., Hwang, W. C., & Lafrombose, T. (2005). State of the science on psychosocial interventions for ethnic minorities. *Annual Review of Clinical Psychology, 1*, 113–142.

Miranda, J., Guillermo, B., Lau, A., Kohn, L., Hwang, W.-C, & Lafroboise, T. (2005). State of the science on psychosocial interventions for ethnic minorities. *Annual Review Clinical Psychology, 1*, 113–142.

Mizrahi, T., & Rosenthal, B. B. (2001). Complexities of coalition building: Leaders' successes, strategies, struggles, and solutions. *Social Work, 46*(1), 63–78.

Moffitt, T. E., Caspi, A., Harrington, H., & Milne, B. J. (2002). Males on the life-course-persistent and adolescence-limited antisocial pathways: follow-up at age 26 years. *Developmental Psychopathology, 14*(1), 179–207.

Molick, R., & Pinkston, E. M. (1982). Using behavioral analysis to develop adaptive social behavior in a depressed adolescent girl. In E. M. Pinkston, J. L. Levitt, G. R. Green, N. L. Linsk, & T. L. Rzepnicki (Eds.), *Effective social work practice* (pp. 364–375). San Francisco: Jossey-Bass.

Mor Barak, M. E. (2000). The inclusive work place: An eco-systems approach to organizational diversity. *Social Work, 45*(4), 339–353.

Mor Barak, M. E., & Cherin, D. A. (1998). A tool to expand organizational understanding of workforce diversity: Developing a measure of inclusion-exclusion. *Administration in Social Work, 22*(1), 47–64.

Morris, T. (2000). *A Personal Account of Leadership in an Academic Setting*. Advancing Women In Leadership. Retrieved from www.advancingwomen.com/awl/summer2000/m2_morris.html.

Mullaly, B. (1997). *Structural social work: Ideology, theory, and practice* (2nd ed.). Toronto: Oxford University Press.

Mullen, E. J., & Bacon, W. F. (2003). Practitioner adoption and implementation of practice guidelines and issues of quality control. In A. Rosen & E. K. Proctor (Eds.), *Developing practice guidelines for social work intervention: Issues, methods, and research agenda* (pp. 223–235). New York: Columbia University Press.

Muniute-Cobb, E. I., & Alfred, M. V. (2010). Learning from evaluation by peer team: A case study of a family counselling organization. *International Journal of Training and Development, 14*(2), 95–111.

Murray, C. (1984). *Losing ground: American social policy 1950–1980*. New York: Basic Books.

Nagel, T. L. (1998). Tips for reaching Generation X. *US Banker, 108*(8), 66.

Najavita, L. M., Weiss, R. D., Shaw, S. R., & Muenz, L. (1998). Seeking safety: Outcome of a new cognitive-behavioral psychotherapy for women with posttraumatic stress disorder and substance dependence. *Journal of Traumatic Stress, 11*, 437–456.

National Association of Social Workers (NASW). (1999). *NASW Code of ethics*. Washington, DC: Author.

National Association of Social Workers. (NASW). (2001). *NASW Standards for Cultural Competence in Social Work Practice*. Washington, DC: Author.

National Association of Social Workers (NASW). (2008). *NASW Code of ethics*. Washington, DC: Author.

Netting, F. E., & O'Connor, M. K. (2003). *Organization practice: A social worker's guide to understanding human services*. Boston: Allyn and Bacon.

Nichols, E. J. (1976). *The philosophical aspects of cultural differences*. Unpublished manuscript, Ibadan, Nigeria: Nichols and Associates. Paper presented at the conference of the World Psychiatric Association, University of Ibadan, Nigeria.

Nichols, E. J. (1976, July). *Introduction to axiological model*. Paper presented to the World Psychiatric Association and the Nigerian Association of Psychiatrists. University of Ibadan, Nigeria.

Nichols, E. J. (1986). Cultural foundations for teaching black children. In E. J. Nichols (Ed.), *Teaching mathematics: Vol. I. Motivation, history and classroom management* (pp. 1–7). Washington, DC: National Science Foundation.

Nicosia, N., MacDonald, J. M., & Arkes, J. (2013). Disparities in criminal court referrals to drug treatment and prison for minority men. *American Journal of Public Health, 103*(6), e77–e84.

Nobles, W. W. (1991). Foundations of Black psychology. In R. I. Jones (Ed.), *Black psychology* (3rd ed., pp. 99–123). Berkeley, CA: Cobb and Henry.

Nutley, S. M., & Davies, H. T. O. (2000). Making a reality of evidence-based practice: some lessons from the diffusion of innovations. *Public Money & Management, 20*(4), 35–42. https://doi.org/10.1111/1467-9302.00234

O'Dell, S. L., O'Quin, J. A., Alford, B. A., O'Briant, A. L., Bradlyn, A. S., & Giebenhain, J. E. (1982). Predicting the acquisition of parenting skills via four training models. *Behavior Therapy, 13*(2), 194–208. doi:10.1016/S0005-7894(82)80063-4

O'Hagan, K. (1999). Culture, cultural identity, and cultural sensitivity in child and family social work. *Child and Family Social Work, 4*(4), 269–281.

Page, S. (2003). Entrepreneurial strategies for managing interagency collaboration. *Journal of Public Administration and Research Theory, 13*(3), 311–339.

Page, T., Iwata, B. A., & Reid, D. H. (1982). Pyramidal training: A large-scale application with institutional staff. *Journal of Applied Behavior Analysis, 75*, 335–351.

Page, T. J., Christian, J. G., Iwata, B. A., Reid, D. H., Crow, R. E., & Dorsey, M. F. (1981). Evaluating and training interdisciplinary teams in writing IPP goals and objectives. *Mental Retardation, 19*(1), 25–27.

Park, Y. (2005). Culture as deficit: A critical discourse analysis of the concept of culture in contemporary social work discourse. *Journal of Sociology & Social Welfare, 32*(3), 11–33.

Patterson, G. (1982). *Coercive family process. Social learning approach series* (Vol. 3). Eugene, OR: Castalia.

Patterson, G., Reid, J., Jones, R., & Conger, R. (1975). *A social learning approach to family intervention: Vol. I. Families with aggressive children.* Eugene, Oregon: Castalia.

Patti, R. J., Poertner, J., & Rapp, C. A. (1987). *Managing for service effectiveness in social welfare organizations.* New York: Hawthorne Press.

Patti, R. J., Rapp, C. A., & Poertner, J. (Eds.). (1988). *Managing for service effectiveness in social welfare organizations.* Binghamton, NY: Hawthorne Press.

Perlman, H. H. (1957). *Social casework, a problem-solving process.* Chicago: University of Chicago Press.

Pew Research Center. (2016). http://www.pewresearch.org/topics/millennials/page/4/

Pewewardy, N., & Almedia, R. V. (2014). Articulating the scaffolding of white supremacy: The act of naming in liberation. *Journal of Progressive Human Services, 25*, 230–253.

Pfau, B. N. (2016). Generational Issues. What Do Millennials Really Want at Work? The Same Things the Rest of Us Do. Harvard Business Review, April 7, 2016.

Pincus, A., & Minahan, A. (1973). *Social work practice: Model and method.* Itasca, IL: F. E. Peacock.

Pinderhughes, E. (1994). Diversity and Populations at Risk: Ethnic Minorities and People of Color. *The Foundation of Social Work Knowledge.* Columbia University Press. New York.

Pinkston, E. M., Friedman, B. S., & Polster, R. A. (1981). Educating parents as behavior change agents for their children. In S. P. Schinke (Ed.), *Behavioral methods in social work: Helping children, adults, and families in community settings* (pp. 29–40). Hawthorne, NY: Aldine.

Pinkston, E. M., & Herbert, J. W. (1975). Modification of irrelevant and bizarre verbal behavior using parents as therapists. *Social Service Review, 49*(1), 46–63.

Pinkston, E. M., Levitt, J., Green, G., Linsk, N., & Rzepnicki, T. (1982). *Effective social work practice: Advanced techniques for behavioral intervention with individuals, families, & institutional staff.* San Francisco: Jossey-Bass.

Pinkston, E. M., & Linsk, N. L. (1984). *Care of the elderly: A family approach.* New York: Pergamon Press.

Pinkston, E. M., Reese, N. M., Leblanc, J. M., & Baer, D. M. (1973). Independent control of a pre-school child's aggression and peer interaction by contingent teacher attention. *Journal of Applied Behavior Analysis, 6*(1), 115–124.

Polster, R. A., & Pinkston, E. M. (1979). A delivery system for the treatment of underachievement. *Social Service Review, 53*(1), 35–55.

Pon, G. (2009). Cultural competency as new racism: An ontology of forgetting. *Journal of Progressive Human Services, 20*(1), 59–71. doi:10.1080/10428230902871173

Poole, M. (2006). *The segregated origins of Social Security: African Americans and the welfare state.* Chapel Hill: University of North Carolina Press.

Porterfield, J., Evans, G., & Blunden, R. (1985). Involving families and staff in service improvement. *Journal of Organizational Behavior Management, 7*(1-2), 117–133. doi:10.1300/J075v07n01_08

President's New Freedom Commission on Mental Health. (2003). *Achieving the promise: Transforming mental health care in America. Final report* (DHHS Publication No. SMA 03-3823). Rockville, MD: US Department of Health and Human Services.

Price, E. G., Beach, M. C., Gary, T. L., Robinson, K. A., Gozu, A., Palacio, A., . . . Cooper, L. A. (2005).A systematic review of the methodological rigor of studies evaluating cultural competence training of health professionals. *Academic Medicine, 80*(6), 578–586.

Pulakos, E. D. (2004). *Performance management: A roadmap for developing, implementing and evaluating performance management systems.* Alexandria, VA: SHRM Foundation.

Quilitch, H. R. (1975). Comparison of three staff-management procedures. *Journal of Applied Behavior Analysis, 8,* 59–66.

Randall, V. R. (2010). Teaching civil rights: Teaching diversity skills in law school. *Saint Louis University Law Journal, 54,* 795.

Randall, V. R. (2002, Fall). Racial discrimination in health care in The United States as a violation of the International Convention on the Elimination of all forms of Racial Discrimination. *University of Florida School of Law & Public Policy, 14,* 45–91.

Rapp, C. A., & Poertner, J. (1992). *Social Administration: A client-centered approach.* New York: Longman Publishing Group.

Raven, B. H. (1965). Social influence and power. In I. D. Steiner & M. Fishbein (Eds.), *Current studies in social psychology* (pp. 371–382). New York: Holt, Rinehart, Winston.

Raven, B. H. (2008). The bases of power and the power/interaction model of inter-personal influence. *Analyses of Social Issues and Public Policy, 8*(1), 1–22.

Razack, N., & Jeffery, D. (2002). Critical race discourse and tenets for social work. *Canadian Social Work Review, 19*(2), 257–271.

Reamer, F. G. (2001). *The social work ethics audit: A risk management tool.* Washington, DC: NASW Press.

Redd, W. H., Porterfield, A. L., & Andersen, B. L. (1979). *Behavior modification: Behavioral approaches to human problems.* New York: Random House.

Reid, W. (1988). Service effectiveness and the social agency. In R. J. Patti, C. A. Rapp, & J. Poertner (Eds.), *Managing for service effectiveness in social welfare organizations* (pp. 41–58). Binghamton, NY: Hawthorne Press.

Reid, W. (2001). The role of science in social work. *Journal of Social Work, 1*(3), 273.

Reid, W. (2004). The contribution of operant theory to social work practice and research. In H. E. Briggs & T. L. Rzepnicki (Eds.), *Using evidence in social work practice: Behavioral perspectives* (pp. 36–54). Chicago: Lyceum Books.

Reid, W. J. (1975). A test of a task-centered approach. *Social Work, 20,* 3–9.

Reid, W. J. (1978). *The task-centered system.* New York: Columbia University Press.

Reid, W. J., & Epstein, L. (1972). *Task-centered casework*. New York: Columbia University Press.

Reilly, T. (2001). Collaboration in action: An uncertain process. *Administration in Social Work, 25*(1), 53–74.

Repp, A. C., & Deitz, D. D. (1979). Improving administrative-related staff behaviors at a state institution. *Mental Retardation, 17*(4), 185–192.

Resnick, H. (1978). Tasks in changing the organization from within (COFW). *Administration in Social Work, 2*(1), 29–44. doi:10.1300/J147v02n01_04

Rigoni, B., & Adkins, A. (2016). Generational Issues. What Millennials Want from a New Job. May 11, 2016, Harvard Business Review.

Roberts, D. (2009). The racial geography of child welfare: Toward a new research paradigm. *Child Welfare, 87*(2), 125–150.

Rogers, D. L., & Whetten, D. A. (1982). *Interorganizational coordination: Theory, research, and implementation*. Ames: Iowa University Press.

Rothman, J., & Thomas, E. J. (1994). *Intervention Research: Design and Development for Human Service*. New York: Haworth Press.

Rountree, M. A., & Pomeroy, E. C. (2010). Social justice research: Bridging the gaps among social justice, research, and practice. *Social Work, 55*(4), 293–295.

Rubin, A., & Parrish, D. (2007). Challenges to the future of evidence-based practice in social work education. *Journal of Social Work Education, 43*, 405–428.

Rzepnicki, T. L. (2009, June 5). *The contributions of William J. Reid to empirical practice in social work: The task centered model and other innovations in practice research*. From The Task-Centered Approach To Evidence Based And Integrative Practice, University of Chicago, School of Social Service Administration Centennial Birthday Celebration.

Rzepnicki, T. L., & Briggs, H. E. (2004). Introduction: Panning for gold—using evidence in your practice. In H. E. Briggs & T. L. Rzepnicki (Eds.), *Using evidence in social work Practice: Behavioral perspectives* (pp. ix–xxiii). Chicago: Lyceum Books.

Rzepnicki, T. L., McCracken, S. M., & Briggs, H. E. (2012). *From task centered to evidence based to integrative practice*. Chicago: Lyceum Books.

Sackett, D. L., Stauss, S. E., Richardson, W. C., Rosenberg, W., & Haynes, R. M. (2000). *Evidence-based medicine: How to practice and teach EBM* (2nd ed.). New York: Churchill Livingstone.

Sankar, Y. (2003). Designing the learning organization as an information-processing system: Some design principles from the systems paradigm and cybernetics. *International Journal of Organization Theory and Behavior, 6*(4), 501–521.

Saunders, J. A., Haskins, M., & Vasquez, M. (2015). Cultural competence: A journey to an elusive goal. *Journal of Social Work Education, 51*, 19–34.

Sawrikar, P., & Katz, I. B. (2014). Recommendations for improving cultural competency when working with ethnic minority families in child protection systems in Australia. *Child & Adolescent Social Work Journal, 31*(5), 393–417. doi:10.1007/s10560-014-0334-8

Schall, E., Ospina, S., Godsoe, B., & Dodge, J. (2004). Appreciative narratives as leadership research: Matching method to lens. *In Constructive Discourse and Human Organization* (Vol. 1, pp. 147–170). (Advances in Appreciative Inquiry; Vol. 1).

Schalock, R. L., Foley, J. W., Toulouse, A., & Stark, J. A. (1985). Medication and programming in controlling the behavior of mentally retarded individuals in community settings. *American Journal of Mental Deficiency, 89*(5), 503–509.

Schorr, L. B., & Mann, T. E. (1998). *The Brookings Institute Governmental Studies Program: Learning what works: Evaluating complex social interventions.* Report on the Symposium October 22, 1997, The Brookings Institute, Washington, DC.

Schueman, J. R., Rzepnicki, T. L., & Littell, J. H. (1994). *Putting Families First: An Experiment in Family Preservation.* New York: Aldine de Gruyter.

Schwartz, A., Goldiamond, I., & Howe, M. W. (1975). *Social casework: A behavioral approach.* New York: Columbia University Press.

Scott, W. G. (1961). Organization theory: An overview and an appraisal. In J. Sharfriz & S. Ott (Eds.), *Classics of organizational theory* (5th ed.). Belmont, CA: Wadsworth Group/Thompson Learning.

Senge, P. (1990). *The fifth discipline: The art and practice of the learning organization.* New York: Random House.

Shlonsky, A., & Gibbs, L. (2004). Will the real evidence-based practice please stand up? Teaching the process of evidence-based practice to the helping professions. *Brief Treatment and Crisis Intervention, 4,* 137–153.

Sims, H. P., & Manz, C. C. (1982). Social learning theory. *Journal of Organizational Behavior Management, 3*(4), 55. doi:10.1300/J075v03n04_06

Simyar, F., & Lloyd-Jones, J. (1988). Strategic management in the health care sector. Englewood Cliffs, NJ: Prentice Hall.

Skinner, B. F. (1938). *The behavior of organisms: An experimental analysis.* Englewood Cliffs, NJ: Prentice-Hall.

Skinner, B. F. (1953). Some contributions of an experimental analysis of behavior to psychology as a whole. *American Psychologist, 8*(2), 69–78. doi:10.1037/h0054118

Skinner, B. F. (1957). *Verbal behavior.* East Norwalk, CT: Appleton-Century-Crofts. doi:10.1037/11256-001

Smagner, J. P., & Sullivan, M. H. (2005). Investigating the effectiveness of behavioral parent training with involuntary clients in child welfare settings. *Research on Social Work Practice, 15,* 431–438.

Smith, B. D., & Mogro-Wilson, C. (2008). Inter-agency collaboration: Policy and practice in child welfare and substance abuse treatment. *Administration in Social Work, 32*(2), 5–24.

Smith, G. P. (2003). Baby boomer versus Generation X: Managing the new workforce. Retrieved from http://www.chartcourse. com/articlebabyvsgenx.htmlS

Snowden, L. R. (2001). Barriers to effective mental health services for African Americans. *Mental Health Services Research, 3*(4), 181–187.

Snowden, L. R. (2012). Health and mental health policies' role in better understanding and closing African American–White American disparities in treatment access and quality of care. *American Psychologist, 67*(7), 524–531. http://dx.doi.org/10.1037/a0030054

Sonnenschein, W. (1997). *The practical executive and workforce diversity.* Lincolnwood, IL: NTC Business Books.

Sowa, J. E. (2008). Implementing interagency collaborations: Exploring variation in collaborative ventures in human service organizations. *Administration & Society, 40*(3), 298–323.

Specht, H., & Courtney, M. E. (1994). *Unfaithful angels: How social work has abandoned its mission.* New York: The Free Press.

Stogdill, R. M. (1974). *Handbook of Leadership: A survey of theory and research.* New York, NY, US: Free Press.

Sue, S., & Zane, N. (1987). The role of culture and cultural techniques in psychotherapy: A critique and reformulation. *American Psychologist, 42,* 37–45.

Sue, S., & Zane, N. (2006). Ethnic minority populations have been neglected by evidence-based practices. In J. C. Norcross, L. E. Beutler, & R. F. Levant (Eds.), *Evidence based practices in mental health* (pp. 329–337). Washington, DC: American Psychology Association.

Sue, S., Zane, N., Levant, R. F., Silverstein, L. B., Brown, L. S., Olkin, R., & Taliaferro, G. (2006). How well do both evidence-based practices and treatment as usual satisfactorily address the various dimensions of diversity? In J. C. Norcross, L. E. Beutler, R. F. Levant, J. C. Norcross, L. E. Beutler, & R. F. Levant (Eds.), *Evidence-based practices in mental health: Debate and dialogue on the fundamental questions* (pp. 329–374). Washington, DC: American Psychological Association. doi:10.1037/11265-008

Suelzle, M., & Keenan, V. (1981). *A family career and individual life cycle perspective on planning residential and vocational options for mentally retarded children.* Springfield, IL: Illinois State Department of Mental Health and Developmental Disabilities.

Tervalon, M., & Murray-Garcia, J. (1998). Cultural humility versus cultural competence: A critical distinction in defining physician training outcomes in multicultural education. *Journal of Health Care for the Poor,* 9(2), 117–125.

Themba-Nixon, M. (2001). Race in the post-Third World. *Colorlines,* 4(3), 14–16.

Thomas, E. J. (1978). Mousetraps, developmental research, and social work education. *Social Service Review,* 52(3), 468–483.

Thomas, E. J. (1984). *Designing interventions for the helping professions.* Beverly Hills: Sage.

Thomas, E. J. (1985). Design and development validity and related concepts in developmental research. *Social Work Research and Abstracts, 21,* 50–58.

Thorndike, E. L. (1998). Animal intelligence: An experimental study of the associate processes in animals. *American Psychologist,* 53(10), 1125–1127. doi:10.1037/0003-066X.53.10.1125

Throsby, D. (2001). *Economics and culture.* Cambridge, UK: Cambridge University Press.

Thyer, B. A. (2004). Science and evidence-based social work practice. In H. E. Briggs & T. L. Rzepnicki (Eds.), *Using evidence in social work practice: Behavioral perspectives* (pp. 74–89). Chicago: Lyceum Books.

Tichy, N. M., & Cohen, E. (2002). *The Leadership Engine: How Winning Companies Build Leaders at Every Level.* HarperCollins.

Timmerman, S., & Mauck, A. (2005). The promises and pitfalls of evidence-based medicine. *Health Affairs, 24,* 18–28.

Tolson, E., Reid, W., & Garvin, C. (2003). *Generalist practice: A task-centered approach* (2nd ed.). New York: Columbia University Press.

Traux, C. B., & Carkhuff, R. R. (1965). Personality change in hospitalized mental patients during group psychotherapy as a function of the use of alternate sessions and vicarious therapy pre-training. *Journal of Clinical Psychology,* 21(2), 225–228. doi:10.1002/1097-4679(196504)21:2<225::AID-JCLP2270210225>3.0.CO;2-Z

Tulgan, B. (2000). *Managing Generation X: How to bring out the best in young talent.* New York: W. W. Norton.

Ulrich, D. (1997a). *Human resource champions: The next agenda for adding value and delivering results*. Boston, MA: Harvard Business Review Press.

Ulrich, D. (1997b). Measuring human resources: An overview of practice and a prescription for results. *Human Resource Management, 36*(3), 303.

US Department of Health and Human Services. (1999a). *Mental health: A report of the Surgeon General*. Rockville, MD: US Department of Health and Human Services, Substance Abuse and Mental Health Services Administration, Center for Mental Health Services, National Institutes of Health, National Institute of Mental Health.

US Department of Health and Human Services. (1999b). *Mental health, culture, race, and ethnicity: A supplemental report*. Rockville, MD: US Department of Health and Human Services, Substance Abuse and Mental Health Services Administration, Center for Mental Health Services, National Institutes of Health, National Institute of Mental Health.

US Department of Health and Human Services (DHHS). (1999). *Child welfare outcomes, 1999: Annual report*. Retrieved from http://www.acf.hhs.gov/programs/cb/publications/cwo99/statedata/il.htm

US Office of Personnel Management, Workforce Compensation and Performance Service (Revised January 2001). *A handbook for measuring employee performance: Aligning employee performance plans with organizational goals*. Performance Management Practitioner Series, PMD-13; Available http:// www.au.af.mil/au/awc/awcgate/opm/handbook_performance.pdf.

Valente, T. W. (1996). Social network thresholds in the diffusion of innovations. *Social Networks, 18*, 69–89.

Vander Stoep, A., Williams, M., Jones, R., Green, L., & Trupin, E. (1999). Families as full research partners: What's in it for us? *Journal of Behavioral Health Services Research, 26*, 329–342.

Walker, P. (2002). Understanding accountability: Theoretical models and their implications for social service organizations. *Social Policy & Administration, 36*(1), 62–75.

Walker, J. S., Briggs, H. E., Koroloff, N., & Friesen, B. J. (2007). Implementing and sustaining evidence-based practice in social work. *Journal of Social Work Education, 43*, 361–375.

Wandersman, A., Imm, P., Chinman, M., & Kaftarian, S. (2000). Getting to outcomes: A results-based approach to accountability. *Evaluation and Program Planning, 23*, 389–395. doi:10.1016/S0149-7189(00)00028-8

Watkins, C. (1999). Grads to grannies, managing the generation gap. *Food Management, 34*(9), 34–35.

Weinberg, M. (2008). Structural social work: A moral compass for ethics in practice. *Critical Social Work, 9*(1), 1–10.

Weisz, J. R., Jensen-Doss, A., & Hawley, K. M. (2006). Evidence-based youth psychotherapies versus usual clinical care: A meta-analysis of direct comparisons. *American Psychologist, 61*, 671–689.

Wells, S. J., & Briggs, H. E. (2009). Cultural competence and evidence based practice: Best friends, strangers, or arch rivals? *Children and Youth Services Review, 31*(11), 1147–1149.

Wells, S. J., Merritt, L. M., & Briggs, H. E. (2009). Bias, racism, and evidence based practice: The case for more focused development of the child welfare evidence base. *Children and Youth Services Review, 31*(11), 1160–1171.

Wenzel, S. L. (1992). Modified self-control schedule. *Journal of Community Psychology, 20,* 57–71.

Wheeler, D., & Briggs, H. E. (2010, October). *Building a culturally competence and diverse leadership for social work education.* Presented at the Council on Social Work Education, Annual Program Meeting, Portland, Oregon.

Williams, C. (2010). Global justice and education: From nation to neuron. *Educational Review, 62*(3), 343–356.

Williams, D. R., & Collins, C. (2001). Racial residential segregation: A fundamental cause of racial disparities in health. *Public Health Reports, 116,* 404–416.

Williams, D. R., & Sternthal, M. (2010). Understanding racial-ethnic disparities in health: Sociological contributions. *Journal of Health and Social Behavior, 51*(1, Suppl), S15–S27. doi:10.1177/0022146510383838

Wilson, G. T., & Evans, I. M. (1977). The therapist-client relationship in behavior therapy. In A. S. Gurman & A. M. Razin (Eds.), *Effective psychotherapy: A handbook* (pp. 309–330). New York: Pergamon Press.

Wilson, P. A. (1999). A theory of power and politics and their effects on organizational commitment of senior executive service members. *Administration & Society, 31*(1), 120–141.

Windsor, L. C., Shorkey, C., & Battle, D. (2015). Measuring student learning in social justice courses: The diversity and oppression scale. *Journal of Social Work Education, 51,* 58–71.

Witkin, S. (1998). Editorial. *Social Work, 43,* 483–486.

Wood, D. J., & Gray, B. (1991). Toward a comprehensive theory of collaboration. *Journal of Applied Behavioral Science, 27,* 139–162.

Xanthos, C. (2008). *The secret epidemic: Exploring the mental health crisis affecting adolescent African-American males.* Atlanta, GA: Community Voices, Morehouse College School of Medicine.

Yollis, M. (2003). The political cybernetics of organisations. *The International Journal of Cybernetics, 32*(9/10), 1253–1282.

Zajda, J., Majhanovich, S., & Rust, V. (2006). Introduction: Education and social justice. *International Review of Education/Internationale Zeitschrift für Erziehungswissenschaft/ Revue Internationale de l'Education. 1/2,* 9.

Zemke, R., Raines C., & Filipczak, B. (2000). *Generations at work: Managing the clash of veterans, boomers, xers, and nexters in your workplace.* New York: AMACOM.

Zlotnick, J. L. (2007). Evidence-based practice and social work education: A view from Washington. *Research on Social Work Practice, 17,* 625–629.

Zule, W. (2008b). Gender differences in the impact of social support on crack use among African Americans. *Substance Use and Misuse, 43*(1), 85–104.

Zule, W. A. (2008a). Perceived neighborhood safety and depressive symptoms among African American crack users. *Substance Use and Misuse, 43*(3-4), 445–468.

INDEX

Note: Tables are indicated by an *t* following the page number

For the benefit of digital users, indexed terms that span two pages (e.g., 52–53) may, on occasion, appear on only one of those pages.